"Through a detailed study of the development of Karl Barth's theology against the background of the Lapsarian Controversy of the seventeenth century, Tseng shows that Barth's professed 'purified supralapsarianism' is in fact a transformed vision of Christology and predestination in which both infralapsarian and supralapsarian elements play an important role. Tseng's headline claim that Barth's mature view is best described (contra Barth himself) as 'basically infralapsarian' is and will no doubt remain controversial. Yet at the same time, his fine-grained presentation of Barth's Christological doctrine of election as a dialectical admixture of supra- and infralapsarian patterns of thinking builds a persuasive case and, moreover, models a hearty mode of theological inquiry that is refreshing in an era grown chary of dogmatic reflection."

Joel D. S. Rasmussen, associate professor of nineteenth-century Christian thought, University of Oxford

"Swimming against the currents of common opinion, Shao Kai Tseng offers a fresh and provocative argument that Karl Barth was not a supra- but infralapsarian. Such a claim will undoubtedly raise eyebrows, but Tseng presents a convincing case rooted in a careful analysis of the original seventeenth-century debate and Barth's own extensive writings. Without hesitation I can say that this is a must-read book for anyone who wants a better understanding of Barth's theology. But this book is also important for anyone who wrestles with how to explain God's relationship with fallen humanity, the doctrine of Christ, time and eternity, and election and salvation."

J. V. Fesko, Westminster Seminary California

"Shao Kai Tseng's text is a most impressive piece of scholarship. His topic of predestination, with a focus on Barth, chimes in with the important debate in Barth scholarship on election in relation to Trinity. This book will take its place as further evaluation and revision of the interpretation of predestination in Barth's theology. I commend the work by this emerging Asian theologian wholeheartedly."

Timothy Bradshaw, University of Oxford

"Shao Kai Tseng's new book tackles a problem that many have regarded as metaphysical and, as such, impossibly obscure. However, Tseng's study shows not only that the choice between a supralapsarian and infralapsarian view was of perennial concern to Barth but that it also dovetails with central aspects of his christological thinking. Tseng approaches the subject by means of a careful scrutiny of key texts as well as of relevant secondary literature. He has an exceptional and welcome ability to juggle the highly technical vocabulary of Reformed dogmatics in such a way as to show how the issues are of importance to all Christian thought."

George Pattison, 1640 Chair of Divinity, University of Glasgow

NEW EXPLORATIONS
IN THEOLOGY

KARL BARTH'S INFRALAPSARIAN THEOLOGY

ORIGINS AND DEVELOPMENT
1920–1953

SHAO KAI TSENG

FOREWORD BY GEORGE HUNSINGER

An imprint of InterVarsity Press
Downers Grove, Illinois

InterVarsity Press
P.O. Box 1400, Downers Grove, IL 60515-1426
ivpress.com
email@ivpress.com

©2016 by Shao Kai Tseng

All rights reserved. No part of this book may be reproduced in any form without written permission from InterVarsity Press.

InterVarsity Press® is the book-publishing division of InterVarsity Christian Fellowship/USA®, a movement of students and faculty active on campus at hundreds of universities, colleges and schools of nursing in the United States of America, and a member movement of the International Fellowship of Evangelical Students. For information about local and regional activities, visit intervarsity.org.

Cover design: Cindy Kiple
Interior design: Beth McGill

ISBN 978-0-8308-5132-4 (print)
ISBN 978-0-8308-9982-1 (digital)

Library of Congress Cataloging-in-Publication Data
A catalog record for this book is available from the Library of Congress.

| P | 23 | 22 | 21 | 20 | 19 | 18 | 17 | 16 | 15 | 14 | 13 | 12 | 11 | 10 | 9 | 8 | 7 | 6 | 5 | 4 | 3 | 2 | 1 |
| Y | 35 | 34 | 33 | 32 | 31 | 30 | 29 | 28 | 27 | 26 | 25 | 24 | 23 | 22 | 21 | 20 | 19 | 18 | 17 | 16 |

To my parents

Contents

Foreword by George Hunsinger   9

Acknowledgments   15

Abbreviations   19

Introduction   21

Part 1: Reappraising Barth's Lapsarian Position

  1 Supra- and Infralapsarianism in the Seventeenth Century: Some Definitions   41

  2 *Church Dogmatics* §33: Barth's Lapsarian Position Reassessed   62

Part 2: Barth's Lapsarian Position in Development, 1920–1953

  3 *Römerbrief* II (1920–1921): Lapsarianism in the "Impossible Possibility" Dialectic   83

  4 The Göttingen-Münster Period (1921–1930): Christology and Predestination in the Subject-Object Dialectic   112

  5 The Bonn Years (1930–1935): Human Talk and Divine Word—New Developments?   148

  6 *Gottes Gnadenwahl* (1936): Infralapsarian Aspects of Barth's Christocentric Doctrine of Election   177

  7 *CD* II/2 (1939–1942): Christ as Electing God and Elected Human—Lapsarianism "Purified"   213

  8 *CD* IV/1 (1951–1953): Adamic History and History of Christ—Infralapsarian Tendencies in Barth's Doctrine of Sin   242

Conclusion   290

Bibliography   301

Author Index   314

Subject Index   315

Foreword

George Hunsinger

In this fine study Professor Shao Kai Tseng makes a solid and creative contribution to Barth studies. By charting how Barth revised his view of election from some of his earliest sketches to his mature views, great light is cast on Barth's theology as a whole. In particular Professor Tseng traces the development of the rather technical, but nonetheless very important, distinction between supralapsarianism and infralapsarianism in Barth's doctrine of election.

Professor Tseng makes the striking proposal that because Barth viewed Jesus Christ as the object of election, his ideas were actually in line with the historic infralapsarians of the Reformed tradition rather than with the supralapsarians with whom Barth explicitly, though not uncritically, aligned himself. Whereas Barth designated his conclusions as "purified supralapsarianism," Professor Tseng argues to the contrary that Barth should be seen instead as "basically infralapsarian." The reason is that in accord with the infralapsarians, but unlike the supralapsarians, Barth saw pretemporal election in Christ as oriented to the salvation of fallen human beings.

Professor Tseng makes a powerful argument. At the level of conceptual analysis and general historical sensitivity, it would be hard to quarrel with it. In that sense it is a fine and original piece of work. I suspect that in many ways the contribution Tseng makes will be a lasting one.

Nevertheless, I have an important reservation. I think it would be better to agree with Barth that in the end he was a "purified supralapsarian," while still accepting the thesis, as advanced by Professor Tseng, that he has strong "infralapsarian" tendencies. With that caveat I think we could say, splitting the difference, that Barth was strongly though not basically infralapsarian. He represented a purified supralapsarianism with strong infralapsarian elements.

To make his case Professor Tseng relies heavily on a remark that I once made about Barth. I observed that Barth did not want to commit himself on the question of whether the incarnation would have occurred without humanity's fall into sin. Barth believed it would be speculative and unwarranted to take a stand on such a matter. So far, so very good. That was Barth's "official" view, and I would stand by my remark.

Nevertheless, it is astonishing how many wheels within wheels Barth's dialectical engine can keep spinning.[1] There are passages in the *Church Dogmatics* that make it sound as though there would indeed have been an incarnation even if the world had not fallen into sin. To this effect there is an almost inconspicuous but still discernible thread that runs through the great, imposing tapestry of Barth's mature dogmatics.

Let me give just one example. Near the beginning of *Church Dogmatics*, volume IV, part 1, Barth has a long section called "The Covenant as the Presupposition of Reconciliation." A careful reading of this material shows that for Barth not only does reconciliation presuppose a logically prior covenant, but the covenant always involves Jesus Christ as its essential content. The covenant is thought to be ontologically basic and prior to reconciliation. Reconciliation is seen as a contingent but not an essential means by which God would fulfill his original covenantal will (*Bundeswillen*) for his creation. There would still have been a covenant even if the world had not fallen into sin. Furthermore, as the eternal Word of God through whom all things came into being, Jesus Christ was at once the covenant's center and the means ordained for its fulfillment—with or without the fall.

Barth's views along these lines are scattered throughout the opening of IV/1. He does not present them thematically or even all in one place. Perhaps the first indication appears in his surprising remark that the creature as such is in need of salvation—not merely the creature qua sinner, but precisely the creature qua creature. "Salvation," Barth states, "is the perfect being which

---

[1] I owe this phrase to Robert W. Jenson. See his "Response" in *Union Seminary Quarterly Review* 28 (1972): 31-34, on 31.

is not proper to created being as such but is still future. Created being as such needs salvation, but does not have it: it can only look forward to it" (IV/1, 8). Salvation for the creature will involve eternal life in communion with God. It will be a gift over and above the gift of creation itself. It will mean nothing less than being given "a part in the being of God" (though without "divinization" in any crude sense) (IV/1, 8).

God's reaction to the creature's fall into sin is a "contingent reaction" (IV/1, 9). The fall is not in itself the occasion for God's original and fundamental will to enter into covenant with his creature. If we start from the incarnation as God's contingent reaction to the fall, we can perceive in it a more primordial divine intention. In Jesus Christ "we see both the fact and also the manner in which it is determined from the very first and already initiated" (IV/1, 36). God's will-to-covenant (*Bundeswillen*) is given with creation as such. It is prior to and independent of the fall. "It is not only a reaction, but a work of the faithfulness of God" (IV/1, 36). From the very outset this covenant is ordained to be carried out in and through Jesus Christ. Hidden in God's contingent reaction is a more primordial intention and plan. The name of Jesus Christ gives us not only the fact of God's primordial will-to-covenant, but also the means appointed for its fulfillment in bringing the creature into the eternal life of God.

"What takes place in Jesus Christ," Barth later continues, "is ... not simply the reaction of God against human sin" (IV/1, 47). The incarnation itself "stands at the heart of the Christian message and the Christian faith, because here God maintains and fulfils his Word as it was spoken at the very first" (IV/1, 47). The incarnation is a matter of affirming and carrying out "the original purpose of God's relationship with us human beings" (IV/1, 47 rev.). "It is the great act of God's faithfulness to himself and therefore to us—his faithfulness in the execution of the plan and purpose which he had from the very first as the Creator of all things and the Lord of all events, and which he wills to accomplish in all circumstances" (IV/1, 47). God's primordial will-to-covenant, which is prior to and in that sense independent of the radical contingency of the fall, finds its irreducible ground—its origin, means and goal—in the election of Jesus Christ.

> For in Jesus Christ we do not have to do with a second, and subsequent, but with the first and original content of the will of God, before and above which

there is no other will—either hidden or revealed in some other way—in the light of which we might have to understand and fear and love God and interpret humankind very differently from how they are both represented in Jesus Christ. (IV/1, 48 rev.)

God's primordial will-to-covenant is "eternally grounded in him," Jesus Christ (IV/1, 48).

> He is the content and form of the divine thought of grace, will of grace and decree of grace in relation to the created world, before the created world was. He is the One for whose sake God willed it and created it. He is the meaning and purpose which it has because God willed to give it to it and did in fact give it to it. The creation, too, and the preservation and direction of the world and man, must be described as pure acts of divine grace. But even here we must think strictly of Jesus Christ in whom these acts had and have their meaning and purpose. The existence and work of Jesus Christ do not follow from the gracious act of creation or the gracious act of divine providence. It is for the sake of Jesus Christ that creation takes place and God rules as the preserver and controller of world-events. These things are all acts of divine grace only because they take place for his sake. (IV/1, 50)

There is more along these lines scattered, almost randomly, throughout Barth's texts. But we have seen enough to grasp why his views break decisively with the older "infralapsarian" mold. The object of election, for Barth, is not merely fallen humanity. It is Jesus Christ as God's primordial will-to-covenant, with or without the fall. The absolute primacy of Jesus Christ from before the foundation of the world—in essential independence of the fall—is what gives Barth's doctrine of election its significantly "supralapsarian" cast.

If we try to locate Barth's views within a seventeenth-century Puritan framework, as Professor Tseng would have us do, he might seem to be "basically infralapsarian," because the incarnation is indeed, for Barth, carried out to counteract the radical contingency of the fall. By making Jesus Christ the object of election, however, Barth established a new and very different framework than any known in the older, historic debates.

For Barth, God's eternal will-to-covenant, as grounded in the election of Jesus Christ—his good will toward the entire human race—is prior to and independent of the fall into sin. In other words, in Jesus Christ God's will-to-covenant (*Bundeswillen*), or benevolence, or loving kindness, would be there for his creation even if the radical contingency of sin had never occurred. In the election of Jesus Christ God's loving kindness (*Menschenfreundlichkeit*) is logically and ontologically prior to the fall. In Christ God then supersedes and overcomes the fall on the cross for the sake of all humankind. There is a prior and universal benevolence in God that persists and makes itself effectual in election despite the fall into sin. We may thus conclude that in his doctrine of election Barth was only contingently infralapsarian, while still remaining essentially supralapsarian—precisely, as he said, in a "refined" or "purified" sense.

Acknowledgments

I WOULD LIKE TO TAKE THIS OPPORTUNITY to thank the persons and institutions whose help and support have made possible the publication of this monograph.

I first began research on the subject matter of this book as a master of theology student at Princeton Theological Seminary. There Professor George Hunsinger, my supervisor, not only taught me how to read Barth but also helped to shape the core insight this monograph now offers.

Originally this book appeared in the form of a doctoral thesis, which I composed at the University of Oxford in 2011–2014 under the supervision of Professor Joel Rasmussen, who expanded my horizons beyond expectations. Those truly inspiring conversations with Professor George Pattison, Dr. Timothy Bradshaw, Professor Johannes Zachhuber and Professor Benno van den Toren also proved to be invaluable.

Professor Paul Dafydd Jones graciously read over my manuscript and offered helpful suggestions for revision. Professor Paul Fiddes and Professor Paul Nimmo, my viva voce examiners, pointed me to necessary revisions without which my thesis would not have been worthy of publication as a monograph.

Professor J. I. Packer, Professor Hans Boersma and Professor Daniel Migliore have been instrumental in laying the foundation for my doctoral research. Hans has always been there for me as a great friend and mentor.

Professor John Fesko of Westminster Seminary, California, kindly read over my chapters on the Lapsarian Controversy and offered invaluable feedback and encouragement. Dr. Hans-Anton Drewes impressed on me a very personal picture of Barth as we chatted over tea at the Swiss theologian's old residence in Basel.

Professor Stephen Chan, my most cherished mentor-friend since the very beginning of my theological pursuits, has always been a source of inspiration for me. Conversations with Dr. Mark Jones, Professor Phee Seng Kang and the Rev. Dr. Paul Kong all contributed significantly to my reflections on the subject matter.

My doctoral studies from which this book emerged have been supported by a number of institutions and individuals. I received grants, funds and honorariums from China Evangelical Seminary, R.E.M. (HK), Evangelical Reformed Church Taipei, Evangelical Formosan Church of Washington, DC, Living Spring Church Zurich, Oxford Chinese Church and the Faculty of Theology at Oxford. The Chinese Community Church of New York gave me a spiritual home and supported me financially through generous honorariums. Elder Lyna Lim's townhouse in Hackensack, New Jersey, has truly been a home away from home since my Princeton days. Princeton Seminary offered me the handsome Presidential Scholarship for my ThM research on the topic that was to become the subject matter of this monograph. Individual friends from my church in Vancouver offered charitable financial and prayer support for my studies. Philanthropist Minde Jiang funded a year's worth of my living expenses in the United Kingdom. The Blessings Foundation in California under the leadership of the Rev. Dr. Grant Chen not only funded my theological studies in the past but also became a trusted spiritual family that has supported me in every way.

Since I joined the faculty at China Evangelical Seminary, Taipei, my colleagues have lovingly supported my work and ministry. I would like to thank the former president Professor Peter Chow for having recruited me to this community of intellect-seeking faith. The current president, Professor Lee-Chen Tsai, and academic dean Professor Wesley Hu have gone out of their way to support my academic pursuits that are sometimes in conflict with my duties at the seminary.

Professor Hong-Hsin Lin and the Fellowship of Theologians at Taiwan Theological College and Seminary have given me wonderful opportunities to interact with leading theological scholars in Sino-Christian circles.

Wycliffe Hall, Oxford, the college of which I was proudly a member, showed me the very best of English and Christian hospitality, enabling me to pursue theological scholarship in a loving community of faith.

While away from Oxford, most of my reading and writing were done alongside unlimited espresso and gratis high-end cuisine at Our Place Café, a small restaurant in Vancouver owned by Cordon Bleu–trained chef Powell Sung, my best friend since childhood.

My buddies from Vancouver, D. L. Ming and B. L. Yun, have been the best listeners to my theological reflections. My extended family back in Taiwan has always encouraged me with loving kindness. Monetary support from Uncle Joe, Aunt Sharon and Uncle Wolfgang, and my godparents Mr. and Mrs. Yen significantly alleviated my financial burdens toward the end of my doctoral studies. The final part of my dissertation was composed in Shanghai, where my parents-in-law loved and supported me as their very own.

Needless to say, the privilege to be published by IVP Academic is beyond what I could have asked for. I would like to thank David Congdon and his team at the press for making this possible. His expertise as an editor and a Barth scholar has made this project truly enjoyable. I am also thankful to Michael Gibson at Fortress Press for having kindly referred my book proposal to Dr. Congdon.

Finally, I am most grateful to my parents and my wife, Jasmine. Despite all my inadequacies, Jasmine decided to marry me and to support me lovingly in every imaginable way. I have my parents to thank for everything, and it is to them that I dedicate this monograph—this is not just proper Chinese etiquette on my part. Above all else, it is through the influence of their piety that I have taken faith—that "firm and certain knowledge"—as the starting point of my theological inquiries.

Soli Deo Gloria
Taipei, 2015

Abbreviations

General Abbreviations

ET English Translation

Karl Barth's Works

GA *Karl Barth Gesamtausgabe.* 51 vols. Zurich: TVZ, 1973–2015.

Römerbrief II *Der Römerbrief 1922.* 16th ed. Zurich: TVZ, 1999.

Romans II *The Epistle to the Romans.* Translated by Edwyn Hoskyns. 1922 ed. London: Oxford University Press, 1933.

Unterricht *Unterricht in der christlichen Religion.* 3 vols. Edited by Hannelotte Reiffen (vol. 1) and Hinrich Stoevesandt (vols. 2-3). Zurich: TVZ, 1985-2003.

GD *The Göttingen Dogmatics.* Vol. 1. Edited by Hannelotte Reiffen. Translated by Geoffrey W. Bromiley. Grand Rapids: Eerdmans, 1990.

MD (*Münster Dogmatics*) *Die christliche Dogmatik im Entwurf, 1. Band: Die Lehre vom Worte Gottes, Prolegomena zur christlichen Dogmatik, 1927.* Zurich: TVZ, 1982.

Anselm *Fides quaerens intellectum: Anselms Beweis für die Existenz Gottes, 1931.* Zurich: TVZ, 1981.

Anselm (ET) *Anselm: Fides Quaerens Intellectum, Anselm's Proof of the Existence of God in the Context of His Theological Scheme.* Translated by Ian Robertson. London: SCM, 1960.

Gottes Gnadenwahl *Gottes Gnadenwahl.* Munich: Kaiser, 1936.

KD *Die Kirchliche Dogmatik.* 4 vols. in 12 parts (I/1–IV/4). Zurich: TVZ, 1932–1970.

CD *The Church Dogmatics.* 4 vols. in 12 parts (I/1–IV/4). Edited by Geoffrey W. Bromiley and T. F. Torrance. Translated by Geoffrey W. Bromiley. Edinburgh: T&T Clark, 1936–1975.

Introduction

SUBJECT MATTER: THE LAPSARIAN PROBLEM

This book is a study on the twentieth-century Swiss theologian Karl Barth's christological and predestinarian treatments of the problem of human sin and fallenness through the successive stages of his career from *Romans* II (1920) to *CD* IV/1 (1953). Is the divine word of election, and along with it God's rejection of sin—Barth maintained throughout his theological career that predestination must be understood as *double* predestination (i.e., as election *and* reprobation)—addressed to its object as fallen or unfallen? In historic Reformed theology, this has been known as the "lapsarian" (from the Latin word *lapsus*, meaning "the fall") problem. Supralapsarianism (*supra-lapsum*: above or before the fall) contends that in God's eternal decisions God has in mind unfallen human beings as the object of election and reprobation; infralapsarianism (*infra-lapsum*: below or after the fall) argues that when God eternally issued the double decision of election and reprobation the human object was considered as fallen.

In our postmetaphysical age, these anglicized Latin scholastic terms may seem obsolete and irrelevant. Particularly in the field of Barth studies, in which terms like "metaphysics" and "natural theology" are often used pejoratively, the whole lapsarian debate may seem all the more repulsively speculative.

However, to simplistically label Barth as altogether antimetaphysical is to misconstrue his intentions. Barth rejects metaphysics as a *method*, but the ontological questions that metaphysics as a subdiscipline of philosophy seeks to answer, such as those of God, of being and beings, of becoming, of nature, of origins and so on, remain central to his theology. As George

Pattison reminds us, "Barthian treatments of the relationship between act and being and the nature of revelatory communication" serve to challenge "recent theologies that use the tropes of post-metaphysical philosophy to position claims for the independence of theological enquiry."[1] The complexity of Barth's antimetaphysical approach to metaphysical questions should caution against any simplistic dismissal of historic theological inquiries that do not seem at first glance to be of interest in our postmetaphysical zeitgeist.

Barth is known for surprising his readers at times by taking up theological problems that others have deemed speculative and unanswerable. In fact, to dismiss the lapsarian problem as "metaphysical" is to miss a crucial part of Barth's theology, namely, his insistence on seeking understanding of the reality of sin in light of God's gracious election. For him, the history of fallen humankind and what he calls nothingness indeed constitute an absurd, irrational and unexplainable reality, but he insists that faith must seek to understand this reality and take it seriously not for its own sake but for the sake of understanding what Christ has done for us and in our stead. Only by explicating this inexplicable reality in light of God's gracious election *and reprobation* in Christ is it possible for the believer to truly understand (and thus not understand) this reality and take it seriously (and thus laughingly). Even though Barth takes issue with certain theological methods that classical supra- and infralapsarians have employed to answer the lapsarian problem, from *Romans* II (1920) he deemed this inquiry worthy of pursuit.

Barth even insists on retaining the supra-/infra- nomenclature, because the logical orders that the terms imply are important for ruling out the possibility of natural theology in his reconstruction of the doctrine of election: he wants to make sure that no eternal act of God and no historical event is understood detachedly from the highest word that God has uttered to humankind, the word of God's gracious election.

Yet, if election is not understood christologically, then—as Barth would consistently argue from 1936 onward—the very doctrine of election would itself become speculatively natural-theological, in which case the theological notion of sin would easily slip into an anthropological category and become

---

[1] George Pattison, *God and Being: An Enquiry* (Oxford: Oxford University Press, 2011), 14.

some sort of a second god. While his christological reorientation of the doctrine of election only began in 1936, from *Romans* II on he always made sure to treat the problem of sin christologically.

For this reason Barth's doctrine of election is deeply related to christological lapsarianism. As a note of explanation, supralapsarian Christology holds that God *would have* become incarnate regardless of humanity's sin: christological supralapsarians claim to possess knowledge of divine purposes to become incarnate other than the purpose to reverse the human plight of fallenness. By contrast, infralapsarian Christology, without necessarily denying that God *could have* become incarnate even if humankind had not fallen into sin, declines to claim knowledge of any divine purpose for which God *would have* done so. Infralapsarian Christology offers only one answer to Anselm's great question, *cur Deus homo* (why God became human): God decided to become incarnate for our salvation.

More detailed definitions of predestinarian and christological supra- and infralapsarianism will be provided anon. Suffice it now to note that although Barth does not apply lapsarian terminology to his Christology, he engages deeply with christological lapsarianism. One aim of this book is to paint a picture of how Barth weaves together his Christology and doctrine of election as a result of his reflections on the lapsarian problem, demonstrating how supra- and infralapsarian patterns of thinking are dialectically interwoven in the development of his christological doctrine of election.

NARRATIO

When I was a student at Regent College, Vancouver, I participated in a seminar on the atonement led by the prominent scholar of Puritan theology, the beloved J. I. Packer. One session was dedicated to Karl Barth. During that session, I suggested that in *CD* II/2, election presupposes the fall. To my assertion Professor Packer responded, "If you are right about Barth, then he would have to be an infralapsarian. I'm quite intrigued, because obviously he calls himself a supralapsarian."

Professor Packer's comment piqued my interest in Barth's lapsarian position, and after Regent I continued on to Princeton Theological Seminary, where I wrote a master of theology thesis on this subject under the supervision of one of the most respected Barth scholars of our day, George

Hunsinger. In my thesis I quoted Loraine Boettner's famous formulation of the lapsarian question: "When the decrees of election and reprobation came into existence were men considered as fallen or as unfallen?"[2]

In the margin next to this quote on the printed copy of my submitted thesis, the master who taught me how to read Barth wrote: "Barth would say 'fallen.'" However, Professor Hunsinger issued the caveat that Barth's mature theology dialectically incorporates both supra- and infralapsarian patterns of thinking while rejecting what he sees as their errors. This key insight eventually became the foundation and a central thesis of this monograph.

While agreeing with my take on Barth's view of the object of election, at that time Professor Hunsinger still preferred to think of Barth as basically supralapsarian. He wrote the following definition of supralapsarianism on my submitted thesis: "Strictly, supralapsarians are those who hold that in pretemporal election God chose to elect some and reject others in order to glorify himself and so created the world to carry out this plan."

I came to realize then that in the circle of Barth studies, supra- and infralapsarianism are defined quite differently than in the circle of Puritan and Reformation studies. To be sure, definitions vary somewhat within Puritan and Reformation studies themselves, but there is at least a minimalist definition to which they would agree.

To further demonstrate the case, during my doctoral research I had a conversation with my friend Mark Jones, who is a prolific young scholar in Puritan studies. I told him that the majority of mainstream Barth scholars believe that Barth sees the object of election as fallen. "That's interesting—and they still call Barth a supralapsarian," responded Jones, in his characteristically calm and unwavering voice, raising his eyebrows as if putting a question mark at the end of the sentence. In fact, whenever I tell friends from evangelical Reformed circles that Barth sees the object of election as fallen, their responses are almost always something like: "Then why does Barth call himself a supralapsarian?" or "Doesn't that make Barth an infralapsarian?"

When I raise these questions among friends from Barthian circles, they usually respond, "No, Barth is a supralapsarian, because, unlike the infralapsarians, he doesn't think of election as 'a reaction to previous events in the

---

[2]Loraine Boettner, *The Reformed Doctrine of Predestination* (Philadelphia: P&R, 1932), 126.

history of God's relations with us.'"³ They might say with Barth: Unlike the infralapsarian, the supralapsarian does not think of "God's overruling of evil . . . as a *later and additional struggle* in which God is dealing with a *new and to some extent disruptive feature* in His original plan."⁴

Yet, a Reformed evangelical might reply by quoting Herman Bavinck: "So, 'was the fall actually a *frustration of God's plan*? But no Reformed believers, *even if they are infralapsarians*, can or may ever say such a thing.'"⁵ She might add: "For supra- and infralapsarians alike, 'God's decision to be for us in Jesus is not a reaction to previous events in the history of God's relations with us, but has a reality in its own right preceding the whole of that history.'"⁶

When I took up this understanding years ago and argued that Barth is in fact basically infralapsarian by virtue of believing that the object of election is fallen, a then doctoral candidate at Princeton Seminary—who agreed with me that for Barth election presupposes humanity's fallenness—responded to me in a short email comprising just one German word: "*Nein!*" Evidently Barth and Barthians define supra- and infralapsarianism quite differently from most Reformed evangelicals, especially specialists in Puritan and Reformation studies.

But why should this matter? Shall those who say "chips" say unto the others, "Thou shalt not say 'fries'"? Certainly not—as far as deep-fried potatoes are concerned. However, the discrepancy between the two groups of scholars at large with regard to the definitions of supra- and infralapsarianism is in fact of a different nature.

For one thing, it shows that evangelical critics of Barth who are familiar with the Lapsarian Controversy have not understood his doctrine of election, which many consider to be the heart of his theology, accurately enough to recognize that he is not entirely a supralapsarian according to the way they would define the word. Conversely, Barth and Barthians have not sufficiently probed into Reformed-orthodox formulations of the doctrine of predestination to disagree with them with complete accuracy.

---

[3] See Kathryn Tanner, "Creation and Providence," in *The Cambridge Companion to Karl Barth*, ed. John Webster (Cambridge: Cambridge University Press, 2000), 114.
[4] *KD* II/2, 137; ET 128-29 (emphasis added).
[5] Herman Bavinck, *Reformed Dogmatics*, vol. 2, *God and Creation*, ed. John Bolt, trans. John Vriend (Grand Rapids: Baker Academic, 2004), 385.
[6] Contra Tanner, "Creation and Providence," 114.

Sorting out the terminology is unlikely to bring Barthians and evangelicals to a complete doctrinal agreement, but I believe it would at least be helpful for ongoing dialogues between these two diverse groups of scholars who, while having different loci of theological norms, share many overlapping theological concerns and convictions.

More importantly, when Barth identifies himself as a supralapsarian, he does so in the context of the Lapsarian Controversy of the seventeenth century. Understanding seventeenth-century Reformed-orthodox definitions of supra- and infralapsarianism would thus help us to place Barth in the context of the broader Reformed tradition, with which he was deeply yet critically engaged. As John Webster, one leading Barth scholar of our day, puts it, Barth's engagement with historic Reformed theology was "deeply formative of the direction of his theological thinking."[7]

Webster laments that "one of the graver weaknesses of some contemporary Christian theology is catechetical: it has simply not learned the traditions of Christianity deeply enough and lovingly enough to be able to move around within them, restate them or even disagree with them with much accuracy."[8] Heeding Webster's call to scholarly reappraisal of Barth's theological development in light of his critical reappropriation of historic Reformed theology, I will show that sorting out Barth's lapsarian position in the context of the broader Reformed tradition is a worthwhile and fruitful endeavor in many ways: it not only helps us gain more insight into Barth's theological development but can also lead to deeper and more accurate appreciation of the tradition so formative to his theological thinking.

The Theodicy Problem

The sociologist of religion Peter Berger has observed that theodicy, which "represents the attempt to make a pact with death," is "central for any religious effort at world-maintenance, and indeed also for any effort at the latter on the basis of a non-religious *Weltanschauung*."[9] This is because theodicy seeks to explain universal experiences of sin, evil and suffering, which con-

---

[7]John Webster, *Barth's Earlier Theology* (London: T&T Clark, 2005), 1.
[8]Ibid., 64.
[9]Peter Berger, *The Sacred Canopy: Elements of a Sociological Theory of Religion* (New York: Anchor, 1969), 80.

stitute an *a posteriori* reality that Barth's version(s) of (neo-)Kantianism has sought to address since the 1910s. Berger argues that Christianity in the modern West is threatening to dissolve because of the difficulty in reconciling faith in an almighty Father with the universal "terror" of "chaos" and "insanity."[10] He warns that "if the Christian explanation of the world no longer holds, then the Christian legitimation of social order cannot be maintained very long either."[11]

The challenge Berger describes here was an especially acute problem for Christians in the first half of the twentieth century, during which traditional Christian explanations of the world had been challenged by centuries of modernization, and neo-Protestant world-explanations from the nineteenth century were struggling for survival amid chaotic forces that culminated in the two World Wars. This was a time when Western Europe saw an outpouring of profound theological reflections from the likes of Dietrich Bonhoeffer, Emil Brunner, Rudolf Bultmann, Hans Urs von Balthasar, Henri de Lubac and others.

Barth, who witnessed firsthand the rise of the Third Reich as a resident alien in Germany, also came to develop during those chaotic days his christocentric doctrine of election as an attempt to testify to the universal lordship of Jesus Christ, the gracious and sovereign God-with-us and God-for-us.

It must be emphasized, however, that strictly speaking Barth's theology was not so much a response to the "crisis" of his time, but rather an endeavor to witness to Christ in defiance of the "crisis." His theology was not really guided or driven by theodicy—which he saw as a prideful human attempt to justify the God who alone is entitled to justify—but rather a deep desire to point the church, so that the church may point the chaotic world, to her Lord and Savior. Increasingly in his career, Barth would see himself as a theologian *for* the church and *of* the church, the community that God has elected and called to proclaim God's Word: hence the title of his magnum opus, the *Church Dogmatics*.

SUPRA- AND INFRALAPSARIANISM

As early as *Romans* II (1920–1921), Barth saw in the seventeenth-century Reformed-orthodox debate between supra- and infralapsarians an im-

---

[10]Ibid., 22.
[11]Ibid., 79.

portant formulation of the theodicy problem. Yet he increasingly came to feel that classical Reformed answers to the problem were inadequate for the task of theology, namely, to proclaim the Word of God as revealed in Christ, because of what he understood (and in many ways misunderstood) to be some of Reformed orthodoxy's basic assumptions.

As a note of recapitulation and further explanation, supralapsarianism is the position that in the double act of election and reprobation God has in mind unfallen humanity as the object of predestination (*obiectum praedestinationis*); this has been variously described as lapsable humanity (*homo labilis*), humanity yet to fall (*homo lapsandus*) and not yet fallen humanity (*homo nondum lapsus*). By contrast, infralapsarianism states that in divine predestination God's conception of the object of election-reprobation is fallen humanity (i.e., *obiectum praedestinationis* as *homo lapsus*). Note that the infralapsarian *obiectum* is God's eternal conception of *homo lapsus*, but not humanity actually created and fallen in history.

When the Lapsarian Controversy had developed into maturity, both sides would generally agree that (1) God is not the author of sin; (2) humankind's fall occurred by an efficaciously permissive decree of God, and this decree is therefore by no means a new or disruptive feature in God's original plan; and (3) election is unconditional, and is thus by no means a later or additional struggle whereby God responds to the actuality of sin.

In the current analysis, the problem over which supra- and infralapsarians of the seventeenth century debated is basically a Reformed formulation of the theodicy problem: given that God is absolutely good and sovereign, how was it that God decreed—even though permissively—humanity's fall, and how was it that the Creator decreed to predestine some of God's own creatures unto perdition?

The diverse answers that supra- and infralapsarians gave to this question will be discussed in chapters one and two. Suffice it now to note that in Barth's view—especially after having started to develop his Christocentric doctrine of election in 1936—there are fatal flaws to this way of framing the lapsarian question. First, Reformed orthodoxy speaks of reprobation and the fall in terms of divine decrees, which for Barth does not sufficiently stress God's absolute nonwilling of the negative element that assails God's covenant partner. Second, according to Barth, Reformed orthodoxy tends to answer the lapsarian problem apart from Christ, as if the freely electing God were above and behind, thus detached from, the God self-revealed in Christ (though this has been one tendency in Reformed orthodoxy, this is not always the case—see chapters one and two). Third, Reformed orthodoxy tends to *explain* the cause and origin of evil in terms of divine sovereignty and purpose, but for Barth the reality of what he later came to call "nothingness" (*das Nichtige*) is absurd and unexplainable. As Barth sees it, nothingness is understood—and thus not understood—as such only in light of Christ's triumph over it from and to all eternity.

Reassessing Barth's Lapsarian Position

The first and shorter part of my twofold thesis in this book is that despite Barth's avowedly "purified supralapsarian" conviction, his mature formulation of the doctrine of election is in fact a dialectical combination of both lapsarian positions. As far as the object of election and the order of divine decrees are concerned, Barth may be described as basically infralapsarian.

But how is this important for a helpful interpretation of Barth? Many in the guild of Barth studies would be tempted to think that what is important is to understand what the theologian means when he calls himself a supralapsarian and why he rejects what he calls infralapsarianism, and whether his definitions are in accordance with seventeenth-century usage is insignificant. True enough, it is important to ask why Barth calls himself a supralapsarian—and I shall surely do that. However, as I have argued, reassessing Barth's lapsarian position in light of the original Lapsarian Controversy would help us to place him in the broader context of the Reformed tradition. This helps us not only gain deeper insights into his critical interactions with the tradition but also compare him to other theologians of the Reformed heritage in order to develop a more robust understanding of his theology. For instance, how does Barth's Christocentrism compare with the common-grace theology of the Dutch supralapsarian Abraham Kuyper, and how might such comparison shed light on Barth's famous debate with Emil Brunner?

In any case, what I am arguing here is that to identify Barth as holding to a complex and dialectical, albeit basically infralapsarian, view of the object of election according to traditional Reformed definitions is not to interpret him with preimposed categories, failing to appreciate his intention in calling himself a supralapsarian. Rather, this reassessment is helpful for a deeper understanding of his theology within a broader historical context.

Barth's definitions of supra- and infralapsarianism are at variance with the original Lapsarian Controversy, especially with regard to the notions of *homo creabilis et labilis* (creatable and lapsable humanity) and *homo creatus et lapsus* (created and fallen humanity). He suggests that *homo creabilis et labilis* refers to God's eternal conception of the object of election as sinful and lost, while *homo creatus et lapsus* refers to humanity actually created and fallen. However, according to Reformed orthodoxy, supra- and infralapsarian alike, the *obiectum praedestinationis* is strictly within God's eternal plan, which is causally independent of actual events in the creaturely sphere. Reformed-orthodox supra- and infralapsarians alike believe that in pretemporal predestination God issued forth election and reprobation for the ultimate purpose of God's glory, and so created the world to carry out this plan.

Part one of this book sets these technical matters straight. Chapter one defines supra- and infralapsarianism in light of seventeenth-century Reformed-orthodox texts and recent secondary literature on the Lapsarian Controversy, while chapter two discusses Barth's definitions of supra- and infralapsarianism, showing that his complex and dialectical scheme is actually more in line with infralapsarianism than supralapsarianism.

As a note of explanation, when I refer to Barth's doctrine as "*basically* infralapsarian" the reader should bear in mind that this term on its own without careful qualification can be potentially unhelpful and misleading. First of all, Barth has rejected some fundamental assumptions shared among both classical supra- and infralapsarians, so he cannot be simplistically identified with either camp. I use the description "basically infralapsarian" only to refer to the basic thesis that the object of double predestination is *homo lapsus*, in contrast to the basic supralapsarian thesis that the object of double predestination is unfallen.

Even here, the caveat must be issued that for Barth, Christ is the first and final object of election, and fallen humankind is elected only in and with Christ. As the proper object of election, Christ in himself is without sin—not even *homo labilis* or *nondum lapsus* but simply "he who knew no sin." Therefore *homo lapsus* describes the human race elected in and with Christ, and Christ "became sin for us" only by imputation through participation (in chapter eight I will counter the interpretation of Barth as having adopted a "fallenness view" of Christ's human nature). In this way, then, Barth's basically infralapsarian view of the *obiectum praedestinationis* dialectically carries a supralapsarian aspect as well.

CHRISTOLOGICAL LAPSARIANISM

The terms *supralapsarianism* and *infralapsarianism* have also been applied to Christology. Supralapsarian Christology states that God *would have* become incarnate regardless of humanity's fall (e.g., Duns Scotus), and infralapsarianism contends that God's primary purpose behind the incarnation is to save humankind from sin (e.g., Anselm). Occasionally some christological infralapsarians have ventured to state that God would not have become incarnate if humankind had not fallen into sin (e.g., Aquinas), but this is not generally characteristic of infralapsarians.

In other words, supralapsarian Christology contends that while the incarnation does take care of the sin problem, "God had . . . other, deeper motives behind the incarnation than only the need for reconciliation."[12] By contrast, infralapsarian Christology, without necessarily denying that God *could have* become incarnate even if humanity had not fallen (i.e., without necessarily ruling out the possibility of incarnation regardless of sin), refuses to claim to know *that* or *why* God *would have* done so. According to infralapsarian Christology, then, "the divine will to become incarnate logically follows (*infra*, after) the divine will to allow sin (*lapsus*, fall)," while for supralapsarian Christology, "the divine will to become incarnate logically precedes (*supra* before) the divine will to allow sin."[13] Note here that both supra- and infralapsarian Christology are concerned with the logical order of God's decisions to become incarnate and to confront sin.

In what follows, when I speak of the incarnation as having been "made necessary" by God's decision to confront sin (infra) or to enter into fellowship with the creature (supra), a language that Barth himself adopts, I refer to a hypothetical necessity constituted by and contingent on God's will.

---

[12]Edwin van Driel, *Incarnation Anyway: Arguments for Supralapsarian Christology* (Oxford: Oxford University Press, 2008), 4.
[13]Ibid.

For both supra- and infralapsarian Christology, the divine ordinance concerning the logical relations between God's decisions to become incarnate and to confront sin or enter into fellowship with the creature pertains to God's *potentia ordinata* (God's power as bound and limited by God's own ordinances with reference to creaturely reality) rather than *absoluta* (the absolute omnipotence of God's being in Godself). When Barth speaks of the "necessity" for God to become incarnate in order to conquer sin (he is not shy to say that "God had to [become incarnate]"), he is also referring to the *hypothetical necessity* arising out of God's *potentia ordinata* (a term he explicitly uses), rather than an *absolute necessity*.[14]

In this language of necessity, supralapsarian Christology claims that the incarnation was made necessary by a divine will other than God's purpose to confront sin, such as God's desire to enter into fellowship with God's own creatures, or God's decision to manifest God's own glory. By contrast, infralapsarian Christology maintains that the incarnation was made necessary by God's decision to save fallen creatures from sin. From the Göttingen years on, Barth consistently maintained that it was God's decision to confront sin on behalf of the creature that made the incarnation necessary. In Bruce McCormack's words, "[the] incarnation was necessary, in Barth's view, because of the Fall."[15]

In this book I will show that Barth's Christology became increasingly infralapsarian through the successive phases of his theological development, although it always retained certain supralapsarian aspects. As his theology becomes increasingly Christocentric overall, his doctrine of election also becomes increasingly infralapsarian, along with his Christology.

It must be acknowledged that my basically infralapsarian reading of Barth's Christology is complexified by the ever-present claim in the *Church Dogmatics* that Jesus Christ is the beginning of all God's ways and works, which surely reflects a strongly supralapsarian conviction. Dialectically, this claim carries both supra- and infralapsarian aspects. Notwithstanding the obviously supralapsarian overtone in this statement, for Barth the Word who was in the beginning, the *Logos* eternally *incarnandus*, is revealed in the concrete history of the incarnation as determined from the very beginning

---

[14]For example, *KD* I/1, 41; ET 37.
[15]Bruce McCormack, *Karl Barth's Critically Realistic Dialectical Theology* (Oxford: Clarendon, 1995), 360.

to be Reconciler between God and fallen sinners.[16] There has never been and will never be a moment in the entire history of Jesus Christ, who is the very beginning of all God's ways and works, in which he is not determined to be the bearer of and victor over humankind's sin. In this way, Barth's mature Christology is basically infralapsarian, though it certainly carries a supralapsarian aspect as well.

True enough, after 1936 Barth would speak of the incarnation as primarily an eternal event, and of the *Logos* as eternally *incarnandus*, which again comes very close to supralapsarian Christology. However, whether a Christology is supra- or infralapsarian does not depend on the chronological order of the events concerned: traditionally the incarnation has almost always been regarded as a temporal event (the few exceptions include Origen, the Actistetae, Meister Eckhart and Menno Simons), and both supra- and infralapsarian Christology would see the incarnation as chronologically occurring *post lapsum*. The point of contention is whether God's will to become incarnate presupposes God's will to overcome sin: that is, whether it was God's decision to confront sin that made the incarnation necessary. In this regard, Barth's mature Christology is basically infralapsarian because the incarnation is the event in which humanity's sin is posited in order to occasion Christ's eternal triumph over it.

Even though Barth is emphatic that Jesus Christ is the beginning of all God's decisions, it should be noted that he identifies the "event in which . . . the Word became flesh" with that "in which . . . the Judge was Himself judged on the cross of Golgotha."[17] Throughout his career, Barth has never claimed knowledge of an "incarnation regardless of sin," even though he does think that "the incarnation resolves a plight [of creation] logically independent of sin, namely, the plight of transitoriness and dissolution into nonbeing."[18] While Barth's view of the incarnation approximates Duns Scotus's supralapsarianism in this particular regard, he has never ventured far enough to make the essential supralapsarian claim that God *would have* become incarnate regardless of sin.

---

[16]*KD* IV/1, 55; ET 52.
[17]Ibid., 394; ET 358.
[18]George Hunsinger, *Disruptive Grace: Studies in the Theology of Karl Barth* (Grand Rapids: Eerdmans, 2000), 204.

Barth's Theological Development

But who cares if Barth is supra- or infralapsarian in his Christology or in his doctrine of election? The second and main part of my twofold thesis is that Barth's struggles with the lapsarian problem (i.e., questions about the sovereign and holy God's dealings with humanity's sin) through the successive phases of his theology are in fact one important factor driving his theological development.

To be sure, Barth would frame the predestinarian-lapsarian problem quite differently from Reformed orthodoxy, hence his use of the term "purified" to describe his own lapsarian position. We shall see in chapters two, six and seven what this adjective means. For now, suffice it to say that Barth would frame the lapsarian problem by asking: how is sin to be understood in light of Jesus Christ and of God's sovereignty in the act of election? After the Christocentric reorientation of the doctrine of election in 1936–1942, the problem would be framed even more concretely: how is the reality of sin to be seen in light of God's gracious election-in-Christ?

Part two of this book (chapters three to eight) traces the development of Barth's christological and predestinarian lapsarianism from its inception in 1920 to its christological revision in 1936–1942, and finally the highly actualistic and "historicized" (as some have put it—I borrow this term with discretion) rendition of Christology and predestination in *CD* IV/1 (published in 1953).

In a nutshell, my thesis in tracing the development of Barth's lapsarian thinking is that Christology and predestination started out as two loosely related doctrines in his theology, but as he drew his doctrine of predestination, which was basically but inconsistently supralapsarian during the first phase of the development, closer to Christology, which carried infralapsarian tendencies at first and became basically infralapsarian in the 1920s, his doctrine of predestination became more and more infralapsarian, and then in 1936–1942 the two doctrines merged and became inseparable, and he became basically infralapsarian in both Christology and predestination, albeit still retaining certain supralapsarian characteristics. Then, in the actualistic and historicized Christology developed in the 1950s he came even closer to christological and predestinarian infralapsarianism.

This development up to 1953 may be divided into five major phases:

1. In *Romans* II (1920–1921), Barth's Christology was moving in an infralapsarian direction while his doctrine of election leaned toward supralapsarianism, though it already carried infralapsarian elements.
2. In the Göttingen-Münster period (1921–1930), Barth's Christology became basically infralapsarian, while his doctrine of election began to move toward infralapsarianism.
3. In the Bonn years (1930–1935) during which *Anselm* and *CD* I/1 were written (as well as most of I/2, published in 1938), Barth made no substantial revision to his theology (here I am in agreement with Bruce McCormack's insight against the "von Balthasar thesis" regarding the centrality of *Anselm* to Barth's theological development), but with the Anselm book, which gave Barth a more robust way of setting forth the concept of revelation, Christology and predestination, both of which were primarily formulated within the category of revelation, became more closely interwoven in *CD* I/1. Meanwhile, in *CD* I/1 Barth became more attentive to the presupposition of human sin in the divine act of revelation in its actual form, which motivated him to adopt a basically infralapsarian orientation in the Christocentric doctrine of election in the next phase of his development.
4. In *Gottes Gnadenwahl* (1936) and *CD* II/2 (1939–1942), the basically infralapsarian Christology from previous phases of Barth's development dictated the basically infralapsarian orientation of his christological revision of the doctrine of election in 1936–1942.
5. In *CD* IV/1 (1951–1953) Barth set forth a Christology that some have labeled as "historicized." In "The Pride and Fall of Man" (§60) he draws from his notion of nothingness in *CD* III/3 but develops it in a more historical-actualistic direction, identifying fallen humanity with Adamic history. Here his discussion of sin in terms of the *Geschichte* of the "pride and fall" of humankind consistently presupposes a basically infralapsarian Christology and continually refers to a basically infralapsarian understanding of election.

In these chapters I also show that Barth had adopted his mistaken definitions of supra- and infralapsarianism as early as 1920, and that the inadequate

German historiography on Reformed orthodoxy by Heinrich Heppe and others that Barth encountered while at Göttingen did little in helping to clarify the terminology.

God's Gracious Reprobation:
Election-in-Christ as *Aufhebung*

To appreciate the basically infralapsarian orientation of Barth's Christocentric doctrine of election is to grasp his concern to understand God's No as a gracious, never-capricious word in Christ for the definite and definitive purpose of God's Yes. For Barth, reprobation is God's eternal negation of humanity's sin that negates God's grace, and this negation of negation in Christ is for the purpose of election as the *Aufhebung* of reprobation.

As a note of explanation, the German word *Aufhebung*, literally meaning "lifting up" and sometimes translated as "sublation" or "supersession," is a Hegelian notion of dialectical progression in which the new abrogates or supersedes the old in form, but the rationality of the old is in one sense preserved in the new, which fulfills the purpose of the old. This is sometimes understood as the logic of the "negation of negation." According to Barth's Christocentric doctrine of election, sin negates God's grace, but the vicarious reprobation Christ suffers, manifested in his death as the death of death, is the negation of negation, and the purpose of the two negatives is fulfilled as they are *aufgehoben* in God's gracious election-in-Christ.

From 1936 (*Gottes Gnadenwahl*) onward, Barth would describe Christ as vicariously reprobated for the sin of all humankind, so that all humankind, partaking of Christ, may be elected *in* him, therefore *by* and *with* him as he is electing God and elected human. The vicarious reprobation Christ suffered, of which Christ is both the subject and the object, is for Barth God's eternal, a priori (*zum Vornherein*) negation of humanity's sin, and this negation of negation is sublated in God's gracious election-in-Christ, which presupposes and in a sense preserves the rationality of divine reprobation as manifested on Golgotha. Barth's understanding of election as the Christocentric *Aufhebung* of fallen human history (the historical aspect of election-in-Christ is especially emphasized in *CD* IV/1) and divine reprobation is basically in line with infralapsarianism: double predestination deals with the element of sin, and the human race elected in and with Christ is *homo lapsus*.

Again, as a caveat, this basically infralapsarian orientation must not be understood in a simple, but in a dialectical manner: Christ as the proper *obiectum praedestinationis* who took on the sin of all humankind is without sin in himself.

For Barth, God's No is not the "caprice of a tyrant" arbitrarily deciding from all eternity to send the reprobate to hell forever (to set the record straight, I do not think Barth is entirely fair to historic Reformed orthodoxy when he thinks of it in these terms). Rather, with his basically infralapsarian formulation of election-in-Christ, Barth portrays reprobation as a gracious word of God against the sin that assails God's covenant partner, a No in Christ negatively posited in order to be sublated for the sake of the Yes, which is God's gracious election of all humankind *in Christo*.

PART ONE

Reappraising Barth's Lapsarian Position

1

Supra- and Infralapsarianism in the Seventeenth Century

SOME DEFINITIONS

THIS CHAPTER SEEKS TO DEFINE supra- and infralapsarianism in accordance with seventeenth-century Reformed orthodoxy. One aim of this book is to challenge the simple perception of Barth as a supralapsarian, an assumption that, to my knowledge, has not yet been explicitly questioned. The fact, I would argue, is that his lapsarian thinking through the successive stages of his theological development has always been complex, dialectically comprising both supra- and infralapsarian aspects. Barth's mature Christocentric doctrine of election, while carrying supralapsarian incentives, may be described as "basically infralapsarian" according to the fundamental and quintessential definitions this chapter will offer: supralapsarianism is the position that the object of God's electing grace is neutral, unfallen humanity, while infralapsarianism contends that the object of divine election is God's eternal conception of fallen humanity.

    I am aware that the label "basically infralapsarian" can be unhelpful and misleading if it is not carefully qualified in such a way that the complex and dialectical nature of Barth's lapsarian thinking is well recognized. I therefore ask the reader to bear in mind that Barth's lapsarian position differs from traditional supra- and infralapsarianism in important ways such that it defies any simple identification as either supra- or infralapsarian, and thus not to lose sight of the complexity of Barth's lapsarian thinking when I use the description "basically infralapsarian."

True enough, Barth, in a detailed and insightful doctrinal-historical excursus on the Lapsarian Controversy of the seventeenth century in *CD* II/2, explicitly sides with supralapsarianism.[1] In fact, as early as *Romans* II (written 1920–1921), he had already taken an avowedly supralapsarian position.[2] However, recent research has shown that his understanding of Reformed orthodoxy relies heavily on the somewhat inadequate works of nineteenth-century German historiographers.[3] In particular, Ryan Glomsrud observes that Barth's "recovery" of seventeenth-century Reformed authors during his Göttingen years "was synonymous with his discovery of Heppe and a coterie of nineteenth-century historiographers of the tradition."[4] It was not "an entirely *ad fontes* event" in that "Barth encountered Reformed orthodoxy almost exclusively in the texts of the nineteenth-century historiographers . . . and not in the primary sources themselves."[5]

Although in his later years Barth had acquired and studied primary texts from Francis Turretin, Petrus van Mastricht, Gisbertus Voetius, Amandus Polanus and others, his collection and knowledge of Reformed-orthodox writers had hardly expanded beyond those mentioned in the secondary literatures of Heinrich Heppe and other nineteenth-century German historiographers. At least this is the case in Barth's excursus on the Lapsarian Controversy in *CD* II/2, §33, where he explicitly states that his discussions are based on the reports of Heppe and Alexander Schweizer.[6] One primary source from the seventeenth century that Barth cites extensively is Francis Turretin's *Institutes of Elenctic Theology*, but, as I shall argue, Barth missed some key passages in Turretin and, as a result, came to a somewhat inaccurate understanding of the latter's definitions of supra- and infralapsarianism.

By the time he was composing *CD* II/2 Barth had begun to consult primary sources, including Turretin and others, and was even able to discern

---

[1]*KD* II/2, 136-57; ET 127-45.
[2]*Römerbrief* II, 163; ET 172.
[3]See Ryan Glomsrud, "Karl Barth Between Pietism and Orthodoxy: A Post-Enlightenment Ressourcement of Classical Protestantism" (DPhil thesis, University of Oxford, 2009).
[4]Ryan Glomsrud, "Karl Barth as Historical Theologian," in *Engaging with Barth*, ed. David Gibson and Daniel Strange (Nottingham: Apollos, 2008), 89. Cf. Bruce McCormack, *Karl Barth's Critically Realistic Dialectical Theology* (Oxford: Clarendon, 1995), 329-36.
[5]Glomsrud, "Karl Barth as Historical Theologian," 86-87.
[6]*KD* II/2, 136; ET 127.

some of Heppe's misrepresentations of primary texts.[7] However, Barth's understanding of Reformed orthodoxy in general and of the Lapsarian Controversy in particular still depended heavily on nineteenth-century historiography. Comparing Barth's lapsarian excursus to Heppe's *Dogmatik*, for instance, reveals that the former's presentation of the Lapsarian Controversy is little more than a selective summary of the latter's quotations of primary sources along with a few passages from Schweizer.

Given such a case, readers trying to learn about the Lapsarian Controversy should exercise discernment when trying to steer through Barth's otherwise brilliant and insightful excursus on the historic debate. This excursus is theologically dense, and, in a manner akin to his small book on Anselm, which "tells us more about Barth than it does about the eleventh-century theologian,"[8] the reader should bear in mind that its chief value lies in what it tells us about his lapsarian thinking, and the historical-theological reports are secondary. After all, Barth is a dogmatician rather than a historical theologian, and technical imprecision in his historical-theological reports do not diminish the worth of his lapsarian excursus.

With regard to the historical-theological aspect of the excursus, Barth's admitted reliance on Heppe should signal a warning, as Richard Muller cautions that "Heppe's *Reformed Dogmatics*... overlooks [the] development of genuine prolegomena [in early Reformed orthodoxy] and presents from the outset a somewhat distorted presentation of Reformed system."[9] Carl Trueman, too, warns that "Heppe's ordering of topics, arrangement of quotations, and running commentary on the whole served to make the result something of a synthesis of Reformed Orthodoxy and the views of Heppe himself."[10]

To be fair, as far as Heppe's presentation of the Lapsarian Controversy is concerned, perhaps "inadequate" would be a more accurate description than "distorted," since Heppe does little more than simply offer a mosaic of quotations from selected primary sources without translating the Latin into

---

[7]E.g., *KD* II/2, 83-84; ET 77-78. Cf. Richard Muller, *Christ and the Decree* (Grand Rapids: Baker Academic, 1986), 9.
[8]McCormack, *Dialectical Theology*, 428.
[9]Richard Muller, *Post-Reformation Reformed Dogmatics*, vol. 1, *Prolegomena to Theology* (Grand Rapids: Baker Academic, 2003), 150.
[10]Carl Trueman, "Calvin, Barth, and Reformed Theology: Historical Prolegomena," in *Calvin, Barth and Reformed Theology*, ed. Neil MacDonald and Carl Trueman (Eugene, OR: Wipf and Stock, 2008), 17.

German. To demonstrate the case, in the sections on the Lapsarian Controversy in Heppe's *Dogmatik* (7.14-15; 8.3-9), the author's own explanations in German constitute less than one-tenth of the text, while the rest consists of direct quotations in Latin.[11] Lacking in these sections are clear definitions of the plenitude of confusing seventeenth-century scholastic terms in the quotations, and in reading these sections Barth's understanding of the terms *homo creabilis et labilis* (creatable and lapsable humanity) and *homo creatus et lapsus* (created and fallen humanity), which are central to the definitions of supra- and infralapsarianism, is not entirely accurate. That is, Heppe does not offer wrong definitions of the terms—he simply does not define them in sufficient detail. What Barth in turn does is to read his own inaccurate definitions, developed as early as *Romans* II (it is unclear how he got these definitions), into Heppe's reports.[12]

Additionally, Barth's complete omission of seventeenth-century Puritans on the other side of the British Isles, including major theologians like Richard Sibbes, Samuel Rutherford, John Owen, Thomas Goodwin and others, is an instance of the inadequacy of nineteenth-century German historiography on Reformed orthodoxy, suggesting that Barth's understanding of the Lapsarian Controversy lacks at least one crucial piece of the puzzle.

To be sure, as far as the definitions of supra- and infralapsarianism are concerned, Continental and British Reformed-orthodox theologians were at one accord. However, British Puritans tended to be more concise in their wording, while Continental Puritans tended to employ more scholastic terminology and *quodam-modo* expressions. One instance, as we shall see, is Francis Turretin's use of the language of divine "foreseeing" in explaining the infralapsarian view of the object of election. Though the Swiss-Italian Puritan is careful to qualify that this "foreseeing," *quodam-modo*, is strictly eternal, and that the "foreseen" *obiectum* is by no means God's foresight of actually created and fallen humanity in history, the writings of the British Puritans might well have made this matter much clearer for Barth.

Meanwhile, just as Barth might have understood Turretin's definitions of supra- and infralapsarianism more accurately had he paid closer attention

---

[11]Heinrich Heppe, *Die Dogmatik der Evangelisch-Reformierten Kirche* (Whitefish, MT: Kessinger, 2010), 108-10, 117-23.
[12]We shall see how Barth defines supra- and infralapsarianism in chap. 2.

to the fuller context and the qualifying details, in Barth's reading of Heppe's selection of primary texts, Barth omits some important passages that might have helped him to define supra- and infralapsarianism with greater accuracy (see chapter two).

In what follows, I shall offer some basic definitions of supra- and infralapsarianism in light of primary sources and recent secondary literature, definitions that are not my own but are in line with the scholarly consensus in Puritan studies. On this basis I shall proceed to chapter two to discuss Barth's definitions of supra- and infralapsarianism, and contend that he is in fact more in line with the basic position of infralapsarianism than with that of supralapsarianism.

Supra- and Infralapsarianism: Shared Assumptions

Divine sovereignty and permission of sin. As mentioned above, Reformed-orthodox supra- and infralapsarians share the same basic understanding of divine predestination and humanity's fall, which is nicely summarized by Calvin's paraphrase of Augustine in explaining the origin of evil.

> We make most sound confession . . . that God the Lord of all things, who made all things very good, foreknew that evil would arise out of this good, and also knew that it contributed more to His glory to bring good out of evil than not to allow evil at all; so He ordained the life of men and angels so that in it He might first show what freewill could do, and then what the gift of His grace and the judgment of His justice could do.[13]

As if this Augustinian language does not sufficiently represent God's sovereignty, Calvin elsewhere stresses that humanity's sin is "no mere 'permission'" on God's part.[14] Insisting on the unity and simplicity of God's will, he states that God "creates light and darkness, that he forms good and bad; that nothing evil happens that [God] himself has not done."[15] Agreeing that evil is in a sense permitted by God, he qualifies that God "does not unwillingly permit it, but willingly; nor would [God],

---

[13] John Calvin, *Concerning the Eternal Predestination of God*, trans. J. K. S. Reid (Philadelphia: Westminster, 1961), 67. Here Calvin is paraphrasing chapter 10 of Augustine, *On Rebuke and Grace*.

[14] John Calvin, *Institutes of the Christian Religion*, ed. John T. McNeil, trans. Ford Lewis Battles (Philadelphia: Westminster, 1960), 1.18.1.

[15] Ibid., 1.18.3.

being good, allow evil to be done, unless being also almighty he could make good even out of evil."[16]

By the late sixteenth century, Reformed theologians had generally come to agree that Adam fell into sin by an "effectively permissive decree" of God: they generally agreed that in God's eternal counsels the element of humankind's fall is in one sense foreseen (in the Augustinian-Calvinist sense as summarized in the block quote above) and permitted by God, though this "foresight," as it were, is strictly eternal, and is by no means God's passive consideration of humankind's actual action in history. For the Reformed orthodox, divine "foresight" of historical events is by no means a cause, efficient or teleological, of any divine decree; rather, all events in the creaturely sphere occurred by the execution of God's sovereign decrees alone, which are logically independent of (i.e., uncaused by) actual human actions.

This *quodam-modo* language of divine "foreseeing," adopted by Calvin in the sixteenth century and the likes of Turretin in the seventeenth century, can of course be misleading, notwithstanding all the careful qualifications that these theologians have attempted to make. It is thus unsurprising that the Canons of Dort, which, as we shall see, adopts an infralapsarian position without repudiating supralapsarianism, consistently avoids the language of divine "foreseeing" in its positive doctrinal assertions, and uses it only in describing the Arminian position that it rejects. One crucial shared assumption among the Reformed, supra- and infralapsarians alike is that none of God's eternal decrees are based on God's passive consideration of any event in historical actuality.

On these shared assumptions, a supralapsarianism began to emerge in the late sixteenth century, most notably advanced by Theodore Beza (1519–1605). Proponents of this supralapsarianism asserted double predestination irrespective of humanity's sin, while agreeing with infralapsarians, who were the majority among the Reformed, that the God who permitted the fall is by no means the author of sin. The English supralapsarian William Perkins (1558–1602), for example, denies that his position makes God culpable for humanity's sin, contending that God "planted nothing in Adam, whereby he should fall into sin, but left him to his own liberty, not hindering his fall

---

[16]Ibid.

when it might."[17] At the Synod of Dort, a confessional consensus was established among the Reformed, where it was agreed that Adam's fall occurred by an efficaciously permissive divine decree.[18]

However, how did the sovereign God allow something so alien to God's holiness to come into existence? In pursuing this question, sixteenth- and seventeenth-century Reformed-orthodox theologians attempted to formulate logically rigorous answers.

Diversity of opinions: Brief taxonomy. From the current analysis it can be inferred that the Lapsarian Controversy was essentially a theodicy inquiry: on the suppositions of God's holiness and sovereignty, how are divine reprobation and permission of sin to be understood? Supra- and infralapsarianism are two formulations of the logical relations between God's eternal decrees of double predestination, creation and permission of the fall, aimed at taking into account the reality of sin and evil without compromising God's sovereignty and holiness.

Note that the terms *supralapsarianism* and *infralapsarianism* represent two general opinions within Reformed orthodoxy, but, as has long been known and as John Fesko's studies have recently shown with greater historical precision, there is diversity within each of the two camps, just as there are intermediate views that attempt to reconcile them.[19] Fesko lists the following taxonomies:

> Turretin identifies three different opinions: those who ascend above the fall (*supra lapsum*), and hence are supralapsarians; those who descend below the fall (*infra lapsum*), and others who stop in the fall (*in lapsu*). . . . In his Conference with Junius, Arminius identifies three positions, two supras, man as to be created or man as created but unfallen, and one infra, man as created and fallen. . . . Edward Leigh confirms Arminius's taxonomy and offers the same: . . . man to be made . . . , man already made, but not fallen, and man

---

[17] William Perkins, *Works*, vol. 2, *A Treatise of the Manner and Order of Predestination, and of the Largeness of Gods Grace*, 619. Quoted in Mark Jones and Joel Beeke, "William Perkins on Predestination," in *A Puritan Theology: Doctrine for Life* (Grand Rapids: Reformation Heritage Books, 2012), 121.

[18] See John Fesko, "Lapsarian Diversity at the Synod of Dort," in *Drawn into Controversie: Reformed Theological Diversity and Debates Within Seventeenth-Century British Puritanism*, ed. Michael Haykin and Mark Jones (Göttingen: Vandenhoeck & Ruprecht, 2011).

[19] John Fesko, "The Westminster Confession and Lapsarianism: Calvin and the Divines," in *The Westminster Confession into the Twenty-First Century*, ed. Ligon Duncan (Fearn, Scotland: Mentor, 2005), 2:477-525; Fesko, "Lapsarian Diversity at the Synod of Dort," 99-123.

made and fallen.... Baxter also offers the same taxonomy.... If these theologians are accurate, then according to the compiled taxonomies, there are at least two kinds of infras and two kinds of supras.[20]

My aim here is not to account for the details of the diversity, but to arrive at general and quintessential definitions that accurately describe supra- and infralapsarianism respectively. I will show that what unifies the supralapsarians is the essential position that the object of election is unfallen, while the infralapsarians at one accord contend that the object of election is fallen.

Unity in diversity: Eternality of the decrees. The point of contention between supra- and infralapsarianism is whether God's consideration of humanity's sin is presupposed in double predestination (election and reprobation). Supra- and infralapsarians agree that humankind's actual fall in history was *eternally* decreed by God, thus Adam's sin was part of God's eternal plan rather than a surprise to God.

The various supralapsarian (*supra-lapsum*: above or before the fall) positions agree that God's eternal decree of humankind's fall presupposes election and reprobation. By contrast, the various infralapsarian (*infra-lapsum*: below or after the fall) positions at one accord contend that election and reprobation presuppose the divine decree of the fall.

Note that in referring to God's *eternal* decrees, supra- and infralapsarians alike have in mind not only an Augustinian understanding of timelessness but also a Boethian notion of successionlessness and simultaneity. Louis Berkhof, despite inadequacies in his reports and analyses, puts it well: "The divine decree is eternal in the sense that it lies entirely in eternity. The decree ... partakes of the *simultaneousness* and the *successionlessness* of the eternal."[21] Thus in both supra- and infralapsarianism, "the order in which the different elements ... stand to each other may not be regarded as temporal, but only as logical. There is a real chronological order in the events as effectuated, but not in the decrees respecting them."[22]

---

[20] John Fesko, *The Theology of the Westminster Standards: Historical Context and Theological Insights* (Wheaton, IL: Crossway, 2014), 105. See also Richard Muller, "Revising the Predestination Paradigm: An Alternative to Supralapsarianism, Infralapsarianism, and Hypothetical Universalism" (lecture for the Mid-America Fall Lecture Series, Mid-America Reformed Seminary, Dyer, Indiana, 2008).

[21] Louis Berkhof, *Systematic Theology* (Edinburgh: Banner of Truth, 1958), 104 (emphasis added).

[22] Ibid.

In fact, Heppe also notes (rather cursorily) that there is no sequentiality to the decrees in God's mental processions.[23] Unfortunately, Barth has not picked up from his reading of Heppe this understanding of Reformed orthodoxy's view of the successionlessness and simultaneity of the divine decrees. (Barth's understanding of eternity involves a certain notion of succession—this pertains to another discussion.)

While Berkhof's *Systematic Theology* and Heppe's *Dogmatik* are somewhat inadequate in their accounts of the Lapsarian Controversy, their comments on the logical independence of the eternal decrees from the actual executions thereof accurately reflect the shared conviction of Reformed-orthodox authors from the seventeenth century. This is evinced by a passage from Richard Sibbes's (1577–1635) preface to Paul Baynes's (1573–1617) 1604 book in which the latter contends for a rigorous supralapsarian position. In this passage Sibbes, in friendly spirit, lists three points of agreement among supra- and infralapsarians of his time.

> Both [supra- and infralapsarians] agree in this: First, that there was an *eternal separation of men in God's purpose*. Secondly, that this first decree of severing man to his ends, is an act of sovereignty over his creature, and *altogether independent of anything in the creature*, as a cause of it . . . ; *sin foreseen cannot be the cause*, because that was common to both [elect and reprobate], and therefore could be no cause of severing. Thirdly, all agree in this, that damnation is an act of divine justice, which supposeth demerit; and therefore the *execution* of God's decree is founded on sin.[24]

Two points may be observed. First, according to Sibbes, supra- and infralapsarians of his time agree that double predestination is *eternal*. Second, for supra- and infralapsarians alike, the eternality of predestination implies that it is by no means caused by anything in the creaturely realm, nor is it logically dependent on the actual execution of any of God's decrees, or even God's foresight thereof ("sin foreseen cannot be the cause").

Heppe shows that this is also the shared understanding among Continental Reformed-orthodox theologians: "Predestination does not first appear temporally after the Fall. On the contrary it belongs to God's eternity,

---

[23]Heppe, *Dogmatik*, 103-4.
[24]Richard Sibbes, "To the Reader," in Paul Baynes, *A Commentary Upon the First Chapter of the Epistle to the Ephesians* (London, 1618) (emphasis added).

to His essential being.—Bucan (XXXVI, 11): 'This decree does not begin precisely after men have been created or have begun to sin; but before the foundations of the world were laid, from eternity, that very thing was purposed by God.'"[25] Heppe rightly concludes: "Thus in no way may the ground of election be sought in anything that is outside God."[26] This is affirmed by a quote from Amandus Polanus (1561–1610), describing the Reformed position in general: "The efficient impulsive cause on account of which our eternal election was made is nothing outside God, and accordingly not the will of man; not a good use of the grace we may have received from God; not our foreseen faith; not men's foreknown merits . . . ; nor yet a prevision of any of these things, which was and is in God."[27] Because of the eternality of the divine decrees strictly defined in Reformed-orthodox terms, the Swiss-French divine Guliemus Bucanus (died 1603) carefully distinguishes between "the decree itself in God's mind to save and reject men" and "the execution of progress of that actual eternal decree through mediate causes."[28]

Patrick Gillespie (1617–1675), a Scottish Puritan who served as principal of Glasgow University in 1653–1659 under Oliver Cromwell's auspices, also emphasizes the eternality of the divine decrees in his discourse on the covenant of redemption (*pactum salutis*, the Reformed notion of an eternal covenant between the persons of the Trinity for the salvation of the elect):

> This transaction having been from eternity, it was a concluded bargain before the creatures had a being. . . . The Father and Son were not only free from all natural necessity and outward compulsion; but also from all hire, allurement or motive from any thing without their own will; there was nothing in man, *no not foreseen*, that could allure or move; far less hire the Father to give Christ, to engage him in this work [of redemption], nor Christ to engage his name in our bond.[29]

Gillespie makes clear here that since the *pactum salutis*, which concerns God's eternal plan to redeem fallen creatures, is "from eternity," it is com-

---

[25]Heinrich Heppe, *Reformed Dogmatics*, ed. Ernst Bizer, trans. G. T. Thomson (London: Wakeman, 2010), 162.
[26]Ibid., 166.
[27]Ibid.
[28]Ibid., 155.
[29]Patrick Gillespie, *The Ark of the Covenant Opened* (London: Parkhurst, 1677), 59. I am indebted to Professor Fesko for pointing me to this work.

pletely free and sovereign on God's part, causally independent from anything God foresaw in the creature. This understanding of the *pactum salutis* has been adopted by supralapsarians such as Gillespie and Thomas Goodwin, as well as infralapsarians like John Owen.[30] We shall discuss the cases of Goodwin and Owen anon.

It would be helpful at this juncture to note that the notion of an intratrinitarian covenant was first developed by the Dutch infralapsarian Johannes Coccerius (1603–1660), "a much-maligned figure" in "the scholarship on Reformed orthodoxy."[31] Readers of Barth will recall that he, following Herman Bavinck, is deeply antagonistic toward many features of Coccerius's theology, not least the notion of an intratrinitarian covenant that later came to be called *pactum salutis* (though in the end Bavinck still retains the notion of this *pactum*). Whether Barth and Bavinck are correct about Coccerius in their attacks is tangential to this book, and I shall leave this matter to experts in the field of Puritan studies.[32]

The point to be noted here is the way Coccerius emphasizes the eternality of God's decrees. This was one of the theological axioms that set the Reformed apart from the Socinians, "who asserted that God's decrees differ from God *realiter* and 'that not all decrees are eternal, but certain ones are temporal.'"[33]

Coccerius begins his refutation of this Socinian view by stating the major premise of the inseparable unity of God's will and essence: "it is superfluous to ask in what respect God's decrees differ from his essence."[34] On this premise, he employs an argument reductio ad absurdum against the Socinians: "If any fresh will exists in God, it exists in time. Therefore the will of God will be subject to time; therefore God himself will be temporal, not eternal."[35]

---

[30]See Ryan McGraw, *Heavenly Directory: Trinitarian Piety, Public Worship and a Reassessment of John Owen's Theology* (Göttingen: Vandenhoeck & Ruprecht, 2014), 155-65.
[31]Glomsrud, "Karl Barth as Historical Theologian," 104.
[32]Suffice it here to say that scholarship over the last decade has shown that Coccerius's theology has been seriously misunderstood in the past. This should caution against any attempt to understand Reformed covenant theology through the lenses of Barth's unoriginal criticisms of the Dutch divine. Ibid., 131-32. See also Willem Van Asselt, *The Federal Theology of Johannes Coccerius (1603–1669)*, trans. Raymond A. Blacketer (Leiden: Brill, 2001).
[33]Van Asselt, *Federal Theology*, 57. Van Asselt is quoting Coccerius's description of Socinianism.
[34]Ibid.
[35]Ibid.

While modern theology might be more open to the idea of divine becoming or process, inserting temporality into God's essence was horrendously unacceptable to the seventeenth-century mind. Yet the Socinian view of the temporality of some of the divine decrees would, on the major premise of the unity of God's decrees and essence, lead to exactly such a conclusion. In this syllogistic reductio ad absurdum, the eternality of the divine decrees is shown to be axiomatic for Cocceius.

It is because of the eternality of the decrees, which as we saw are axiomatic to Reformed orthodoxy, that Cocceius felt the need to develop the notion of an eternal, intratrinitarian covenant in addition to the temporal covenants of works and of grace. Some contemporary proponents of historic Reformed theology share Barth's opinion that the *pactum salutis* is a superfluous and speculative idea, while others take this notion to be a significant and praiseworthy feature of Reformed theology. Whatever the case, the point to be noted here is how the notion of an intratrinitarian pact demonstrates the classical Reformed understanding of the eternality of divine decrees. Cocceius, an infralapsarian, developed this notion in order to ensure that God's will, which he takes to be strictly eternal, is distinguished from the historical "execution" of the decrees through the covenants of works and of grace.[36] The later doctrine of the *pactum salutis* developed on the basis of Cocceius's covenant theology was adopted by many supralapsarians as well as infralapsarians of the seventeenth century.

In short, the eternality of the divine decrees is an inviolable axiom in Reformed orthodoxy. Supra- and infralapsarians are completely at one accord with regard to this axiom, and they are always careful to emphasize that God's eternal decisions are completely sovereign, logically independent of any historical event or human decision. This is crucial for a correct understanding of the Lapsarian Controversy.

Supra- and Infralapsarianism Defined

Obiectum praedestinationis. Central to the Lapsarian Controversy is the question of the object of predestination (*obiectum praedestinationis*), the watershed dividing supralapsarians from infralapsarians: "When the decrees

---
[36]Ibid., 57-58.

of election and reprobation came into existence were men considered as fallen or as unfallen?"[37]

While diverse arguments and schemes have been developed by both camps, what unifies the infralapsarians is their central thesis that the object of *obiectum praedestinationis* is created and fallen humanity (*homo creatus et lapsus*), whereas supralapsarians at one accord contend that the *obiectum praedestinationis* is unfallen humanity (variously referred to, e.g., as *homo creabilis et labilis, homo creatus sed nondum lapsus, homo creandus et lapsandus sed nondum lapsus*).

Note that these terms refer to God's eternal conception of the object of predestination, rather than humans in created actuality. Thus the Swiss-Italian Reformed-orthodox infralapsarian Francis Turretin (1623–1687) says that in the Lapsarian Controversy "it is not inquired whether the creation of man and the permission of the fall come under the decree of God (for it is acknowledged on both sides that this as well as that was determined by God). But the question is . . . whether God in the sign of reason [*in signo rationis*] is to be considered as having thought about the salvation and destruction of men before he thought of their creation and fall."[38] This makes clear that for supra- and infralapsarians alike, the logical relations between election/reprobation and creation/fall are strictly within God's eternal mental processions.

Echoing the Canons of Dort in stating that divine election is not caused, teleologically or efficiently, by historical actuality, Turretin says in the heading of section eleven, fourth topic of his celebrated *Institutes*, under the rubric "The Cause of Election": "Is election made from the foresight of faith, or works; or from the grace of God alone? The former we deny; the latter we affirm."[39]

It is true that Turretin occasionally uses the language of divine "foreseeing" in setting forth his infralapsarian view of God's decree of Adam's fall (in fact, this Augustinian language has been employed by supra- and infralapsarians alike to explain God's permission of sin), in a way that may

---

[37]Loraine Boettner, *The Reformed Doctrine of Predestination* (Philadelphia: P&R, 1932), 126.
[38]Francis Turretin, *Institutes of Elenctic Theology*, ed. James Dennison Jr., trans. George Giger (Phillipsburg, NJ: P&R, 1992), 1:342.
[39]Ibid., 1:355.

cause readers unfamiliar with Reformed orthodoxy to confuse infralapsarianism with Arminian or semi-Pelagian understandings of divine foreknowledge as the ground of election. Yet note that when Turretin speaks of divine foresight of the *obiectum praedestinationis*, he is careful to point out that "although the object of predestination is determined to be fallen humanity, it does not follow that predestination is actually made in time. Fallen humanity is understood as to his known and foreseen being, not as to his *real* being. Also the prescience of the fall and its permissive decree is no less eternal than the predestination itself."[40] The second to last sentence in this quote is important for clarifying what Turretin does *not* mean by the language of divine "foreseeing": it is not God's foresight of actually fallen human beings in history ("not as to his *real* being"). Rather, according to the last sentence in the quote, God's foresight, *quodam-modo*, is strictly within God's eternal predestination. This shows that Turretin's notion of *homo lapsus* as divine foresight, as it were, of sinful humanity does not place the *obiectum praedestinationis* in temporal actuality. Rather, *homo lapsus* is strictly God's eternal conception of the object of election-reprobation in God's mind.

On that note, English Puritan Stephen Charnock (1628–1680) explains the Reformed-orthodox understanding of divine prescience, which is shared by supra- and infralapsarians:

> God's foreknowledge is not, simply considered, the cause of anything.... Nothing is because God knows it, but because God wills it, either positively or permissively; God knows *all things possible*; yet, because God knows them they are not brought into actual existence, but *remain still only as things possible* . . . ; the will is the immediate principle, and the power the immediate cause.[41]

From this Reformed-orthodox principle it follows that for supra- and infralapsarians alike, God's prescience of humankind's actual fall could not have been the cause or ground of election-reprobation.

---

[40]Ibid., 1:349. Translation revised. Giger's translation is misleading, rendering "non sequitur Praedestinationem *demum* factam in tempore" as "it does not follow that predestination is made *only* in time" (Turrettino, *Institutio Theologicae Elencticae* 1.4.9.26).

[41]Stephen Charnock, *The Existence and Attributes of God* (Grand Rapids: Baker, 1996), 1:448 (emphasis added).

If this is not clear enough, the infralapsarian John Edwards (1637–1716) makes it unmistakable that for infralapsarians, just as supralapsarians, "the decree of election is absolute in as much as 'tis founded wholly on God's free will and pleasure, and . . . not on any thing that was fore-seen in man."[42] Strictly speaking, then, the infralapsarian *homo lapsus* does not even refer to God's foresight of actually created and fallen humanity, but only to God's eternal conception of human beings as sinful and lost.

With regard to the supralapsarian *obiectum*, it is worth pointing out that there are variations in terminology and understanding. The supralapsarian Samuel Rutherford (1600[?]–1661), for instance, uses the future-passive participle to describe the *obiectum* as "*homo creandus [et lapsandus sed] . . . nondum creatus [et lapsus]*," "certain to be created/to fall, but not-yet created/fallen."[43] In using this terminology, Rutherford shares with other supralapsarians the conviction that God eternally conceives of unfallen humanity as the *obiectum praedestinationis*.

On the supralapsarian view, election-reprobation is causally independent of the decrees of creation and the fall. That is (as most supralapsarians would have it), in God's eternal plan, election-reprobation is both the final and efficient cause (purpose and basis) of the subsequent decrees. As Beza puts it, "Predestination . . . is nothing else than His will unto the fixed end of the destination of either salvation or destruction . . . and the subordinate means unto these two ends."[44] Most supralapsarians would agree with Beza in contending that God predestined some unto salvation and others unto destruction simply because God decided to do so.[45] On this view, double predestination is not a decree in which God conceives of humanity as sinful. God is sovereign and thus free to predestine humans for damnation even if God does not conceive of them as guilty of sin and deserving punishment.

Varying formulations of the ordo decretorum. Related to the question of the object of election is the question of logical precedence in God's eternal decrees: does the double decree of election-reprobation logically precede or follow God's decrees to create the world and permit the fall?

---

[42]John Edwards, *Veritas Redux* (Andover, UK: Gale, 2010), 71.
[43]Guy Richards, "Samuel Rutherford's Supralapsarianism Revealed," *Scottish Journal of Theology* 59 (2006): 29.
[44]Theodore Beza, *Tractationum theologicarum* (Geneva, 1582), 3:402 (translation mine).
[45]Beza, *Tractationum* (Geneva, 1570), 1:173-74.

The following logical order has often been attributed to infralapsarianism: "1. the decree to create the world and (all) men; 2. the decree that (all) men would fall; 3. the election of some fallen men to salvation in Christ (and the reprobation of the others); 4. the decree to redeem the elect by the cross work of Christ; 5. the decree to apply Christ's redemptive benefits to the elect."[46]

By contrast, the following *ordo* is often used to describe supralapsarianism: "1. The election of some men to salvation in Christ (and the reprobation of the others); 2. The decree to create the world and both kinds of men; 3. The decree that all men would fall; 4. The decree to redeem the elect, who are now sinners, by the cross work of Christ; 5. The decree to apply Christ's redemptive benefits to these elect sinners."[47]

To present supra- and infralapsarianism with these *ordines*, however, is somewhat simplistic. First, these are generalizations of the supra- and infralapsarian *ordines*, but there are variations to these orderings within both camps.[48] For instance, Heppe provides Beza's schematic diagram of the *ordo*, which reveals that Heppe's own five-step presentation would be quite an oversimplification if applied to Beza's *ordo*.[49]

Second, while the five-step generalization would be an oversimplification in the case of Beza, it is often an overcomplication in other cases. Rutherford, for instance, never developed a rigorous *ordo*, but merely maintains that "God's electing of us cannot be after the consideration of our creation and fall."[50] Fesko comments: "While Rutherford's treatment resonates with supralapsarianism . . . , an *ordo decretorum* [is not] stated."[51]

In the case of John Owen (1616–1683), a supralapsarian in his earlier years, the *ordo* is usually presented in a subtle and narrative way, rather than in a five-step-point form. The following is an example from *The Death of Death in the Death of Christ*:

---

[46]Robert Reymond, *A New Systematic Theology of the Christian Faith* (Nashville: Thomas Nelson, 1998), 480.
[47]Ibid., 488. Cf. Boettner, *Reformed Doctrine*, 126; Heppe, *Dogmatik*, 110; Herman Bavinck, *Reformed Dogmatics*, vol. 2, *God and Creation*, ed. John Bolt, trans. John Vriend (Grand Rapids: Baker Academic, 2004), 382-83.
[48]Reymond, *Systematic Theology*, 488-89.
[49]Heppe, *Dogmatik*, 109-10.
[50]Richards, "Rutherford's Supralapsarianism," 29.
[51]Fesko, "Westminster Confession and Lapsarianism," 499.

God hold[s] the lump of mankind in his own power, as the clay in the hand of the potter, determining to make some vessels unto honour..., and others to dishonour..., and to this end suffer[s] them all to fall into sin and the guilt of condemnation, whereby they became all liable to his wrath and curse; his purpose to save some of these doth not at all exempt or free them from the common condition of the rest, in respect of themselves and the truth of their estate, until some actual thing be accomplished for the bringing of them nigh unto himself: so that notwithstanding his eternal purpose, his wrath, in respect of the effects, abideth on them until that eternal purpose do make out itself in some distinguishing act of free grace.[52]

It is only a little more than implicit here that Owen ascribes logical priority to the decree of election-reprobation over the decree to permit the fall. His main purpose in this treatise is to contend that Christ died only for the elect.

The first indication of Owen's conversion to infralapsarianism came in 1653 in the publication of *A Dissertation on Divine Justice*, where he takes up the task to "discourse and dispute on the vindicatory justice of God, and the necessity of its exercise, on the supposition of the existence of sin."[53] While the earlier, supralapsarian Owen asserted that the satisfaction of divine justice is predicated on the double decree of election-reprobation, the infralapsarian Owen now contends that God's will to punish creatures is "on the supposition of the existence of sin."[54] Throughout the *Dissertation*, Owen's concern is the satisfaction of God's punitive justice, and his infralapsarian conviction that election-reprobation presupposes *homo lapsus* as the *obiectum* underlies his argumentation without being fully spelled out in the form of an *ordo*.[55]

Another case is Thomas Goodwin (1600–1680), a contemporary of Owen. Goodwin's lapsarian position is quite complex. On a cursory reading Michael Horton identifies Goodwin as an infralapsarian, but Carl Trueman has shown that Goodwin is in fact a supralapsarian.[56] Goodwin's formulation of

---

[52] John Owen, "The Death of Death in the Death of Christ," in *The Works of John Owen*, vol. 10, *The Death of Christ* (Philadelphia: Banner of Truth, 1991), 275.
[53] John Owen, "A Dissertation on Divine Justice," in *Death of Christ*, 486.
[54] Ibid., 510 (emphasis added).
[55] Ibid., 596-600.
[56] Mark Jones, *Why Heaven Kissed Earth: The Christology of the Puritan Reformed Orthodox Theologian, Thomas Goodwin (1600–1680)* (Göttingen: Vandenhoeck & Ruprecht, 2010), 128. Cf.

the "covenant of redemption" (*pactum salutis*)—"the eternal transactions between the Father and the Son" in which "the Son promised to act as a surety for the elect and so 'satisfy his Father for all the Wrong [...] done to him'"—is clearly "considered in the context of man as fallen."[57] It is for this reason that Horton took Goodwin to be an infralapsarian. However, there is a distinction between election and the *pactum salutis*. Mark Jones has convincingly shown that Goodwin takes a supralapsarian position when it comes to the doctrine of election.[58]

With regard to the doctrine of election, Goodwin distinguishes between election and predestination in a nuanced way. Election is the end of God's eternal decrees, while predestination is the means toward the end. Jones clarifies:

> The end is either God's glory, what Goodwin calls the "supreme end of all," or the "ultimate end," which refers to the glory God designed to bring the elect into. . . . The latter end—the "ultimate end"—has in view the perfection of Christ's elect. This is what Goodwin has in mind when he affirms that the decree regarding the end was not upon the consideration of the fall. . . . However, the means to the "ultimate end" considers man as fallen.[59]

In this way, Goodwin's supralapsarian doctrine of election, which views the object of election as unfallen but the object of predestination as fallen, is to be distinguished from what he calls "pure supralapsarianism," which "takes into the means to [the ultimate] end, the creation, and the permission of the fall, and calls them means to bring about that intention or decree to that ultimate end or glory specified."[60] Goodwin contends against "pure supralapsarianism" that the decrees of creation and permission of the fall are not directly means unto the supreme end of election. Rather, Christ's soteric

---

Michael Horton, "Thomas Goodwin and the Puritan Doctrine of Assurance: Continuity and Discontinuity in the Reformed Tradition, 1600–1680" (PhD diss., Wycliffe Hall, Oxford and Coventry University, 1995), 66; Carl Trueman, *The Claims of Truth: John Owen's Trinitarian Theology* (Carlisle: Paternoster, 1998), 138.

[57] Jones, *Why Heaven Kissed Earth*, 128.

[58] Mark Jones, "Thomas Goodwin's Christological Supralapsarianism," in Jones and Beeke, *A Puritan Theology*, 148-59. Also see Thomas Goodwin, *A Discourse of Election*, in *The Works of Thomas Goodwin, D.D.* (Grand Rapids: Reformation Heritage Books, 2006), 9:94. By "Christological Supralapsarianism" Jones is mainly contending that Goodwin's christological doctrine of election is supralapsarian, rather than describing a supralapsarian Christology, though, as Jones points out, Goodwin's Christology is also supralapsarian.

[59] Jones, "Christological Supralapsarianism," 155.

[60] Ibid.

works are God's means of bringing the elect unto the ultimate end of glory. In Goodwin's doctrine of election, then, the *ordo* is presented as a complex scheme of means and ends.

Goodwin does not fundamentally disagree with those whom he calls "pure supralapsarians." Beza, too, distinguishes between the ends and means of God's eternal decrees, and identifies the *obiectum praedestinationis* as *homo creabilis et labilis* only with regard to the ends of election-reprobation.[61] Though Beza would identify the decrees of creation and the fall as part of the means toward election, his emphasis is on Christ's soteric works as well. With regard to the decrees concerning salvation as the means unto election-reprobation in Beza's *ordo*, humanity is considered fallen, as these subordinate decrees are logically subsequent to the subordinate decrees of creation and the fall.[62]

Another "pure supralapsarian" is Johannes Maccovius (1588–1644), whose supralapsarianism and condemnation of infralapsarianism were a subject of controversy at the Synod of Dort. He distinguishes between election unto the ultimate end of eternal glory (*electio ad finem*) and election unto grace as the means unto that end (*electio ad media*). Maccovius's notion of election unto grace is primarily concerned with Christ's soteric works, though he would see the decrees of creation and the fall as part of *electio ad media*. For Maccovius, the "object" of *electio ad media* is "fallen human beings."[63] However, in *electio ad finem*, God's eternal decree concerns "humans before they have done anything good or bad."[64] Here we see that Maccovius's supralapsarianism is primarily defined by the position that the *obiectum praedestinationis* is *homines antequam quidquam fecissent boni vel mali*, that is, unfallen humanity.

Much more can be said about Goodwin and Maccovius. My point here is that their lapsarian thinking, just as that of Rutherford and Owen, is primarily defined in terms of the object of election as fallen or unfallen, rather

---

[61] Beza, *Tractationum*, 3:402.
[62] Ibid., 404–5.
[63] *Haec electio [ad media] pro objecto habet hominen lapsum*. Johannes Maccovius, *De aeterna Dei electione* (Franeker, 1618), thesis 5. See Willem Van Asselt, "On the Maccovius Affair," in *Revisiting the Synod of Dordt*, ed. Aza Goudriaan and Fred van Lieburg (Leiden: Brill, 2006), 238.
[64] Ibid., thesis 8: *Namque dum eadem agit de electione ad finem asserit Deum in aeterno decreto suo eligisse homines antequam quidquam fecissent boni vel mali* (translation mine).

than a rigorous or expressly listed *ordo rerum decretarum*. While Beza holds to a rigorous *ordo*, what unifies him with other supralapsarians is not so much his *ordo*, which varies from one theologian to another, but his contention that the object of election-reprobation is unfallen humanity.

Yet another case is Turretin, whose arguments against supralapsarianism shed light on the fundamental difference between the two lapsarian positions. Turretin's definition of the two positions constitute two main parts in the fourth topic of his *Institutes*: he first deals with the question of the *obiectum*, and then with the question of the *ordo*. While he acknowledges the significance of the *ordo*, his repudiation of supralapsarianism focuses on the *obiectum*, since this is the most fundamental watershed between supra- and infralapsarianism. Turretin advances four arguments against the supralapsarian thesis that "the decree of [double] predestination should be made to precede the decree of creation and the permission of the fall."[65] First, if God decides to punish humans whom God considers nonguilty, then "the first act of God's will towards some of his creatures [would be] made to be an act of hatred," and since God's will corresponds to God's nature, this would render hatred essential to God's being.[66] Second, the supralapsarian belief that God decided to create humans "for the purpose of illustrating his justice in their damnation" would "indicate that he is neither perfectly good nor perfectly wise and just."[67] Third, if the object of election is "neither miserable nor guilty; yea, . . . not even conceived of as yet existing," then God's mercy in election would be quite meaningless.[68] Last, the supralapsarian thesis that election-reprobation is the final cause of the decree of the fall is really another way of saying that God caused Adam to sin in order to reprobate some of God's creatures, which would render God a tyrant.[69]

According to Turretin, the supra-infra debate hinges on one simple question: is the object of election fallen or unfallen?[70] The question of the *ordo* stems from the question of the *obiectum*: if the object of election is fallen, it follows that election logically follows God's decree to permit the fall,

---

[65]Turretin, *Institutes*, 1:418.
[66]Ibid.
[67]Ibid.
[68]Ibid.
[69]Ibid.
[70]Ibid., 341.

and if the *obiectum* is unfallen, then vice versa. All four of Turretin's arguments are specifically targeted at the supralapsarian notion that the *obiectum praedestinationis* is unfallen humanity—"neither miserable nor guilty." While the *ordo* is indeed significant for Turretin, he sees the *obiectum* as the main contention between supra- and infralapsarians.

Conclusion

The cases presented in this chapter show that the basic watershed between supra- and infralapsarianism is whether God eternally conceives of the object of election-reprobation as fallen. This is not to say that the *ordo decretorum* is unimportant. As Fesko comments, "There are two basic considerations regarding lapsarianism: (1) the *ordo decretorum* . . . and (2) the object of predestination."[71] However, "the number and order of the decrees can vary from theologian to theologian; therefore the question ultimately hinges upon how a theologian understands the object of predestination."[72] In other words, the point of contention between supra- and infralapsarianism is primarily defined by the question, "Does God take into account man's sin in the divine decree of election?"[73] Though there is diversity within both supra- and infralapsarianism, what defines supralapsarianism in general is the thesis that in election-reprobation God considers humanity as unfallen, while what defines infralapsarianism is the view that in eternal double predestination—before the actual creation of the world—God conceives of fallen humanity as the object of election-reprobation. These definitions will serve as the basis on which I proceed to discuss Barth's lapsarian position in the following chapters.

---

[71]Fesko, "Lapsarian Diversity," 100.
[72]Ibid.
[73]Ibid.

2

Church Dogmatics §33

BARTH'S LAPSARIAN
POSITION REASSESSED

THIS CHAPTER EXAMINES BARTH'S lapsarian excursus in *CD* II/2, §33, to demonstrate that despite his avowed favor toward supralapsarianism, his doctrine of election is more in line with the basic position of infralapsarianism, namely, that the object of election is fallen humanity. I should point out from the outset that his doctrine of election does not square nicely with either classical supra- or infralapsarianism. However, as far as the object of election is concerned, it would be fair to say that he is *basically*, though not *simply* infralapsarian.

With regard to the question of the *obiectum*, though Barth is basically in line with the infralapsarian thesis, there is also a deeply supralapsarian aspect in his Christocentric doctrine of election: he identifies Christ, who took on humanity's sin but is without sin in himself, as the proper object of election; sinful humanity becomes the object of election only by *participatio Christi*. There is thus a profound sense in which Barth sees the object of election as without sin. Christ as the primary object of election can be *secundum quid* described as *homo lapsus* only in the sense that he who knew no sin is made to be sin for us, that he who is without sin participates in our *status corruptionis*.

As for the question of the *ordo*, Barth may be described as basically infralapsarian in that he sees election as presupposing creation and the fall. However, there is also a strongly supralapsarian side in Barth's treatment of the *ordo* question. For him, God's decisions to create the world and, as it were, permit the fall (as we shall see in chapter seven and eight, Barth speaks of God's *permissio* of sin strictly in terms of God's rejection of it) would be incomprehensible if they were not understood in light of God's gracious election in Christ. In this sense, Barth does see God's decisions to create the world and permit the fall as presupposing election. As a result, Barth's lapsarian thinking dialectically comprises a supralapsarian and an infralapsarian *ordo*. Yet if we go back to the more basic question of the *obiectum* from which the *ordo* question stems, we would find that what the supralapsarian *ordo* wants to say is that election does *not* presuppose God's decision to permit the fall (i.e., the object of election is *un*fallen), a contention that would contradict Barth's lapsarian thinking. Meanwhile, the infralapsarian *ordo* is meant to assert positively that election *does* presuppose divine permission of the fall (i.e., the object of election is fallen), which is basically in agreement with Barth's lapsarian thinking, albeit far from conveying its full complexity. In this regard, and with all the foregoing qualifications, Barth's treatment of the *ordo* may be described as basically infralapsarian.

The problem this chapter tackles is as follows: given that Barth explicitly calls his doctrine a "purified supralapsarianism," how can the description "basically infralapsarian" be reasonably applied to his Christocentric doctrine of election? In answering this question, I will argue that Barth's definitions of supra- and infralapsarianism in the *CD* §33 excursus are not precise enough for him to see that he is in fact closer to the infra side than he thinks. In identifying himself as a supralapsarian his focus is primarily on the *ordo* question, without giving enough weight to the more fundamental question of the *obiectum*. Furthermore, his definitions of supra- and infralapsarianism in terms of the *obiectum* involves a certain degree of confusion, and what he calls *homo labilis* is in fact closer to the infralapsarian *homo lapsus*. Again, this degree of imprecision in Barth's historical-theological reports does not diminish the value of the lapsarian excursus, if we come to appreciate that it tells us more about his own lapsarian thinking than about the seventeenth-century controversy.

Why Barth Avowedly Favors Supralapsarianism

To appreciate what the *CD* §33 excursus tells us about Barth's lapsarian thinking, one question requires consideration before we move on to reassess his lapsarian position: Why does he call his doctrine of election developed in 1936–1942 a "purified supralapsarianism"? What theological incentives lie behind his avowed favor for supralapsarianism? Here I offer a brief discussion, and I shall go into more detail in chapter seven.

Before answering this question, bear in mind that Barth is critical of both classical supra- and infralapsarianism primarily because of their common assumption of a *decretum Dei absolutum* (absolute divine decree) whereby humankind is inflexibly divided into elect and reprobate from and to eternity. As he sees it (rightly or wrongly), this classical Reformed formulation of double predestination posits an arbitrarily electing God above and behind the God self-revealed in Christ, thus ascribing to God a "demonic aspect."[1] Yet he thinks that the lapsarian question (namely, whether double predestination presupposes humanity's fall) is crucial to a sound theological discussion of sin, evil and death in light of divine predestination. He wants to salvage supralapsarianism by bringing it into christological light to eliminate that "demonic aspect" (as he sees it).

In a nutshell, Barth's mature understanding of double predestination is that election is *in Christ*—it is *by* him and *with* him. Christ is the electing God—this is primary to Barth's doctrine of election. Only as electing God does Christ become the object of election in whom all humankind, partaking of Christ, is elected. Now, if Christ is the object of election, then the divine act of double predestination can only be understood in light of the Christ event. Christ's death and resurrection reveal that reprobation and election do not stand in a balanced equilibrium, but rather Christ as elected human was reprobated in the stead of all humankind so that all humankind may be elected in him.

For Barth, reprobation is God's No against the nothingness that negates God and God's covenant partner in Christ, and election, in which reprobation as negation of negation is sublated (*aufgehoben*), is God's Yes for all humankind in Christ, who is at once the subject and object of God's No and Yes. By electing to become human, the electing God who remains without sin in the whole person of Christ participates in the human state of corruption into which God's No has concluded all humanity, so that all humanity may stand under God's gracious Yes.

---

[1]*KD* II/2, 154; ET 142.

With this rendition of double predestination, Barth calls his own doctrine a *"purified* supralapsarianism." Again, he is critical of both classical supra- and infralapsarianism, while he finds strengths in both. He thinks that classical supralapsarianism is more prone to render God the author of evil, while infralapsarianism tends to compromise God's sovereignty. By the same token, the strength of infralapsarianism, according to Barth, is that it successfully avoids ascribing the origin of sin to God, and one advantage of supralapsarianism is that it consistently upholds God's sovereignty. Because of these strengths and weaknesses, as Barth perceives them, at one point he comes close to ambivalence in his lapsarian excursus.[2]

However, moving beyond these strengths and weaknesses, Barth identifies what he sees as one definitive feature of supralapsarianism, and he deems it crucial for a right understanding of election-in-Christ: according to Barth, at the heart of supralapsarianism is the teleological priority of election-reprobation over all other divine decrees, such that "to this proper divine will and decree of God everything else that God wills is subordinate, as an interrelated means to its accomplishment."[3]

On Barth's understanding, this teleological priority of election is missing in infralapsarianism. The result, as he sees it, is that infralapsarianism fails to describe creation and the fall in light of God's highest purpose in election. Rather, as Barth understands it, infralapsarianism attempts to deduce God's eternal purpose by observing the historical sequentiality of God's works. For Barth, this deduction constitutes metaphysical speculation and natural theology. To be sure, he thinks that classical supralapsarianism is on the brink of natural theology as well because of the assumption of a nonchristological *decretum absolutum*, but it can be salvaged when election is understood to be *in Christo*.

As we saw earlier, Barth replaces the classical Reformed understanding of double predestination with an understanding of election-in-Christ as *Aufhebung* of sin and reprobation. This logic of *Aufhebung* involves a one-directional teleology: God's purpose for rejecting humanity's sin in Christ is—to use a phrase from *CD* IV/1—"served by [the] evil instrument [of sin],"

---

[2]Ibid., 150; ET 139.
[3]Ibid., 137; ET 128.

and this divine purpose is the election of all in Christ.[4] For Barth, election-in-Christ stands at the top of the teleological order in all God's acts, hence the ever-present claim in his writings that Christ is the beginning of all God's ways and works. With this nuanced Christocentric approach to the *ordo* question, Barth asserts that "with no material alteration" he has "developed [supralapsarianism] in a Christological direction."[5]

In this whole reconstruction (and perhaps deconstruction) of classical lapsarianism, we see a consistent attempt on Barth's part to stay true to his theological axiom: God is God, and world remains world, therefore there can be no human knowledge of God apart from God's self-revelation in Jesus Christ. The corollary is that natural theology with its metaphysical speculation is doomed to fall into Feuerbach's charge of anthropocentric idolatry. In his analyses of classical lapsarianism and development of what he calls a "purified supralapsarianism," Barth makes a consistent attempt to avoid natural theology, and so his treatment of the lapsarian problem is part and parcel of his Christocentric doctrine of election and epistemology.

According to Barth, the God of his "purified Supralapsarianism is not the God who in holy self-seeking is so preoccupied with Himself and the revelation of His own glory.... He is the God who loves man. He is the God who in love makes man a companion."[6] In other words, against classical supralapsarianism (as he sees it) Barth stresses that election-in-Christ is the overflowing of the free love that God's being-in-act is. However, like classical supralapsarians, he thinks that all God's acts and decisions in relation to the creature are subordinate to God's purpose in election-in-Christ.

This teleological subordination of all God's ways and decisions to election-in-Christ is indeed a strongly supralapsarian aspect of Barth's doctrine of election. However, as we shall see from a rather unique instance from the seventeenth century, the English Puritan John Owen, this teleological aspect is not irreconcilable with the more fundamental infralapsarian conviction that the object of election is fallen humanity.

---

[4] *KD* IV/1, 441; ET 399.
[5] *KD* II/2, 154; ET 143.
[6] Ibid., 153; ET 142.

Barth's Definitions of Supralapsarianism and Infralapsarianism

As we saw from chapter one, infralapsarianism does not portray predestination as having taken place temporally after the fall, or as God's response to an actual human decision made prior to God's decree of double predestination: this is a common misunderstanding to which Barth is partly responsible for having given rise. Robert Letham corrects this misunderstanding, which he finds in John T. McNeill's misinterpretation of Calvin as favoring supralapsarianism:

> McNeill . . . misunderstands Calvin's comment in his *Institutes* 2, 12, 5 when he claims that Calvin favours the supralapsarian view of the decrees of God. . . . Calvin points out that the decree of election was before the creation of the world, not subsequent to the fall of Adam. Both infralapsarian and supralapsarian would agree to that. The point at issue between them is not whether the decree of election precedes the fall but whether the decree of election precedes the decree concerning the fall.[7]

That is, the fact that Calvin sees the decree of election as having been made before the actual events of creation and fall does not make him a supralapsarian.

In a similar way, many scholars have relied on Barth's lapsarian definitions to come to the view that Jonathan Edwards is a supralapsarian.[8] Those who adopt the traditional definitions handed down from the seventeenth century, however, would either identify Edwards as an infralapsarian or at least holding to a complex view proximate to infralapsarianism.[9]

In the same way that McNeill describes Calvin as favoring supralapsarianism, many scholars think of Barth as "supralapsarian" in the sense that "God's decision to be for us in Jesus is not a reaction to previous events in the history of God's relations with us, but has a reality in its own right

---

[7]Robert Letham, "Theodore Beza: A Reassessment," *Scottish Journal of Theology* 40 (1987): 28.
[8]Stephen Holmes, *God of Grace and God of Glory: An Account of the Theology of Jonathan Edwards* (Grand Rapids: Eerdmans, 2001), 33; Ross Hastings, "Discerning the Spirit: Ambivalent Assurance in the Soteriology of Jonathan Edwards and Barthian Correctives," *Scottish Journal of Theology* 63 (2010): 447.
[9]John Gerstner, *The Rational Biblical Theology of Jonathan Edwards* (Sanford, FL: Ligonier, 1992), 2:161; Michael Allen, "Jonathan Edwards and the Lapsarian Debate," *Scottish Journal of Theology* 62 (2009): 299-315.

preceding the whole of that history."[10] As we saw in the last chapter, however, according to seventeenth-century Reformed-orthodox definitions, this description fits both supra- and infralapsarianism, and does not make Barth a supralapsarian.

Obiectum praedestinationis: *Barth's Definitions*. Now we shall look into how the Swiss theologian himself defines supra- and infralapsarianism. Again, the lapsarian excursus in *CD* §33 is valuable in its dogmatic-theological aspect, as it tells us much more about Barth's own lapsarian thinking than it does the Lapsarian Controversy.

In the historical-theological aspect, the lapsarian excursus seems to begin on sound footing, as Barth rightly identifies the "point at issue" as "the *obiectum praedestinationis*."[11] It is thus curious why, having stated the central significance of the *obiectum* question from the outset, his avowed favor for supralapsarianism later in the excursus is primarily based on his consideration of the *ordo* rather than the *obiectum*.

In any case, Barth moves on to spell out the "point at issue": "is the one elected or rejected *homo creabilis et labilis*, or is he *homo creatus et lapsus*?"[12] He defines the former as "man as not yet created but still to be created . . . , not yet fallen but still to fall by divine permission and human action," and the latter as "man as already created and already fallen in virtue of this divine permission and human action."[13]

So far so good—but an inadequacy in these definitions is immediately apparent: Barth has not clarified that the predicates *creabilis/labilis* and *creatus/lapsus* refer to God's conception of human individuals in God's eternal plan, rather than humans in created actuality. His definition of *homo lapsus* as humanity "fallen in virtue of . . . human *action*" seems to suggest this term refers to humanity that has *actually* committed the act of sin in time. That is, he uses the right terms at the beginning of the excursus, but as he proceeds he offers definitions of the terms that are at least ambiguous if not misleading or inaccurate—this will become clearer anon.

---

[10]Kathryn Tanner, "Creation and Providence," in *The Cambridge Companion to Karl Barth*, ed. John Webster (Cambridge: Cambridge University Press, 2000), 114.
[11]*KD* II/2, 136; ET 127.
[12]Ibid.
[13]Ibid.

Although Barth emphasizes that infralapsarians, just as supralapsarians, speak of God's decrees as eternal, and the *ordo* as logical rather than chronological, he complains that infralapsarians fail to take seriously the eternality of the decrees, as they "do not take into account the deity of the eternal God, and the possibility that with Him the last could actually be the first."[14]

This complaint probably resulted from one particular misreading of Heppe and Turretin. Many supralapsarians have argued that in God's eternal intention double predestination must logically precede the decrees of creation and the fall, because, as Heppe and Turretin rightly report on the supralapsarian argument, "what is last in occurrence is first in intention."[15] This argument is widely employed by supralapsarians. It is one of the central arguments set forth by the German-English supralapsarian William Twisse (1578–1646) in *Vindiciae Gratiae, Potestatis, Et Providentiae Dei*, a Latin title influential among Continental Reformed theologians, and *The Riches of God's Love unto the Vessels of Mercy*. Barth might not have been familiar with the exact manners in which this argument has been used. He relies on the reports of Heppe and Turretin to infer that infralapsarians reject "the possibility that with [God] the last could actually be the first." However, Barth does not give an example of an infralapsarian who denies that with God "the last could actually be the first." Some infralapsarians have indeed critiqued the supralapsarian argument that with God "the last in execution was *always* the first in intention," but this is not to deny that "the last could be the first."[16]

In any case, Barth sees supralapsarianism as doing greater justice to the eternality of the divine decrees. He sets forth the supralapsarian view of predestination, quoting Bucanus from Heppe:

> What is the decree of predestination? Whereby God, determining the purpose for which God would create humans, before God created them, has according to God's power and sheer good will decreed to extend God's own glory, that

---

[14]Ibid., 146; ET 135-6.
[15]Heinrich Heppe, *Reformed Dogmatics*, ed. Ernst Bizer, trans. G. T. Thomson (London: Wakeman, 2010), 157. Theodore Beza is most well known for having advanced this argument, which is adopted by William Perkins. See Joel Beeke and Mark Jones, *A Puritan Theology: Doctrine for Life* (Grand Rapids: Reformation Heritage Books, 2012), 121. Cf. Turretin's critique in Francis Turretin, *Institutes of Elenctic Theology*, ed. James Dennison Jr., trans. George Giger (Phillipsburg, NJ: P&R, 1992), 1:348.
[16]This is Jonathan Edwards's refutation of supralapsarianism. See Gerstner, *Rational Biblical Theology*, 2:161.

some of them should be vessels and examples of God's benevolence and mercy, but others vessels and matters [*vasa et ὑποκείμενα*] for God's wrath.... And this decree is such as that it sets forth the causes of the execution, while by no means dependent thereupon.[17]

Barth explains the supralapsarian view in his own words: "What Supralapsarianism was trying to say was that in the beginning of all things, in the eternal purpose of God before the world and before history, there was the electing God and elected man, the merciful and just God, and over against that God from all eternity *homo labilis*, man *sinful and lost*."[18] This is a curious passage, and one is left to wonder what Barth might mean by "sinful and lost." As shown in the previous chapter, this description of God's pretemporal conception of humanity as "sinful and lost" is really the definition of the infralapsarian *homo lapsus* in Reformed orthodoxy. One might wonder: did Barth claim to hold to the supralapsarian *homo labilis* when in truth he is closer to the infralapsarian contention of the object of election as *homo lapsus*?

How Barth defines *homo creatus et lapsus* is also curious: "[God] made that choice [of election/reprobation] from all eternity, *but* with reference to man as already created and fallen."[19] Could the conjunction "but" here be taken to imply that "man as already created and fallen" refers not to God's eternal conception of fallen humankind, but to God's predestining decision with reference to humans in historical actuality?

Yet another curiosity has to do with Barth's opinion, shared by many Barthians, that according to the infralapsarian scheme sin and evil somehow disrupted God's plan. Barth comments that supralapsarianism differs from infralapsarianism in that supralapsarians do not present "God's overruling of evil . . . as a *later and additional struggle* in which God is dealing with a *new and to some extent disruptive feature* in His original plan."[20]

Barth thinks that the same cannot be said of infralapsarianism, according to which "predestination has to do with a being which has already been raised from non-being to being. It has to do with an already existent being,

---

[17]*KD* II/2, 137; ET 128. The quote is originally in Latin (translation mine).
[18]Ibid., 154; ET 143 (emphasis added).
[19]Ibid., 141; ET 131.
[20]Ibid., 137; ET 128-29 (emphasis added).

and with a specific form of the existence of this being."²¹ Here Barth is paraphrasing passages found in Heppe and Turretin (*Institutes*, fourth topic, section 9) that are ambiguous when taken out of context. For instance, Heppe quotes Leonard van Rijssen's (ca. 1636–1700) infralapsarian argument that "*non ens* cannot be the object of predestination, for predestination does not make its object, like creation, but supposes it. But *homo creabilis vel labilis* is *non ens*, because by creation he was brought from non-being into being."²² This passage is ambiguous when taken out of context because it has not clarified that *homo creabilis vel labilis* is nonbeing *in God's mind* alone, and *homo creatus et lapsus* is a concrete being also *in God's mind* alone rather than in the actuality of the divine economy.

That the *obiectum praedestinationis* exists in God's mind alone is made clear in a passage Heppe quotes from Swiss Reformed-orthodox infralapsarian Johann Heinrich Hottinger (1620–1667) in the paragraph just preceding the quote above: "The object [of predestination] is the human race to be created and about to fall in Adam or, *considered in the mind of God predestinating*, as created, fallen and corrupted by original sin."²³ That is, for infralapsarians, the *obiectum praedestinationis* is created and fallen only as "considered in the mind of God predestinating," but not in historical actuality.

Had Barth paid closer attention to this passage from Heppe, he might have changed the way he describes the infralapsarian thesis: "before God could decide in mercy and justice, there must have been a *corresponding constitution* of individuals and an *actualisation of their existence*."²⁴ In view of Barth's definition of the infralapsarian *obiectum* as having an actualized existence before the divine decisions of election and reprobation were issued, it is hardly surprising that he would think of the infralapsarian understanding of election as, in Kathryn Tanner's words, "a reaction to previous events in the history of God's relations with us."²⁵ As we have seen in chapter one, however, supra- and infralapsarians alike speak of God's decrees as causally independent of created actuality.

---

[21] Ibid., 141; ET 130-31.
[22] Heppe, *Dogmatics*, 159.
[23] Ibid., 158.
[24] Ibid., 145; ET 135 (emphasis added).
[25] Tanner, "Creation and Providence," 114.

The **ordo decretorum.** Another inadequacy in Barth's report of the Lapsarian Controversy is one shared among other nineteenth-century dogmaticians, namely, the presentation of the *ordo decretorum* as primarily, if not exclusively, a chain of final (teleological) causes. With this narrow understanding of the *ordo*, Herman Bavinck, whose *Gereformeerde Dogmatiek* served as an important source of Barth's understanding of Reformed orthodoxy during the latter's first semester at the University of Göttingen, critiques both supra- and infralapsarianism: "the counsel of God and the cosmic history that corresponds to it must not be pictured exclusively—as infra- and supralapsarianism did—as a single straight line describing relations only of before and after, cause and effect, means and end."[26] On this understanding Bavinck complains about infralapsarianism:

> [If] in the divine consciousness the decree of reprobation did not occur until after the decree to permit sin, the question inevitably arises: . . . why did God, by an act of efficacious permission, foreordain the fall? Infralapsarianism has no answer to this question other than God's good pleasure. . . . Reprobation cannot be explained as an act of divine justice, for the first sinful act at any rate was permitted by God's sovereignty.[27]

Barth critiques infralapsarianism in a similar way: "Unlike the Supralapsarian . . . , the Infralapsarian does not think that he has any exact knowledge . . . of the *reasons* for the divine decree in respect of creation and the fall. On the contrary, he holds that the *reasons* for this decree are ultimately unknown and unknowable."[28]

The fact is, however, that neither supra- nor infralapsarianism is concerned narrowly with final causality. Rather, it is quite common among the lapsarian theologians to construe their respective *ordines* in larger frameworks of various causalities. Heppe quotes the supralapsarians Amandus Polanus (1561–1610) and Johann Alsted (1588–1638) as follows: "the *causa efficiens primaria* [primary efficient cause] is God Himself, the *causa* προηγουμαι [antecedent cause] is God's free will, i.e., the *decretum Dei absolutum* [absolute divine decree, referring to the decree that divides hu-

---

[26]Herman Bavinck, *Reformed Dogmatics*, vol. 2, *God and Creation*, ed. John Bolt, trans. John Vriend (Grand Rapids: Baker Academic, 2004), 392.
[27]Ibid., 385.
[28]*KD* II/2, 138; ET 129 (emphasis added).

manity into elects and reprobates].... Its *finis summus* [chief end] is the *Gloria Dei*, its *finis subordinatus* [subordinate end] is the *salus electorum* [salvation of the elect]. Its *effectus* [effect] are the creation of intelligent beings and the permission of sin."[29] Here, God's very being, the divine decrees and their relations to the economy of salvation are obviously not presented as merely a linear chain of teleological causes.

The seventeenth-century infralapsarian John Owen makes clear that although the "first spring or original [of the eternal counsels of God] was in the divine will and wisdom alone" such that "no reason can be given, no cause be assigned, of these counsels, but the will of God alone," "the *design* of their accomplishment was laid in the person of the Son alone. As he was the essential wisdom of God, all things were at first created by him. But upon a prospect of the ruin of all by sin, God would in and by him—as he was fore-ordained to be incarnate—restore all things."[30] What Owen means is that when the infralapsarian *ordo* is understood as a chain of final causality, the origin of the decrees (i.e., God's ultimate purpose) would be unknowable, but the way all the decrees are centered on God's works in Christ reveals that predestination is designed to manifest God's self-giving glory in the incarnate Son.

Here we see that at least in the case of Owen, arguably the most influential English Puritan of the seventeenth century, Barth's critique of what he sees as the infralapsarian teleology does not apply very well: Barth comments that supralapsarians ascribe teleological priority to double predestination, and "to this proper divine will and decree of God everything else that God wills is subordinate, as an interrelated means to its accomplishment,"[31] but "the same cannot be said of Infralapsarianism."[32] He thinks that no unifying purpose can be found in the infralapsarian *ordo* except an arbitrary good pleasure of God prior to the decree of creation that stands at the top of a chain of means and ends.

Recall that Barth's primary incentive in adopting a "purified supralapsarianism" is that supralapsarianism, as he understands it, allows for a Christo-

---

[29]Heppe, *Dogmatics*, 155.
[30]John Owen, "The Person of Christ," in *The Works of John Owen*, vol. 1, *The Glory of Christ* (Philadelphia: Banner of Truth, 1991), 62.
[31]Ibid., 128.
[32]Ibid., 143.

centric reinterpretation in which election-in-Christ is the divine decree to which everything else that God wills is subordinate, teleologically and otherwise. While this aspect of Barth's lapsarian thinking indeed leans heavily toward the supralapsarian side, the case of Owen shows that infralapsarianism is not necessarily at odds with Barth's insistence that election-in-Christ is the highest divine purpose from which all God's decisions proceed.

Reconsidering Edwin van Driel's Supralapsarian Reading of Barth

Though Barth's avowed favor for supralapsarianism has received frequent mention in the secondary literature since his own time, a clear explanation or proper definition of the term has not been offered until recently, by Edwin van Driel.[33] Most authors speak of Barth's "supralapsarianism" in the sense that "God's decision to be for us in Jesus is not a reaction to previous events in the history of God's relations with us, but has a reality in its own right preceding the whole of that history."[34] As we have seen, this description applies to Reformed-orthodox supra- and infralapsarian alike.

In his book, van Driel offers clear and accurate definitions of the terms. Yet, curiously, he describes Barth as a supralapsarian without any qualification: "God's electing act is supralapsarian in the twofold sense of the word . . . , both predestinarian and Christological."[35] While we have been looking at supra- and infralapsarianism primarily in terms of predestination, van Driel gives a helpful definition of supra- and infralapsarian Christology: "We can call such a Christology *infralapsarian*: the divine will to become incarnate logically follows (*infra*, after) the divine will to allow sin (*lapsus*, fall). . . . By contrast . . . , we can call such an understanding of the incarnation *supralapsarian*: the divine will to become incarnate logically precedes (*supra*, before) the divine will to allow sin."[36] To describe Barth as a supralapsarian in both the christological and predestinarian senses implies that for Barth "God had motives to become incarnate that

---

[33]Edwin van Driel, *Incarnation Anyway: Arguments for Supralapsarian Christology* (Oxford: Oxford University Press, 2008).
[34]Tanner, "Creation and Providence," 114.
[35]Van Driel, *Incarnation Anyway*, 67.
[36]Ibid., 5.

were not contingent upon sin."³⁷ Van Driel argues that since election on Barth's view *is* God's decision to become incarnate, Barth's doctrine of election is also supralapsarian.

Though van Driel's definitions of predestinarian and christological supra- and infralapsarianism are accurate, labeling Barth as a supralapsarian according to these definitions seems too simplistic, as this reading has yet to be reconciled with the infralapsarian aspect of Barth's theology, which has in fact been well documented in the secondary literature, albeit without being described as infralapsarian.

First, with regard to Christology, mainstream Barth scholars would agree with R. Scott Rodin that "to hold to such a distinction between incarnation and atonement, between the assuming of human essence and the assuming of sinful humanity, is to misread Barth's intentions. Barth never sees God as envisaging a creation which would be fulfilled by incarnation alone."³⁸ George Hunsinger also points out that "whether God would have become incarnate even if the world had not fallen into sin was . . . a question that" Barth regarded "as speculative and unanswerable."³⁹

Second, in his supralapsarian reading of Barth, van Driel repeatedly appeals to Barth's exegesis of John 1:1, which Barth takes to mean that Jesus Christ is the beginning of all God's ways and works.⁴⁰ This is indeed a supralapsarian aspect in Barth's Christology, as I have shown. Yet van Driel does not seem to have done justice to the infralapsarian aspect of Barth's identification of Christ as the beginning of all God's ways: the *Logos* eternally *incarnandus* as revealed in the concrete history of the incarnation was determined from the very beginning to be the Reconciler between God and sinners. According to Barth's exegesis of John 1:14 ("the Word became flesh . . ."), which must be understood in the same context as John 1:1, "the message of Christmas *already includes within itself* the message of Good Friday. For 'all flesh is as grass.' The election of the man Jesus means, then, that a wrath is kindled, a sentence pronounced and finally executed, a rejection actualized. . . . *From*

---

³⁷Ibid., 4.
³⁸R. Scott Rodin, *Evil and Theodicy in the Theology of Karl Barth* (New York: Peter Lang, 1997), 87.
³⁹George Hunsinger, *Disruptive Grace: Studies in the Theology of Karl Barth* (Grand Rapids: Eerdmans, 2000), 204.
⁴⁰Van Driel, *Incarnation Anyway*, 65-67. Cf. *KD* II/2, 101; ET 94.

all eternity judgment has been foreseen."[41] Clearly, for Barth, what stands "at the beginning" is not an election-incarnation independent of God's consideration of humanity's sin.

To be sure, for Barth, while election-in-Christ presupposes humanity's sin, the converse is also true: sin as that which God has rejected for the sake of God's gracious Yes could not have existed apart from God's election of the covenant partner in Christ. God's rejection, and thereby *permissio*, as it were, of humanity's sin presupposes election-in-Christ. Thus, again, we must recognize the dialectical nature of Barth's lapsarian thinking: there is both a supra- and an infralapsarian side to his christological doctrine of election.

If Barth may be described as *basically* infralapsarian, it is because the fundamental supralapsarian thesis, in both the predestinarian and christological senses, entails that election-incarnation does *not* presuppose sin (i.e., election is without regard to humanity's fallenness; the incarnation was made necessary by a primal decision of God other than confrontation with sin). This thesis clearly contradicts Barth, while he would agree with the basic predestinarian and christological infralapsarian theses that election presupposes God's consideration of sin (i.e., the object of election is fallen) and that the incarnate was made necessary by God's will to overcome sin.

Third, van Driel asserts that for Barth "the ontological and epistemic principles that govern divine revelation are not a result of sin, but given with the nature of Creator and creation. Incarnation, as the necessary means of divine self-disclosure, is therefore a supralapsarian event."[42] In other words, van Driel thinks that according to Barth, divine self-revelation in election-incarnation is necessary even for unfallen humanity, if humanity is to participate in God's self-knowledge and thus come to true knowledge of God. This contradicts Barth's explicit position since *Romans* I (published in 1919). As we shall see in chapters three and four, in both his *Romans* I (1915–1919) and II (1920–1921) phases as well as the Göttingen-Münster period (1921–1930), Barth states that the paradisiacal human was immediate to God and thus in need of no revelation in the form of the incarnation, and that revelation as a dialectic of divine self-veiling and unveiling is predicated on the

---

[41]*KD* II/2, 131; ET 122.
[42]Van Driel, *Incarnation Anyway*, 77.

sin of humankind.[43] This is a position Barth would continue to hold in *CD* I/1, albeit with some modifications (see chapter five). Even in *CD* IV/1 (see chapter eight), Barth would still state that it was "the disruption of the relationship between God and man which made this event [of the incarnation] necessary and which was overcome by this event."[44]

Thus van Driel's simplistic identification of Barth as a supralapsarian, which not only neglects but also rules out the infralapsarian aspect of his Christology and doctrine of election, places him at odds with the majority of mainstream Barth scholars. David Ford, for instance, states that "Barth . . . understands election through the events of the story. Election is to suffering at Golgotha, where Jesus substituted for men and revealed the divine wrath in his suffering. . . . The other side of election is the overcoming of evil and death. . . . Evil is there and so must have been permitted by God, but its function is to occasion the cross."[45] Rodin also comments that for Barth, humanity's state of fallenness is fully assumed in the election of Christ: "God did not positively will the Fall . . . , but in His eternal election of Jesus Christ as *homo labilis* [this should read *homo lapsus*], the Fall is fully assumed as the state of humanity."[46] Bruce McCormack, with reference to Barth's covenant theology, also stresses this: "It must be emphasized that the covenant is with *sinful man*. Not the 'neutral' human who lives in a paradisiacal situation but the sinful human is the object of God's electing grace."[47] These authors might not have recognized their own statements as basically infralapsarian, but these descriptions clearly point out that for Barth, the *obiectum praedestinationis* is "sinful humanity" (*homo lapsus*).

In fact, in an earlier article, in which van Driel does not refer to lapsarianism explicitly, he already intimates a supralapsarian reading of Barth, asserting that in Barth's theology, election is "followed by creation."[48] Against

---

[43] *Römerbrief* II, 254; ET 251. *Unterricht* 1:190; ET 155.
[44] *KD* IV/1, 395-96; ET 359.
[45] David Ford, *Barth and God's Story* (Eugene, OR: Wipf and Stock, 1985), 75.
[46] Rodin, *Evil and Theodicy*, 113 (emphasis added).
[47] Bruce McCormack, "*Justitia aliena*: Karl Barth in Conversation with the Evangelical Doctrine of Imputed Righteousness," in *Justification in Perspective: Historical Development and Contemporary Challenges*, ed. Bruce McCormack (Grand Rapids: Baker Academic, 2006), 191 (emphasis original).
[48] Edwin van Driel, "Karl Barth on the Eternal Existence of Jesus Christ," *Scottish Journal of Theology* 60 (2007): 53.

McCormack's so-called "revisionist" (a label that McCormack himself has rejected)[49] interpretation of Barth, which claims that election-incarnation constitutes the Trinity, van Driel offers a so-called traditionalist (namely, God is necessarily triune, and election-incarnation logically presupposes the Trinity) reading of Barth with a supralapsarian *ordo*:

> We have . . . , on Barth's side, as the starting point God's Trinitarian nature, with the Trinitarian processions being natural and necessary . . . ; followed by the decree of election, which is not part of God's nature, but dependent on the divine will, and contingent, since God could have been God without being the God of election; followed by creation, also voluntary and contingent.[50]

After McCormack's response to van Driel,[51] Hunsinger published an article challenging McCormack's view.[52] Although Hunsinger agrees with van Driel's understanding that Barth sees election as presupposing the Trinity, he disagrees with van Driel's unilateral, undialectical assertion that Barth sees creation as presupposing election. Hunsinger states: "[The tripersonal God] would exist whether the world had been created or not; [election] presupposes the creation and fall of the world."[53]

The logical relation that Hunsinger describes here is in fact precisely the defining element in the infralapsarian *ordo*. Of course, Hunsinger well recognizes the dialectical character of Barth's lapsarian thinking: election presupposes the fall, but the fall also presupposes election. The *ordo* that van Driel describes is true to Barth, but it lacks the other emphasis in Barth that in divine election humanity's fall is fully presupposed—this is the aspect that Hunsinger accents.

This infralapsarian emphasis is brought to light in Barth's excursus on the Lapsarian Controversy: "It is God's will that *elected man* should repudiate what He repudiates. . . . God does not will and affirm evil and the fall . . . , but for the sake of the fullness of His glory, for the sake of the completeness of His covenant with man . . . , He wills and affirms this man *as sinful man* . . . , as the one

---

[49]See Bruce McCormack, "Election and the Trinity: Theses in Response to George Hunsinger," *Scottish Journal of Theology* 63 (2010): 204.
[50]Van Driel, "Karl Barth on the Eternal Existence of Jesus Christ," 53.
[51]Bruce McCormack, "Seek God Where He May Be Found: A Response to Edwin Chr. Van Driel," *Scottish Journal of Theology* 60 (2007): 62-79.
[52]George Hunsinger, "Election and the Trinity: Twenty-Five Theses on the Theology of Karl Barth," *Modern Theology* 24 (2008): 179-98.
[53]Ibid., 193.

foreordained to utter the same No *and thus* to corroborate the divine Yes."[54] Here, the italics I have added show that (1) Barth thinks of the *obiectum praedestinationis* as "sinful man," and (2) election proper (the Yes) presupposes God's No to sin. To overlook this infralapsarian emphasis and the basically infralapsarian orientation of Barth's christological doctrine of election is tantamount to a failure to do justice to the full complexity of Barth's lapsarian thinking.

Conclusion

In this chapter I have focused on Barth's lapsarian excursus in *CD* §33, considering both his robust dogmatic-theological analyses and his ambiguous, if not imprecise or perhaps even inaccurate, historical-theological reports. My attempt has been to challenge the simplistic perception of Barth as a supralapsarian, to briefly outline the complex and dialectical nature of his lapsarian thinking, and to claim that his doctrine of election in *CD* II/2 may be described as *basically* infralapsarian.

It is not *simply* infralapsarian because its emphasis on the teleological priority of election-in-Christ is closer to supralapsarianism, though this emphasis does not necessarily contradict infralapsarianism, as the case of Owen has shown. With regard to the *obiectum praedestinationis*, Barth is also not *simply* infralapsarian, because he identifies Christ, who is without sin in himself, as the proper object of election; sinful humanity becomes the object of election only by partaking of Christ.

In chapters three and four I will show that Barth had already adopted definitions of supra- and infralapsarianism in *Romans* II and the *Göttingen Dogmatics*, which would cause readers familiar with Reformed orthodoxy to raise some eyebrows. What I have yet to show is how Barth's predestinarian and christological lapsarianism evolved from *Romans* II to *CD* II/2. Additionally, this chapter is narrowly focused on the lapsarian excursus for the purpose of initial clarification of Barth's position, and I have yet to give a fuller exposition of Barth's christological doctrine of election set forth in *CD* II/2, and explain in greater detail why in that particular christological context he finds it important to "purify" and adopt a complex but basically infralapsarian position. I now proceed to part two for these tasks.

---

[54]*KD* II/2, 152; ET 141 (emphasis added).

PART TWO

Barth's Lapsarian Position in Development, 1920–1953

3

Römerbrief II (1920–1921)

Lapsarianism in the "Impossible Possibility" Dialectic

The aim of this chapter is to examine Barth's lapsarian tendencies in Christology and predestination in *Romans* II (published in 1922). I will show that in this phase of his development, Barth's Christology is moving toward an infralapsarian understanding while his formulation of predestination may be described as inconsistently supralapsarian.

Historical Introduction

The reason for my choice to begin with *Romans* II is simple: this is the first major work in which Barth explicitly engages with the lapsarian problem and takes an avowedly supralapsarian position.[1] To be sure, at this point, Barth, writing in Safenwil during his final year (October 1920–October 1921) of parish ministry, was not yet acquainted with specific arguments set forth by various participants in the Lapsarian Controversy, nor was he yet seriously reflecting on what he perceived as strengths and inadequacies in confessional Reformed theology. While Barth would later begin to wrestle with the theologies of Calvin, Zwingli and the classical Reformed confessions during his Göttingen-Münster phase (1921–1930), the main struggle for Barth in his last Safenwil year was with over a century of neo-Protestant theology dominated and challenged by Immanuel Kant.

---

[1]*Römerbrief* II, 163; ET 172.

Bruce McCormack summarizes the "fundamental problem being addressed by Barth throughout the phase of *Romans* II": "how can God make Himself known to human beings without ceasing—at any point in the process of Self-communication—to be the *Subject* of revelation?"[2] This central theological concern is in line with an earlier phase of Barth's theological development in Safenwil (1915–1918) during which *Romans* I (published in 1919) was written, where "Barth everywhere presupposed: 1. The validity of Kant's epistemology (where it touched upon knowledge of empirical reality), and 2. the success of Kant's critique of metaphysics."[3]

Unquestionably, in *Romans* II Barth remains well within Kant's epistemological boundaries. As McCormack puts it, "that the knowledge of God given in revelation was a problem at all was, in Barth's view, because of two factors: the limits of human knowing on the one side, and divine election on the other."[4]

This basically (neo-)Kantian "problem" becomes deeply lapsarian when Barth adds the crucial element of human fallenness to the ontological and epistemological gulf between God and humanity. The "limits of human knowing" of which McCormack speaks describe not only the (neo-)Kantian idea of the "bounds of bare reason." It is more sharply a Kierkegaardian notion of an "infinite qualitative difference" between God and humanity, which involves a profound understanding of the noetic effects of sin.[5]

---

[2] Bruce McCormack, *Karl Barth's Critically Realistic Dialectical Theology* (Oxford: Clarendon, 1995), 207.
[3] Ibid., 130. As a note of clarification, Barth's appropriation of Kant has been a debated subject in the secondary literature. Neo-orthodox interpreters like T. F. Torrance tend to downplay Kant's influence on Barth. Those who acknowledge Barth's reliance on Kant have debated whether Barth is closer to Marburg neo-Kantianism or classical Kantianism. As I see it, Clifford Anderson is right that while "Barth's transcendental argument was more neo-Kantian than straightforwardly Kantian," Barth's appropriation of Kant is unique and not identical to any other version of Kantianism than his own. See Clifford Anderson, "A Theology of Experience? Karl Barth and the Transcendental Argument," in *Karl Barth and American Evangelicalism*, ed. Bruce McCormack and Clifford Anderson (Grand Rapids: Eerdmans, 2011), 94. Cf. Johann Lohmann, *Karl Barth und der Neukantianismus* (Berlin: de Gruyter, 1995); T. F. Torrance, *Karl Barth: An Introduction to His Early Theology, 1910–1931* (Edinburgh: T&T Clark, 1962), 99.
[4] McCormack, *Dialectical Theology*, 207.
[5] McCormack believes that "there is no good reason to think that [Barth] read the *Philosophical Fragments* or *Concluding Unscientific Postscript*—at least not in this period before the publication of *Romans* II." See McCormack, *Dialectical Theology*, 236. McCormack's view has been challenged by Sean Turchin in *Examining the Primary Influence on Karl Barth's "Epistle to the Romans"* (MARS thesis, Liberty University, 2008), 5, as well as his PhD thesis at Edinburgh University. The fact is that Barth's dialectic of "impossible possibility" in *Romans* II draws heavily on Kierkegaard's *Sickness Unto Death* and *Concluding Unscientific Postscript*.

In 1963 Barth recounts: "[Kierkegaard] only entered my thinking seriously, and more extensively, in 1919, at the critical turning-point between the first and second editions of my *Romans*. . . . What we found particularly attractive, delightful and instructive was his inexorable criticism. . . . We saw him using it to attack all speculation which wiped out the infinite qualitative difference between God and man."[6]

For the Barth of *Romans* II, there had in fact been a prelapsarian state of humanity's "life of immediacy [with God]" (*das unmittelbare Leben*),[7] which he calls the "Origin" (*Ursprung*) in *Romans* I, a key term that he continues to use in *Romans* II.[8] This is a position that Barth would continue to hold in *GD*, in which he says that humanity was once "immediate to God."[9] In *Romans* II, Barth posits an *Ursprung* from which humanity has fallen, and identifies human fallenness as the primary problem for humanity's knowledge of God in a way akin to Kierkegaard's view of the noetic effects of sin: sin makes revelation subjectively impossible on the human side.[10]

The dialectic of impossibility and possibility in *Romans* II, which relies heavily on Kierkegaard, is Barth's way of describing how God's election ultimately overcomes human sin for the sake of divine self-revelation.[11] It is as such deeply lapsarian: it addresses the relations between predestination—in fact double predestination—and human fallenness. Yet the matter is not so simple. Rather, the "impossible possibility" dialectic would be played out layer by layer through multiple impossibilities on the human side, each overcome—negated—by a divine act of *Aufhebung*.

In the rest of this chapter, I shall show how the impossible-possibility dialectic undergirds and holds together Barth's overall theological framework

---

[6]Eberhard Busch, *Karl Barth: His Life from Letters and Autobiographical Texts*, trans. John Bowden (London: SCM, 1975), 116.
[7]*Römerbrief* II, 254; ET 251. Note: ET renders "direct union with God."
[8]*Römerbrief* I, 45.
[9]Karl Barth, *Unterricht in der christlichen Religion* (Zurich: TVZ, 1985), 1:190 (*unmittelbar zu Gott*); ET 155.
[10]For a discussion of Kierkegaard's view of sin as obstacle for knowing God, see Joel Rasmussen, *Between Irony and Witness: Kierkegaard's Poetics of Faith, Hope and Love* (London: T&T Clark, 2005), 101.
[11]The Kierkegaardian categories of possibility and impossibility are set forth through the pseudonyms Anti-Climacus and Johannes Climacus in *Sickness Unto Death* and *Concluding Unscientific Postscript*. See Søren Kierkegaard, *Sickness Unto Death*, trans. Alastair Hannay (Radford: Wilder, 2008), 30-31; Kierkegaard, *Concluding Unscientific Postscript to the Philosophical Crumbs*, ed. and trans. Alastair Hannay (Cambridge: Cambridge University Press, 2009), 485-88.

in *Romans* II. The basis of the impossible-possibility dialectic in *Romans* II is the axiom, "Impossible with man; possible with God!"[12] I shall show that with this central dialectic in *Romans* II, Barth develops a Christology moving in the direction of infralapsarianism, and a basically supralapsarian doctrine of election that carries infralapsarian elements.

The Impossible-Possibility Dialectic as Central Theme of *Romans* II

Interestingly, the impossible-possibility dialectic in *Romans* II has not received its due attention in the secondary literature. Aside from John Webster, who briefly pinpoints "the possibility of impossibility" as key to understanding "the imperative movement of grace into human history and activity" in *Romans* II, few have noted the centrality of this dialectic in the commentary.[13]

It is little exaggeration to say that the impossible possibility is the most dominating dialectic in *Romans* II. The word "possibility" (*Möglichkeit*) in all its grammatical declensions appears 591 times in the German edition, which comprises 567 pages, pervading virtually every chapter and almost every single section. This number does not include the adjectival form of the same word, which totals 117 occurrences. Similarly, the adjective "impossible" appears 157 times in the German edition, and the noun "impossibility" fifty-seven times.[14] In nearly all these occurrences, the words "impossible" and "possible" in various grammatical forms appear in the context of the impossible-possibility dialectic. The synthesis of the two terms of the dialectic, the "impossible possibility" (*die unmögliche Möglichkeit*), appears twenty-five times in *Romans* II, in contrast to only once in the major dogmatic opus of the next phase of Barth's development, the *Göttingen Dogmatics*.[15]

The impossible-possibility dialectic not only marks one chief distinction between *Romans* II and Barth's major works in dogmatic cycles thereafter; that the impossible possibility was also a new way of thinking for Barth in *Romans* II is evident from the fact that in *Romans* I (578 pages) the word

---

[12]*Römerbrief* II, 55; ET 75. See Matthew 19:26; Mark 10:27; Luke 18:27.
[13]John Webster, *Barth's Moral Theology: Human Action in Barth's Thought* (London: T&T Clark, 1998), 29; see also 27-28.
[14]These word counts are made possible by the search function on the Karl Barth Digital Library, 2015, http://solomon.dkbl.alexanderstreet.com/.
[15]*Unterricht* 2:400; ET 164.

"possibility" occurs only ninety-eight times—without any technical or special meaning—and the impossible possibility formula is not used at all.

In a word, to appreciate the uniqueness of this commentary among the successive phases of Barth's theological development, it is important to understand the central significance of the impossible-possibility dialectic in *Romans* II.

Grasping the centrality of the impossible-possibility dialectic is also important for understanding Barth's treatment of the lapsarian problem in *Romans* II. For the Barth of *Romans* II, whether revelation as the event of faith that recognizes Christ's resurrection through his death—an event impossible in this world because of its fallenness—becomes a possibility ultimately hinges on God's decision in double predestination. To understand how Barth formulates his understanding of double predestination as God's act to overcome humankind's sin as well as its noetic and moral effects, it is important to understand the role that the notion of sin plays in the overall framework of Barth's impossible-possibility dialectic, as well as how each human impossibility is sublated by a divine act. Conversely, an understanding of Barth's predestinarian-lapsarian position in *Romans* II sheds light on its overall theological framework, predicated on the impossible-possibility dialectic.

Seven impossible possibilities. At the outset of an exposition of *Romans* II in light of the impossible-possibility dialectic, it should be noted that whereas the later Barth, having almost completely abandoned this dialectic in the first two volumes of the *Church Dogmatics*, would pick up the same rhetoric again to describe negative elements such as "nothingness" (*CD* §50), humanity's repudiation of divine providence (*CD* §49) and the sin of unbelief (*CD* §60), in *Romans* II the impossible possibility always refers positively to God's sovereign and gracious act that overcomes human impossibilities.

As mentioned earlier, this dialectic is built on the axiom "Impossible with man; possible with God!"[16] The "impossible" resides with humanity, but God's act makes the impossible possible, therefore the dialectic is not a balanced paradox, but a process of *Aufhebung*: God's grace ultimately breaks through and triumphs over human limitations. What is impossible on the

---

[16]*Römerbrief* II, 55; ET 75.

human side, however, is not any human act: the acts of sin and false religion are straightforward, undialectical possibilities and actualities for humanity (contrast this to *CD* §60, where sin is described as impossible possibility—see chapter eight). Rather, the "impossibilities" describe God and God's act, which are, to be sure, not impossible in themselves, since all things are possible for God. To use the language that Barth would later adopt in Göttingen, divine revelation is an "objective possibility" that renders humanity inexcusable for not knowing God (see chapter four). Thus revelation is not objectively, but subjectively impossible for humanity because of the limitations of the human condition.

Seven human impossibilities found in *Romans* II may be ordered as follows:

1. Revelation: humanity's knowledge of God
2. Revelation: humanity's knowledge of itself as Adam
3. Revelation: humanity's knowledge of the Krisis
4. Redemption and Justification
5. The resurrection of Christ
6. Faith in Christ
7. Election

Except the first, all these impossibilities are linked as a series of God's acts, turning the previous impossibility into an impossible possibility. The first impossibility includes all the others. The main problem that Barth tackles in *Romans* II is this: Given that God has revealed Godself to enable human knowledge of God, what is it that made this impossibility possible? The key to answering this question lies in the doctrine of election, as Robert Jenson rightly points out that "the doctrine of predestination is the heart of the *Commentary on Romans*, and the most succinct expression of its basic pattern."[17]

First impossibility: Revelation—humanity's knowledge of God. For Barth, that God has made Godself knowable is an unquestionable given, and the possibility and actuality of revelation is Barth's theological starting point. The possibility of divine revelation is, to borrow a term from *GD*, an

---

[17]Robert Jenson, *God After God: The God of the Past and the God of the Future as Seen in the Work of Karl Barth* (Minneapolis: Fortress, 2010), 28.

"a posteriori" given (note the neo-Kantian thought form).[18] However, this is not an uncritical, straightforward possibility. Rather, it is impossible possibility—an impossibility made possible and yet remaining impossible in this world. Thus Barth comments on the Jews whom Paul describes as keepers of divine revelation (bear in mind that Barth is no Marcionite!): "By their [the Jews'] recollection of the *impossible* they are themselves the [a posteriori] *proof* that God stands within the realm of *possibility, not as one possibility among others*, but—and this is precisely what is made clear in their case—as the *impossible possibility*."[19]

But what was it that made revelation impossible in the first place? For the Barth of *Romans* II, humans cannot know God not because they are human, but because they are sinners. Since the impossibility of revelation—the event central to which is God's act of election—is predicated on an understanding of the world and of human beings as *fallen*, the lapsarian problem (namely, whether predestination presupposes humanity's sin) is highly pertinent to the overall theological framework of *Romans* II. As we shall see anon, in *Romans* II Barth's treatment of eternal election carries supralapsarian tendencies, but on the temporal-actualistic level Barth sees election as presupposing humanity's fallenness.

For now, simply note that for Barth revelation is impossible because of humanity's sin: "To us God is, and remains, unknown; we are, and remain, homeless in this world; sinners we are and sinners we remain."[20] Barth defines the notions of "humanity" and "history" in lapsarian rather than neutral terms: "The word 'humanity' means *unredeemed* men and women; the word 'history' implies limitation *and corruption*; the pronoun 'I' spells *judgment*."[21] Because the subject "I" is fallen and sinful, it cannot intuit God as object.

Barth follows Kant in stating that "the only world we can know is the world of time, of things, and of men," distinguishing between "Nature, which is mere 'world,'" and "Creation."[22] The former comprises "what we are able

---

[18] *Unterricht* 1:185; ET 151.
[19] *Römerbrief* II, 58; ET 79 (emphasis added).
[20] Ibid., 65; ET 85.
[21] Ibid. (emphasis added).
[22] Ibid., 254; ET 251.

to observe"; it denotes "visible history, which is only process."[23] Creation, on the other hand, is "beyond our observation."[24] That "irrevocable . . . Moment of eternal creation" is posited in a prelapsarian state of humanity in which time and transience had not yet plagued the human condition.[25]

Barth posits a pretemporal, nonhistorical, suprahistorical and yet *real* (not just metaphoric) state of original humanity characterized by "purity and peace of that existence in which God and men were one and not two."[26] God and humanity existed in a "unity of life,"[27] a "life of immediacy" (*das unmittelbare Leben*) with God.[28] In its "direct relationship with God,"[29] human knowledge of God was immediate because God was directly intuitable to humanity. "Creation" denotes this prelapsarian state of humanity, which is its "Origin" (*Ursprung*) that even today still "evokes in us a memory of our habitation with the Lord of heaven and earth."[30]

"The world," however, is to be distinguished from "Creation."[31] "The world is our whole existence, as it has been, and is, conditioned by sin. There has come into being a COSMOS which, because we no longer know God, is not Creation."[32] This entrance of sin into the world is "the Fall which lies behind time."[33] By this maneuver Barth reacts against the historicism and psychologism of nineteenth-century neo-Protestantism: "The entrance of sin into the world through Adam is in no strict sense an historical or psychological happening."[34]

For Barth, humanity's fall is a real event even if it is ahistorical, and it has a real consequence beyond and effect on history. The supratemporal fall destroys humanity's original immediacy to God.[35] Thus death also entered

---

[23] Ibid.
[24] Ibid.
[25] Ibid.; ET 250 (translation mine). ET omits "eternal." Original: "Unwiderruflich vorbei ist nun der Augenblick der ewigen Schöpfung."
[26] Ibid.
[27] Ibid.
[28] Ibid.; ET 251, revised. ET renders "direct union with God." Barth uses the word *Unmittelbarkeit* frequently in *Romans* II.
[29] Ibid., 159; ET 168.
[30] Ibid., 73; ET 92.
[31] Ibid., 159; ET 168.
[32] Ibid.
[33] Ibid.
[34] Ibid.
[35] Ibid., 159; ET 168.

the world, not just death in its physical manifestation, but death that "is the mark of that passing of eternity into time, which is, of course, not an occurrence in time, but a past happening in primal history."[36]

As a result of sin and death, "now everything is concrete and indirect."[37] "Our direct union with God was destroyed."[38] Human knowledge of God is now impossible, because objects of human knowledge can only be found within this fallen world that has passed from eternity into time, a world in which the eternal God cannot be found. In a word, divine self-revelation leading to humanity's knowledge of God has now become impossible for the human subject.

The problem that Barth tries to solve at this point is not how humanity can attain to any knowledge of God—asking this wrong question was for Barth one chief reason for what he saw as the failure of nineteenth-century neo-Protestant theology. For Barth, divine self-revelation is a given, and the question that he seeks to answer is this: *given that* God has revealed Godself, how did the impossibility of human knowledge of God become impossible possibility? This question undergirds the following series of impossible possibilities, the last of which is election. As we shall see, since Barth's notion of impossible possibility in *Romans* II is predicated on an understanding of the world and humans as *fallen*, his treatment of double predestination inevitably has to deal with the lapsarian problem: Do election and reprobation presuppose humanity's sin?

Second impossibility: Revelation—humanity's knowledge of itself as Adam. In inquiring about the possibility of divine revelation, Barth points to a Calvinistic dialectic: "Without knowledge of self there is no knowledge of God," and "without knowledge of God there is no knowledge of self."[39] For Barth the impossibility of human knowledge of God also implies that fallen humanity is unable to know itself as such, that is, as Adam. To be "in Adam" (see Rom 5) is to be an "old, fallen, imprisoned creature."[40] For a human person to come to faith in Christ's resurrection—which, for the Barth of

---

[36]Ibid., 254; ET 250.
[37]Ibid.
[38]Ibid., 253; ET 251.
[39]John Calvin, *Institutes of the Christian Religion*, ed. John T. McNeil, trans. Ford Lewis Battles (Philadelphia: Westminster, 1960), 1.1.1-2.
[40]*Römerbrief* II, 155; ET 165.

Romans II, is the definitive locus of divine self-revelation—it is necessary that she comes to the knowledge of Christ's death, but no knowledge of Christ's death can be attained without knowledge of humanity's *Krisis*, that is, the crisis of standing under God's wrath and judgment as sinners.

Note that Barth's use of the word *Krisis* is not simply negative. Rather, the word denotes God's *negating* grace: by wrath and judgment, reprobation and punishment, God negates humanity's sin that negates God and creation. Thus the *Krisis* is the negation of negation, and it leads to election and resurrection as *Aufhebung* of the *Krisis*. Thus human knowledge of this *Krisis* presupposes the epistemic awakening to the fact that all sinners are "in Adam." For Barth, this epistemic awakening is impossible.

The reason is as follows: "Adam has no existence on the plane of history and of psychological analysis."[41] As human knowledge is confined to the realm of space and time, knowledge of the true, nonhistorical Adam is impossible. That is, the "non-temporal fall of all men from their union with God," though "manifested in that they imprison the truth in ungodliness and unrighteousness," is unintuitable.[42]

Therefore Barth asks: "Whence have we the competence to understand what 'fallen—from God' means?"[43] The answer, according to Barth, is Christ's resurrection, the definitive locus of revelation in *Romans* II. "The Adam who [fell from God] is not Adam in his historical unrelatedness, but Adam in his non-historical relation to Christ."[44] The only way "we [could] form any conception of Adam's Fall" is to have "in mind the exaltation of Christ from death to Life."[45] The reason is that both Adam's fall and Christ's resurrection are "timeless and transcendental," and Christ's resurrection is the only means whereby humanity may gain knowledge of Adam's nonhistorical fall.[46] In a word, the impossibility of humanity's knowledge of itself as Adam is made possible by Christ's resurrection.

Third impossibility: Revelation—humanity's knowledge of its Krisis. Yet faith in Christ's resurrection is no simple matter. First, the resurrection is

---

[41] Ibid., 162; ET 171.
[42] Ibid.
[43] Ibid.
[44] Ibid., 161; ET 170.
[45] Ibid., 162; ET 171.
[46] Ibid.

itself timeless and nonhistorical, and as such it cannot be directly intuitable to fallen humans. In fact, not only is faith in Christ's resurrection impossible; the resurrection itself is impossible.[47] The impossible possibilities of faith and the resurrection will be discussed in more detail later.

There is another difficulty with faith in Christ's resurrection: knowledge of the resurrection is necessarily indirect, not only because it is unhistorical but also because it is a process of *Aufhebung*. That is, Christ's resurrection is the result of "the negation of negation";[48] it is, in Luther's words, the "death of death."[49] Christ's death is grace, "because its negation is positive."[50] To understand the resurrection, then, is also to understand the negation that Christ's death negates.

That first negation is the entrance of death into the world through sin: "through sin, death entered into the world—as KRISIS."[51] This "penetrating and ultimate KRISIS" is "an irresistible and all-embracing dissolution of the world of time and things and men," "the supremacy of a negation by which all existence is rolled up."[52]

This *Krisis* did not arise from the natural order of creation. Rather, it is God's "wrath" and "judgment" as the "Lawgiver who as such is above His law."[53] Yet it is also God's gracious intervention, lest the world fall completely away from God. The *Krisis* of humanity is that it is under a "double predestination" and not just dereliction—here Barth is hinting at a supralapsarian tendency in his understanding of predestination (as we shall see later).[54] The *Krisis* is "the sign of the wrath of God and the signal of His imminent salvation. In any case, death is the divine command—'Stop'—and we cannot disobey it."[55] In other words, salvation includes not only Christ's death and resurrection but also the first negation. Salvation is the entire process of *Aufhebung*, the negation of negation. Thus knowledge of the resurrection necessarily involves knowledge of the human *Krisis*.

---

[47]Ibid., 190; ET 195.
[48]Ibid., 333; ET 322.
[49]Ibid., 189; ET 194.
[50]Ibid.
[51]Ibid., 160; ET 169.
[52]Ibid., 72; ET 91.
[53]Ibid., 160; ET 169.
[54]Ibid., 358; ET 343.
[55]Ibid., 160; ET 169.

The question is, "whence comes our recognition of [the KRISIS] and our ability to comprehend it?"[56] God is known as God, the unknown God, only "in light of ultimate and all-embracing KRISIS," but "such realization and perception lie beyond the *possibility* of our knowledge, and are the becoming possible of that which is *impossible*."[57]

Here, again, Barth begins with an a posteriori given, namely, the possibility of human knowledge of the *Krisis*. His questions, quoted above, are thus framed very carefully. He does not ask whether knowledge of the *Krisis* is possible, but *how* this impossibility became possible.

But why does Barth think that this knowledge is impossible in the first place? The reason goes hand in hand with the impossibility of humanity's knowledge of itself as Adam. Adam's fall is nonhistorical; it is this original fall, rather than the visible sins of human individuals, that determines the status of all humans. It is through Adam's nonhistorical sin that death came into the world. "Death is the reverse side of sin."[58] Physical death is only a manifestation of the death that entered the world through sin, the true death that robbed the creature of true life, "which is the relationship of men to God."[59] Of this true *Krisis* humanity can know nothing, because it is beyond the bounds of human reason. Despite all the physical manifestations of sin and death that make God's wrath clear to all (Rom 1:19-21), sinners fail to know God as the "Unknown."[60]

So what was it that made this impossibility possible? Barth's answer, again, is Christ's resurrection. The resurrection must be understood in relation to the *Krisis*, but at the same time the *Krisis* can only be known in light of the resurrection. "In the Resurrection, the full seriousness and energy of the veritable negation, of our being buried, are displayed and ratified."[61]

Only the resurrection reveals death—the death that entered the world through Adam's sin as well as Christ's death that put death to death—as grace.[62] On the other hand, grace would not be grace had it not involved

---

[56] Ibid., 72; ET 91 (emphasis added).
[57] Ibid. (emphasis added).
[58] Ibid., 160; ET 169-70.
[59] Ibid.
[60] Ibid., 22-24; ET 45-47.
[61] Ibid., 190; ET 195.
[62] Ibid., 189; ET 194.

the *Krisis*: "Grace is not grace, if he that receives it is not under judgement."[63] It is "in light of the Resurrection of Jesus from the dead" that "we are able to recognize" death as *Krisis*, that is, as both God's judgment and salvation.[64] The impossibility of humanity's knowledge of its *Krisis* has become possible only through Christ's resurrection.

Fourth impossibility: Redemption and justification. Put another way, knowledge of death as *Krisis* is knowledge of the *Krisis* as redemption. But how is redemption, which is "movement from Adam to Christ,"[65] the "union of 'here' and 'there,'"[66] possible? That is, what made it possible for humanity to be in the kingdom of God, which is not of this world? For Barth, the infinite qualitative difference between God and the world means that "this world, because it is our world, is the world into which sin found entrance," and "in this world, on this earth, and under this heaven, there is no redemption, no direct life [*kein unmittelbares Leben*, that is, no immediate relationship with God]."[67] In a word, as the world remains world, and God remains God, redemption is impossible.

Noteworthy here is the eschatological character of Barth's soteriology in *Romans* II. For Barth the impossibility of redemption in this world means that "redemption can only take place at the coming Day, when there shall be a new heaven and a new earth."[68] In the present world, however, redemption is not simply absent, though it is not directly present. Redemption stands as a *dialectical possibility* in the present: "By His death He declares the impossible possibility of our redemption, and shows Himself as the light from light uncreated, as the Herald of the Kingdom of God."[69]

Yet Christ's death in itself is not redemption as such. Christ's death is atonement "*by blood*" (Rom 3:25).[70] It is the negation of negation, but not yet the sublation. In and of itself it is neither timeless nor nonhistorical. Thus it can only declare redemption as a possibility, with the dialectical emphasis that this possibility remains impossible. As long as humanity remains in this world,

---

[63]Ibid., 181; ET 187.
[64]Ibid.
[65]Ibid.
[66]Ibid., 135; ET 148.
[67]Ibid., 160; ET 169 (translation mine).
[68]Ibid.
[69]Ibid., 87; ET 105.
[70]Ibid., 90; ET 108.

we are deprived of the possibility either of projecting a temporal thing into infinity or confining eternity within the sphere of time. Similarly, it is impossible for us to detach a fragment of our behaviour from its human context and to pronounce it to be justified before the judgment seat of God, just as it is impossible for us to detach one element from the righteousness of God and to regard it, in its detachment, as capable of being comfortably inserted within the structure of human behaviour as it is.[71]

Thus, just as redemption is impossible possibility, the possibility of justification remains impossible. That is, justification has been opened up as a possibility in the present, but the locus of its reality is in the future beyond time. "The righteousness of God is a vast impossibility.... We have nothing of which to boast, nothing past or future, nothing before or after the 'Moment'—which is no moment in time—when the last trumpet shall sound and men stand naked before God, and when, in their nakedness, they shall be clothed upon with the righteousness of God."[72]

Note that this is not what Luther would describe as *simul iustus et peccator*. In *Romans* II the present reality of sin is nothing dialectical or perplexing to Barth; sin is not described here as an impossible possibility as it is in *CD* III/3 and IV/1 (see chapter eight). The redeemed human, the "new man," is an impossible possibility, with which "it always remains . . . a burning question whether we can and do venture to reckon," but "there is no question at all but that the *possible possibility of sin* is excluded by it."[73]

For the new human, "continuance in sin" is indeed rendered impossible—"excluded"—by Christ's resurrection, and this is not just a "parable."[74] Yet it is not a present reality either. The exclusion and impossibility of sin is strictly eschatological, because the resurrection is strictly nonhistorical. That believers continue to sin in this life is therefore not at all a paradox of Luther's *simul*: redemption and justification are not present realities but only paradoxical possibilities in the here and now. "Because the world is the world, and time is time, and men are men, so long as they remain what they are, my new life must exist 'beyond' them."[75]

---

[71] Ibid.
[72] Ibid.
[73] *Römerbrief* II, 191; ET 196 (emphasis added).
[74] Ibid., 190; ET 195.
[75] Ibid.

As we shall see in chapter eight, when Barth picks up the impossible-possibility dialectic again in CD III/3–IV/1, his emphasis well shift to the other side, focusing on the "already" of God's objective work in Christ eternally accomplished before the creation of the world. For now, suffice it to say that in *Romans* II the impossible possibility of redemption and justification denotes the "not yet" of a heavily eschatological soteriology.

As we shall see later, this strict dichotomy of the here and now and the futuristic there and then gives rise to double predestination on two levels, the eternal-eschatological and the present-actualistic. On the eternal-eschatological level, Barth tends to be supralapsarian in that he identifies the election of all humans as the purpose for which God "shut up all in disobedience" (Rom 11:32 NASB); on the present-actualistic level, Barth sees double predestination as presupposing humanity's sin.

Fifth impossibility: The resurrection of Christ. From the foregoing discussions it has become clear that in *Romans* II, Christ's resurrection is the decisive locus of God's grace and revelation, rendering possible all human impossibilities. The problem, however, is that the resurrection is itself impossible in this world. Barth not only asserts that knowledge of the resurrection is impossible but also names the resurrection as one of three great impossibilities along with knowledge of God and the "union of 'here' and 'there.'"[76] So how is it that the impossibility of the resurrection became possible?

Barth's answer is both ontic and noetic. The ontic part of the answer is simple: "Impossible with man; possible with God!"[77] The noetic part of the answer has to do with Barth's theological method in *Romans* II. Simply stated, the preliminary answer is that the resurrection just *has to be* possible, because without the possibility of the resurrection, the a posteriori given of the possibility of revelation cannot be explained, nor can the possibility of the new life, which is not simply absent in the here and now, but exists sharply as a dialectical possibility that observably "presses upon my *continuing in sin*" and "as the criticism of my temporal existence and thought and will."[78]

---

[76]Ibid., 135; ET 148.
[77]Ibid., 55; ET 75.
[78]Ibid., 190; ET 195.

The new ego is not a figment of metaphysical imagination: "I am *veritably* [*in der Tat*] dead to sin."[79] Employing a (neo-)Kantian transcendental argument, Barth asserts that it is "because we have perceived this," namely, the present impossible possibilities of grace, righteousness and life, that "we are able to recognize—in the light of the Resurrection of Jesus from the dead—the power and meaning of the Coming Day: the Day of the New World and of the New Man."[80]

It is also in light of the impossible possibility of the resurrection that death is revealed as grace, the *Krisis* as the power of the gospel and the crucifixion as salvation: "We encounter the power of the Resurrection: *Christ was raised from the dead through the glory of the Father*: impossibility becomes possibility. In the Resurrection, the full seriousness and energy of the veritable negation, of our being buried, are displayed and ratified."[81]

The resurrection as such is revelation of the death of death and of the new life. The new life, again, is not just a parable.

> My new life is the "ought" and "can," the "must" and "will," of my new EGO which has been created in Christ: it is the assurance of my *citizenship in heaven*; . . . it is the invisible point of observation and of relationship, the judgement exercised by my infinite upon my finite existence; it is the threatening and promising which is set beyond time, beyond all visibility, beyond all the finite and concrete events of my life.[82]

In a word, Christ's resurrection, though beyond space and time, ought to be a possibility because of the veritability of the new life.

It has to be emphasized, however, that this "ought to" must not be understood as the metaphysical conclusion of a logical reductio ad absurdum. How faith in Christ's resurrection becomes a possibility will be explained in the next section. Suffice it to keep in mind here that Barth's theological method is, as McCormack puts it, "strictly 'anti-metaphysical' at all points and in all phases of his development."[83] That is, Barth refuses to deduce first principles from observable phenomena.[84] For *Romans* II, this would imply

---
[79]Ibid., 191; ET 196 (emphasis added).
[80]Ibid., 181; ET 187.
[81]Ibid., 190; ET 195.
[82]Ibid.
[83]McCormack, *Dialectical Theology*, 246.
[84]Ibid.

that the resurrection is not the result of deduction, but the starting point and presupposition in light of which every other veritable impossible possibility can be understood.[85]

Now, what is the event through which the resurrection becomes comprehensible to human reason? In answering this question, Barth remains consistently within Kant's epistemological boundaries: this event of revelation has to be within the realm of objects intuitable to human senses; it has to have taken place on the plane of temporal history. Since the new life began when the old one was put to death, Barth argues that the truth of the resurrection is to be comprehended through the crucifixion, the negation of negation, the putting to death of death.

> The truth that we ARE new men is . . . comprehensible to us only at its starting-point. And this starting-point means for us the end of the old man. This is the only aspect of the truth visible to us; only in the Cross of Christ can we comprehend the truth and meaning of His Resurrection.[86]

To be sure, however, the crucifixion in and of itself cannot be revelational, because revelation *from* God has to be nonhistorical and nontemporal. Only Christ's resurrection is revelation as such. Meanwhile, revelation *to* humans has to be conveyed through some historical medium in order to be humanly intuitable. The crucifixion, according to Barth, is the divinely appointed medium through which the light of the resurrection shines. The cross in itself is not revelational as such; it is an improper medium for revelation. However, since for God all things are possible, God can use this historical medium as a vehicle for that which is truly revelation, namely, the resurrection. Barth compares resurrection and crucifixion to sun and sunlight: "Below in the valleys rise the mighty oaks" whose "topmost branches" block our sight of the sun itself, but "the light catches us in the early morning, and we see what none other can see: we see the sun of the coming day, and we cry out our welcome—'Come, Lord!'"[87]

Yet, as discussed earlier, the crucifixion is negation. The cross in and of itself is but a sign of death, weakness, violence, injustice and negativity. God

---

[85]In this respect Barth's methodology runs in the reverse direction of Paul Tillich's deduction of the "New Being." See Tillich, *Systematic Theology* (Chicago: University of Chicago Press, 1957), 2:170.
[86]*Römerbrief* II, 137; ET 150.
[87]Ibid.

is utterly hidden by the negativity of the cross. If the light of the resurrection is to shine forth by the cross and break through its veil, no eye can perceive it except eyes of faith: "Only in the Cross of Christ can we comprehend the truth and meaning of His Resurrection. We can only BELIEVE in what is new, and, moreover, our capacity reaches no further than to believing that we do believe."[88] In other words, the impossible noetic comprehension of the resurrection becomes a possibility through the crucifixion of Christ as perceived by faith.

Sixth impossibility: Faith in Christ. Faith in Christ, however, is yet another impossibility. This is because Christ as Jesus of Nazareth who died on the cross is an improper medium of revelation.[89] In (neo-)Kantian manner Barth insists that Jesus cannot be directly identical to revelation, and with Kierkegaardian overtones he comments that "the vision of the New Day remains an *indirect* vision; in Jesus revelation is a *paradox*, however objective and universal it may be. That the promises of the faithfulness of God have been fulfilled in Jesus the Christ is not, and never will be, a self-evident truth, since in Him it appears in its *final hiddenness* and its most profound secrecy."[90]

However, it is for the purpose of self-revelation that God hides Godself in Christ. Echoing Luther's *theologia crucis* Barth writes: "In Him [Jesus] He [God] conceals Himself utterly, in order that He may manifest Himself to faith only."[91] It is true that the faithfulness of God is simply "not accessible to our perception."[92] It cannot be known through occult powers or intellectual inquiry.

Yet God's faithfulness can be known by faith, and by faith alone. Again with reference to Kierkegaard, Barth defines faith as "always a leap into the darkness of the unknown, a flight into empty air," because "the revelation which is in Jesus, because it is the revelation of the righteousness of God, must be the most complete veiling of His incomprehensibility."[93] There are "no preliminaries necessary to faith"—faith admits no precondition or

---

[88] Ibid.
[89] Ibid., 78; ET 97.
[90] Ibid. (emphasis added).
[91] Ibid., 353; ET 369. Cf. McCormack, *Dialectical Theology*, 249-50.
[92] *Römerbrief* II, 79; ET 98.
[93] Ibid.

deduction—but rather "faith is its own initiation, its own presupposition."⁹⁴ Thus "for all faith is both simple and difficult; for all alike it is a scandal; . . . to all it presents the same embarrassment and the same promise; for all it is a leap into the void. And it is possible for all, only because for all it is equally impossible."⁹⁵

In short, faith in Christ is impossible because "Jesus of Nazareth, *Christ after the flesh*, is one amongst other possibilities of history; but He is THE possibility which possesses all the marks of impossibility."⁹⁶ Yet God "is intelligible only by faith," and given that intelligibility of God has been made impossibly possible by revelation—this is Barth's theological starting point— how did the impossibility of faith become possibility?

Barth's answer is the "impossible possibility of the faithfulness of God."⁹⁷ Recall that whenever Barth uses the term "impossible possibility," it refers to an act of God. The "impossible possibility of the faithfulness of God" is such that "in the paradox of faith the faithfulness of God is sufficient; for through it we stand on firm ground and move forward with assurance."⁹⁸ Therefore "the faithfulness of God is where faith is."⁹⁹

God's faithfulness turns faith into an impossible possibility. Faith is God's work, which lies beyond and puts to death all human possibilities. Faith as impossible possibility—as God's work—corresponds to God's faithfulness (see Rom 1:17).¹⁰⁰

But how does God awaken faith in the sinful human subject, and how does this temporal act of God relate to God's eternal being? This is where Barth's doctrine of election, along with his treatment of the lapsarian problem, in *Romans* II sets in.

Seventh impossibility: Election. As suggested earlier, Barth's notion of impossible possibility is deeply eschatological. Revelation is impossible in this world because the eternal cannot be directly identified with anything temporal or historical—God is "wholly Other."¹⁰¹ Though by God's sovereign

---

⁹⁴Ibid.
⁹⁵Ibid., 81; ET 99.
⁹⁶Ibid., 85; ET 103.
⁹⁷Ibid., 96; ET 113.
⁹⁸Ibid.
⁹⁹Ibid., 97; ET 114.
¹⁰⁰Ibid., 18; ET 41.
¹⁰¹Ibid., 253; ET 250.

and gracious act revelation has been made possible in the present, this possibility is impossible for the world, so long as the world remains world and God is God. Only in the eschaton where creation is no longer plagued by temporality and transience will revelation cease to be impossible. Before the end of time, the works of God in this world shall ever remain impossible possibilities.

From the perspective of the present world, then, election—defined in *Romans* II as God's act of awakening faith in human subjects—also carries the mark of impossible possibility: "Men encounter the *possibility* of election only in the form of a *promise*."[102] God's "promise," moreover, "is *comprehended* in everything that points to the Truth, that is to say, to miracle, to the Spirit, to *impossibility*."[103] This means that for fallen humans as subjects of comprehension, election may be encountered only as impossible possibility.

Because the possibility of election retains the mark of impossibility in the present world, reprobation goes hand in hand with election. That is, the impossibility of election entails the possibility of reprobation, which Barth defines in *Romans* II as God's act of withholding faith from human individuals and leaving them in unbelief. Note, however, that this "double predestination," synonymous with the impossible possibility of election, only describes predestination as manifested in the present world.

Eschatologically speaking, the "possibility of rejection" has been "eternally overcome" in God.[104] Thus McCormack rightly observes that "Barth's doctrine of election in this phase functioned on two distinct levels."[105] In the eternal eschaton, reprobation is only tentative, posited only to be eternally overcome by election, which is universal in scope. On this level, reprobation is God's act of subjecting humanity to the plight of time, and election is God's negation of time through Christ's resurrection whereby humanity is lifted up into eternity. As Robert Jenson puts it, "The relation between the two sides of double predestination . . . is but another form of the relation we have traced between time and eternity; for the meaning of time, as different

---

[102]Ibid., 327; ET 344 (emphasis added).
[103]Ibid. (emphasis added).
[104]Ibid., 363; ET 348.
[105]Bruce McCormack, "So That He May Be Merciful to All: Karl Barth and the Problem of Universalism," in McCormack and Anderson, *Karl Barth and American Evangelicalism*, 243.

from eternity, is rejection, and the meaning of eternity for time is acceptance. In time we are all rejected; in eternity we are all chosen."[106]

As discussed earlier, Christ's death has put to death all human possibilities and overcome the *Krisis* that threatens all humanity, and in the nonhistorical and nontemporal event of the resurrection, the life of immediacy with God is freely given to all. Thus Barth says that in the eternal-eschatological sense, predestination "involves no equilibrium, but . . . it is the eternal victory of election over rejection, of love over hate, of life over death."[107] As McCormack puts it, this is the "movement from a universal reprobation to a universal election, which took place in the death and resurrection of Jesus Christ."[108]

On the level of temporal history, however, election is defined as "something that takes place in the here and now of our lives in that God awakens faith in us."[109] Election as such takes place as impossible possibility, with the threat of reprobation and unbelief ever looming. God may elect or reject one individual at any moment in time. An individual's faith or unbelief depends entirely on God's sovereign decision. In this sense, Matthias Gockel helpfully recognizes "Barth's emphasis [in *Romans* II] on divine predestination as the sole basis for human knowledge of God."[110] God has complete freedom in first revealing Godself to the Jews and withholding faith from the Gentiles, then blinding the Jews and electing the Gentiles (Rom 9–11). Although predestination on the eternal-eschatological level is the victory of election over reprobation, "this victory is hidden from us in every moment of time."[111] Therefore, in this temporal world, the possibility of reprobation always accompanies the impossible possibility of election, and predestination is always twofold.

Note, however, that according to Barth, even this double predestination on the level of the present world must not be thought of as a *decretum absolutum* that divides the human race into two fixed masses for faith and

---

[106] Jenson, *God After God*, 28.
[107] *Römerbrief* II, 363; ET 347.
[108] McCormack, "So That He May," 243.
[109] Ibid.
[110] Matthias Gockel, *Barth and Schleiermacher on the Doctrine of Election: A Systematic-Theological Comparison* (Oxford: Oxford University Press, 2006), 114.
[111] *Römerbrief* II, 363; ET 347.

unbelief. Against the Reformers, Barth contends that the "secret" of double predestination "concerns not this or that man, but all men. By it men are not divided, but united. In its presence they all stand on one line—for Jacob is always Esau also, and in the eternal 'Moment' of revelation Esau is also Jacob."[112]

In this sense, "the inevitable doctrine of eternal 'Double Predestination' is not the quantitative limitation of God's action, but its qualitative definition."[113] For Barth, double predestination does not mean that this person is an elect, or that person is a reprobate. Rather, it means that in every moment of every person's life, God has the freedom to give and to take away. One who is elected this moment might be derelict at the very next moment. Thus Barth contends that faith is given to humans as impossible possibility, and as a corollary, "revelation can never be extended onto the plane of time, so as to be thought of as a concrete possession" (note the Kierkegaardian overtones).[114] Therefore "Christian assurance" is a notion that exists "only in the imagination of theologians."[115] (Barth will continue to attack the notion of Christian assurance until 1936.)

Thus understood, double predestination in *Romans* II is, on the level of temporal history, a dialectic between faith and unbelief that results from the impossible possibility of revelation in the present world. Because of humanity's fall and God's sovereign grace, "men are compelled to advance along a road which ends in 'Double 'Predestination.'"[116]

This double predestination, however, is not a balanced equilibrium: "for God hath shut up all unto disobedience, that he might have mercy upon all" (Rom 11:32)—for Barth this is the statement whereby "the final meaning of 'Double Predestination' seeks to make itself known."[117] This understanding of double predestination is for Barth "the 'key to the whole of the epistle to the Romans'" as well as the whole theology of Paul.[118] According to Romans 11:32, as Barth interprets it, double predestination is such that on the level of

---

[112]Ibid., 362; ET 347.
[113]Ibid., 361; ET 346.
[114]Ibid., 334; ET 322.
[115]Ibid.
[116]Ibid., 253; ET 250.
[117]Ibid., 407; ET 421.
[118]Ibid. Quoted and translated by McCormack in "So That He May," 242.

the eternal eschaton, the reprobation of "all" is posited only in order to be defeated by the election of "all" unto mercy; in the present world of temporality, double predestination is a description of the impossible possibility of revelation that results in an "actualistic" (the notion that God's act sovereignly corresponds to creaturely activity—at this stage Barth is far from having developed the final version of his actualism, with the central concept of God's "being-in-act") dialectic of faith and unbelief in the lives of "all" human individuals.

The present impossible possibility of election, moreover, just like predestination on the eternal level, is not a balanced paradox: "Impossible with man; possible with God!"—and God's grace is always sovereign over human limitations.[119] Thus the church shall continue to stand by faith—the miraculous work of God—to testify to God's faithfulness in the election of all humans unto mercy.[120]

Lapsarian Tendencies in Romans II

Inconsistently supralapsarian formulation of predestination. In identifying Romans 11:32 as the definitive statement for the doctrine of predestination, Barth's formulation of election and reprobation in *Romans* II inevitably takes on lapsarian character, for this passage states that "God hath shut up all unto disobedience." That is, humanity's fall is considered here in light of divine activity, and a doctrinal formulation of the relation or nonrelation between predestination and the fall becomes necessary.

Barth confronts the lapsarian problem head on, stating that humanity's "active disposition" to "imprison the truth in ungodliness and unrighteousness" is "explained—and yet not explained—by the divine predestination of men to destruction which follows their divine election in Christ as the shadow follows the light."[121] The dialectical phrase "explained and yet not explained" suggests that humanity's fall is to be understood in light of double predestination, which is nevertheless beyond understanding. Thus double predestination is to be grasped by faith, and the higher understanding of faith, as it were, is an impossible possibility. Barth is thus sug-

---

[119]Ibid., 55; ET 75.
[120]Ibid., 363; ET 348.
[121]Ibid., 163; ET 172.

gesting here that the fall is to be understood by faith as having been predestined by God, and this decree of the fall, as it were, is preceded by and thus serves the purpose of election in Christ, "as the shadow follows the light."

Note that in the passage above Barth is describing double predestination in the eternal-eschatological sense (as opposed to present-actualistic faith and unbelief—recall that Barth's doctrine of predestination in *Romans* II comprises two levels of reality). His predestinarian thinking on this level is clearly supralapsarian: "election in Christ" precedes "the divine predestination of men to destruction," and it is for the purpose of election that God predestined the fall.

Additionally, note that in *Romans* II, reprobation on the eternal-eschatological level is almost synonymous with the fall, which consists of sin and death. Sin rent asunder the bond of immediacy between God and humanity, and death is "the mark of that passing of eternity into time," which, as "a past happening in primal history," was God's eternal reprobation of humankind.[122] Thus Barth equates eternal reprobation with the nonhistorical and nontemporal fall of Adam, which precedes any historical manifestation thereof. As a result, when Barth asserts that reprobation took place only for the purpose of being defeated by election,[123] he is essentially making the supralapsarian statement that in eternity God predestined the fall for the purpose of election.

In *Gottes Gnadenwahl* (1936) and *CD* II/2 (1942), Barth would again contend that reprobation serves the purpose of election (see chapters six and seven). However, by that time he would no longer equate reprobation with humanity's fall. Rather, he would define reprobation as God's eternal rejection of humankind's sin in Christ, who is at once electing God and elected human. As elected human, Christ overcomes sin by suffering divine reprobation vicariously for all humankind that is in him, so that all humankind may be elected in and with him. According to this scheme, in the act of election humanity is considered as *homo lapsus*, as we saw in chapter two. Therefore, although Barth seems to be saying the same thing in *Gottess Gnadenwahl* and *CD* II/2 as he said in *Romans* II when he asserts that reprobation serves the purpose of election, he in fact moves closer to infralapsarianism in the former two.

---

[122]Ibid., 254; ET 250.
[123]Ibid., 362-3; ET 347.

Furthermore, in *Romans* II, when Barth speaks of election on the temporal-actualistic level as impossible possibility, the *obiectum praedestinationis* (object of predestination) is clearly *homo peccator* (sinful humanity). That is, election on this level is defined as God's act of awakening faith in fallen sinners, and reprobation, which dialectically accompanies the present impossible possibility of election, as leaving sinners in the state of unbelief. As Gockel puts it, throughout *Romans* II "Barth correlates the concepts of predestination, election and reprobation to the duality of faith and unbelief. ... In correspondence to the Reformers' idea of justification by grace through faith, he maintains that a person's faith in Christ is characterized by his or her acceptance of God's opposition to the human predicament of sin and death."[124]

Remember that the whole dialectic of impossible possibility is predicated on humanity's fall from the *Ursprung*. Of course, this formulation does not make Barth an infralapsarian in the classical sense, because on his scheme predestination in the temporal realm actualistically corresponds to its eternal and definitive reality, which, as shown above, is formulated in a supralapsarian way in *Romans* II. The historic debates between supra- and infralapsarians are concerned about predestination strictly in the eternal sense; the notion of a present-actualistic double predestination is foreign to Reformed orthodoxy. Therefore, Barth's formulation of double predestination on the present-actualistic level does not fit neatly into any lapsarian theory of historic Reformed theology, even in the minimalist sense. Even so, the pervasiveness of the dialectic of impossible possibility in *Romans* II suggests that infralapsarian patterns of thought are already present in Barth's theological reflections during this phase of his development. The fact that on one level of his doctrine of predestination the *obiectum* is *homo peccator* means that his predestinarian thinking in 1920–1921 is not thoroughly supralapsarian, but carries a hint of infralapsarianism as well.

Romans *II as early source of Barth's lapsarian misnomers*. Despite this infralapsarian element, on the eternal-eschatological level Barth's formulation of double predestination in *Romans* II is unmistakably supralapsarian, and in fact he explicitly identifies himself as a supralapsarian in this com-

---

[124]Gockel, *Barth and Schleiermacher*, 105-6.

mentary.[125] However, his definition of supralapsarianism at this point in time already appears curious for readers familiar with Reformed orthodoxy: "The Fall is not occasioned by the transgression of Adam; but the transgression was presumably its first manifest operation. In this context the venerable Reformation doctrine of 'Supralapsarianism' becomes intelligible. According to it, predestination unto rejection precedes the 'historical' fall."[126]

Barth's *description* of supralapsarianism here is not wrong, but it is not much of a *definition* in that it does not distinguish supralapsarianism from the opposing view. It can be inferred from this definition of supralapsarianism that he thinks of infralapsarianism as claiming that eternal reprobation presupposes the *historical actuality* of the fall. In reality, however, the infralapsarian thesis in the original Lapsarian Controversy was that reprobation presupposes the *eternal divine decree* of the fall rather than its historical actuality.

As I showed in the previous chapter, these imprecise definitions of supra- and infralapsarianism are exactly the ones Barth gives in the excursus at the end of *CD* §33. It is now clear that Barth already held to this understanding as early as his Safenwil years. This means that before his encounter with the works of Heinrich Heppe and other nineteenth-century German historiographers during the Göttingen years, he had already adopted these inaccurate definitions on his own.

Toward an infralapsarian Christology. While Barth's formulation of predestination in *Romans* II may be described as inconsistently supralapsarian, the Christology in this phase of his theological development leans toward infralapsarianism. Recall that a supralapsarian Christology is one in which God would have become incarnate regardless of whether humanity had fallen into sin. By contrast, an infralapsarian Christology describes the incarnation as having been made necessary by God's decision to deal with humanity's sin.

It should be noted in the first instance that Barth's Christology in *Romans* II does not fit nicely into either category, because, as McCormack points out, "Barth was not really interested in *Romans* II in the incarnation."[127] However,

---

[125]Ibid., 163; ET 172.
[126]Ibid.
[127]McCormack, *Dialectical Theology*, 253.

the whole dialectical scheme of impossible possibilities that undergirds Barth's commentary indicates that his Christology at this stage is moving in a strongly infralapsarian direction.

First, the language of "impossible possibility" is predicated on and expresses the central notion that revelation in this world is impossible as long as God remains God and the world remains a domain of existence that has fallen into temporal transience. As we saw earlier, in the prelapsarian *Ursprung* humanity's communication with God was immediate. Mediation between God and humanity through the death and resurrection of Jesus—which constitutes the core of Barth's Christology in *Romans* II—became necessary only in the temporal world into which humanity has fallen. In this way, the notion of Christ as the *medium* for divine self-revelation presupposes humanity's fall, thus leaning toward an infralapsarian Christology.

In fact, Barth's Christology in *Romans* II is expressed in an almost explicitly infralapsarian manner in a few instances. For example, Jesus as the incarnate Christ is described as "impossible possibility" (again, a dialectic presupposing humanity's fall): "Jesus of Nazareth, *Christ after the flesh*, is one amongst other possibilities of history; but He is THE possibility which possesses all the marks of impossibility."[128] Here, to say that Jesus was "one amongst other possibilities of history" is to say that he was truly human, truly belonging to this temporal world. Meanwhile, to say that he "possesses all the marks of impossibility" is to say that he, as a historical person, is "fraught with eternity."[129] The eternal cannot exist in this fallen world; thus all the marks of eternity in the person of Jesus of Nazareth are described as "marks of impossibility." In this way, the "Christ after flesh" is described in almost infralapsarian terms as having entered into a fallen world and taken on the plight of human fallenness. In a passage that we discussed earlier, Barth explicitly states that "Jesus stands among sinners as a sinner; He sets Himself wholly under the judgement under which the world is set."[130]

Note, however, that here Barth is very careful not to identify Jesus of Nazareth as God eternal, though he does not explicitly deny this either. In *Romans* II, Barth has not yet developed an incarnational Christology. If

---

[128] *Römerbrief* II, 85; ET 103.
[129] Ibid., 87; ET 105.
[130] Ibid., 78; ET 97.

Jesus of Nazareth really "occupies a position in time, in history, and in the presence of men," then difficult problems would arise if he is to be identified as God eternal.[131] Barth could describe Jesus as "fraught with eternity," even saying that "God was *in* Christ reconciling the world unto himself,"[132] but in *Romans* II he consistently avoids speaking of Jesus as truly and fully the eternal God. He would rather avoid the doctrine of the incarnation and focus on the death and resurrection of Christ as the locus of divine self-revelation.

The definitive infralapsarian phrase "God became human for us and for our salvation" does not apply to Barth's Christology in *Romans* II, because in insisting on the critical distance between God and the world, he consistently avoids the notion that God has become anything that is in this world. As we shall see, when Barth begins to adopt a basically Nicene-Chalcedonian view of Christ's two natures during the Göttingen years, his understanding that mediation between God and humanity presupposes the fall—which is already present in the impossible-possibility dialectic in *Romans* II—will determine the basically infralapsarian nature of his Christology. In 1920–1921, however, Barth's Christology is best described as moving in an infralapsarian direction.

Chapter Summary

To sum up, four concluding remarks are in order. First, Barth's doctrine of predestination in *Romans* II may be described as inconsistently supralapsarian: it is supralapsarian on the eternal-eschatological level, but on the present-actualistic level it reflects infralapsarian patterns of thinking.

Second, Barth's Christology in *Romans* II is moving in an infralapsarian direction in that Christ's person and works are predicated on humanity's fall, but it cannot be properly described as supra- or infralapsarian because Barth consistently tries to steer away from any proper discussion of the incarnation during this phase of his theological development.

Third, the questionable definitions that Barth gives to supra- and infralapsarianism in *CD* II/2, as we saw in the previous chapter, are already found in *Romans* II. These definitions are Barth's own rather than Heppe's: as we

---
[131]Ibid., 87; ET 105.
[132]Ibid. (emphasis added).

saw in chapter two, Heppe's definitions are basically in line with the original Lapsarian Controversy. However, Heppe's selection of texts and his running commentary are not organized well enough to have helped Barth arrive at more accurate definitions.

Fourth, the dialectic of impossible possibility is predicated on the fall of humanity. Although Barth would drop this rhetoric in his later works, he would retain a strong notion of humanity's fall and the consequent impossibility of God's direct presence in this world. This would be an important factor leading to Barth's theological development in the direction of christological and predestinarian infralapsarianism in the 1920s and 1930s, as we shall see in subsequent chapters.

4

The Göttingen-Münster Period (1921–1930)

CHRISTOLOGY AND PREDESTINATION IN THE SUBJECT-OBJECT DIALECTIC

THIS CHAPTER EXAMINES THE lapsarian tendencies in Barth's Christology and doctrine of election during the Göttingen-Münster period (1921–1930). *The Göttingen Dogmatics* (*GD*) marks Barth's first dogmatic treatment of incarnational Christology, which I will show to be basically infralapsarian. This chapter also aims to demonstrate that Barth's doctrine of election during this period began to lean toward infralapsarianism. Additionally, in *GD* Barth sets forth his first dogmatic treatment of the Lapsarian Controversy, declaring himself a supralapsarian. I will demonstrate how his definitions of supra- and infralapsarianism in *Romans* II became in *GD* more elaborately out of sync with the original Lapsarian Controversy.

PRIMARY SOURCES AND HISTORICAL INTRODUCTION

I begin with a brief introduction to the primary sources used in this chapter. For practical purposes I have chosen to focus mainly on *GD*, a published collection of Barth's lectures at the University of Göttingen from 1924 to 1925. These lectures were published posthumously in 1985 as a three-volume collection in Barth's *Gesamtausgabe* under the title *Unterricht in der christlichen Religion* (Instruction in the Christian religion), echoing Calvin's *Institutes of the Christian Religion*.¹ The English translation of these lectures is divided into two volumes, the second of which is yet unpublished.

Dogmatics in Göttingen and Münster. *GD* represents the major corpus of Barth's dogmatic output during the Göttingen-Münster period. Although he offered another cycle of courses at the University of Münster in 1926–1927, the contours of his theology during the two dogmatic cycles remains essentially unchanged. Bruce McCormack points out that the Münster dogmatics "added little that was decisively new.... And even on a material level, though there is certainly expansion and clarification at some important points, Michael Beintker is undoubtedly right in his suggestion that Barth had the Göttingen material constantly before him as he wrote this book."²

The reason for my choice to focus on the Göttingen rather than the Münster lectures is practical: only the first volume of the Münster dogmatics, originally planned as a three-volume project, has been published, under the title *Die Christliche Dogmatik im Entwurf* (Christian dogmatics in outline).³ The published volume comprises the prolegomena alone, and only four sections are directly relevant to the study of this chapter: §14 *Die objektive Möglichkeit der Offenbarung* (The objective possibility of revelation); §16 *Die Geburt des Herrn* (The birth of the Lord); §17 *Die subjektive Möglichkeit der Offenbarung* (The subjective possibility of revelation); and §19 *Die Glaube und der Gehorsam* (Faith and obedience). The doctrine of predestination is not included in this volume. These sections, moreover, are mostly just rearrangements of what Barth has already set forth in *GD*. For these reasons, I will cite the Münster dogmatics only when it helps to better explain certain issues.

Barth's encounter with Reformed orthodoxy. When Barth first arrived at Göttingen as Professor of Reformed Theology in 1921, the Lutheran faculty did not expect him to give lectures in dogmatics. Rather, he began his teaching there by offering courses on the theologies of Calvin (1922),⁴

---

¹*GA* 2.17, 20, 38.
²Bruce McCormack, *Karl Barth's Critically Realistic Dialectical Theology* (Oxford: Clarendon, 1995), 375. See Michael Beintker, "Unterricht in der christlichen Religion," *Verkündigung und Forschung* 30, no. 2 (1985): 46.
³*GA* 2.14.
⁴*GA* 2.23.

Zwingli (1922/1923),[5] the Reformed confessions (1923),[6] Schleiermacher (1923/1924)[7] and so on.

Preparing these lectures in historical theology gave Barth the opportunity to become acquainted with Reformed orthodoxy. In my first two chapters I discussed his encounter with the works of Heinrich Heppe and other German historiographers of the Reformed tradition while at Göttingen. Relying on the historiography that was available to him, Barth gave his own expositions of Calvin, the Heidelberg Catechism and the Reformed confessions.

One major insight that Barth retrieved from his study of the Reformed tradition was the economy of the Holy Spirit. This would become the foundation of one of his two major theological breakthroughs in the Göttingen-Münster period. The historic Reformed doctrine of the pneumatological *ordo salutis* provided Barth with a new way of thinking of the subjective possibility of revelation: God is *in* and *with* the believer by the Holy Spirit in the here and now when the believer as subject comes to know God who has become object. Although humans possess no organ capable of receiving revelation, God becomes this very organ in the person of the Holy Spirit so that revelation becomes subjectively possible for the believer.

This pneumatological emphasis in Barth's theology during the Göttingen-Münster phase would give rise to an actualistic[8] doctrine of election that focuses on the active faith and obedience of the believer in the concrete moments of the here and now. This may be contrasted with what some have called the "christological objectivism" of Barth's Christocentric doctrine of election in *Gottes Gnadenwahl* (1936) and *CD* II/2 (1942), where the objectively accomplished reality of eternal election-in-Christ becomes the definitive ground of Barth's theology. The Göttingen-Münster period, then, represents a phase of Barth's theological development that is most trinitarian in terms of his treatment of the divine economy. As George Hunsinger notes,

---

[5]*GA* 2.40.
[6]*GA* 2.30.
[7]*GA* 2.11.
[8]Barth has not yet developed the notion of God as "being-in-act" at this stage. Rather, his actualism in this phase describes God's "revelation in act," in which God is completely sovereign in his active relations to the recipients of revelation. See George Hunsinger, "Karl Barth's *The Göttingen Dogmatics*," *Scottish Journal of Theology* 46 (1993): 374.

"It is one of the most surprising features of *The Göttingen Dogmatics* that Barth is much more explicitly Trinitarian than christocentric."[9]

Barth's other major discovery in his encounter with classical Reformed theology during the Göttingen years was the two-nature Christology of Nicene-Chalcedonian orthodoxy.[10] McCormack recounts: "In May 1924 Barth made a momentous discovery. During the course of his first lectures in dogmatics, he came upon the anhypostatic-enhypostatic Christological dogma of the ancient Church in a textbook of post-Reformation theology."[11] The two-nature Christology of Chalcedon may be summed up in a phrase frequently used by the Nicene fathers: "God became human without ceasing to be God."[12] This Chalcedonian logic, as we shall see, constitutes the core pattern of Barth's thinking as well as the theological problem he tries to tackle in *GD*.

In Chalcedonian Christology Barth saw one of Christianity's definitive answers to Kant's challenge, namely, the epistemological gulf between God and humanity, which gave rise to what T. F. Torrance calls a "fatal deistic disjunction between God and the world which does not allow for any real Word of God to cross the gulf between God and the creature or therefore to permit man in space and time any real knowledge of God as he is in himself."[13]

Confronting this central theological problem, Barth found in the ancient christological dogma a theological method that fit nicely with insights he picked up from Kierkegaard, the thrust of which is that God entered into the veil of humanity and became "incognito" in order to reveal Godself, thus allowing an indirect, albeit true, subjective human knowledge of God.[14] As we shall see, this has much to do with the basically infralapsarian character of Barth's Christology at this stage of his development.

---

[9]Hunsinger, "*Göttingen Dogmatics*," 377.
[10]Paul Jones has questioned how helpful it is to label Barth's Christology at this stage as "Chalcedonian." See Paul Jones, *The Humanity of Christ: Christology in Karl Barth's Church Dogmatics* (London: T&T Clark, 2008). In chap. 8 I shall discuss Jones's viewpoint.
[11]McCormack, *Dialectical Theology*, 327.
[12]Most famously, Cyril of Alexandria: see, e.g., *Letters* 55.23.
[13]T. F. Torrance, *Space, Time and Resurrection* (Edinburgh: T&T Clark, 1976), 2.
[14]In this phase, Barth seems particularly interested in Kierkegaard's *Training in Christianity* and *Fear and Trembling*. See, e.g., *GD* 1:37, 143, 332-33, 460. Also dominant in this period of Barth's theological development is the Kierkegaardian theme of subjectivity.

Subjective and Objective Possibilities of Revelation

We now turn to *GD*. A sharp contrast between *Romans* II (see chapter three) and *GD* is the complete absence of the rhetoric of "impossible possibility" in the latter. In fact, Barth now explicitly rejects the impossible-possibility dialectic: since the "possibility" of knowledge of God in Christ by faith "can be a *reality* at any time by the Holy Spirit, we must not say that the conditional nature of revelation through Christ and the obedience of faith is the same as the unknowability of God, as the *impossibility* and unreality of a true and adequate and satisfactory knowledge of God."[15]

Two key differences between *Romans* II and *GD* are apparent in this passage. First, divine self-revelation in Christ and human knowledge of God by faith are no longer described as "impossible possibilities," but as "possibilities" that "*can* become a reality" in the here and now. To be sure, in *GD* Barth still rejects the historicism and psychologism of neo-Protestantism, continuing to refer to the "psychological impossibility" of faith and "historical impossibility" of revelation as he did in *Romans* II.[16] However, unlike *Romans* II, Barth now clearly acknowledges the present possibility of a true, adequate and satisfactory human knowledge of God.

The reason for this difference lies in the second point to be noted in the passage above—the economy of the Holy Spirit. In *Romans* II, this notion is almost completely absent, even in the exegetical passages on Romans 8. For the Barth of *Romans* II, God cannot be present in this temporal world in any true sense. In *GD*, however, not only is the human Jesus described as truly and fully God—a statement that Barth consistently avoided in *Romans* II—but also God is said to be really present in the here and now by the Holy Spirit, so that on the subjective human side of the divine-human communication, God Godself becomes the receptive organ for revelation.

This pneumatological insight is Barth's other definitive answer to Kant's epistemological challenge. As Hunsinger summarizes it: "because our participation in this drama 'is a psychological impossibility, just as revelation is a historical impossibility' (p. 197), only in the midst of this drama is our ability to receive revelation 'a real ability' (p. 346). In other words, we 'have

---

[15] Karl Barth, *Unterricht in der christlichen Religion* (Zurich: TVZ, 1985), 2:21; ET 333 (emphasis added).
[16] Ibid., 1:243; ET 197.

a share in revelation' only 'by the Holy Spirit, that is, by God himself, and not in any other way' (p.451)."[17]

Because of these new emphases, the central theological problem in *GD* is framed differently from that of *Romans* II. In *Romans* II, the question is unilateral—it is only concerned with the possibility of revelation from God's side downward: Given that human knowledge of God is impossibly possible, how was impossibility made possible? In *GD*, however, Barth sets forth his question in two directions: Given that humans *do* stand before God, (1) "How can God come to us without ceasing to be God," and (2) "how can we humans stand before God without ceasing to be human?"[18]

These two questions rely heavily, albeit critically, on Chalcedon and the Reformation. The starting point here, just as in *Romans* II, is that revelation is a given. The difference is that in *Romans* II, revelation is given as impossible possibility, but in *GD*, revelation is given as the reality of humanity's standing before God—the Reformation rally cry of *coram Deo*. Additionally, these two questions are reminiscent of the patristic phrase "God became human without ceasing to be God." The emphasis in the second question, moreover, underscores the abiding distinction between God and humanity in Chalcedonian Christology.

The two questions above lead Barth to a very different way of working out the possibility of revelation than in *Romans* II. In *Romans* II, as we saw in chapter three, the dialectic was primarily between impossibility and possibility. In *GD*, however, the dialectic is between God as subject and as object, which gives rise to two kinds of possibilities for revelation—the objective and the subjective. The possibility for God to come to us without ceasing to be God, the subject of the *Deus dixit*, is the objective possibility of revelation; the possibility for humans to stand before God without ceasing to be human is the subjective possibility of humankind's knowledge of God. Barth finds the answer to the objective side of the question in the doctrine of the incarnation, whereas he approaches the subjective side of the question with his newly discovered economic pneumatology.[19]

---

[17] Hunsinger, "*Göttingen Dogmatics*," 375.
[18] *Unterricht* 1:214; ET 174.
[19] Ibid., 2:21; ET 333.

While Barth no longer considers the possibility of revelation as remaining ever impossible in this world, his subject-object dialectic in *GD*, just as the now abandoned impossible-possibility dialectic, is still predicated on the notion of humanity's fallenness—this will be important for my discussion of Barth's lapsarian thinking. With reference to the I-Thou philosophy popular among Barth's contemporaries such as Friedrich Gogarten, Barth says that the original relationship between God and humanity was that of an *Ich-und-Du*—God is neither a "He" nor an "It" but an "I."[20] He stresses God's utter aseity: "I am who I am (Exod. 3:14). . . . This subject is not giving an objective definition of himself but positing himself again as subject."[21]

Here we see that Barth's axiom "God is God" now takes on biblical-exegetical character. Eberhard Busch rightly observes that in *GD* "the statement 'God is God' is nothing but a paraphrase of the name of God in Exodus 3:14: 'I am that I am.'"[22] Barth repeatedly uses the term *actus purus* in *GD* to describe God's act in the person of the Holy Spirit.[23]

Here is an instance where Barth is not ashamed to draw from theological insights with which he does not entirely agree—in this case Thomism. Thomists interpret Exodus 3:14 as a statement that God is pure actuality in which all potentialities are actualized. Of course Barth's stance against natural theology means that his "actualism," as it has often been called, is incompatible with the Thomist-Aristotelian notion of an Unmoved Mover: metaphysical deduction of the existence of God as Unmoved Mover from the observable motions of the world constitutes a theological method that fails to presuppose the infinite qualitative difference between God and the

---

[20]Ibid., 2:13-15; ET 327-29. See Martin Buber, *I and Thou*, trans. Walter Kaufmann (New York: Charles Scribner's Sons, 1970), 84. In *GD* Barth does not refer to Buber explicitly by name. In Barth's correspondences during the 1920s, Thurneysen mentions Buber a few times in his letters to Barth, but Barth never mentions Buber in his letters during this period. Barth's personal bookshelf, preserved at the Barth-Achiv in Basel, shows that he owned Buber's books and had taken notes while reading them, but it is unclear when this happened. Given Buber's prominence in Germany during Barth's lifetime, however, there is no question that Barth knew of Buber's *Ich und Du* (published in 1923, the year before Barth started his Göttingen lectures on dogmatics) and was using Buber's language in this particular discourse. For more on Barth and Buber, see Dieter Becker, *Karl Barth und Martin Buber, Denker in dialogischer Nachbarschaft? Zur Bedeutung Martin Bubers für die Anthropologie Karl Barths* (Göttingen: Vandenhoeck & Ruprecht, 1986).
[21]*Unterricht* 2:13; ET 327.
[22]Eberhard Busch, *Die Anfänge des Theologen Karl Barth in seinen Göttinger Jahren* (Göttingen: Vandenhoeck & Ruprecht, 1987), 28 (translation mine).
[23]E.g., *Unterricht* 1:155; ET 127.

world, and the result of the deduction is similarly a god standing at the top of a chain of efficient causes that cannot be described as truly transcendent.[24] For Barth this blatantly contradicts Exodus 3:14.

What is noteworthy is that Barth's understanding of the axiom "God is God" in light of Exodus 3:14 is an improvement on the theology of *Romans* II, in which he asserted that as God is God and the world remains world, human knowledge of God in this world is ever impossible. Werner Ruschke helpfully explains the "the ground of dialectic" in *Romans* II: "We know that God is the one whom we do not know, the one whom we cannot know, because God is God."[25] In *Romans* II, "humanity has no possibility to draw near to God" or come to any knowledge of God because of God's "absolute otherness" over against the world.[26] Recall from chapter three that according to *Romans* II the "world" is not God's original creation, but a realm of existence that has fallen into temporality in which it is impossible that the transcendent God be revealed or known. Here Barth assumes a basically Kantian argument: the axiom "God is God" means that God cannot be known within the realm of intuitable objects. Thus in *Romans* II, God's transcendence goes hand in hand with humanity's supratemporal fall and the impossibility of human knowledge of God.

Barth improves on this understanding of the axiom "God is God" in *GD* when he interprets it in light of the subject-object dialectic he finds in Exodus 3:14. Busch is right that according to Barth's subject-object dialectic in *GD*, "God's hiddenness is not to be confused with God's transcendence."[27] The reason is that the paradisiacal human stands directly before the transcendent *Ich* without any veil—she is "immediate to God."[28] God was transcendent over humankind even in the prelapsarian state, but the transcendent God was not hidden to the paradisiacal human. This was indeed what Barth would have also maintained in *Romans* II, but it would have been inconsistent with his argument there that God's absolute otherness over against the world was due to the latter's fall into temporality.

---

[24] Amy Marga has suggested that during the Göttingen-Münster period Barth left room for the viability of the *analogia entis*. See Amy Marga, *Karl Barth's Dialogue With Catholicism in Göttingen and Münster: Its Significance for His Doctrine of God* (Tübingen: Mohr Siebeck, 2010).
[25] Werner Ruschke, *Entstehung und Ausführung der Diastasentheologie in Karl Barths zweitem Römerbrief* (Neukirchen: Neukirchener Verlag, 1987), 14 (translation mine).
[26] Ibid.
[27] Busch, *Göttingen Jahren*, 28 (translation mine).
[28] *Unterricht* 1:190 (*unmittelbar zu Gott*); ET 155.

In *GD*, God's transcendence is no longer associated with humanity's fall. It is rather God's hiddenness that resulted from the fall. For fallen humanity, direct knowledge of God is impossible. As we shall see, this basic position is important for understanding Barth's lapsarian thinking at this stage.

Referring back to the twofold questions of the possibility of revelation, Barth comments: "When God truly reveals himself truly to us, this presupposes ... (a) that God meets us and (b) that we stand before God. For our problem this means that God is an object of knowledge and we the subject. God becomes an object of knowledge by becoming man in Christ. We become the subject of knowledge by faith and obedience."[29] In this "twofold event" of revelation God enters into "the concealment of the subject-object relation."[30] Concealment, or nonrevelation, *is* God's self-revelation, and conversely, revelation *is* nonrevelation. Barth repeatedly refers to this as a "dreadful equation": "*Offenbarung = Nicht-Offenbarung*."[31]

But is revelation as nonrevelation really revelation? In the Münster dogmatics Barth gives a "critically realistic dialectical" (McCormack) answer: revelation is really revelation even and precisely in its being nonrevelation. The critical realism of this dialectic of revelation and nonrevelation is not philosophical or metaphysical, but rather a thinking-after (*Nach-denken*) of the matter-of-fact (*Tatsache*) of revelation.

> The question of which form of philosophy one is intentionally or unintentionally devoted to is entirely irrelevant; epistemological conversion to some critical realism would be completely meaningless in light of the matter-of-fact—that God is a hidden God precisely because He is the self-revealing God, the God before whose deity we can neither flee from transcendence into immanence nor vice versa, the God who is never so far away since He is completely near us, and near us precisely in being far from us, the One who can never be an object because He is God. So, is revelation as such non-revelation?[32]

---

[29]Ibid., 2:17; ET 330.
[30]Ibid., 2:17-19; ET 330-32.
[31]E.g., ibid., 1:166; ET 135. ET does not use the equals sign. Original: "So wäre also gerade Offenbarung = Nicht-Offenbarung?" ET: "Is revelation, then, 'nonrevelation'?"
[32]Karl Barth, *Die christliche Dogmatik im Entwurf, I. Band: Die Lehre vom wortes Gottes, Prolegomena zur christlichen Dogmatik, 1927* (Zurich: TVZ, 1982), 291-92 (translation mine). D. Paul La Montagne makes a minor mistake in commenting that the term "critical realism" was not readily available to Barth. See Montagne, *Barth and Rationality: Critical Realism in Theology* (Eugene,

Put differently, the revelation that "we see, hear, feel, touch, what we can inwardly or outwardly perceive—that something else, an opposite, a second thing, an object, an 'I'—is it not this 'I' [the "*I am that I am*"]?"[33] Barth's answer is affirmative: "Yes, so it is, and it always remains so."[34] The fact that revelation *is* nonrevelation means that the *Deus revelatus* and the *Deus absconditus* are one and the same God.[35]

Revelation as such is an event in which God never ceases to be the *Ich*. The divine subject became a creaturely object without ceasing to be the divine subject. In the event of the *Deus dixit*, God remains ever the subject. In *GD* Barth explains: "God does not set aside or reverse his irremovable and irreversible I. He does not cease to be God in his revelation. But he conceals his I in a relation in which we can share in his self-knowledge, in which he can meet us, in which we can stand before him."[36]

Note here that fallen humans cannot know God directly. This would mean that even when God has become an object, the human subject cannot know God through God's self-concealment. So how is revelation subjectively possible? Barth's answer is that only God knows Godself truly, and fallen humans come to know God only by participating in God's self-knowledge.

This notion of God's self-knowledge is deeply trinitarian: it is the Holy Spirit's knowledge of God who objectifies Godself in the incarnate Son. Christologically, God becomes knowable as object when God "conceals his I in a human It or He"; pneumatologically, God as object becomes knowable to the human subject when God the Spirit "conceals himself in a human seeing, hearing, touching, and tasting of this objective reality."[37]

Therefore, revelation, again, means concealment: God enters into the concealment of the subject-object relation in order to reveal Godself. With reference to Kierkegaard, Barth states that this concealment is the "medium" of revelation, "which under the condition of revelation we know in Christ by the obedience of faith, is only the veil, the incognito, in which the divine subjective, I am who I am, the living God, conceals himself and

---

OR: Wipf and Stock, 2012), 10.
[33]*MD* 292 (translation mine).
[34]*MD* 292 (translation mine).
[35]*MD* 293 (translation mine).
[36]*Unterricht* 1:17; ET 330.
[37]Ibid.

wills to be known."[38] This means that human knowledge of God is necessarily "indirect."[39]

Meanwhile, Barth emphasizes that human knowledge of God in the two-way event of revelation, albeit indirect, is true and adequate knowledge.[40] This stands in sharp contrast to the one-sidedly eschatological theology of *Romans* II, where the possibility of human knowledge of God in this temporal world shall always remain impossible. In the Göttingen-Münster period, the reality of revelation and human knowledge of God is both an "already" (it is already true and adequate) and a "not yet" (it is not yet direct). This shift in Barth's eschatological thinking is, again, reflected in his abandonment of the "impossible possibility" rhetoric in favor of the subject-object dialectic, which, as we shall see, is intimately related to his lapsarian thinking.

Objective Possibility: The Incarnation

Christology "a posteriori." Despite these differences between *Romans* II and *GD*, some of Barth's fundamental convictions remain unchanged. Among these is his insistence that the possibility of revelation is an a posteriori given: he does not ask whether revelation is possible, but *how* it has become possible. He states: "We can seriously raise and treat the problem of the possibility of revelation only when we know its reality. Fundamentally we can construct it only a posteriori. All reflection on how God *can* reveal himself is in truth only a 'thinking after' [Nach-Denken] of the fact that God *has* revealed himself."[41] The same position is reiterated in Münster. Discussing the "objective possibility of revelation," Barth writes: "Precisely speaking, our construction is . . . not a construction a priori, but a construction a posteriori."[42] This is so for revelation in general, and not just its objective possibility: "One can seriously pose and treat the problem of the possibility of revelation only by knowing its reality; as a basic principle one can only construct it a posteriori."[43]

---

[38]Ibid., 2:21; ET 333.
[39]Ibid., 2:20; ET 332.
[40]Ibid., 2:21; ET 333.
[41]Ibid., 1:185; ET 151.
[42]*MD* 307 (translation mine).
[43]*MD* 339 (translation mine).

For this reason, in adopting an enhypostatic-anhypostatic Christology, Barth is not seeking to deduce Christ's two natures from intuitable phenomena or rational first principles. Rather, the incarnation is presupposed as an a posteriori given. As a concluding remark to his basically Chalcedonian[44] construal of Christ's two natures, Barth writes:

> What I have constructed ... was obviously a construction a posteriori. ... I have not been talking hypothetically ... but about the actually existent possibility of revelation, about Jesus Christ. ... I could not speak specifically about the condition without finally, as you have noted, adopting the terms of the Chalcedonian Definition, in which the church gave classical formulation, not to a deduction of Christ a priori, but to an account of the actual reality of Christ.[45]

Christology in Chalcedonian patterns. Barth's Christology as such is explicitly Chalcedonian in its form. Note, however, that in *GD* he is trying to find in Chalcedon a soteriological solution to a modern epistemological problem that was not Chalcedon's central concern. The problem that he poses and treats is that of "the *Deus dixit* to which the Bible testifies as our first scientific dictum. In light of this testimony ... we face the question of the objective possibility of this *Deus dixit*. We ask, then, how according to the biblical testimony God brings it about that he comes to us with his Word without ceasing to be God."[46]

Here we see that Barth is trying to treat the problem by appealing to the biblical witness. What he saw in Chalcedon was a sound summary of Scripture's testimony to the *Deus dixit* in Christ. The incarnation, to which Scripture attests, is the very starting point of proving itself to be the only way whereby revelation becomes objectively possible.

> According to our proof (our a posteriori proof, even though the presupposition is assumed), revelation is not objectively possible except by God's in-

---

[44]Some have protested against the use of this term to refer to Barth's mature theology. Bruce McCormack and Paul Jones have done so with specific agendas of interpreting Barth's Christology as "historicized." Paul Nimmo, rationalistically deducing from Barth an "actualistic ontology," argues that the term "Chalcedonian" as a description of Barth's Christology can carry misleading connotations. In chaps. 7 and 8 I provide more details as to why I think we should retain "basically Chalcedonian" as a proper description of Barth's theology.
[45]*Unterricht* 1:173; ET 141.
[46]Ibid., 1:176; ET 144.

carnation. Now God's revelation in any case means God's revelation in his concealment. It means the radical dedivinization of the world and nature and history, the complete divine incognito, God's dealings with us exclusively by indirect communication.[47]

Barth outlines four basic points to describe the incarnation in Chalcedonian patterns. First, "God will have to be wholly God in this concealment that makes him comprehensible."[48] This is the Chalcedonian definition of Christ as fully and truly God. God in concealment cannot be any less or other than God in Godself. Otherwise what is revealed through the concealment would not be God at all.

Second, "the human being through whom God conceals himself and makes himself comprehensible must be no less fully human."[49] The reason, according to Barth, is that if God is not fully concealed in full humanity, if any part of God (were God divisible!) is revealed directly, the incomplete concealment would "again withdraw [God] from our perception. God must really meet man, and that means that he himself must be truly and totally human and nothing else."[50]

Third, "the real deity and the real humanity must be so united that neither can be changed into the other or mixed with it. . . . Otherwise it would no longer be God that meets us, or he would cease to meet us truly."[51] Here Barth is referring to the famous Chalcedonian adverbs describing Christ's deity and humanity as having been united "unchangeably" and "unconfusedly." These two adverbs underscore the Chalcedonian principle of the *abiding distinction* between Christ's deity and humanity. Barth sets forth this principle while emphasizing the other principle, the *inseparable union* of Christ's two natures, as described by the other two Chalcedonian adverbs, "inseparably" and "indivisibly": "The deity and humanity must be distinguished in such a way that we cannot *detach* the one from the other or consider the one *apart from* the other."[52]

Barth takes special note of the dialectical nature of the so-called four fences of Chalcedon, commenting that the union of Christ's two natures is

---

[47]Ibid.
[48]Ibid., 1:169; ET 138.
[49]Ibid.
[50]Ibid.
[51]Ibid.
[52]Ibid., 1:170; ET 138-39 (emphasis added).

a "strictly dialectical union," "a differentiation in union."[53] For Barth, this ancient dialectic was key to solving the modern-critical problem of the objective possibility of revelation.

Fourth, Barth emphasizes the Chalcedonian principle of the *uniqueness* of the incarnation: "By its very nature this union of deity and humanity cannot be general or multiple but only once and for all."[54] If there could have been multiple God-humans, argues Barth, it would have meant that the incarnation could have taken place many times, and God could have separated Godself from the human to whom God is united many times. Not only would this violate the Chalcedonian principle of the inseparability of the union of Christ's two natures, but also, more importantly, this would have meant that there is more than one revelation. However, it is axiomatic for Barth that "revelation is one" since God is one.[55] Thus there can only be one incarnation.

Barth's argument for the singularity of the incarnation is modern. In the Chalcedonian tradition the uniqueness of the incarnation is described in terms of the enhypostatic-anhypostatic union, rather than the uniqueness of revelation. This is not to say that Barth fails to see the importance of the enhypostatic-anhypostatic union. In fact, this notion is of such central importance to him that he treats it separately, under the topic of Christ's *assumptio* of human nature.

> Early writers called the act of union an assumption. It is not, then, a changing or alteration of the divine nature of the Son, but with his divine mode of existence the Son takes a human made of existence, uniting it . . . to his person, just as the divine mode of existence is eternally united to his person, yet without in any way altering his divine mode of existence.[56]

This means that "the kenosis of the Son in the incarnation is not that he wholly or partially ceases to be the eternal Son of the Father (otherwise the incarnation would not be revelation) but that as the Son of God he is also made the Son of Man."[57] This is an understanding of the kenosis that Barth

---

[53]Ibid.
[54]Ibid.; ET 139.
[55]Ibid.
[56]Ibid., 1:192; ET 156.
[57]Ibid.

would retain in his mature theology, on which McCormack rightly comments that the kenosis is "by addition and not by subtraction": "Nothing proper to deity is 'left behind' when the 'Son' takes on the form of a servant."[58] This view of the kenosis underscores the Nicene-Chalcedonian axiom that "God does not cease to be God in becoming human."[59]

Such an *assumptio* of human nature by the Logos would require that the person of the God-human is one divine person taking on human nature, not—in the words of Chalcedon—"as parted or divided into two persons, but one and the same Son and only-begotten God the Word, Lord Jesus Christ." Nor is Christ a human hypostasis taking on divine nature—that would be the Nestorian heresy rejected by the Chalcedonian term *Theotokos*. Barth emphasizes the idea that Christ's human nature "did not exist prior to its union with the Logos. It has no independent existence alongside or apart from him. . . . It is *anhypostatos*."[60] This apophatic *anhypostatos* can also be expressed positively: "It is *enhypostatos*. It has personhood, subsistence, reality, only in its union with the Logos of God."[61]

For Barth, the central significance of the enhypostatic-anhypostatic union is again epistemological: it is the only way in which revelation is possible. "Those who want to see revelation in Jesus as a human individual" without recognizing his person as that of the Logos, says Barth, are "necessarily groping in the void."[62] Barth would continue to emphasize this epistemological significance of the incarnation in his treatment of the *assumptio carnis* in the Münster dogmatics, which Barth begins by commenting that the *assumptio* and the kenosis have to be described in line with Chalcedon, "otherwise the incarnation would not be God's revelation."[63]

From the foregoing discussions it is clear that Barth's Christology at this stage takes on Chalcedonian patterns. However, it does not share Chalcedon's central soteriological concern: according to Chalcedon the incarnation was "for us humans and for our salvation."

---

[58] Bruce McCormack, "Karl Barth's Christology as Resource for a Reformed Version of Kenoticism," *International Journal of Systematic Theology* 8 (2006): 248.
[59] Ibid.
[60] *Unterricht* 1:193; ET 157.
[61] Ibid.
[62] Ibid.
[63] *MD* 347 (translation mine).

In the Göttingen-Münster years, Barth's central concern in his Christology is revelation rather than salvation. Barth explicitly states that his construction of two-nature Christology is not in a "soteriological setting."[64] He admits that the setting of his christological construction in GD not only differs from that of Chalcedon but is also "not in the same specifically soteriological setting as what Anselm did in Book II of his *Cur deus homo?*, and after him the authors of the Heidelberg Catechism in Questions 12-17."[65] In this regard, during the Göttingen-Münster period the *setting* of Barth's Christology is different from both that of Chalcedon and Reformed orthodoxy, the latter of which owes a great debt to Anselm's satisfaction theory. This is not to say that Barth's Christology in this phase is not soteriological. However, the primary theological problem he tackles is epistemological, even if the solution has to be soteriological.

Infralapsarian Christology. To say that Barth's Christology in the Göttingen-Münster period is not explicitly or primarily soteriological, however, is not to say that it does not regard sin as the fundamental problem that the incarnation confronts. As Christopher Asprey observes, to take seriously the Christology of GD "would mean seeing the 'two-natures' Christology not in isolation, but as ingredient within soteriology, as the focal point of the reconciliation between God and humanity."[66] Of course, the soteriology of GD is primarily concerned with how revelation overcomes human sin, rather than with salvation as usually understood in traditional Christian theology.

In any case, according to GD, sin is the very cause of the epistemological gulf between God and humans, and the purpose of the incarnation is precisely to take care of the problem of sin in history, thus "the incarnation is not an eternal relation."[67] As McCormack puts it, "revelation in the form of incarnation was necessary, in Barth's view, because of the Fall."[68] McCormack even stresses that there was never "an independent, second ground

---

[64]*Unterricht* 1:172; ET 140.
[65]Ibid.
[66]Christopher Asprey, *Eschatological Presence in Karl Barth's Göttingen Theology* (Oxford: Oxford University Press, 2010), 175.
[67]*Unterricht* 1:190; ET 155.
[68]McCormack, *Dialectical Theology*, 360.

of the necessity of the incarnation."⁶⁹ Therefore, Barth's Christology in the Göttingen-Münster phase clearly leans toward infralapsarianism.

Recall that supralapsarian Christology maintains that the incarnation was made necessary by God's primal decisions that were regardless of sin. Barth, however, explicitly states the very opposite:

> Revelation, or, more precisely, incarnation . . . is the divine answer to the human question concerning the overcoming of the contradiction of human existence. To anticipate an expression from dogmatics proper, it takes place *because of the fall*, to reverse the fall. . . . It is because of man and his contradiction that God must leave his self-resting deity for a second time after creation and come into action.⁷⁰

Would the incarnation have been necessary for humanity to know God and be with God, had humankind not fallen? Barth's answer at this stage is unequivocally negative: "Man as God created him, paradisal man, needed no divine revelation or incarnation. . . . He stood before the revelation that was always and everywhere given to him directly. He was what the Romantics would have liked to have been, that is, *immediate to God*."⁷¹

In the Münster dogmatics Barth reiterates and explicates the very same position under the section "The Birth of the Lord" (§16): "The human, as created by God, the paradisiacal human, did not need the paradox of reconciliation. . . . He would be what Romantic theology would have wanted to describe him to be by wrongly extracting him out of the situation of fallenness: he would be immediate to God. . . . God was not a problem to him."⁷²

In short, for the Barth of Göttingen-Münster, God's decision to become incarnate logically follows God's decision to reverse the fall, thus his Christology during this period leans very clearly toward infralapsarian, even more so than in his mature Christocentric doctrine of election, in which he claims that Christ eternally *incarnandus* is the beginning of all God's ways and works. The Christology of *GD* does not carry this supralapsarian overtone.

In *GD* Barth even adds that in the eschaton wherein "the Son hands over the kingdom to the Father (1 Cor. 15:28)," the incarnation "is no longer

---

⁶⁹Ibid., 361.
⁷⁰*Unterricht* 1:190; ET 155.
⁷¹Ibid. (emphasis added).
⁷²*MD* 345 (translation mine).

needed."[73] To be sure, the incarnation is once and for all; the hypostatic union is inseparable. Therefore, "not that [Christ] ceases to be the incarnate Son any more than we cease to be men and women . . . , but in such a way that his humanity is no longer needed and revelation ends as it began."[74] In short, God's decision to become incarnate is predicated on humanity's separation from God—and this is precisely the infralapsarian view.

From 1936 onward, Barth would modify his eschatological Christology and assert that even in the eschaton, humanity's union with God presupposes *participatio Christi*. Despite this supralapsarian overtone, the basic orientation of the Christology of *Gottes Gnadenwahl* and *CD* II/2 still remains infralapsarian—I will explain why in chapters six and seven. Suffice it now to say that Barth's Christology in the Göttingen-Münster period is quite clearly on the infralapsarian side.

Subjective Possibility: Pneumatology and Predestination

Calvin and Reformed orthodoxy. Having established the objective possibility of revelation in the incarnation, Barth proceeds to consider the subjective possibility: how can fallen sinners see and hear God in the incognito of Christ? Once again we note that human fallenness is presupposed in Barth's discussion of the subjective possibility of revelation—this will be important for our consideration of Barth's predestinarian lapsarianism. Barth's answer to this question is faith and obedience, and he appeals to Reformed pneumatology to describe faith-obedience as the Holy Spirit's work.

Barth's discourse on faith-obedience as the subjective possibility of revelation is indebted to his studies on Calvin. Though by 1911 Barth had already read Calvin's 1559 *Institutes*, his encounter with Reformed orthodoxy in Göttingen gave him new insights on Calvin's writings. In his lectures on Calvin's theology delivered in the summer of 1922, Barth talks about the two-sidedness of the unity of revelation in Calvin's thought. Barth says that according to Calvin, Scripture is inspired by the Holy Spirit, but a sinner can grasp the truth of Scripture only by "the inner testimony of the Holy Spirit,

---

[73]*Unterricht* 1:192; ET 156.
[74]Ibid.

the voice of truth that makes itself heard not merely in the Bible but also in the believing reader or hearer."[75]

What Barth picks up from Calvin in this line of thought is the "unity" of the "subjective and objective" sides of revelation.[76] For Barth, revelation is the act of the *one* God who enters into *one* subject-object concealment. Having commented on Calvin's view of the unity of the objective and subjective aspects of inspiration, Barth continues: "The same may be said about the thinking of Calvin on the appropriation of revelation, on faith. More strongly than the other reformers Calvin stresses the purely other-sided basis and content of faith. Faith does not come from us, not even as the recognition of our need."[77] Faith is the Holy Spirit's work, as book 3 of Calvin's *Institutes* consistently stresses.

The notion of faith as the Holy Spirit's work to effect the subjective possibility is a new insight that Barth retrieves from Calvin and Reformed orthodoxy. In *GD* §7, "Faith and Obedience," Barth writes in his introductory note: "As the miracle of faith and obedience, this knowledge and action are both effected by the Holy Spirit, whom no one and nothing can replace as the subjective possibility of revelation," with a marginal note: "Heppe 381! 384-85."[78] From these pages of Heppe's *Dogmatik* Barth has learned the Reformed-orthodox doctrine of the "efficacious call" of the Holy Spirit in the so-called *ordo salutis* of economic pneumatology.[79] According to this doctrine, fallen humans are dead in their sins and transgressions, so totally depraved that they are utterly unable to perceive the call of Christ's gospel. Thus the Holy Spirit regenerates the sinner, inwardly calling her to accept the gospel by faith. This inward call of the Holy Spirit is said to be "efficacious," because it is God's grace that sovereignly overcomes the obstructions of sin, a grace that Reformed orthodoxy describes as "irresistible."

Actualistic pneumatology. This understanding of the Holy Spirit's economy leads to the important topic of Barth's actualistic pneumatology in

---

[75]Karl Barth, *Die Theologie Calvins 1922*, GA 2.23 (Zurich: TVZ, 1993), 223; ET *The Theology of John Calvin*, trans. G. W. Bromiley (Grand Rapids: Eerdmans, 1995), 167-68.
[76]Ibid.
[77]Ibid.
[78]*Unterricht* 1:207; ET 168.
[79]Heinrich Heppe, *Die Dogmatik der Evangelisch-Reformierten Kirche* (Whitefish, MT: Kessinger, 2010), 367-91.

the Göttingen-Münster period, which determines the basic shape of his doctrine of election. Reappropriating the Reformed doctrine of total depravity, Barth begins his subsection titled "The Subjective Possibility of Revelation" (*GD* §7.I) with the statement: "We must now discuss the subjective possibility of revelation, that is, human receptivity for it. . . . What we have in view is the element in the concept which as attention or openness to it confronts directly our *constitutional inability* to grasp God's incarnation."[80]

This "element" is the work of the Holy Spirit *in nobis*, which ensures that "revelation is not a light that shines among the blind but real revelation."[81] For Barth, if revelation is not subjectively possible as it is objectively, then it is not revelation at all. The particular content of the Holy Spirit's work effecting this subjective possibility is thus the believer's "faith and obedience."[82]

The central theological problem here is as follows: "How can we humans stand before God without ceasing to be human?"[83] Again, Barth's a posteriori "presupposition" is that "revelation exists," and that "we humans who cannot stand before God are the very ones who do stand before God."[84]

But how is it that humans could not stand before God in the first instance? Here Barth, as in *Romans* II, adopts a "critical philosophy": the question of the subjective possibility of revelation "would be fine if we might be able to escape it with a little conversion from critical philosophy to a more friendly philosophy. . . . But we have made the presupposition that man stands before *God*, and precisely on the basis of the presupposition we must now say rather oddly that man cannot stand before God."[85]

In the Göttingen-Münster period, Barth's critical philosophy takes on Calvinistic overtones: it "means . . . that we have no organ by which to receive God's revelation. . . . We have no quality, capacity, or possibility whereby to stand before God. . . . We would no longer be human if any such could be ascribed to us."[86] Of course, Barth is here referring to fallen humanity, not paradisiacal humanity. He is describing the subjective impos-

---

[80]*Unterricht* 1:207; ET 168.
[81]Ibid.
[82]Ibid.
[83]Ibid., 1:215; ET 174.
[84]Ibid., 1:215-16; ET 174-75.
[85]Ibid., 1:216; ET 175.
[86]Ibid., 1:215; ET 174.

sibility of revelation in a way akin to the Calvinist doctrine of total inability—this will be important for our consideration of his lapsarian tendency during the Göttingen-Münster period.

Stating that humans have no organ whereby to receive revelation, Barth explains: "For God himself is the content as well as the subject of revelation. What element in human self-consciousness can come into consideration as an organ by which to grasp this reality?"[87]

If humans are incapable of receiving revelation, the only way that revelation becomes subjectively possible is that "God does what we ourselves cannot do."[88] Just as "God can step out of his deity, so we can step out of our humanity, although without surrendering but rather *activating* it; that we can step out of ourselves, out of our being and our awareness of being caught in the contradiction, and be with God and even in God, learning from God to know God in his revelation with eyes that God has opened."[89] In this event, God posits "himself as the beginning, middle, and end of this human activity, granting us his good pleasure of his own free grace, that is, granting us meaning, truth, power, and success, being himself the organ and way and movement in this human activity, so that it is no longer without an object but has God himself as its object."[90]

Again, this event does not erase the believer's humanity—Barth wants to ensure that he describes humans as standing before God *without ceasing to be human*. Therefore, this event is an "activation of our humanity which is from God and in God."[91] It is from God, because it is God's work "in the third person, the Holy Spirit. *His* work is the activation of our humanity that is caught in contradiction to the extent that this work of his enables us to see and hear and receive and accept, that it makes us receptive to God, that it places us before God incarnate in Christ, that it sets us in fellowship with God."[92]

In other words, humans have no organ whereby to receive revelation, so Godself in the person of the Holy Spirit became this very organ. God is now not only the object of human knowledge, but also its subject: "God stands

---

[87] Ibid.
[88] Ibid., 1:216; ET 175.
[89] Ibid. (emphasis added).
[90] Ibid.
[91] Ibid., 1:216-17; ET 175-78.
[92] Ibid., 1:218; ET 177.

before them as an object but also because, for all their impotence, God is with them and indeed in them as the subject, so that God makes the connection, building the bridge that cannot be built."[93]

In this way, true human knowledge of God corresponds to God's self-knowledge, because only God knows Godself truly. Human knowledge of God is true and adequate only insofar as it is the Holy Spirit's knowledge of the triune God, as the Holy Spirit is *with* and *in* the believer as the subject of this knowledge.

More concretely, the Holy Spirit's work is to "create faith and obedience in us and thus place us before God."[94] Just as in *Romans* II, Barth now describes faith and obedience as God's work of creation and a miracle.

> That is to say, as he [God] creates the world out of nothing, and as he makes a particle of human nature in the body of the virgin the dwelling of the Logos, so he makes a piece of broken humanity into human knowing and doing, with himself in his revelation as the object. As in creation and the incarnation, so here, too, we have a *miracle*, an event which has its only ontic and noetic basis in the freedom and majesty of God.[95]

This last point about God's freedom and majesty in the event of faith and obedience points to an *actualistic* understanding of the Holy Spirit's work. Remember, Barth's *actualism* carries the implication that God is completely free and sovereign in God's active relations with everything that is not God. The actualism of Barth's later theology would be defined in terms of God's being-in-act, but in the Göttingen-Münster period, Barth only speaks of a revelation-in-act. Even so, in this period Barth already describes revelation as God's free and pure act whereby God gives Godself to be known. The subjective possibility of revelation, in particular, can be understood as just the *enactment* or *activation* of God's self-disclosure in the subjective-human sphere.

Therefore, the actual human relation of faith and obedience to God "has to be a conversation, a drama, a struggle, in which there are dangers and turning points, surprises and discoveries, repulses and advances, victories and defeats, standings and fallings."[96] Humankind's relation of faith and

---
[93]Ibid., 1:217; ET 176.
[94]Ibid.
[95]Ibid.
[96]Ibid., 1:222; ET 180.

obedience to God "must not set up anything constant or given, any natural necessity."[97] Rather, "it must be a relation which, in order to remain true, must be renewed every moment both by God's work and word and in our own knowing and doing. Is not this unavoidable if God's free good pleasure on the one side, and faith and obedience as our own free acts on the other, are really the deciding factors?"[98]

In this rhetorical question, Barth is invoking the actualistic principle of *correspondence*: "faith and obedience as our own free acts" are set up in correspondence to "God's free good pleasure." Recall that faith and obedience are truly human acts, but they are the act of the Holy Spirit *in nobis*, which is God's sovereign will *in actu*. This means that human faith and obedience are not given to believers to be in their constant possession. Rather, faith and obedience are the temporal enactment of God's free self-revelation in the believer's life, thus "each moment must be unique and nonrepeatable, for our other partner is God and he demands that we hazard our whole existence."[99] Barth's actualistic formulation of the Holy Spirit's work as such implies, then, in simple terms, that faith and obedience are a free gift of God that God can choose to give or withhold at any moment in time.

Double Predestination

Barth's actualistic pneumatology implies that the ultimate ground of a person's concrete situation of faith or unbelief is not ultimately her own choice—even though these are truly her own acts—but God's eternal decision. Human choices of faith and unbelief are "but the human and temporal shadow, manifestation, repetition, and outworking of a divine and eternal reality."[100]

A sinner has no choice between faith and unbelief apart from God, since unbelief is inherent to fallen humanity. This is because God's objective revelation is an act of self-concealment, and the sinner has no capacity to perceive the divine in the incognito of the incarnation. Thus faith, as we saw, is impossible without the Holy Spirit's work *in nobis*. This means that whether a person will come to faith depends entirely on God's sovereign decision and act.

---

[97] Ibid.
[98] Ibid.
[99] Ibid.
[100] *Unterricht* 2:170; ET 443.

Now, if a person can come to faith only by God's free decision through the Holy Spirit's work, this would imply that "the possibility of unbelief" can be understood "only in terms of a divine nonwilling, nonawakening, and noneffecting, a planned and purposeful attitude of God, a specific holding back, a presence and activity that produces a vacuum on the human side."[101] Conversely, "If we could find a basis for unbelief in ourselves apart from God, at least in part, then we could find a total or partial basis . . . for a faith that God did not will or awaken or effect, or did not do so totally, but that is totally or partially the result of our own piety or inspiration or conflict. But this faith would not be faith, faith in revelation."[102]

Therefore, God's decision has to be the total ground for human situations of faith and unbelief, and "the Holy Spirit, through whose power our weak faith and obedience become the subjective possibility of revelation, is the special thing in the election of grace."[103] In the case of unbelief "we are passed by or rejected by God"; in the case of faith and obedience "we are elected or accepted by God."[104] This "twofold possibility" is God's act of double predestination.

The reality of double predestination as such is of course God's *eternal* decision. However, Barth insists that this "eternal" decision must not be understood detachedly from concrete actualities perceptible to human beings. He criticizes the classical Calvinist doctrine of a *decretum absolutum*, which teaches that God eternally chose a fixed group of people as vessels of mercy and reprobated all others as vessels of wrath, as speculatively metaphysical, calling it a "Trojan Horse" of pagan thought that would eventually ruin Reformed orthodoxy from within.[105] For Barth, the classical Reformed understanding of the *decretum absolutum* is "an illegitimate abstraction" that "anthropologizes or psychologizes a thought which strictly makes sense only as a concept of the knowledge of God."[106]

Against historic Reformed theology, Barth sets forth two theses that are similar to but different from his own position in *Romans* II. First, he insists

---

[101]Ibid., 2:181; ET 451-52.
[102]Ibid.; ET 452.
[103]Ibid., 2:200; ET 466.
[104]Ibid., 2:167; ET 440.
[105]Ibid., 2:186; ET 455.
[106]Ibid., 2:185; ET 454.

that predestination must be understood *actualistically*: "Precisely as eternal predestination, predestination is the divine decree in action, the divine decreeing concerning us in which at every moment God is free in relation to us and goes forward with us from decision to decision."[107] With this actualistic formulation, Barth rejects the traditional understanding of God's decree as "eternal" in the sense of being rigidly fixed from all eternity. Rather, "God's eternity means that 'my time is in thy hands.' It is not an ossified eternity but his living eternity, the eternity of his will, the eternity in which he is Lord."[108]

As we saw in chapter three, the Barth of *Romans* II also holds to an actualistic understanding of predestination. However, in *Romans* II, Barth does not conflate eternity with present actualities as he does in *GD*. In *Romans* II, predestination operates on two levels: on the present-actualistic level, double predestination is manifest through faith and unbelief; on the level of divine eternity, predestination moves from reprobation to election. In *GD*, however, Barth identifies divine eternity as eternity-in-actuality.

Such a view of eternity is indeed strange, as it seems to destroy the transcendence of this very concept and conflate it with temporal actualities. In 1936–1942 Barth would give up this actualistic understanding of predestination in favor of an "election-in-Christ" to maintain the utterly objective reality of God's eternal decision (see chapters six and seven). In 1954, he would combine the two insights and develop a highly actualistic rendition of his notion of election-in-Christ (see chapter eight). During the Göttingen-Münster period, however, Barth still defines God's eternal will in terms of temporal actualities.

Does this mean that God's eternal will is mutable? In *GD* Barth argues that if God's immutability is truly God's, then we cannot perceive it directly. God's unchangeable will must not be sought "in the comprehensibility of a fate which we can abstract from the givenness of a particular station on the way."[109] To claim knowledge of such a "fate"—the *decretum absolutum*—is to "isolate an event in time from the event in the divine eternity instead of relating it to it."[110]

---

[107]Ibid.
[108]Ibid.
[109]Ibid.
[110]Ibid.

For this reason Barth insists that we can only perceive God's immutable will *in actu*, that is, in God's actions in the concrete moments of time. "God is free not only to elect and reject different people but also to elect or reject a particular individual at different times. It is in the eternal act of predestinating, as comes out in the different situations of a person face-to-face with it, that this divine freedom triumphs."[111]

Barth's second thesis is that while predestination does not mean God's "fixed will of election and rejection," it must not be understood as "vacillation between the two" either, for "its point and goal are always election, not rejection, even in rejection."[112] Thus double predestination must be understood *teleologically*: election is irreversibly the purpose of reprobation. Barth again cites Romans 11:32, as he did in *Romans* II, to claim that "the way leads fundamentally from rejection to election, not vice versa. God has shut up all in disobedience in order to have mercy upon all."[113] Just as God's self-concealment is not a goal in itself but serves the purpose of revelation, so "rejection does not take place for its own sake" but for the sake of election.[114] "In his election the judged as such are also the elect."[115]

With these two theses, Barth's doctrine of predestination in *GD* operates from two perspectives, but not on two levels as in *Romans* II: according to *GD* "the elect might also perish (i.e. on their own side) . . . , but they cannot fall away on the side of the decree, of God."[116] Note that unlike *Romans* II, Barth no longer differentiates between God's eternal will and actualistic work. Rather, the distinction is now between the will of the elect and the decree of God. In other words, Barth now understands God's eternal decree actualistically such that the tension is no longer between God's eternal decree and temporal act—the Barth of *GD* refuses to claim knowledge of an eternity above and behind the eternity-in-actuality humanly intuitable in space and time—but between the decisive actuality of God's eternally electing decree and the paradoxical will of God to permit sinners in their attempts to oppose this decree.

---

[111] Ibid.
[112] Ibid., 2:192; ET 460.
[113] Ibid., 2:193; ET 461.
[114] Ibid., 2:192; ET 460.
[115] Ibid., 2:199; ET 465.
[116] Ibid., 2:200; ET 465-66.

With his attention on this actual tension in the here and now, Barth no longer asserts in *GD* any explicitly universalist eschatology as he did in *Romans* II. Instead, he now focuses on "our actual situation," in which "all are at every moment under the divine either-or and can be either elect or rejected. No one is hopeless, and no one is yet in port. All can and must seek the decision where from all eternity (but from God's living eternity) it has been made for time, and will now be made in time one way or another according to *God's* will."[117] Thus Barth rejects the notion of an absolute assurance of having been "plucked out of the mass of perdition" once and for all.[118]

There is, however, "a relative assurance of God, and therefore also of election and salvation, as surely as we know God in his revelation in Christ as the one whose will is to save and not to judge."[119] With reference to Calvin, Barth states that "Christ is the mirror of election."[120] Christ reveals crucifixion, judgment and condemnation to be the means for salvation and election. "In this *teleology* of *God* that is revealed in *Christ* (we must stress all three words) there is the source of our certainty of election and salvation. Thus again, not in ourselves, not in an abstract idea of God, but in God's revelation, and there most certainly, we too, as we look there, can and should be most certain."[121] This is a certainty found only in Christ—it is not the "absolute certainty" of what Barth considers (and, in my opinion, misunderstands) to be a speculatively constructed doctrine of *decretum absolutum*.

As to the question of whether all humans will eschatologically pass from reprobation to election, Barth's answer in *GD* is far more ambiguous than in *Romans* II. In *GD* he warns: "That election and not rejection is the goal of the ways of God is the most that we can and must say.... The idea of apocatastasis, of the elimination of rejection, cannot derive from knowledge of this [electing, free and majestic] God."[122]

Here Barth is refusing to speculate about predestination apart from what is objectively revealed in Christ. He insists that "we must stand by the *revelation in Christ* and thus start with what predestination is in the first in-

---

[117]Ibid., 2:207; ET 471.
[118]Ibid., 2:199; ET 465.
[119]Ibid., 2:207; ET 471.
[120]Ibid.
[121]Ibid.
[122]Ibid., 2:211; ET 475.

stance, that is, election."[123] For the Barth of *GD*, all that revelation in Christ allows him to say is that election is the goal of reprobation, but it says nothing about the elimination of reprobation. Thus in *GD* universal election is only a possibility of which no one can be certain.

Recall that in *Romans* II Barth sees the death and resurrection of Christ as the revelation of an eternal movement from universal reprobation to universal election. Accordingly, no universal election is to take place in time; double predestination in the temporal realm will always remain actualistic. Thus Barth's doctrine of election in *Romans* II also differs from the doctrine of an *apocatastasis*. However, in contrast to *GD*, wherein eternity is no longer detached from present actualities, the eternal-eschatological aspect of predestination as described in *Romans* II is truly universal in scope.

This difference between *Romans* II and *GD* has to do with a shift in the locus of revelation in Barth's mind. According to *Romans* II Christ's resurrection alone is revelation in the strictest sense, and this event manifests a supratemporal, nonhistorical triumph of election over reprobation. In *GD*, however, incarnation is the event in which God enters into a veil in order to unveil Godself, and divine self-disclosure is never complete without the Holy Spirit's work on the subjective human side. On this view, theological reflection may never venture beyond what is revealed in the temporal veil. Thus Barth can no longer speak with certainty about an eternal predestination of God apart from what he perceives to have been given in the actuality of revelation. All his view of revelation would allow him to say is that reprobation serves the purpose of election. Romans 11:32 hints at a universalistic character in the teleology of predestination, but this is to be taken as nothing more than a mere hint.

Toward Infralapsarianism

Recall from Chapter 3 that in *Romans* II Barth is basically supralapsarian because the universal movement from reprobation to election on the eternal-eschatological level constitutes the purpose of the divine predestination of humanity unto fallenness. Such a statement is nowhere to be found in *GD*, because the epistemological confines of revelation-in-Christ would

---

[123]Ibid., 2:210; ET 474 (emphasis added).

not allow Barth to venture this far. That is, the *actual* event of God's self-veiling and self-unveiling does not tell us whether God predestined the fall as a means to fulfill God's purpose in double predestination.

According to *GD*, what we know in the *actual* event of God's self-concealment and self-disclosure, of unbelief and faith, is that "our rebellion against God is a fact"; thus those whom God rejects are already sinners.[124] Against the Catholic and Lutheran accusation that the Reformed doctrine of predestination renders God the "author of sin," Barth contends that "sin, which rules in the circumscribed area to which the reprobate are banned, is not God's work, though it is certainly God's work that the reprobate are banned there and thus left to their own device."[125]

Barth argues: "It is nothing but justice if God leaves people to themselves, for it is they who sin. . . . The fact that God passes people by and therefore condemns them adds nothing new to sin, which is not of God. . . . The only point is that sin is recognized and taken seriously [in God's act of reprobation]. Thus sin is the cause of ruin, not God."[126]

In this line of thought, Barth is basically using the classical infralapsarian argument to counter the charge that the Reformed doctrine portrays God as the author of sin. Recall that according to infralapsarianism, God eternally conceives of the object of predestination as fallen humanity (*homo lapsus*)—and here Barth is appealing to the infralapsarian thesis in saying that those whom "God passes by" are "the hardened, for it is they who sin." This argument is an implicit denial of the supralapsarian thesis that God decreed the fall of humanity in order to issue forth election and reprobation.

It is worth noting how Barth's argument here echoes the infralapsarian position of the Canons of Dort. At the Synod of Dort, Johannes Maccovius was accused of rendering God the author of evil for holding to a strongly voluntaristic version of supralapsarianism. While the synod finally found Maccovius not guilty of heterodoxy, the Canons of Dort make clear that in the decree of reprobation God is by no means the author of sin.[127] The

---

[124]Ibid., 2:191; ET 459.
[125]Ibid.
[126]Ibid.
[127]John Fesko, "Lapsarian Diversity at the Synod of Dort," in *Drawn into Controversy: Reformed Theological Diversity and Debates Within Seventeenth-Century British Puritanism*, ed. Michael Haykin and Mark Jones (Göttingen: Vandenhoeck & Ruprecht, 2011), 120-22.

infralapsarian argument that Dort offers is precisely the one that Barth makes here: reprobation is God's act whereby God passes over those whom God had already permitted to voluntarily fall into sin.

In fact, in his Göttingen lectures on the Reformed confessions (1923), Barth already indicated that he agrees with Dort's rebuttal of "the idea that 'God is the author of sin.'"[128] He takes issue with the *decretum absolutum*, but agrees with Dort that "God's *action* is election; God's *non*action is merely *to leave* the rejected in the condition that is by rights that of all people—that is rejection. . . . The rejected are simply the 'nonelect' ('nonelecti'), 'those who are passed by' ('praeteriti'). The idea that 'God is the author of sin' ('deus autor peccati') can in this way be successfully rebutted."[129]

What Barth does not seem to have realized is that these statements constitute precisely the infralapsarian position that Dort sets forth against the supralapsarian delegates, Gomarus and Maccovius.[130] John Fesko's recent study on the lapsarian debates at Dort shows that the Canons of Dort "specify that *homo creatus et lapsus* is the object of predestination," and that Dort uses this "infralapsarian position" to define the "decree of reprobation" in order to ensure that it "by no means makes God the author of sin."[131]

Thus we see that in 1923 Barth had already adopted Dort's infralapsarian thesis. We have also seen that Barth uses the same thesis in *GD* to argue that double predestination does not render God the author of sin.

This does not mean that the description "basically infralapsarian" can be applied to Barth's doctrine of election from the Göttingen-Münster period. The reason is that this infralapsarian argument only applies to "eternal" predestination as manifested in present actualities, but says nothing about God's eternal election and reprobation before the foundation of the world. In other words, Barth's infralapsarian argument applies to predestination as a divine *economy* in the here and now, rather than a divine *will* in eternity. Supra- and infralapsarians in the seventeenth century would all agree that in terms of soteriological economy, the object of salvation is *homo peccator*.

---

[128]Karl Barth, *Die Theologie der reformierten Bekenntnisschriften 1923*, GA 2.32 (Zurich: TVZ, 1998), 333; ET *Theology of the Reformed Confessions*, trans. Darrell L. Guder and Judith J. Guder (Louisville, KY: Westminster John Knox, 2002), 215.
[129]Ibid.
[130]Also see Fesko, "Lapsarian Diversity," 114-15.
[131]Ibid., 116.

Since the Barth of Göttingen-Münster treats predestination as a soteriological economy, he may not be considered basically infralapsarian even if he has been emphatic that the *obiectum praedestinationis* is *homo peccator*.

In 1936 Barth would identify the incarnation with God's eternal predestination, and from then on Barth would no longer hesitate to speak with clarity about God's eternal acts in light of Christ. Yet during the Göttingen-Münster period Barth's doctrine of election has not yet merged with his Christology, and there is still a gap between what he thinks we may know in Christ and what he thinks we may not know about God-in-eternity. Put another way, in the Göttingen-Münster phase, Barth had only developed the notion of God's "revelation-in-act," but not yet God's eternal "being-in-act." Thus Barth would still hesitate to discuss God's eternal decisions in light of temporal actualities. This means that the infralapsarian thesis he adopted from Dort really applies to his actualistic pneumatology only (which describes God's sovereignty in awakening faith or abandoning people in unbelief), rather than a proper doctrine of election describing God's *eternal* decision and act.

In this sense, it would be appropriate to say that during the Göttingen-Münster period Barth's doctrine of predestination is moving in an infralapsarian direction. However, Barth will not become basically infralapsarian in his doctrine of election until he marries this doctrine with his Christology in 1936, as we shall see in chapter six.

Barth on the Lapsarian Controversy

The foregoing discussions alluded to the fact that during the Göttingen-Münster period Barth had already adopted definitions of supra- and infralapsarianism that would seem curious to readers familiar with the Lapsarian Controversy. In the final subsection of *GD* §18, "The Election of Grace," he offers a historical-dogmatic discussion of the Lapsarian Controversy for the first time in his career, and identifies himself as a supralapsarian.[132] As we shall see, however, his definitions of supra- and infralapsarianism in *GD* §18, just as in *Romans* II and *CD* §33, are not exactly in line with the original seventeenth-century debate.

---

[132]*Unterricht* 2:202-3; ET 468.

Barth begins his treatment of the Lapsarian Controversy at the end of *GD* §18 by stating that "the issue here is the relation of predestination to the creation of the world and humanity and the fall of the human race. What is the first, primary, and original thing in the one will of God that we see in some way in all these acts?"[133]

To define the point of contention between supra- and infralapsarians this way is, of course, not necessarily erroneous. However, this definition is inadequate, because Barth does not specify that supra- and infralapsarians are concerned about the logical relations between election-reprobation and God's *eternal decrees* of creation and the fall. Rather, in introducing the contended issue he makes it sound as if the Lapsarian Controversy were about predestination in relation to God's *actual* work of creation and *actual* permission of humanity's fall.

To be sure, he qualifies his statement above by clarifying that "what we have here is not, of course, a temporal *prius* but a logical and material *prius*."[134] Still, it would have been preferable for Barth to have emphasized that the supra-infra debate is about God's *pretemporal* decrees of creation and the fall, rather than the corresponding events in history.

Barth continues to explain the point of contention: "Are creation and the fall presupposed in predestination? Or is predestination the presupposition of creation and the fall? Is the object of predestination created and fallen humanity or humanity that may be created and may fall?"[135] Here Barth defines the supra-infra debate in terms of the *obiectum praedestinationis* as either *homo creabilis et labilis* (creatable and lapsable human) or *creatus et lapsus* (created and fallen). Again, this is all in line with seventeenth-century Reformed-orthodox terminology, but Barth still has not clarified that the object of predestination in both supra- and infralapsarianism is strictly God's eternal conception of human individuals in election-reprobation rather than actually created or uncreated, fallen or unfallen human beings in history.

Barth's understanding begins to show signs of detachment from the original Lapsarian Controversy when he moves on to define infralapsari-

---

[133]Ibid.
[134]Ibid.
[135]Ibid.

anism: "God first created humanity to his own glory, and then, again to his glory, to bring to light the incapacity of the unfree will . . . , permitted it to fall into sin, and only then, once again to his glory, brought into force the decree of election or reprobation in relation to this fallen humanity."[136] Here Barth is defining *homo creatus et lapsus* as humanity *actually* created and fallen, in terms of the temporal economy of salvation. According to this definition, God actually created humanity and allowed it to fall into sin before *bringing into force* the decrees of election and reprobation. But as we saw in chapter one, supra- and infralapsarians alike would subscribe to this temporal economy of salvation.

Barth's description of the supralapsarian position is also in need of greater precision. He begins by stating that unlike infralapsarianism the supralapsarian view "relied constantly on Eph. 1:4 . . . : 'he chose us in him before the foundation of the world.'"[137] This report is quite curious, since at the Synod of Dort, Ephesians 1:4 was precisely one key passage that Polyander, Thysius and Walaeus, three Dutch infralapsarian professors from Leiden, cited to refute Gomarus's supralapsarian argument from Romans 9:21.[138] The three professors argued: "For we are elect in Christ, so that we might be holy, Eph 1.4 and predestined to be adopted as sons, v. 5. Therefore we were outside of Christ previously, unrighteous, and unsuitable of the adoption of sons."[139] Instead of acknowledging Ephesians 1:4 as a passage often cited by infralapsarians to refute supralapsarianism, Barth asserts the very opposite. One might wonder if this is not because his doctrinal and historical understandings of the Lapsarian Controversy are not precise enough for him to recognize the party relying constantly on Ephesians 1:4 as infralapsarian.

Moving on, Barth comments that infralapsarians have had to turn Paul's statement in Ephesians 1:4 "into the platitude that predestination did not *merely* arise in time with the fall but belongs to God's eternal being."[140] This comment again begs for greater precision, if not accuracy, because of the adjective "merely." For supra- and infralapsarians alike, predestination *never* arose in time but belongs *strictly* to God's eternal will.

---

[136]Ibid.
[137]Ibid.
[138]Fesko, "Lapsarian Diversity," 113.
[139]Ibid.
[140]*Unterricht* 2:201; ET 467 (emphasis added).

Barth goes on to define supralapsarianism:

The Supralapsarians claim that God created humanity immediately and originally with the destiny of manifesting his glory by manifesting mercy and righteousness. He thus created the human being as a rational creature in his own image, that is, as a being in which he might cause his own attributes to shine forth. The human was thus a creature that could fall, having a will of its own. Election and rejection are then the execution of this first and original decree, affecting created humanity.[141]

Such a description of election and rejection as the "execution" of some "first and original decree" rather than as a very divine decree in itself is quite foreign to Reformed orthodoxy. In Reformed orthodoxy, election-reprobation *is* the very decree itself, not the execution. Additionally, Barth defines the supralapsarian *obiectum praedestinationis* as "a creature that could fall," a "creature" that he describes in the passage above as actually having been created, but in the original Lapsarian Controversy, neither supra- nor infralapsarianism would treat the *obiectum* as actually created. Moreover, Barth says here that election and rejection *affected created humanity*, but the supralapsarian thesis is that the object of predestination is uncreated and unfallen (see chapter one).

Having given his doctrinal-historical introduction to supra- and infralapsarianism, Barth states: "I myself take the Supralapsarian position."[142] He explains: "As I see it, predestination is set at the *beginning* of God's ways. The decision before and under which we are set by God's Word in Christ is so decisive that we are not permitted to go back to an indecision, indefiniteness, or neutrality in God prior to this decision."[143] Given the definitions of supra- and infralapsarianism in the original Lapsarian Controversy, it is uncertain how this conviction would make Barth a supralapsarian.

Barth continues to explicate his conviction, which he thinks belongs to supra- rather than infralapsarianism: "From and to all eternity we are simply the objects of the mercy and righteousness of the divine will. How can God's omnipotence, wisdom, and goodness be anything other alongside these?

---

[141] Ibid.
[142] Ibid., 2:202; ET 468.
[143] Ibid.

Predestination is the secret of creation *and* redemption *and* consummation."[144] Yet, as we saw in chapter one, this description suits infralapsarianism just as well as supralapsarianism, because for the Reformed orthodox in general, predestination is strictly eternal, and God's will in double predestination grounds all God's actual works (distinct from eternal decrees) from creation to consummation.

Additionally, as noted earlier, in resorting to the Synod of Dort to argue that the freely predestining God is not the author of sin, Barth has in fact subscribed himself to the infralapsarian conviction that the object of reprobation is sinful humanity, and that in God's act of reprobation "sin is recognized and taken seriously."[145] That is, in the Göttingen-Münster period Barth has adopted an infralapsarian logic that divine reprobation was issued upon God's consideration of human fallenness. Given these considerations, the Barth of Göttingen and Münster is in fact closer to infralapsarianism than he thinks.

Chapter Summary

In this chapter I have shown that during the Göttingen-Münster period, Barth's Christology is basically infralapsarian, for he describes the incarnation as having been made necessary by God's decision to deal with the creature's sin. This is not to say that God *could not have* become incarnate if humanity had not fallen into sin. To say that the incarnation presupposes sin is to say that in God's eternal plan, "the divine will to become incarnate logically follows . . . the divine will to allow sin."[146] This is the divine ordinance by which the incarnation was made necessary upon the supposition of sin.

Both supra- and infralapsarian Christology agree that the incarnation de facto confronts sin. Supralapsarian Christology, however, contends that God *would have* become incarnate even if humanity had not fallen into sin, since "the divine will to become incarnate logically precedes . . . the divine will to allow sin," and "God had . . . other, deeper motives behind the incarnation

---

[144] Ibid.
[145] Ibid., 2:191; ET 459.
[146] Edwin van Driel, *Incarnation Anyway: Arguments for Supralapsarian Christology* (Oxford: Oxford University Press, 2008), 4.

than only the need for reconciliation."[147] By contrast, infralapsarian Christology contends that God has not revealed any purpose behind the incarnation other than dealing with sin. It does not deny that God *could have* become incarnate if humanity had not sinned, but refuses to claim to know *that* or *why* God *would have* done so, since by the divine ordinance revealed in Christ, as infralapsarian Christology sees it, God's will to become incarnate presupposes God's consideration of humanity's fall.

I have demonstrated that in the Göttingen-Münster period, Barth denies that there is a ground of the necessity of the incarnation other than the divine purpose to overcome sin, which is in line with infralapsarian Christology. I have also demonstrated how Barth's actualistic pneumatology in this period caused him to lean toward predestinarian infralapsarianism. Finally, I have demonstrated the ambiguity, if not inaccuracy, of Barth's definitions of supra- and infralapsarianism, initiated in *Romans* II (see chapter three) and fully explicated in *CD* §33 (see chapters two and seven), during the Göttingen-Münster period. If Barth calls himself supralapsarian on the basis of these descriptions, then this invites the question as to whether he really is as supralapsarian as he thinks. In the next chapter, we move on to the Bonn years, during which Barth brought his Christology and doctrine of election closer together in his doctrine of the Word of God.

---

[147]Ibid., 4-5.

5

The Bonn Years (1930–1935)

HUMAN TALK AND DIVINE WORD— NEW DEVELOPMENTS?

IN MARCH 1930 BARTH LEFT MÜNSTER to join the theology faculty at Bonn. Barth scholars of an older generation paradigmatically described the Bonn years as the final methodological turning point in the Swiss theologian's development: according to this paradigm it was a watershed opus titled *Anselm: Fides Quaerens Intellectum* written during the Bonn years that marked the beginning of Barth's "turn from dialectic to analogy." Scholars who subscribed to this older paradigm believed that *Anselm* provided Barth a new methodology that forced him to abandon *Die christliche Dogmatik* and begin anew his major dogmatic corpus under the title *Die kirchliche Dogmatik*.[1] This earlier view of the importance of Barth's theological development in Bonn has generally fallen out of favor since Bruce McCormack's paradigm-shifting opus, *Karl Barth's Critically Realistic Dialectical Theology: Its Genesis and Development 1909–1936*, in which the author argues, among other theses, that with regard to methodology and material content there is no essential difference between Barth's theology during the Göttingen-Münster phase and the Bonn years.

This chapter examines the lapsarian position of Barth's Christology and doctrine of predestination during 1930–1935 in light of McCormack's thesis. My aim is to show that during the Bonn years Barth still held to the

---

[1] This early paradigm is generally attributed to Hans Urs von Balthasar, *Karl Barth: Darstellung und Deutung Seiner Theologie* (Cologne: Jakob Hegner, 1951); ET: *The Theology of Karl Barth*, trans. Edward Oakes (San Francisco: Ignatius, 1992).

same christological and predestinarian lapsarianism that he had developed in Göttingen-Münster. Meanwhile, I shall argue that during the Bonn years Barth developed a more robust understanding of the Word of God as presupposing human fallenness, and this view of the Word of God paved the path to the basically infralapsarian christological revision of the doctrine of election in 1936–1942. (Recall that infralapsarian Christology is the view that God's will to become incarnate presupposes the divine will to deal with sin, while predestinarian infralapsarianism is the position that the object of double predestination is fallen humanity; the opposite positions, namely, that God's will to become incarnate does not presuppose God's decision to permit the fall, and that the object of double predestination is unfallen humanity, would be christological and predestinarian supralapsarianism respectively.)

This chapter focuses on *CD* I/1 (1932), which, I shall show, best represents among Barth's works produced during the Bonn years the lapsarian position of his Christology and doctrine of predestination in this phase of his development. Before proceeding to *CD* I/1, however, I will discuss the Anselm book. My thesis regarding *Anselm* is that it is generally unconcerned with the lapsarian question, since it is primarily a book on Anselm rather than one in which Barth sets forth his own theology, which, as we have seen, has been increasingly lapsarian in each successive phase of his development. As far as lapsarianism is concerned, *Anselm* is not a turning point in Barth's theological thinking.

Additionally, as some have spoken of "the Barth of *CD* I/1 and 2" with reference to his doctrine of election, I will argue that *CD* I/2 (completed in 1937 and published in 1938) is an opus in between two successive phases of Barth's development, carrying influences from both phases but not fitting nicely into either.[2]

Anselm: *Fides Quaerens Intellectum*

McCormack's thesis. I begin with a discussion of the role of *Anselm* in Barth's theological development. McCormack recounted in the 1990s: "For over forty years now, interpretation of Karl Barth's theological development

---

[2]Suzanne McDonald, "Barth's 'Other' Doctrine of Election in the *Church Dogmatics*," *International Journal of Systematic Theology* 9 (2007): 134-47.

has stood beneath the massive shadow cast by Hans Urs von Balthasar's 1951 book, *Karl Barth: Darstellung und Deutung seiner Theologie*."[3] Part of Balthasar's thesis is that *Anselm* (1931) either constitutes a radical break from his previous theology, or at least it marks the beginning of a gradual "turn from dialectic to analogy" that saw its maturation in *CD* II/1 (1938).[4] Under Balthasar's influence, scholars of an older generation such as Hans Frei and T. F. Torrance, while taking varying approaches to understanding Barth's theological development, generally ascribed to *Anselm* the status of a watershed between the dialectical and analogical phases of Barth's thought.[5]

Since the 1980s, attempts to challenge or correct the Balthasar thesis began to emerge from scholars such as Eberhard Jüngel, Ingrid Spieckermann, Michael Beintker and others.[6] However, there is little dispute today that the decisive paradigm shift came with McCormack's 1995 book, *Karl Barth's Critically Realistic Dialectical Theology*. Part of McCormack's paradigm is the thesis that Barth's theology has always remained dialectical even after the so-called turn to analogy, and that the Anselm book with its emphasis on the *analogia fidei* did not give rise to any essentially new methodology or theological material in Barth's thinking.[7]

McCormack's paradigm dominates much of recent scholarship, and there has been little attempt to challenge it. Among those who have expressed disagreement with McCormack is Stephen Wigley, who is of the opinion that McCormack has misunderstood Balthasar. Yet Wigley does not directly challenge McCormack's paradigm per se. His opinion is that "while McCormack may be right on Barth, he is wrong on von Balthasar on Barth."[8] Wigley says, "McCormack maintains that Barth's theology remained dialec-

---

[3] Bruce McCormack, *Karl Barth's Critically Realistic Dialectical Theology* (Oxford: Clarendon, 1995), 1.
[4] Ibid.
[5] Ibid., 4-5, 422. Cf. Hans Frei, "The Doctrine of Revelation in the Thought of Karl Barth, 1909 to 1922" (PhD diss., Yale University, 1956), 194; T. F. Torrance, *Karl Barth: An Introduction to His Early Theology 1910–1931* (Edinburgh: T&T Clark, 1962), 133.
[6] McCormack, *Dialectical Theology*, 5-14. See Eberhard Jüngel, "Von der Dialektik zur Analogie: Die Schule Kierkegaards und der Einspruch Petersons," in *Barth-Studien* (Gütersloh: Mohn, 1982); Ingrid Spieckermann, *Gotteserkenntnis: Ein Beitrag zur Grundfrage der neuen Theologie Karl Barths* (Munich: Kaiser, 1985); Michael Beintker, *Die Dialektik in der 'dialektischen Theologie' Karl Barths* (Munich: Kaiser, 1987).
[7] McCormack, *Dialectical Theology*, 14-19.
[8] Stephen Wigley, "The von Balthasar Thesis: A Re-Examination of von Balthasar's study of Barth in the Light of Bruce McCormack," *Scottish Journal of Theology* 56 (2003): 345.

tical into the *Church Dogmatics*. But von Balthasar recognises this too."⁹ That is, Wigley does not directly challenge McCormack's view that there has never been a "turn from dialectic to analogy" in Barth's career.

As I see it, there are good reasons to accept McCormack's thesis regarding the role of *Anselm* in Barth's theological development. Wigley, without directly opposing McCormack, suggests that McCormack's view contradicts "Barth's expressed opinion" from which Balthasar takes his cue: "The real work that documents my conversion . . . from the residue of a philosophical or anthropological . . . grounding of Christian doctrine . . . is not the much-read tract against Emil Brunner but my 1931 book on Anselm of Canterbury's proofs for the existence of God."¹⁰ In so doing, however, Wigley has neglected McCormack's argument that "missing from von Balthasar's quotation is the larger context—which might have turned the interpretation in a very different direction from the one von Balthasar took."¹¹

Furthermore, Wigley—and Balthasar—have not accounted for Barth's own comment in the preface to *CD* I/1 that in this new prolegomenon he is simply reexpressing the materials from the *Christliche Dogmatik im Entwurf* (prolegomenon to the Münster dogmatics), "saying the same thing, but in a very different way."¹² That is, although in *CD* I/1 Barth denounces the *analogia entis* while turning against so-called dialectical theology, the Anselm book never gave rise to essentially new materials in Barth's theology that occasioned the composition of the *Church Dogmatics*. Rather, it simply gave him new ways of expressing his theology: "My new task was to rethink everything far more clearly, unambiguously and simply, in accordance with the church's belief, and yet far more freely, openly and comprehensively than I could ever have said it before."¹³

McCormack points out one further interpretative problem regarding *Anselm*: "This is a book on Anselm. It is not a book on Barth's theology—however true it may be at the end of the day that it tells us more about Barth

---

⁹Ibid., 350.
¹⁰Ibid., 348. See Balthasar, *Karl Barth*, 93; McCormack, *Dialectical Theology*, 1. Balthasar is quoting from Karl Barth, "Parergon," *Evangelische Theologie* (1948): 272.
¹¹McCormack, *Dialectical Theology*, 1.
¹²*KD* I/1, Vorwort; ET xi.
¹³Eberhard Busch, *Karl Barth: His Life from Letters and Autobiographical Texts*, trans. John Bowden (Munich: Kaiser, 1976), 210.

than it does about the eleventh-century theologian."[14] Therefore, "it is most likely that we should distinguish between Anselm (as Barth understands him) and Barth's own theological viewpoint at one decisive point."[15]

While McCormack applies this interpretative strategy to the "one decisive point" concerning "the relation (and distinction!) of the *ratio veritatis* and the *ratio fidei*, of the Word and the Creed,"[16] I will focus on a different aspect, showing that although the predestinarian and christological lapsarianism developed during the Göttingen-Münster period is recognizable as an underlying assumption in *Anselm*, Barth makes it far less explicit here than he will in *CD* I/1, where he sets forth his own theology.

Barth on Anselm: Brief exposition. One primary contention in Barth's 1931 book on Anselm is that the methodology the theologian of Canterbury assumes in the often-so-called ontological proof set forth in *Proslogion* 2–4 is an analogy of faith (*analogia fidei*) that seeks to rationally demonstrate the existence of God, taking faith, which conforms to the Word, as its presuppositional starting point. In other words, Barth contends that for Anselm, to "prove" is to "rationally demonstrate" or "explicate." The notion of "faith seeking understanding" (*fides quaerens intellectum*) as such, according to Barth's interpretation of Anselm, runs contrary to any natural theology or analogy of being (*analogia entis*) that takes its starting point in metaphysical first principles or empirical observations.

For Barth, it is necessary to first inquire about Anselm's motivation in seeking understanding.[17] Barth emphasizes that for Anselm, understanding does not lead to faith. Rather, true understanding is the "understanding of faith" (*intellectus fidei*).[18] This means that desire for understanding is inherent to faith: "What we are speaking of is a spontaneous desire of faith. Fundamentally, the *quaerere intellectum* is really immanent in *fides*."[19] Barth thus recognizes an irreversible order in Anselm's program of *fides quaerens intellectum*.

> Anselm wants "proof" and "joy" because he wants *intelligere* and he wants *intelligere* because he believes. Any reversal of this order of compulsion is

---

[14] McCormack, *Dialectical Theology*, 428.
[15] Ibid., 431.
[16] Ibid.
[17] *Anselm* 14; ET 16.
[18] Ibid.
[19] Ibid.

excluded by Anselm's conception of faith. That is to say, for Anselm, "to believe" does not mean simply a striving of the human will towards God but a striving of the human will into God and so a participation (albeit in a manner limited by creatureliness) in God's mode of being and so a similar participation in God's aseity, in matchless glory of his very Self, and therefore also in God's utter absence of necessity.[20]

Underlying this interpretation of Anselm is Barth's own actualism.[21] As we saw in the previous chapter, Barth borrows a term from medieval scholasticism, describing God as "pure act" (*actus purus*).[22] With sharp contrast to Thomist metaphysics, however, Barth insists with the idea of *actus purus* that the transcendent God cannot be known except by the divine act of revelation. Revelation is God's act, and God's revelation is *in actu*. Human knowledge of God through revelation-in-act is possible only by faith, which is itself God's act, hence *fides quaerens intellectum*. According to Barth's interpretation of Anselm, the believer noetically participates in God's revelation in an actualistic way, that is, with relations of actualistic distinctions and correspondences. Put more concretely, the understanding of faith conforms to God's self-revelation in such a way that the latter grounds the former, and it is by God's act that the former is actualized. Thus faith and the understanding to which it gives rise stand in a relation of analogy to divine revelation. The analogy is between human faith and divine act, not human being and divine being, hence Barth's insistence on the *analogia fidei* and rejection of the *analogia entis*.

It is in light of this actualistic *analogia fidei* that Barth interprets Anselm. For Barth, the term *ratio* (reason) is a "decisive concept" crucial to a correct understanding of Anselm. Barth distinguishes between an "ontic *ratio*" and a "noetic *ratio*" in Anselm.[23] The latter is "noetic" in the sense that it is the "knowing *ratio* of the human faculty of making concepts and judgments"; the "ontic" *ratio*, by contrast, is "peculiar to the object of faith."[24] The believer attains understanding when her noetic *ratio* conforms to the ontic *ratio* of God's truth.

---

[20]Ibid., 15; ET 17.
[21]McCormack, *Dialectical Theology*, 432.
[22]Karl Barth, *Unterricht in der christlichen Religion* (Zurich: TVZ, 1985), 1:155; ET 127.
[23]*Anselm* 45; ET 45.
[24]Ibid.

Yet this conformity is no simple matter. Barth identifies a further distinction in Anselm's notion of the ontic *ratio*. There is first the truth of God in itself, the *ratio veritatis*, which is "identical with the *ratio summae naturae*, that is with the divine Word consubstantial with the Father. It is the *ratio* of God."[25] The human intellect cannot directly comprehend the Word because of an ontological divide between God and creatures that makes God incomprehensible to creatures.[26] Any creaturely understanding of God must begin with faith.[27]

Distinct from the *ratio veritatis* is thus the *ratio fidei*—the rationality of faith. The *ratio fidei* is a special kind of human reason that grasps the Word of God: it is the *credo* of the church. While for Anselm, the Bible is *ratio veritatis* in the stricter sense, Barth places the Bible on the same plane with the *credo* as *ratio fidei*. Simply put, Barth's understanding of Anselm is such that the Word gives rise to the *credo*, the *ratio fidei*, by God's active decision. The *ratio fidei* is not something that creatures may possess by their own powers; the believer possesses *ratio fidei* by God's act, and thus the *ratio fidei* actualistically corresponds to the *ratio veritatis*. This actualism also implies that the *ratio veritatis* is strictly distinct from the *ratio fidei*.

Now, human intellect cannot directly comprehend the *ratio veritatis*, but understanding of the ontic *ratio* is possible when human reason seeks to explicate the *ratio fidei*, which corresponds to the *ratio veritatis*. Yet, once again, this event of understanding as noetic participation in God's mode of being would be subjectively impossible from the human side; it is made possible only when God becomes its author. As McCormack puts it, "The attainment of the *ratio intellectus* that is in conformity with the *ratio veritatis* hidden in the *ratio fidei* depends upon a divine decision, and therefore upon grace."[28] It is in this way that the noetic *ratio* actualistically corresponds to the ontic *ratio*.

Much more should be said if a full summary of *Anselm* is to be given, but for my purposes the foregoing discussions should suffice. Three observations are now in order. First, in *Anselm* Barth has not yet developed the

---

[25]Ibid.
[26]Ibid., 57-58; ET 57-58.
[27]Ibid.
[28]McCormack, *Dialectical Theology*, 430.

mature version of his actualism—the notion of God's being-in-act. The actualism in *Anselm* remains the same as that in the Göttingen-Münster period: it is still the notion of a revelation-in-act. The first hint of the notion of God's being-in-act, as I shall briefly show in my exposition of *CD* I/1, will not appear until *CD* §9, where Barth begins to explicate the import of the doctrine of the Trinity for divine revelation. In this regard, *Anselm* stands in continuity with the Göttingen-Münster period and does not mark the beginning of a new phase in Barth's actualism.

Second, the *analogia fidei* in *Anselm* is but a new way for Barth to express the same "critically realistic dialectical theology" (McCormack) that he has already set forth in the previous phases of his development. From the foregoing discussions it is clear that the actualistic correspondences and distinctions between the different *rationes* are essentially just a set of new terminology to describe the dialectic of God's self-veiling and unveiling in the objective and subjective possibilities of revelation from the Göttingen-Münster period.

As we have seen, this dialectic is grounded on Barth's critical realism, the conviction that God is objectively real in and of Godself (as opposed to the claims of modern consciousness theology) and that human reason cannot attain to any immediate knowledge of God (following Kant's critique of reason). This critical realism means that the dialectic of veiling and unveiling is necessary for any true human knowledge of God, and that this knowledge is necessarily indirect and mediated. This "neo-Kantian framework," as Graham Ward observes, is also the ground of Barth's *analogia fidei*.

> Barth, following Kant, accepts that we cannot know "things in themselves"; we work with the mediated representations of these things and, on this basis, we live in the world "as if" we had immediate awareness.... Only the noetic operation of the Spirit of Christ, establishing *analogia fidei*..., can enable us to have some understanding of the world as it is. Only God sees things as they are. This theological position, as I pointed out, critiques notions of "presence" and "identity," for the world (and God's unveiling of himself within the world) is always and only mediated to us.[29]

---

[29]Graham Ward, "Barth, Modernity, and Postmodernity," in *The Cambridge Companion to Karl Barth*, ed. John Webster (Cambridge: Cambridge University Press, 2000), 285.

All this is to say that Barth's *analogia fidei* set forth in *Anselm* is simply another way of describing his "critically realistic dialectical theology." It is not a new theological method, but one to which Barth has remained committed in all phases of his development.

Lack of lapsarianism in Anselm. The third observation constitutes my main contention for this section: there is no explicit lapsarianism in *Anselm*, either predestinarian or christological. Barth interprets Anselm as saying that humanity's noetic participation in God is "limited by creatureliness," but it is unclear whether this means prelapsarian or postlapsarian creatureliness.[30] To be sure, Anselm's Christology is unmistakably infralapsarian, and Barth acknowledges that in *Cur Deus Homo* "sin as man's eternal guilt before God" is one of the "vital presuppositions" underlying "the necessity . . . of the Incarnation."[31] However, Anselm, as understood by Barth, seems to suggest that revelation in the actualistic form of God's indirect speech is necessary for humankind to know God in the prelapsarian state (i.e., the necessity of revelation-in-act for human knowledge of God is not predicated on the fall). As we saw, the noetic *ratio* cannot be directly identical to the ontic *ratio*, and the *ratio fidei* cannot be simply identical to the *ratio veritatis*, but is this because of human fallenness, or simply God's ontological transcendence over humanity regardless of humanity's sin?[32] The fact is that quite unlike the Göttingen and Münster dogmatics—as well as *CD* I/1 for that matter—the notion of sin is brought up only twice in the entire Anselm book.[33] This would have been uncharacteristic of Barth if his primary aim in *Anselm* were to set forth his own theology, but as McCormack puts it, "This is a book on Anselm. It is not a book on Barth's theology."[34]

Of the two places where sin is mentioned in *Anselm*, however, Barth gives a slight hint of his own infralapsarian leaning in Christology against the view that he sees in Anselm's *Proslogion*, which seems to deem the lapsarian question irrelevant when it comes to the necessity of revelation-in-act for humanity's knowledge of God. (When it comes to the question, *Cur Deus Homo*, Anselm's Christology is of course infralapsarian—the incarnation

---

[30] *Anselm*, 15; ET 17.
[31] Ibid., 55; ET 55.
[32] Ibid., 57-8; ET 57-8.
[33] Ibid., 55, 71; ET 55, 71.
[34] McCormack, *Dialectical Theology*, 432.

took place for soteric purposes.) "Perhaps Anselm did not know any other way of speaking of the Christian *Credo* except by addressing the sinner as one who had not sinned . . . on the basis of the great 'as if' which is really not an 'as if' at all, but which at all times has been the final and decisive means whereby the believer could speak to the unbeliever."[35]

Barth's comment on Anselm here implies that for Anselm (as Barth understands him) fallen and prelapsarian creatures alike are able to attain *intellectus fidei*. This would entail that the necessity of the Word-*in-actu*, the *analogia fidei*, the act of God whereby the understanding of faith in conformity to the *ratio veritatis* is actualized, is not predicated on sin, but perhaps merely on the ontological divide between Creator and creatures. Put more simply, Barth seems to be suggesting that for Anselm the necessity of revelation-in-act for human knowledge of God does not presuppose human fallenness, as revelation in this form for Anselm (on Barth's interpretation) would be necessary even for creatures in the prelapsarian state if they were to attain *intellectus fidei*. In opposing this view, Barth is implying the infralapsarian patterns of thinking in his own understanding of the twofold event of revelation (i.e., incarnation and election) that only upon the presupposition of humanity's fallenness is revelation in this form necessary for humans to attain to any true knowledge of God (see chapter four).

Aside from this slight hint of Barth's own infralapsarian leaning in Christology, *Anselm* is generally unconcerned about the noetic effects of sin in relation to the necessity of revelation for human knowledge of God. This, again, is because this is Barth's book on Anselm, rather than a straightforward presentation of Barth's own theology.

On this point, one fallacy that Balthasar commits is to read *CD* I/1 into *Anselm*. With particular regard to the role of the doctrine of sin in *Anselm*, Balthasar neglects the fact that mention of human fallenness is almost completely absent in the book. Thus Balthasar comments that the "relevance" of Barth's teaching (it is really Barth's understanding of Anselm!) on the ontic and noetic *rationes* is that "the ontic *ratio* of things (for which truth is something inherent) has not been affected by sin, while the discovery of the truth (which occurs only on the noetic side) has been damaged. In other words,

---

[35]*Anselm* 71; ET 71.

man could be blinded by sin, as it were, and no longer recognize God's revelations of the eternal *ratio* in the ontic *ratio* of creation."[36]

Balthasar brings up this point in order to counter Barth with the Catholic understanding that "the spontaneity of human knowing belongs to its very nature, which has not been destroyed by sin."[37] In any case, Balthasar's interpretation of *Anselm* errs partly in that he sees it as Barth's own theology rather than a book on Anselm. With regard to the necessity of God's revelation-in-act for humanity's knowledge of God, *Anselm* does not offer a full picture of Barth's view, because it lacks the infralapsarian Christology whereby Barth's theology in the Göttingen-Münster period and the Bonn years stand in continuity.

With regard to predestinarian lapsarianism, as far as I can see there is no trace of it at all in *Anselm*. In this regard, too, Balthasar commits the error of confusing Barth with Anselm-according-to-Barth. Strangely, in discussing the significance of sin in *Anselm*, Balthasar reads the infralapsarian Christology of *CD* I/1 into it, but in discussing Barth's view of faith and reason, Balthasar reads Anselm's supralapsarian view of revelation ("supralapsarian" in the sense that the necessity of revelation in its present form for humanity's knowledge of God is not predicated on humanity's sin) into Barth. Balthasar comments:

> Let us first take up the case that so puzzled Anselm and Barth: the conundrum of the "possibility of denying the existence of God" [*Anselm* 186-87]. How can the fool say in his heart that there is no God, when he cannot really think such a thought? . . . Barth no longer answers the question as he did in the dialectical period, asserting that creaturely existence born in sin is itself a contradiction to itself. . . . What, then, are we to say about the fool? . . . The unbelief of the fool can consist in nothing other than the contradiction that the fool does not *will* to accept and believe his faith as true. He chooses not to believe what he already believes. This shall have important consequences for Barth's doctrine on predestination, whose roots and power of synthesis lie here in this insight about faith.[38]

---

[36]Balthasar, *Karl Barth*, 159. Hans Boersma offers a concise and inspiring discussion of Balthasar's agreements and disagreements with Barth on the *analogia entis* in *Nouvelle Théologie and Sacramental Ontology: A Return to Mystery* (Oxford: Oxford University Press, 2009), 131-34.
[37]Balthasar, *Karl Barth*, 160.
[38]Ibid., 146-47.

What Balthasar does here is to treat the "possibility of denying the existence of God" as the seed of Barth's later notion of sin and unbelief as "impossible possibility" (*CD* III/3), a notion to which his mature Christocentric doctrine of predestination (*CD* II/2) gives rise (see chapter eight).[39] In drawing this connection, Balthasar fails to recognize one crucial difference between Barth and Anselm-according-to-Barth: the latter sees human nature as inherently capable of believing the Word, but the Barth of *CD* II/2 and III/3 insists that sinners have no inherent ability to participate in God apart from Christ. It is only because all humans are a priori elected in Christ and that nothingness has been eternally negated by Christ's vicarious reprobation that sin and unbelief are described as impossible possibilities. In other words, as Balthasar elsewhere puts it, for Barth, the human ability of "the discovery of truth ... has been damaged [by sin]," and human beings have no innate ability to know God—this is a point that I have just discussed. Note here that Balthasar contradicts himself, since, as we have just seen, he also says that for Barth the human possibility of denying God's existence is not a result of sin.

All this is to say that Balthasar fails to recognize the incompatibility between Anselm's supralapsarian view of revelation and the basically infralapsarian character of Barth's mature doctrine of predestination. The self-contradiction in Balthasar's interpretation of *Anselm* would be easily resolved if we acknowledge that this book is Barth's attempt to understand and learn from Anselm rather than one in which Barth paints a full picture of his own theology. There is really no connection between "the possibility of denying the existence of God" in *Anselm* and the "impossible possibility" of sin and unbelief in Barth's later doctrine of election. Predestinarian lapsarianism (that is, the role of sin in the doctrine of predestination) is simply not an issue that Barth addresses in *Anselm*.

In sum, *Anselm* tells us precious little about Barth's lapsarian thinking, christological or predestinarian. Bear in mind that, as I have shown, lapsarianism plays an increasingly central role in the successive phases of Barth's theology. To treat *Anselm* as a key to understanding the shifts in the methods and contents of Barth's theology is thus to miss out a crucial aspect of his theological development.

---

[39]Ibid., 186.

CHURCH DOGMATICS I/1

As I have contended, *CD* I/1 is the opus that best represents Barth's theology in 1930–1935. In this section I will show that with regard to christological and predestinarian lapsarianism, Barth's position during these years remains essentially the same as in the Göttingen-Münster period, but because of the complexity of Barth's presentation of the matter in the framework of the *analogia fidei* in *CD* I/1 and his new emphasis on the very concept of the Word of God itself (rather than the subjective-objective distinction), Christology and predestination now become much more closely interwoven.

Preface and introduction. In the preface to *CD* I/1 Barth makes it clear that there is no essential difference between this part-volume and the Münster prolegomena insofar as material contents are concerned: on his own admission, he is "saying the same thing, but in a very different way."[40] The difference, then, lies primarily in the way he presents his thought.

One difference between the Münster dogmatics (*Christliche Dogmatik im Entwurf*) and *CD* I/1 (*Kirchliche Dogmatik*) is suggested by the titles of the works, as Barth comments: "In substituting the word 'Church' for 'Christian' in the title, I have tried to set a good example of restraint in the lighthearted use of the great word 'Christian' against which I have protested."[41]

This is where the influence of *Anselm* on Barth's presentation of his theology becomes apparent. Barth has now come to think that to claim the word "Christian" for his own dogmatics could suggest a kind of unwarranted audacity in confusing the theologian's understanding of faith (*intellectus fidei*) with the divine Word itself. In substituting "Church" for "Christian," Barth is emphasizing that "dogmatics is not a free science. It is bound to the sphere of the Church, where alone it is possible and meaningful."[42]

That is, in line with *Anselm*, Barth now stresses that theological reflection must conform to the church's *credo*. This is of course nothing new: as we saw in chapter four, Barth was already drawing from Nicene-Chalcedonian orthodoxy and critically reliant on confessional Reformed theology during the Göttingen-Münster period. He also insisted on being faithful to the biblical

---

[40]*KD* I/1, Vorwort; ET xi.
[41]Ibid.; ET xii.
[42]Ibid.; ET xiii.

witness, which he considered to be in a shared genre with church proclamation. Thus John Webster: "Like the *Göttingen Dogmatics*, the *Church Dogmatics* sees its task as critical examination of the church's proclamation."[43] The difference between Göttingen-Münster and *CD* I/1, then, is a matter of emphasis in presentation: Barth's appeal to church tradition and his biblical exegesis is much more explicit and extensive in *CD* I/1 than in previous dogmatic cycles.

In light of *Anselm*, Barth now clearly spells out his conviction that the science of dogmatics is an "inquiry" (*Forschung*)—*quaerere*.[44] In the introduction to *CD* I/1 (§§1–2) Barth asserts that dogmatic inquiry "presupposes that the true content of Christian talk about God can be known by man. It makes this assumption as in and with the Church it believes in Jesus Christ as the revealing and reconciling address of God to man."[45]

In one sense, to conform to the church is to conform to Christ the Word: "Talk about God has true content when it conforms to the being of the Church, i.e., when it conforms to Jesus Christ."[46] This is because "Jesus Christ is the essence of the Church."[47] Yet Christ and the church are not simply identical. Rather, Christ the Word "is the truth, not merely in Himself, but also for us as we know Him solely by faith in Jesus Christ."[48] Here Barth distinguishes between Christ the Word, who is *ratio veritatis*, "truth in Himself," and the *ratio fidei*, "truth . . . as we know Him . . . by faith in Jesus Christ."

Theology as rational explication of the *ratio fidei* corresponds to the Word only by God's act: "In the event of the divine action corresponding to the promise given to the Church, it is possible for it to be knowledge of the truth."[49] Here Barth's appeal to the actualistic notion of *analogia fidei* from *Anselm* is apparent: "The fulfilment of this knowledge, the *event* of human *action*, the appropriation *corresponding* to this address in which, through the stages of intuitive apprehension formulated comprehension, the reve-

---

[43]John Webster, *Karl Barth* (London: Continuum, 2004), 54.
[44]*KD* I/1, 10; ET 11.
[45]Ibid., 12; ET 13.
[46]Ibid., 11; ET 12.
[47]Ibid.
[48]Ibid.
[49]Ibid.

lation of the *analogia fidei* to resultant clarity in dogmatics..., is, of course, a second event compared with the divine *action* itself, *united* with it in faith, yet also in faith to be *distinguished* from it."[50]

While here Barth is obviously using the pattern of thought developed in *Anselm*, his actualistic description of the possibility of human knowledge of God is essentially the same as that found in *GD*: God's action gives rise to human action that corresponds to it. That is, the act of faith corresponds to the act of revelation; faith is the subjective actualization of revelation. Thus, just as in *GD*, Barth's actualism in *CD* I/1 still speaks of a "revelation-in-act" rather than God's "being-in-act." The only place in *CD* I/1 where Barth hints at the notion of God's being-in-act is §9, "The Triunity of God," where Barth states that "to the unity of Father, Son and Spirit among themselves corresponds their unity *ad extra*. God's essence and work are not twofold but one."[51] Yet before having developed a Christocentric rendition of election in 1936, the Barth of *CD* I/1 still describes election as revelation-in-act. That is, the human act of faith corresponds to the divine act of election in the event of the *Deus dixit*.

Recall from chapter four that during the Göttingen-Münster period Barth also spoke actualistically of the event of faith in terms of the event of election: God can elect a person for faith at any moment in time, and freely reject the same person in the next moment. In the introduction to *CD* I/1 we find this rendition of election still serving as the underlying principle of Barth's *analogia fidei*.[52]

> Faith ... is not a determination of human action which man can give to it at will or maintain at will once it is received. On the contrary, it is the gracious address of God to man, the free personal presence of Jesus Christ in his activity. Hence, if we say that dogmatics presupposes faith, or the determination of human action by hearing and as obedience to the being of the Church, we say that at every step and with every statement it presupposes the free grace of God which may at any time be given or refused as the object and meaning of this human action. It always rests with God and not with us whether our hearing is real hearing and our obedience real obedience, whether our dog-

---

[50]Ibid. (emphasis added).
[51]Ibid., 391; ET 371.
[52]See McDonald, "Barth's 'Other.'"

matics is blessed and sanctified as knowledge of the true Christian utterance or whether it is idle speculation.[53]

The question now is whether in *CD* I/1 Barth still thinks election, the event wherein the understanding of faith (*intellectus fidei*) conforms to God's truth (*ratio veritatis*), which manifests itself through the reason of faith (*ratio fidei*), presupposes humanity's fallenness (i.e., whether it is supra- or infralapsarian).

Still leaning toward predestinarian infralapsarianism. That Barth's robust doctrine of the Word of God in *CD* I/1 is predicated on a doctrine of election moving toward infralapsarianism (see chapter four) developed during the Göttingen-Münster period is immediately obvious from the very outset. In the very first paragraph of chapter one of *CD* I/1, Barth states that "talk about God" and "Church proclamation" are possible only on the basis of the event of election, the object of which is "one who is fallen, lost and condemned."[54]

The central problem in Barth's new prolegomena is this: how can theology as human talk be truly talk about God? Eberhard Jüngel explains: "[Barth] does not ask what it *means* to speak of God, but, rather, in what sense God *must* be spoken of in order that our speaking is about *God*."[55] Barth observes that "not all human talk is talk about God."[56] This fact reflects a contradiction in the present state of human existence. Barth takes as his starting point that human talk "could be and should be" talk about God, as all realities and truths distinct from God "exist from Him and to Him," and thus "there is no genuinely profane speech. In the last resort there is only talk about God."[57] However, Barth observes that "this is not at all the case, that it is quite impossible to interpret human talk as such as talk about God."[58]

This contradiction is a result of human fallenness. Just as in *Romans* II and the Göttingen-Münster period, in *CD* I/1 Barth still speaks of an "original estate" from which humanity has fallen: "Of this [original] man it

---

[53]*KD* I/1, 17-18; ET 18.
[54]Ibid., 47; ET 47.
[55]Eberhard Jüngel, *God's Being Is in Becoming: The Trinitarian Being of God in the Theology of Karl Barth*, trans. John Webster (Grand Rapids: Eerdmans, 2001), 1.
[56]*KD* I/1, 47; ET 47.
[57]Ibid.
[58]Ibid.

might well be said that all his talk is talk about God. But we do not know ourselves as this man. We know ourselves only as the man to whom mercy is shown as one who is fallen, lost and condemned."[59]

I have noted in chapter four that while in *Romans* II Barth speaks of revelation as "impossible possibility," the Barth of Göttingen-Münster finds his dialectical starting point in both the impossibility of fallen humanity's attainment unto any true knowledge of God and the empirically observable and verifiable matter of fact (*Tatsache*) that human beings do possess true knowledge of God. This is also the case for *CD* I/1, albeit with a new emphasis on the role of the church: human talk about God in the church does become God's Word despite the inherent secularity (*Welthaftigkeit*: this word carries the connotation of being confined to the world) of all human talk.

From the very outset, Barth makes it clear that true theology (i.e., theology that really talks about God) is possible only on the basis of divine election. He reiterates the position that he developed in Göttingen:

> [As] man in the kingdom of grace . . . we stand under the sign of a *decision* constantly taken between the secularity and the sanctification of our existence, between sin and grace, between a being as man which forgets God, which is absolutely neutral in relation to Him and therefore absolutely hostile, and one which in His revelation is *awakened by faith* to *being in the Church*, to the appropriation of His promise.[60]

While the Barth of Göttingen-Münster did not stress the inseparable connection between true personal faith and the *credo* of the church as he does in *CD* I/1, every other element in the quote above is taken from the actualistic doctrine of election developed in *GD*. This actualism becomes more apparent at the end of the same paragraph: "The ongoing event of the final distinction [between secular and sanctified existence], the event in which God Himself acts, casts its shadow before in the event of this provisional distinction [between a believing and religious and an unbelieving and worldly attitude] in which man is at work."[61]

While the doctrine of election undergirding *CD* I/1 remains essentially the same as that of *GD*, Barth now introduces the new emphasis that election

---
[59]Ibid.
[60]Ibid., 47-48; ET 47-48 (emphasis added).
[61]Ibid., 48; ET 48.

is not only God's act of awakening faith in the human subject but also that of gathering believers into the church. This, again, reflects Barth's conviction in *Anselm* that *intellectus fidei* must conform to the *credo* of the church, which in the first instance must conform to God's Word. Thus Barth says, "The event in which God acts consists wholly in the fact that men are visibly awakened, separated and gathered by God to being in the visible Church."[62]

This event of which Barth speaks is precisely divine election: "A visible distinction which arises within the secular sphere between religious and profane is now, not intrinsically but in this *event of divine election*, confirmed and maintained and therefore characterised as a genuine indication of the antithesis of judgment and grace in which, even though men do not act towards others, God Himself acts towards men."[63]

How this divine act of election is accomplished is explained in *CD* I/1, §12, "God the Holy Spirit." Barth begins this paragraph with the problem of the subjective possibility of revelation: "We begin . . . with the New Testament witness: Jesus is Lord. But . . . we add the query: How do men come to say this?"[64] In other words, "How does this predicate, this faith, come to this subject, the subject man?"[65]

To this question Barth gives the same answer as he did in *GD*: "This special element in revelation is undoubtedly identical with what the New Testament usually calls the Holy Spirit as the subjective side in the event of revelation."[66] Moreover, "the creature needs the Creator to be able to live. It thus needs the relation to Him. But it cannot create this relation. God creates it by His own presence in the creature and therefore as a relation of Himself to Himself. The Spirit of God is God in His freedom to be present to the creature, and therefore to create this relation, and therefore to be the life of the creature."[67]

But how is it that the creature came to need the Holy Spirit to create this relation to the Creator? Does not the creature, by virtue of being created, already exist in an intimate relation with its Creator? Barth's answer is that

---

[62]Ibid.
[63]Ibid., 49; ET 48-49 (emphasis added).
[64]Ibid., 470; ET 448.
[65]Ibid.
[66]Ibid., 472; ET 449.
[67]Ibid., 473; ET 450.

this was indeed the case in the original state of human existence.[68] Fallen human beings, however, need the Holy Spirit to create in them this new relation of faith to the Creator. Barth takes as a basic theological principle the Reformed-orthodox conviction that *homo peccator non capax verbi divini*: the sinful human is not capable of hearing God's Word. For Barth, to ask how humans can come to faith in God is to ask, "How does *homo peccator* become *capax verbi divini*?"[69] Barth's answer is divine election, the event wherein the Holy Spirit sovereignly creates faith in fallen sinners.

Although this doctrine of election does not occupy center stage in *CD* I/1, the fact that Barth lays it down as a foundational concept at the very outset of chapter one suggests that it undergirds the first half-volume of his doctrine of the Word of God—I will show that this is indeed the case. For now, suffice it to note that the actualistic doctrine of election in *CD* I/1, which Barth had developed while in Göttingen, clearly leans toward infralapsarianism because its *obiectum praedestinationis* is "*homo peccator*."[70] Without humanity's sin, election would not have been necessary (for humankind's knowledge of God) or even meaningful, since election is God's act whereby sinners are "visibly awakened, separated and gathered by God to being in the visible Church."[71]

In chapter four I have already indicated the reason why I do not consider this doctrine of election to be fully infralapsarian, but only "leaning toward infralapsarianism": in Barth's actualistic account of the doctrine, the *obiectum praedestinationis* is sinful humans in temporal history, rather than God's eternal conception of fallen human individuals in double predestination prior to the work of creation. This doctrine of election leaning toward infralapsarianism, which Barth developed in Göttingen, underlies the doctrine of the Word of God in *CD* I/1.

Doctrine of the Word of God: Infralapsarian Christology. As we saw in chapter four, in *GD* and *MD*, Barth's infralapsarian Christology and the infralapsarian tendency in his doctrine of election are tied together by the conviction that the necessity of divine revelation-in-act for humanity's

---

[68] Ibid., 47; ET 47.
[69] Ibid., 479; ET 456.
[70] Ibid.
[71] Ibid., 48; ET 48.

knowledge of God presupposes human fallenness. Humanity in its original state of creation existed in immediate relationship with God and needed no revelation in the form of the incarnation. The necessity of revelation in both its objective-christological and subjective-pneumatological aspects is predicated on human fallenness.

The same goes for *CD* I/1, where Barth asserts that revelation *is* reconciliation.[72] Revelation of the Word of God in its doubly indirect form is necessary because of human sinfulness, without which humanity in its original estate would have enjoyed immediate knowledge of God.[73] "To the image of God in man which was lost in Adam but restored in Christ there also belongs the fact that man can hear God's Word. Only as the Word of God is really spoken in spite of his sin and to his sin, only in the grace with which God replies to sin, can this possibility revive."[74] Note here that Barth's entire discourse on the Word of God is predicated on the supposition of humanity's sin—this is what gives rise to the infralapsarian character of both predestination and Christology in *CD* I/1.

That this is so is apparent in Barth's famous notion of the Word of God in its threefold form as preached, written and revealed. God's Word preached is the church's proclamation qua proclamation. Proclamation and the church are not "simply and visibly there . . . as that which they want to be and should be . . . , as realities of revelation and faith."[75] Proclamation and the church are earthly media that are inherently secular because believers are sinners. Ecclesial proclamation in itself is not simply or visibly God's Word. "The Word of God is the event itself in which proclamation becomes real proclamation."[76] The event in which proclamation becomes God's Word, then, is contingent on God's free and gracious decision.

Scripture, too, is not simply or visibly God's written Word, as its historical form and medium are inherently secular. Scripture becomes God's Word in the event of God's free decision and action: "Recollection of God's past reve-

---

[72]Ibid., 430; ET 409. See George Hunsinger, *Disruptive Grace: Studies in the Theology of Karl Barth* (Grand Rapids: Eerdmans, 2000), 149. Hunsinger comments that for Barth, revelation and reconciliation are inseparable realities that are both identical to the incarnation.
[73]*KD* I/1, 47; ET 47.
[74]Ibid., 254; ET 241.
[75]Ibid., 89-90; ET 88.
[76]Ibid., 95; ET 93.

lation ... is also an event, and is to be understood only as an event. In this event the Bible is God's Word."[77] "The Bible, then, becomes God's Word in this event" in which "God's action on man has become an event ... , and the Bible has grasped at man."[78]

Just as Barth had asserted in *GD* (see chapter four), Scripture as revelation must be indirect because of its inherent secularity. That is, through Scripture—and proclamation for that matter—God unveils Godself only by veiling Godself in the "fallible human word."[79] Thus we must not "equate [Scripture] directly with this other, with revelation itself."[80]

To be sure, Scripture and revelation are "indeed one," but "their union is really an event."[81] Therefore, "in the statement that the Bible is God's Word the little word 'is' refers to its being in this becoming. It does not become God's Word because we accord it faith but in the fact that it becomes revelation to us."[82] In this sense the Word of God preached and written belong to "a single genus, Scripture as the commencement and present-day preaching as the continuation of one and the same event,"[83] even though God's Word "in its writtenness as 'Bible' ... must be distinguished from and given precedence over the purely spiritual and oral life of ecclesial tradition."[84]

From the foregoing discussions we can see how the actualistic doctrine of election from the Göttingen-Münster cycle undergirds Barth's understanding of God's Word preached and written. We can also see how Barth places these discussions in the context of the *analogia fidei* developed in *Anselm*. The *ratio fidei* (Scripture and the church's *credo*) conforms to the *ratio veritatis* (God's Word itself) only by the event of God's free decision and action, namely, election.

This event of election, moreover, presupposes the inherent secularity—which results from human fallenness—of proclamation and Scripture as God's chosen media of revelation. Thus we find in Barth's discussion of "the Word

---

[77]Ibid., 112; ET 109.
[78]Ibid.
[79]Ibid., 118; ET 116.
[80]Ibid., 115; ET 112.
[81]Ibid., 116; ET 113.
[82]Ibid., 113; ET 110.
[83]Ibid., 104; ET 102.
[84]Ibid., 108; ET 106.

of God preached and written" an actualistic doctrine of election carrying infralapsarian overtones: the *obiectum praedestinationis* is sinful humanity.

Moving on, Barth sets forth his notion of "the Word of God revealed." He begins by stressing that Scripture is God's Word only in the form of "attestation."[85] Scripture "is not in itself and as such God's past revelation. As it is God's Word it bears witness to God's past revelation, and it is God's past revelation in the form of attestation. . . . Witnessing means pointing in a specific direction beyond the self and on to another."[86] This "other" to which the biblical witness points is the Word of God revealed.

Unlike Scripture and proclamation, which are "derivatively and mediately" (*abgeleitet und mittelbar*) God's Word, revelation is "originally and immediately" (*ursprünglich und unmittelbar*) the *Deus dixit*.[87] Revelation is not the *Deus dixit* veiled by the *Paulus dixit*.[88] Rather, "revelation denotes the Word of God itself in the act of its being spoken in time."[89] More concretely, revelation *is* incarnation, the *Logos ensarkos*: "Revelation in fact does not differ from the person of Jesus Christ nor from the reconciliation accomplished in Him. To say revelation is to say 'The Word became flesh.'"[90]

Here, the infralapsarian orientation of Barth's Christology begins to emerge. While in the last quote Barth equates revelation to Jesus Christ and his work of reconciliation, in §11, "God the Son," Barth states that "revelation *is* itself reconciliation."[91] That is, revelation (which is identical to the incarnation) is an act whereby God overcomes the gulf of sin between Godself and fallen humanity. Revelation as such is God's Word spoken to sinners through the improper medium of this fallen world: "The place where God's Word is revealed is objectively and subjectively the cosmos in which sin reigns."[92] Therefore, "the speech of God is and remains the mystery of God supremely in its secularity."[93]

---

[85]Ibid., 114; ET 111.
[86]Ibid.
[87]Ibid., 120; ET 117.
[88]Ibid., 116; ET 113.
[89]Ibid., 121; ET 118.
[90]Ibid., 122; ET 119.
[91]Ibid., 430; ET 409.
[92]Ibid., 172; ET 166.
[93]Ibid., 171; ET 165.

Not only is this so for Scripture and proclamation, which are in themselves fallible human words, but also the Word of God revealed carries the attribute of a "twofold indirectness": "The secularity of the Word of God does not imply only that it meets us in the garment of creaturely reality. Because this creaturely reality is that of fallen man and because the Word of God meets us in this reality, we have to say that its form is not that of a pure nature which as such stands in immediate contrast with the distorted nature of its environment."[94]

Barth's notion of the secularity and twofold indirectness of the Word of God entails an infralapsarian orientation in his Christology.

> This secularity, this twofold indirectness, is in fact an authentic and inalienable attribute of the Word of God. Revelation means incarnation of the Word of God. But incarnation means entry into this secularity. We are in this world and are through and through secular. If God did not speak to us in secular form, He would not speak to us at all. To evade the secularity of His Word is to evade Christ.[95]

In fact, the incarnation as doubly indirect revelation would have been unnecessary for humanity's knowledge of God in its original state of immediacy with God, in which Adam could hear God's Word directly and not indirectly. "To the image of God in man which was lost in Adam but restored in Christ there also belongs the fact that man can hear God's Word. Only as the Word of God is really spoken in spite of his sin and to his sin, only in the grace with which God replies to sin, can this possibility revive."[96]

This understanding of the *Deus dixit* in spite of and to humanity's sin leads to the central meaning of Barth's *analogia fidei*: "Man acts as he believes, but the fact that he believes as he acts is God's act. Man is the subject of faith. Man believes, not God. But the fact that man is this subject in faith is bracketed as a predicate of the subject of God, bracketed in the way that the Creator encloses the creature and the merciful God sinful man."[97]

It is true that in its original state humanity also needed to hear God's Word in order to know God. This is because of the principle "*finitum non*

---

[94]Ibid., 172; ET 166.
[95]Ibid., 174; ET 168.
[96]Ibid., 254; ET 241.
[97]Ibid., 258; ET 245.

capax infiniti."⁹⁸ Yet "the abrogation of this principle is not the real mystery of the revelation of the Son of God."⁹⁹ That is, the abrogation of this prelapsarian principle of human inability to know the transcendent God was accomplished by God's direct speech to Adam in Eden. This prelapsarian principle is not the one that the incarnation abrogates. Rather, "the real mystery" of the incarnation, the doubly indirect Word of God, is "the abrogation of the other and much more incisive principle: *homo peccator non capax verbi divini* [fallen humanity cannot hear God's Word]."¹⁰⁰

The infralapsarian orientation of Barth's Christology is clear: God's will to become incarnate presupposes God's intention to confront humanity's sin, without which God's speech to humanity would have been direct, and the Word incarnate would not have been necessary for human knowledge of God.

CD I/2: Opus "Zwischen den Zeiten"

Up to this point I have shown that *Anselm* and *CD* I/1 stand in continuity with the Göttingen-Münster period as far as Barth's christological and predestinarian lapsarianism is concerned. One might wonder whether *CD* I/2 belongs to the same phase of Barth's development as *CD* I/1 or the one that is to begin in 1936 with the composition of *Gottes Gnadenwahl*. In this section I briefly address this question, arguing that most of *CD* I/2 was written prior to 1936, but before its completion in 1937 Barth had probably revised the doctrine of election therein so that it does not contradict the one developed in 1936.¹⁰¹ In this respect, *CD* I/1 is an opus "between the times."

My position on this topic differs from that of Suzanne McDonald, who thinks that "in the Barth of *CD* I/1 and 2 we continue to see the implications of his doctrine of election in *GD*."¹⁰² McDonald believes that in *CD* I/2, Barth still holds to the doctrine of election that he developed in *GD*. She comments that "the same dynamics we have noted in *CD* I/1 is likewise in

---

⁹⁸Ibid., 427; ET 407.
⁹⁹Ibid., 428; ET 407.
¹⁰⁰Ibid.
¹⁰¹Paul Jones paints a different picture of *CD* I/2 in relation to II/1–II/2. See Paul Jones, *The Humanity of Christ: Christology in Karl Barth's Church Dogmatics* (London: Continuum, 2008), 62–102. I dialogue with Jones in chap. 8.
¹⁰²McDonald, "Barth's 'Other,'" 141.

evidence in I/2, where Barth gives his account of the outworking of God's act of revelation in its objective form *for* us (§13, The Incarnation of the Word) and subjective fulfilment *in* us (§16, The Outpouring of the Holy Spirit)."[103] Yet, as I shall show, McDonald does not seem to recognize that in *CD* I/2 Barth no longer associates the doctrine of election with pneumatology. To be sure, in §16 Barth speaks of election in connection with the Holy Spirit's work, but this is the election of Israel and the church, election in the special sense that Barth would later treat in *CD* II/2, §34, "The Election of the Community," rather than the actualistic rendition of "eternal" predestination found in *GD*.

Of course, there is no question that §13 and §16 constitute an expansion of the subjective and objective possibilities of revelation that Barth sets forth in *GD*. Aside from the fact that he no longer associates election with pneumatology, the slight difference between *GD* and *CD* I/2 is a new emphasis on God's freedom in the latter. Thus Barth reframes his question of the subjective and objective possibilities of revelation.

> A better way of putting the questions is to ask, (1) how far God in His revelation is free for us, i.e., free to reveal Himself to us, free to be our God without at the same time ceasing to be God the Lord; and (2) how far God in His revelation is also free in us, i.e., free to deal with us as His own, who belong to Him and obey Him, although we are but men, and sinful men at that.[104]

Barth's answer to this twofold question is this: "God is not prevented either by His own deity or by our humanity and sinfulness from being our God and having intercourse with us as with His own. On the contrary, He is free for us and in us. That is the central content of the doctrine of Christ and of the doctrine of the Holy Spirit."[105] With regard to God's freedom in the objective aspect of revelation, Barth explicitly states that "God was able and *had to* reveal Himself to us in this familiar form [of the incarnation]."[106] In contending that God *had to* reveal Godself through the incarnation, Barth appeals to the medieval-scholastic and Reformed-orthodox distinction between the *potentia ordinata* and *potentia absoluta Dei*:

---

[103]Ibid.
[104]*KD* I/2, 2; ET 2.
[105]Ibid.
[106]Ibid., 41; ET 37 (emphasis added).

When we say that He had to act otherwise [in the form of the incarnation in order to reveal Godself], we honour the actual will of God visible in the event of His revelation, as the source and inner concept of all necessity. We are thus repeating what was previously told us [by God's self-revelation]. By such repetition we shall and must acknowledge the necessity of His actual manifest will, His *potentia ordinata*.[107]

In ascribing to God's *potentia ordinata* the necessity of the incarnation for God to reveal Godself to fallen humanity, the infralapsarian orientation of Barth's Christology is clear: in God's actually revealed ordinance, God's will to become incarnate presupposes God's intention to confront sin. (Supralapsarian Christology contends that God's *potentia ordinata* makes the incarnation necessary regardless of sin.) God has revealed no other ground of the necessity of the incarnation than God's will to reveal Godself to *sinners*.

The following statements from *CD* I/2 show that Barth's Christology indeed remains infralapsarian: "Jesus Christ . . . is a man as we are, equal to us as a creature, as a human individual, but also equal to us in the state and condition into which our disobedience has brought us. And in being what we are He is God's Word"; "Flesh is the concrete form of human nature marked by Adam's fall. . . . The Word is not only the eternal Word of God but 'flesh' as well. . . . In this way, and only in this way, is He God's revelation to us. He would not be revelation if He were not man. And He would not be man if He were not 'flesh' in this definite sense."[108]

While Barth's Christology in *CD* I/2 remains basically the same as that of *GD* with some new nuances, his actualistic doctrine of election is nowhere to be found in the entire half-volume of 1938. In particular, in *CD* I/2 Barth no longer associates "eternal" election with the actualistic work of the Holy Spirit. The only place in §16 where Barth explicitly discusses election is in the middle of an excursus.[109] There Barth talks about election only in the

---

[107]Ibid. *Potentia absoluta* is the notion that "the omnipotence of God [is] limited only by the law of noncontradiction. . . . God can effect all possibility, constrained only by his own nature." By contrast, *potentia ordinata* is the idea of "a limited and bounded power [of God] that guarantees the stability and consistency of the orders of nature and of grace." See Richard Muller, *Dictionary of Latin and Greek Theological Terms Drawn Principally from Protestant Scholastic Theology* (Grand Rapids: Baker, 1985), 231-32.
[108]*KD* I/2, 165; ET 151.
[109]Ibid., 246; ET 225.

special sense of Israel's being chosen as a "sign" to signify the objective reality of the incarnation.

> Let us think of a sign which is the most visible and in a certain sense includes all the rest, the sign of the election of the people of Israel. It is not identical with objective revelation, the incarnation. Yet in an extremely comprehensive way it obviously corresponds to it. It belongs to objective revelation, to the extent that that revelation does not remain objective. [110]

What Barth says here is quite different from his actualistic doctrine of election in *GD*. As we saw in chapter four, in *GD* human faith and obedience as the Holy Spirit's act *in nobis* corresponds to "God's free good pleasure"; election is God's sovereign will *in actu*.[111] The relation of correspondence becomes quite different in *CD* I/2, where, as we saw in the block quote above, the election of the community of faith (i.e., of Israel) is described as "corresponding" to the objective reality of Jesus Christ.

This line of thought seems to anticipate Barth's mature christological objectivism, which in a nutshell refers to his idea of the objective *participatio* of all humans in Christ, as all human beings are a priori (*zum Vornherein*) elected in Christ. Israel and the church are actualistic manifestations of this eternally objective *participatio*, and in this sense they are elected in a special way. This actualistic election of the community of faith is not to be confused with the eternally objective reality of election-in-Christ to which it corresponds. On this view, Barth's understanding of the election of Israel in *CD* I/2, §16, seems to be more in line with this mature christological objectivism than with the actualistic doctrine of election in *GD*.

Furthermore, in *GD* the Holy Spirit is the divine person who takes on the primary role in the act of election, but in *CD* I/2 Barth describes the Son as the electing God: "The Son of God elects and calls and justifies and sanctifies His own people in and from the midst of the world."[112] This is also in line with the Christocentric doctrine of election that Barth had developed in 1936, though here Barth does not explicitly speak of the *incarnate* Son as the electing God as he does in *CD* II/2 yet (see chapter seven).

These evidences may be taken to suggest that before its completion in 1937

---

[110] Ibid.
[111] *Unterricht* 1:222; ET 180.
[112] *KD* I/2, 246; ET 225.

and publication in 1938, Barth had revised *CD* I/2 so that the doctrine of election in it would more or less conform to the Christocentric one he developed in 1936. My theory is plausible if one considers the fact that *CD* I/2 was completed in the summer of 1937, when the composition of *CD* II/1 was already underway.[113] It would be reasonable to think that before the completion of *CD* I/2, Barth had spent some time revising the work in accordance with his new theological discovery from 1936 while beginning to work on the next volume of his dogmatics. After all, why would Barth publish *CD* I/2 in 1938 if the doctrine of election in it was still the actualistic rendition from *GD* and thus contradicted his new Christocentric doctrine published in 1936, which he deemed to be so momentous in his own theological development?

Of course, given the fact that most of *CD* I/2 was composed between 1932 and Barth's Christocentric revision of his doctrine of election, this half-volume still stands in the shadow of the Göttingen-Münster period. While the subsequent volumes of *CD* would come to be increasingly dominated by Barth's Christocentric doctrine of election and its christological objectivism, most of *CD* I/2 is still free from its influence. That is, Barth's mature doctrine of election developed in 1936–1942 does not undergird *CD* I/2 as it does subsequent volumes of *CD*.

For one thing, still lacking in *CD* I/2 is what Webster calls "an almost ruthless particularity, a concentration of the imagination on one point and one point only: the name of Jesus, his absolute specificity as 'this one,' the first and the last and the most simple thing."[114] This is not to say that Barth's "particularism" ("Barth's theology makes a concerted attempt always to move from the particular to the general") was not already in place early on in his career.[115] Barth's theology has always been characterized by a strictly antimetaphysical particularism. Yet it would not be until 1936 that Barth would begin his attempt to concentrate all his theology on the one particular point of Jesus Christ, and this christological concentration would not find its full-fledged expression until *CD* II/2 (1942). In *CD* I/2, for instance, Barth's pneumatological consideration of the subjective possibility of revelation is still quite independent of Christology.

---

[113]Busch, *Life from Letters*, 282-84.
[114]Webster, *Karl Barth*, 62.
[115]George Hunsinger, *How to Read Karl Barth* (Oxford: Oxford University Press, 1991), 32.

The only impact Barth's Christocentric doctrine of election from 1936 had on *CD* I/2 is that he had done his best to eliminate vestiges of the actualistic doctrine of election developed in *GD*. In this regard, *CD* I/2 is a work *zwischen den Zeiten*, "between the times," in the successive phases of Barth's theological development: it bears the marks of both phases (before and after 1936) of Barth's thought.[116]

Incidentally, during the composition of *CD* I/2 Barth underwent not only the inception of a decisive turning point in his theological development but also the last physical removal in his life: in 1935 he was dismissed from Bonn in the midst of political turmoil, and within three days he received an invitation from the University of Basel for a special chair. Soon thereafter he moved back to his Swiss hometown and would take up residence there until his death in 1968.

---

[116]This is the name of the theological journal that Barth cofounded with Eduard Thurneysen and Friedrich Gogarten in 1922.

6

Gottes Gnadenwahl (1936)

INFRALAPSARIAN ASPECTS OF BARTH'S CHRISTOCENTRIC DOCTRINE OF ELECTION

SINCE THE PUBLICATION OF Bruce McCormack's *Karl Barth's Critically Realistic Dialectical Theology*, it has been generally accepted that Barth's Christocentric doctrine of election developed in 1936 marks, in one way or another, the beginning of the mature phase of Barth's theology. This view of the significance of the 1936 *Gottes Gnadenwahl* (God's gracious election) is one of McCormack's great contributions to contemporary Barth studies. Unquestionably, any student of Barth's theology today is indebted to McCormack's work.

Meanwhile, as we saw in chapter five, the implications of Barth's new Christocentric doctrine of election did not immediately come to govern all aspects of his theology. McCormack himself would later "admit that the picture [he] drew in [his] book, of a sudden shift in Barth's doctrine of election which was alleged to have taken place immediately after hearing Pierre Maury's lecture on Calvin's doctrine of predestination at the International Calvin Congress of 1936, needs to be revised a bit. The change was not immediate but gradual."[1]

This view of a gradual change in Barth's formulation of predestination from *Gottes Gnadenwahl* (1936) to *CD* II/2 (1942) was initially proposed by

---

[1]Bruce McCormack, "The Actuality of God: Karl Barth in Conversation with Open Theism," in *Engaging the Doctrine of God: Contemporary Protestant Perspectives*, ed. Bruce McCormack (Grand Rapids: Baker Academic, 2008), 213.

Matthias Gockel in his 2002 doctoral dissertation at Princeton Theological Seminary under McCormack's supervision.[2] Gockel argues that in 1936 Barth had only formulated the thesis that Christ is both the subject and object of predestination, but it was not until the winter semester of 1939/1940, during which he began to compose *CD* II/2, that he would develop an understanding of "election as God's self-determination to be God in a covenant with humankind."[3] In an article published in 2007, McCormack modifies his earlier thesis of a "sudden shift" in Barth's doctrine of election in 1936, agreeing with Gockel that Barth's "identification of 'Jesus Christ' with the electing God . . . did not appear until *CD* II/2."[4]

While I agree with Gockel's view that the final turning point in Barth's theological development was not immediate but gradual, there are some specific details that, as I see it, Gockel and McCormack have yet to sort out.

First, Gockel and McCormack's portrayal of the development of Barth's doctrine of election suggests that the Christocentric revision of the doctrine in 1936 was primarily occasioned by the historical contingency of Barth's audition of Maury's lecture. Gockel takes his cue from McCormack's comment in *Barth's Critically Realistic Dialectical Theology* that "more than any other influence in Barth's life, it was Maury who deserves credit for opening the way to that form of 'christocentrism' which became synonymous with the name of Karl Barth," while qualifying that the decisively new ideas in *CD* II/2 are mostly Barth's own rather than Maury's.[5] Even though McCormack would later come to concur with Gockel's corrective that "Maury never quite reached the point of equating divine reprobation with the reprobation of Jesus Christ" and that "the identification of 'Jesus Christ' with the electing God is also Barth's invention,"[6] both of them still retain the view that Barth "owed to his good friend Pierre Maury" the core contention of *Gottes Gnadenwahl*, namely, "the correlation of election and reprobation with the crucifixion of Jesus."[7] In a word, McCormack and

---

[2] Now published as Matthias Gockel, *Barth and Schleiermacher on the Doctrine of Election: A Systematic-Theological Comparison* (Oxford: Oxford University Press, 2006).
[3] Ibid., 167.
[4] Bruce McCormack, "Seek God Where He May Be Found: A Response to Edwin van Driel," *Scottish Journal of Theology*, 60 (2007): 64.
[5] Bruce McCormack, *Karl Barth's Critically Realistic Dialectical Theology* (Oxford: Clarendon, 1995), 455.
[6] McCormack, "Seek God," 64.
[7] Gockel, *Barth and Schleiermacher*, 202.

Gockel's emphasis is that most of the materials in *CD* II/2 are Barth's own inventions rather than Maury's, but they (McCormack more so than Gockel) still think of Maury as the primary cause of Barth's christological revision of the doctrine of election in *Gottes Gnadenwahl*.

But why was Barth so impressed by Maury's lecture, if Barth's own theology, with all its basic convictions, was not already developing in a direction and at such a point of maturity that would demand him to embrace the inspiration he found in Maury's christological rendition of predestination? Would it not be more reasonable to say that Barth was occasioned by his own theological maturation to find himself inspired by Maury's lecture to develop a Christocentric version of the doctrine of election, rather than suggesting that Maury gave Barth a sudden change of mind, leading him to revise his theology?

On this point, I will show in this chapter that Maury's lecture indeed served as a catalyst, but the primary cause of Barth's christological revision of the doctrine of election in 1936 was the direction in which his own theology, especially the lapsarian aspect of his Christology and doctrine of election, was already developing. That is, in confronting the lapsarian problem (i.e., whether the incarnation and double predestination are primarily aimed at dealing with humankind's sin), Barth's doctrine of election was already moving toward a christological concentration, and Maury's lecture gave Barth little more than a final push.

So, what is so innovative about *Gottes Gnadenwahl*? And what was it in Barth's own theology from the previous phases of his development that gave birth to this new idea upon hearing Maury's lecture? Here lies the second point on which McCormack and Gockel's presentation of the development of Barth's mature doctrine of election still leaves room for further scholarly contributions: they have not addressed the marriage of Christology and predestination in *Gottes Gnadenwahl*—the decisively new idea—in relation to Barth's lapsarian treatment of the two doctrines.

One important thesis of this chapter is that Barth's basically infralapsarian understanding of the event of the Word of God (see chapter five) was a chief factor that demanded a christological revision of his doctrine of election. When Barth heard Maury's lecture on predestination, its Christocentric orientation made sense to Barth, because in it he saw a rendition of election that tied the loose ends in his previous attempt to understand God's sovereign grace in spite of and to humankind's sin. As I have shown in chapters four and five, Barth's previous attempts at explicating this matter was undergirded by basically infralapsarian patterns of thinking about sin and grace. This would remain so in *Gottes Gnadenwahl*, and it is precisely because of Barth's basically infralapsarian orientation in Christology that he felt the need to replace his actualistic account of election with a thorough Christocentrism.

My main aim in this chapter on *Gottes Gnadenwahl*, then, is to demonstrate the inception of a Christocentric doctrine of election imbued with a robustly complex and dialectical lapsarian scheme that, albeit basically infralapsarian with regard to the object of election, exhibits both supra- and infralapsarian incentives and patterns of thinking.

Barth's Development: The Central Import of the Lapsarian Problem

The seed of the idea: Maury's lecture or Barth's own theology? In 1936, Barth attended a lecture by Pierre Maury on Calvin's doctrine of predestination at the *Congrès international de théologie calviniste* in Geneva. Maury stated in his lecture a thesis that Barth found to be of central significance to the doctrine of election, if not the entire enterprise of Christian theology.

> Outside of Christ, we know neither of the electing God, nor of His elect, nor of the act of election.... One cannot speak of damnation as a decision of God otherwise than on the basis of the cross on Golgotha, but on this basis one must speak of it.... The cross on which Christ was damned, does not damn us. It makes us children of God.[8]

As mentioned earlier, McCormack and Gockel believe, the former more strongly than the latter, that Maury's thesis was by far the most important factor leading to Barth's marriage of Christology and predestination.

McCormack could have appealed to a passage in *CD* II/2 to lend support to his argument, had he not thought that in *CD* II/2 Barth "omitted to say that it was only as a result of his hearing of ... a paper given by Pierre Maury,

---

[8]Pierre Maury, "Erwählung und Glaube," in *Theologische Studien* 8 (Zollikon-Zurich: Evangelischer Verlag, 1940), 7-12. Quoted in McCormack, *Dialectical Theology*, 457.

that he had been led to make the critical correction which, in *Church Dogmatics* II/2, he introduced against the view he had once held."⁹ The fact is, in *CD* II/2 Barth does not neglect to point out Maury's significance. Barth credits Maury for being the one who brought out "the Christological meaning and basis of the doctrine of election . . . in our own time."¹⁰ Barth recounts that "this service has been rendered by Pierre Maury in the fine lecture which he gave on 'Election et Foi' at the *Congrès international de théologie calviniste* in Geneva, 1936."¹¹

However, was it really "*only* as a result of his hearing of . . . a paper given by Pierre Maury," as McCormack claims, that Barth was led to a Christocentric revision of his doctrine of election? In other words, is Maury's lecture really to be credited as the chief agent that caused Barth's shift from an actualistic to a Christocentric rendition of predestination? McCormack himself has in fact suggested that during the composition of *CD* I/2, "already there were strong indications that [Barth] would like to revise this ontology [of his Christology]."¹²

Moreover, the immediate context of Barth's excursus in *CD* II/2 from which I quoted above, in which Barth gives Maury his due credit, suggests that Barth had other motivations for his 1936 theological revision besides Maury's lecture: "Historically there are to hand all kinds of important materials which should encourage and even necessitate an adoption of this thesis [that Jesus Christ is the central mystery of election and reprobation]."¹³

The "important materials" that Barth identifies here include John Knox's Scots Confession of 1560, Athanasius, Augustine, Cocceius, the Lapsarian Controversy and the "general Reformation assertion that Christ is the *speculum electionis*."¹⁴ These are important influences that Barth places alongside Maury's lecture, suggesting that it was not "only as a result of his hearing" the lecture that he was led to his christological reorientation of the doctrine of election. Interestingly Gockel points out this passage in the *CD*

---

⁹McCormack, *Dialectical Theology*, 456.
¹⁰*KD* II/2, 168; ET 154.
¹¹Ibid.
¹²Bruce McCormack, "Karl Barth's Historicized Christology: Just How 'Chalcedonian' Is It?," in *Orthodox and Modern: Studies in the Theology of Karl Barth* (Grand Rapids: Baker Academic, 2008), 207.
¹³*KD* II/2, 168; ET 155.
¹⁴Ibid.; ET 154-55.

II/2 excursus and mentions the Scots Confession, but stops short of correcting McCormack's view of the significance of Maury's influence on Barth, and does not discuss Barth's lapsarian thinking at all.[15]

Before encountering Maury's thesis in 1936, Barth was already wrestling with a host of historical materials that he felt to demand a Christocentric revision of the doctrine of election. Maury's lecture was a catalyst—a significant one to be sure—but Barth's engagement with the history of doctrine was already prompting him to move in the direction of a Christocentric doctrine of election.

More important than these historical materials, I would argue, were Barth's own struggles with the lapsarian problem through the successive phases of his development. As we have seen in the previous chapters, much of his theological development was driven by his attempts to explicate the problematic reality of humanity's sin on the supposition of God's free grace. Thus in the excursus in which he credits Maury for advocating a Christocentric rendition of election, he begins not with Maury's lecture but by commending Knox's Scots Confession for pointing in the direction of a christological doctrine of predestination.

Barth stresses that Knox was driven by his struggles with the lapsarian problem to seek the marriage of Christology and predestination: "It can hardly be denied that in the *Conf. Scotica* the specific conception of sin is intimately connected with the peculiar Christological conception of predestination."[16]

Having developed the thesis that incarnation lies at the heart of election, Barth explicitly states in the same excursus that "we can appeal in support of our thesis . . . to the inevitability of such a solution in the light of the Supralapsarian [sic] controversy."[17] In other words, Barth explicitly states that the theological problem of the Lapsarian Controversy inevitably demands a Christocentric rendition of the doctrine of election.

Barth's development thus far: A brief review. To be sure, Barth would deny that the Christocentric doctrine of election could be deduced from the lapsarian problem—that would make it natural-theological speculation. For

---

[15]Gockel, *Barth and Schleiermacher*, 177 n. 70.
[16]*KD* II/2, 168; ET 154.
[17]Ibid.; ET 155.

him, the lapsarian problem demands a Christocentric-predestinarian "solution" in the sense that only in light of this marriage of Christology and predestination can humanity's fallenness be explicated—and that means nonexplicated (see chapter eight)—in relation, or, better put, nonrelation, to the sovereignty and immutability of God's eternal decree.

As we have seen in previous chapters, Christology and predestination became more and more closely interwoven in each successive phase of Barth's development by a view of revelation as having been necessitated by sin. In *Romans* II, Barth had not yet adopted Chalcedon's two-nature Christology, but he understood revelation, the central locus of which is Christ's resurrection, as necessary (for humanity's knowledge of God) on the supposition of the human condition of sin, without which humanity would have been immediate to God and would have needed no revelation in the form of God's indirect self-disclosure to humankind. With regard to predestination, Barth's understanding during this period was supralapsarian on the eternal-teleological level, but on the temporal-actualistic level the *obiectum praedestinationis* is *homo peccator*. Thus in *Romans* II, only the temporal-actualistic aspect of predestination is incorporated into Barth's infralapsarian understanding of revelation. Christology and predestination in *Romans* II as such are not yet closely knit.

In *GD*, Barth's actualism is such that God's eternity is not an "ossified eternity" but one that is inseparable from history. There is no longer an "eternal" predestination above and behind God's present act in the person of the Holy Spirit. This actualism eliminates the eternal-supralapsarian aspect of Barth's understanding of predestination developed in *Romans* II, and the actualistic doctrine of election in *GD* begins to move toward infralapsarianism. In *GD* the actualistic-pneumatological rendition of election is related to the enhypostatic-anhypostatic Christology by means of Barth's basically infralapsarian understanding of revelation: humanity in its original state existed in immediacy to God and needed no revelation in the form of God's indirect speech, and the very concept of revelation in this form presupposes humanity's sin. The incarnation as the objective aspect and election as the subjective aspect of revelation as such are both predicated on humanity's fallenness.

In *CD* I/1 Barth's understandings of incarnation and election remain essentially the same as *GD*. However, the Anselm book gave him a more robust way of presenting the doctrine of the Word of God. The emphasis now shifts from the subjective-objective distinction (as found in *GD*) to the very concept of the Word of God itself, presented in the framework of the *analogia fidei* that reflects basically infralapsarian patterns of thinking (i.e., prelapsarian humanity would have known God directly; it is for fallen humans that the *intellectus fidei* can only indirectly and actualistically correspond to the ontic *ratio*). In terms of presentation, then, Barth's Christology and doctrine of election in *CD* I/1 become much more closely interwoven than in *GD*. He no longer gives separate treatments of the two doctrines as he did in *GD*, but discusses both under the rubric of the doctrine of the Word of God, which, as I have contended, is predicated on humanity's fallenness, aiming to explicate the a posteriori reality that inherently secular human talk in this fallen world can and does become talk about God.

From the foregoing discussions we see that in each of the previous phases of Barth's development, Christology and predestination have become more and more closely interwoven by his view of revelation as presupposing the fall, which undergirds both doctrines. As Barth himself comments, which we saw earlier, the lapsarian problem inevitably demands a marriage of Christology and predestination.

On this view, one chief driving force behind the christological reorientation of Barth's doctrine of election is really his basically infralapsarian view of the event of revelation. Maury's thesis gave Barth the final push to develop what the previous phases of his theology had already anticipated, but it is not the seed of Barth's Christocentric doctrine of election. The seed of this doctrine is Barth's basically infralapsarian patterns of thinking in his understanding of revelation, which has been expressed through both Christology and predestination in all phases of his development since *Romans* II.

GOTTES GNADENWAHL (1936)

***Brief outline of* Gottes Gnadenwahl.** Having discussed the import of lapsarianism in Barth's theological development leading up to 1936, I now turn to an exposition of *Gottes Gnadenwahl*. This small book comprises a set of lectures published in *Theologische Existenz heute* in 1936. In this book there are four main parts and a lengthy *Fragebeantwortung* (Q&A).

In part one Barth defines the concept of grace and explains what it means to say that predestination is God's grace. The lapsarian problem is stated here as the central theological question that the doctrine of God's gracious election seeks to address—the lapsarian problem really is one, if not *the*, chief driving force behind Barth's christological reorientation of the doctrine of election!

Part two consists of methodological considerations, identifying predestination as "truth of revelation" (*Offenbarungswahrheit*), which is "truth in Jesus Christ."[18] Part three presents double predestination as a process of sublation: reprobation, which Christ suffered vicariously in place of sinful humankind, is God's negation of humanity's sin that negates God's grace, and this negation of negation is for the purpose of God's gracious election of all humans in Christ. In part four Barth revisits double predestination, this time setting forth the thesis that the elect and the reprobate are not two masses of people inflexibly predetermined by a *decretum absolutum Dei*, but rather all humans are elected in Christ, who was vicariously reprobated for all.

Part one: Centrality of the lapsarian problem. Barth begins part one with exegetical considerations, retaining his position in *Romans* II that Romans 9:11-13, which historic Reformed theology customarily cites as proof for the doctrine of double predestination as *decretum absolutum Dei*, must be read in the larger context of Romans 9–11, the theme of which "is not so much the development of the notion of predestination, but—while drawing on this notion—the proclamation of the merciful and yet severe, severe and yet merciful, freely-electing in every step, will of God for the people of Israel."[19] So, too, in all other biblical passages "where we encounter this notion [of predestination] expressly or *en substance*," the doctrine "always occupies the role of a most highly emphatic, nay determinative and never-to-be-overlooked, statement with respect to other predications. It emerges and becomes important not for its own sake but for the sake of these other predications, appearing as salt in the food, so to say, and not as the food itself."[20]

Implicit in this statement about the place of the notion of predestination in Scripture is Barth's understanding of the place of the doctrine in dogmatics,

---

[18]Karl Barth, *Gottes Gnadenwahl* (Munich: Kaiser, 1936), 11. This work exists only in German, and in what follows I shall offer my own translation for passages quoted.
[19]Ibid., 4.
[20]Ibid.

as he comments in the *Fragebeantwortung* on the question whether predestination belongs to the doctrine of the economy of salvation: "The doctrine of predestination may not come to be understood as the food itself, but merely as salt in the food. It must stand at the beginning and behind all Christian thinking, but it is not an element in the description of how humanity comes into union with God."[21] Therefore, "in the economy of salvation the doctrine of predestination does not have its own place."[22] Rather, Barth follows Reformed orthodoxy, as he did in *GD*, in contending that predestination belongs to the doctrine of God. Predestination is thus a presupposition that sheds light on all Christian doctrines and all biblical passages about God's works of salvation.

What all these biblical passages have in common, says Barth, is that the notion of predestination undergirding them "is always about the proclamation that God encountered certain humans in special and direct ways, attending to them and using them for God's own glory and for their own salvation."[23] He appeals to passages such as 1 Peter 2:9, 2 Thessalonian 2:13, Romans 8:30, Mark 4:11 and Ephesians 1:3-4, claiming that "all these and other passages tell us . . . that God would act as such towards these humans on these grounds, because they were chosen by God on account of God's own election and decision. In and of themselves, they are unable, nor have they determined, to receive God's grace. Rather, that this should happen is itself the grace of God: 'So it depends not on human will or exertion, but on God who shows mercy' (Rom. 9:16)."[24]

For Barth, to grasp the core of the doctrine of predestination is to understand it as concrete grace (from part two onward he will show that grace must be understood concretely as grace in Christ) that underlies all God's acts and works attested in Scripture, rather than treating it as an abstract first principle apart from the actuality of God's grace: "The doctrine of predestination is biblical doctrine as long as it consists in this exegesis. It loses its biblical grounding and therewith the right-of-residence in the Church immediately, when it becomes an autonomous proposition, such as: something

---

[21]Ibid., 35.
[22]Ibid.
[23]Ibid., 4.
[24]Ibid., 5.

about the sovereignty and immutability of God, or: about the meaning and content of the divine world-plan, or: about the various essences and fates of human individuals."[25]

Thus in part one Barth's central contention is that predestination must be understood as grace: "it means grace, the reception of grace—that is the general and axiomatic meaning of the doctrine of predestination."[26] But what is grace? Having given the examples of the gift of the Holy Spirit, the summoning of the communion of the saints, the resurrection of the dead, the second coming of Christ and so on—"that is all grace"—Barth defines grace as "the free, Fatherly beneficence, in which God adopts and treats us, *in time* and *for eternity*, as his children."[27] This understanding of grace encompasses the whole doctrine of election: "The Word of God's election is nothing more than the Word of God's grace."[28]

So, what is the central theological problem that this doctrine of God's gracious election—this understanding of election as God's grace—seeks to answer? This is a crucial question that many Barth scholars have overlooked, despite the fact that the theological problem in question is explicitly stated in part one of *Gottes Gnadenwahl* with obvious rhetorical emphasis: "Is man in the place to receive grace, God's grace? Is he not by nature in conflict with grace? Is it not his need from which he would have to be freed by grace in the first instance: that he is by nature sinful, which means that he does not will to live by God's grace?"[29] With humanity's sin in view, "where and how is this decision made, in which it comes to this step" in which sinners come to accept the offer of grace?[30]

"This question," says Barth, "is the one that the doctrine of God's gracious election answers."[31] In other words, the central theological question that he tackles in *Gottes Gnadenwahl* is the lapsarian problem. He wants to take sin seriously in light of the freedom of God's grace. Humanity's fallenness is for the Barth of *Gottes Gnadenwahl* an a posteriori given, and his whole doctrine

---

[25]Ibid.
[26]Ibid., 6.
[27]Ibid. (emphasis added).
[28]Ibid.
[29]Ibid.
[30]Ibid., 7.
[31]Ibid.

of election seeks to address the relation (in *CD* II/2 this relation, as it were, will be emphatically described as nonrelation) between the freedom of God's grace and the sin of humanity, with truth-in-Jesus-Christ as his starting point. To miss this lapsarian problem in *Gottes Gnadenwahl* is to miss the core of Barth's doctrine of election.

Part one: Barth's lapsarian definitions. In fact Barth explicitly refers to the lapsarian problem in part one of *Gottes Gnadenwahl*. In answering the lapsarian problem, he takes an avowedly "supralapsarian" position: God chose humankind "'from the beginning' (2 Thess. 2:13), even 'before the creation of the world' (Eph. 1:14) . . . , in Godself independent of the actualization and of the entire sinful or righteous state of our existence."[32] He continues to comment that in this "so-called supralapsarian view of election . . . , one may see no scholastic sophistry. It was really no speculation, but it was opposed to the infralapsarian view . . . , which tried to distinguish God's omnipotence, goodness and wisdom in the work of creation from God's justice and mercy in the work of reconciliation as something primary and something actual."[33]

Barth continues to emphasize what he calls the "supralapsarian view" against this "infralapsarianism" (as he understood it): "However, there is in God . . . no higher will than his gracious will. . . . We cannot cancel out our being determined through grace on the ground of another higher determination of humankind."[34]

As we have already seen numerous times in previous chapters, the definition Barth gives to supralapsarianism here, which he had adopted as early as *Romans* II, actually describes both supra- and infralapsarianism in the original Lapsarian Controversy. Infralapsarians, as much as supralapsarians, stress that the divine act of election took place in eternity before the actual creation of the world, and none of God's decisions constitutes a passive response to any historical actuality that caught God by surprise, not even humanity's fall. What Barth calls "infralapsarianism" here—which he takes to imply that double predestination is a passive divine reaction to the "actual" human choice of sin—has in fact been rejected by Reformed-orthodox theologians in general, supra- and infralapsarianism alike.

---

[32]Ibid., 8.
[33]Ibid.
[34]Ibid.

Barth calls himself supralapsarian because he thinks supralapsarians are distinguished from infralapsarians by the conviction that even "the human decision over against the decision of the gracious God... took place... on the ground of divine predestination."[35] However, as we saw in chapters one and two, this is a conviction shared by supra- and infralapsarians. It does not make Barth a supralapsarian according to the definitions given in the original Lapsarian Controversy.

In sum, in part one of *Gottes Gnadenwahl* Barth's purpose is to establish an understanding of predestination as God's free and sovereign grace, which he, on his reading of the Lapsarian Controversy, identifies as a distinct feature of supralapsarianism over against the opposing view: "Gracious election, predestination, means: grace-in-grace. Grace-in-grace is God's freedom and sovereignty in grace."[36] Barth takes this to be a supralapsarian conviction, though in reality it characterizes Reformed orthodoxy in general.

In any case, at this point in *Gottes Gnadenwahl*, Barth has not yet explicitly offered his christological reorientation of the doctrine of election, and the basic lapsarian shape of his new understanding of predestination is still unclear. This becomes clear in part two.

Part two: Election "in Christ." Having established in part one that predestination means God's freedom and sovereignty in grace, Barth proceeds in part two to set forth the thesis that election is "in Christ." He arrives at this thesis by methodological considerations, stating at the very outset that "God's gracious election is the truth of revelation [*Offenbarungswahrheit*]; it is confession of faith [*Glaubensbekenntnis*]" (note in passing how the language he uses here resonates with *Anselm*—see chapter five).[37] This statement carries two negative implications: "It is not conceptual necessity [*Denknotwendigkeit*], and it is not an object of experience [*Erfahrungsgegenstand*]."[38]

Here Barth employs Kantian terminology with reference to the analytic/synthetic and a priori/posteriori distinctions. *Denknotwendigkeit* refers to analytic judgments in which the predicate is analytically contained in the

---
[35]Ibid., 9.
[36]Ibid., 10.
[37]Ibid., 11.
[38]Ibid.

subject (e.g., "all boys are male"): the rationalists of Kant's day relied on analytic a priori judgments to attain knowledge, but analytic judgments, though necessarily true, are tautological and do not render new information. By contrast, *Erfahrungsgegenstand* refers to a posteriori propositions attained through empirical judgment. Empiricists such as John Locke and David Hume relied on synthetic a posteriori judgments to obtain knowledge, but a posteriori judgments, though providing new information, are not necessarily true. For Kant, only synthetic a priori judgments can provide new knowledge that is necessarily true. Yet he comes to the conclusion that synthetic a priori propositions are impossible in metaphysics.

As we have seen in previous chapters, this Kantian critique of metaphysics is one fundamental theological starting point to which Barth has held all through his career. If revelation is to be revelation (that is, revelation perceptible to human reason), then the medium of revelation must be of this phenomenal world, which Barth describes as fallen: for Barth, the noumena-phenomena gulf was caused by humanity's fall, as creation in its original state was immediate to God and no mediation was needed between God and humanity. We saw in the last chapter that this is indeed so in *CD* I/1, where Barth asserts the inherent secularity and necessary indirectness of the Word of God.[39] Only when God veils Godself in the garment of fallen creaturely reality can humans perceive God's self-revelation.

In fact, as we saw in chapter four, in *GD* Barth already developed a christological notion of the objective possibility of revelation, stating that God becomes knowable to fallen humans only by becoming human without ceasing to be God. In *GD* this christological understanding of revelation is placed side by side with an actualistic-pneumatological rendition of predestination as the subjective aspect of revelation. In *CD* I/1, the emphasis in Barth's understanding of revelation began to shift from pneumatology to Christology: of the threefold forms of the Word of God, only Christ is in the strictest sense and not in any derivative or secondary sense the very Word of God. However, whether a human individual will come to faith in Christ is still determined by the Holy Spirit's actualistic work of election in the here and now.

---

[39] *KD* I/1, 172; ET 166.

This means that in *CD* I/1 Barth still considers election as an act of God apart from Christ who is the very Word of God, who *is* revelation in the strictest sense. This approach to the doctrine of predestination would contradict Barth's own methodological conviction that humans can never talk about God without Christ. In fact, this contradiction was already present in *GD*. As we saw in chapter four, Barth had already asserted in *GD*, following Calvin, that Christ is the "mirror of election."[40] There he stated: "We must stand by the *revelation in Christ* and thus start with what predestination is in the first instance, that is, election."[41] Yet despite this methodological conviction, Barth still treated predestination apart from Christology. This self-contradiction in *GD* and *CD* I/1 must be resolved, and it anticipated the christological reorientation of the doctrine of predestination in 1936.

In *Gottes Gnadenwahl*, Barth again contends as he did in *GD* that Christ is the "mirror of election."[42] By this he now means that the doctrine of God's gracious election is not *Denknotwendigkeit* or *Erfahrungsgegenstand* but *Offenbarungswahrheit*. With this statement, Barth is making a Copernican shift in his understanding of predestination from a center in pneumatology to a center in Christology: "God's gracious election is the truth of revelation. More concretely: it is biblical truth. With complete concreteness: it is truth in Jesus Christ. Its confession can thus be nothing—really nothing other than an exact form of confession of Jesus Christ."[43]

This has direct implications for the doctrine of *double* predestination: if double predestination can only be understood christologically, then reprobation, just as election, must be considered in light of Christ. For Barth this means that reprobation cannot be a metaphysical proposition based on analytic or empirical judgments—recall that predestination is not *Denknotwendigkeit* or *Erfahrungsgegenstand* but *Offenbarungswahrheit*: "It is with this axiom that we—in Jesus Christ and only in him and thus not in a logically deduced thought-form [*Denkbild*] or in the images [*Bildern*] of our experience—recognize what election and reprobation mean."[44]

---

[40] Karl Barth, *Unterricht in der christlichen Religion* (Zurich: TVZ, 1985), 1:207; ET 471.
[41] Ibid., 1:210; ET 474 (emphasis added).
[42] *Gottes Gnadenwahl*, 13.
[43] Ibid.
[44] Ibid.

But how can double predestination be understood christologically? Barth, inspired by Maury's lecture, interprets double predestination in light of the incarnation: "'Chosen in Christ'—we must now return to the central mystery of the Christian message, namely to the incarnation, in order to understand [this statement]."[45]

In a word—and this is the very core of Barth's mature doctrine of election—election *is* God's eternal decision to become incarnate: "It was the decision and act of the eternal Son and Word, by virtue of which this man, conceived of the Holy Spirit and born of the Virgin Mary, began to be the Son and the Word of God as he began to be human. That is election!"[46]

This identification of election as incarnation carries the profound implication that Barth no longer sees predestination as an indirect work of God in the here and now as he did from *GD* to *CD* I/1: "[Incarnation] is election! And that also means our election is completely direct and immediate."[47] This is because the incarnation is now identified with God's eternal act of election—and this time Barth really means it. (Recall that in *GD* Barth spoke of an actualistic eternity in time that is not really eternity.) The central locus of humankind's being chosen-in-Christ, that is, chosen in union with Christ's human nature, is not found subjectively or existentially in time, but objectively in eternity. Christ's birth in history is an act of God that corresponds to the eternal election of God's being—Barth's notion of God's being-in-act is now in place even though the expression of the notion still awaits maturation.

Barth's understanding of our participation in Christ, then, also undergoes a Copernican shift from a center in history to a center in eternity. Recall that in *GD* Barth states that "the incarnation is not an eternal relation," and election is the Holy Spirit's act in time.[48] In *Gottes Gnadenwahl*, however, Barth asserts that our being chosen through Christ's incarnation took place not in time but in eternity, so he can now say that election is "completely direct and immediate" (recall that for Barth, any temporal-historical human relation to God is necessarily indirect and mediated), something that he

---

[45]Ibid., 15.
[46]Ibid.
[47]Ibid.
[48]*Unterricht* 1:190; ET 155.

could not have said during the actualistic phases of his doctrine of election.

So how does such an understanding of election as incarnation shed light on *double* predestination, especially the dreaded doctrine of reprobation? Barth's christological answer with regard to reprobation is this: "The completion [*Vollendung*] and the last word of the incarnation, the proof of its full and absolute actuality, is the suffering and death of Jesus Christ."[49] That is, Golgotha is the historical actuality of divine reprobation. "As God elected this man Jesus to be in union with himself in his Son, God gave himself up for us . . . : 'My god, my God, why have you forsaken me?' (Mk. 15:34)."[50]

But how does this manifest God's lordship, given that reprobation must be God's sovereign act? "Where is God's sovereignty now?"[51] Barth's ultimate answer is that Christ's resurrection reveals God's sovereignty in double predestination. But before arriving at this conclusion, he argues that even in Christ's suffering and death, God's sovereignty is manifested.

> It is with grave seriousness, that God made himself one with sinful and mortal man, taking man's sin and death upon himself. But God's union with himself, the union of the Father with the Son, cannot be broken, nor can his lordship be degraded, and because of this, the Son—that he is truly God and truly human—does not have to truly bear the entire sin of humankind and truly suffer humankind's entire death. Sure he had to, but this is because he willed to. It is precisely the will of God that he executes. Yet as he executes the will of God, as he executes his own will as very God, how should the lordship of God not become even greater: not in itself but for us and unto us, as revealed and reconciling lordship?[52]

In other words, it is by his very sovereign decision that Christ "had to" bear humanity's sin and suffer humanity's death. But this "revealed and reconciling lordship" is precisely the meaning of Christ's resurrection: "This is Easter, the resurrection of Jesus Christ: the revealed and reconciling lordship of the crucified Son of God, his lordship for us and unto us as newborn ones in his birth. Carried by him, our sin and our death are conquered and carried

---

[49] *Gottes Gnadenwahl*, 16.
[50] Ibid.
[51] Ibid.
[52] Ibid. Note in passing that in *Gottes Gnadenwahl*, the triunity of God's being-in-act is eternally necessary, while election-incarnation is contingent on God's will.

away."⁵³ Again, the definitive locus of the reality of Christ's death and resurrection is not the historical actuality but God's eternal election: "What took place on Golgotha for us and unto us, which became manifest on Easter—although it took place in time—is our eternal election."⁵⁴

In short, the actuality of Christ's birth, death and resurrection reveals to us the truth of God's double predestination in the eternal act of incarnation. For the Barth of *Gottes Gnadenwahl*, it is through the *Offenbarungswahrheit* of Christ's birth, death and resurrection that we come to an understanding of double predestination as the unity of God's will that moves from reprobation to election.

Part two: Christological and predestinarian infralapsarianism. Note that the Christology to which Barth marries his doctrine of election in *Gottes Gnadenwahl* is, just as in *GD* and *CD* I/1-2, basically infralapsarian. As we have seen, the meaning of Christ's eternal incarnation is manifested in his death and resurrection. This means that the incarnation is God's eternal act whereby "God made himself one with sinful and mortal man, taking man's sin and death upon himself."⁵⁵ In other words, for Barth, the incarnation is by definition to take care of the problem of humanity's sin (infralapsarian), rather than the result of God's decision to be with humanity regardless of humanity's fallenness (supralapsarian).

The infralapsarian orientation in the Christology of *Gottes Gnadenwahl* implies a basically infralapsarian doctrine of election, since Barth has now identified predestination with God's eternal decision to be incarnate. Predestination involves reprobation, just as the "completion and the last word of the incarnation . . . is the suffering and death of Jesus Christ."⁵⁶ Predestination moves from reprobation to election, as it is God's choice to take on and then triumph over humanity's sin and death. Therefore sin—not just its historical happening but as an element posited in God's eternal decision to elect humankind in Christ—is presupposed in the divine act of double predestination. The human race that is elected in Christ from eternity, the human race for which God decided to become human without ceasing to

---

⁵³Ibid.
⁵⁴Ibid., 17.
⁵⁵Ibid., 16.
⁵⁶Ibid.

be God, is on this view *homo lapsus*. It is precisely for this reason that Barth calls predestination the "reconciling will of God."[57] This gives to Barth's doctrine of election in *Gottes Gnadenwahl* a basically infralapsarian tone, notwithstanding his own claim to be a supralapsarian.

Recall that in *GD* and *CD* I/1 Barth's doctrine of election was only moving toward infralapsarianism but had not yet adopted the basic infralapsarian thesis, because he had not yet developed the notion of predestination as a truly *eternal* act of God. Now that he marries Christology to predestination and shifts the center of the doctrine from historical actuality to true eternity, the basic infralapsarian thesis has been taken into Barth's doctrine of election.

This christological-predestinarian leaning toward infralapsarianism was in fact latent in the very first statement at the beginning of part two of *Gottes Gnadenwahl*: "God's gracious election is the truth of revelation."[58] As we have seen, this statement entails that humankind cannot attain to the truth of divine election by synthetic a priori judgments, since fallen human beings do not possess immediate rational knowledge of God. Revelation is necessary in order for sinners to come to recognize God's gracious election. As we have seen, Barth's notion of revelation has always been predicated on the sin of humanity. Just as Christology and predestination are woven into his infralapsarian understanding of the event of the Word of God in *CD* I/1, Barth's christological-predestinarian leaning toward infralapsarianism in *Gottes Gnadenwahl* is implicit in his identification of God's gracious election as *Offenbarungswahrheit*. Here again we see how Barth's christological reorientation of the doctrine of election was already anticipated in what I call his infralapsarian view of revelation (i.e., revelation in the form of the Christ event presupposes human fallenness; unfallen humanity knew God directly without the need of divine incarnation) in the previous phases of his theological development.

***Part three: Double predestination as* Aufhebung.** Having identified election as Christocentric *Offenbarungswahrheit* and discussed the meaning of double predestination in light of the incarnation, Barth proceeds in part three to further explicate the notions of election and reprobation: "Election means . . . to see an act of freedom and lordship upon the elect. . . . There is no

---
[57]Ibid.
[58]Ibid., 11.

election, where there is not also nonelection, omission and reprobation. The doctrine of predestination must thus be the doctrine of double predestination."[59]

However, Barth insists that reprobation must not be treated as a "logical postulate" that goes hand in hand with election, as if predestination had to be twofold because "there is no Yes without No, no day without night."[60] Treating double predestination as such would be to speak of election and reprobation as existing in the "tidiness of an equilibrium [*Gleichgewicht*]," which Barth finds to be speculatively metaphysical: as he sees it, such a view, taught by Calvin, Beza and classical Reformed theology (namely, the *decretum absolutum*), renders double predestination an unspeakably arbitrary will of God above and behind the God self-revealed in Jesus Christ.[61]

But "is Jesus Christ merely the bearer of the divine Yes to humankind? Is he not at the same time the bearer of the divine No? Is he—and he alone—not also the divine Judge on the Left Hand? Then how did we come to speak of divine reprobation as if we knew it from somewhere else other than our knowledge of Jesus Christ?"[62] In a word, for Barth double predestination is a christological doctrine—it cannot be derived from any sources other than the Christian knowledge of Christ.

Having established this Christocentric conviction, Barth proceeds to state his thesis:

> We cannot recognize our election in Jesus Christ without first and above all recognizing our reprobation in him. The Son of God, who took on human nature, is certainly the rejected Son of man (Mk 8:13), who in Gethsemane prayed in vain that this cup be removed from him (Mt 26:24), who saw himself abandoned by his heavenly Father on Golgotha (Mk 15:34), who, in the words of the Heidelberg Catechism Q. 37, "sustained in body and soul, the wrath of God against the sins of all mankind."[63]

In a word, through Golgotha we come to recognize Christ as the human vicariously reprobated *from* eternity for the sins of all humankind, for the purpose of God's gracious election of all *from* and *to* all eternity.

---

[59]Ibid., 18.
[60]Ibid.
[61]Ibid., 19.
[62]Ibid.
[63]Ibid., 20.

In view of Golgotha, Barth stresses that reprobation and election do not exist in a balanced equilibrium. Rather, reprobation serves the purpose of election, as Christ died in order to conquer death. Thus even the crucified Christ was reprobated as God's elect. "Mark well: even Jesus Christ on the cross is surely God's elect," for he was the "only one who willed and did the will of God."[64] In other words, Christ as God's elect was chosen to be reprobated in the place of sinful humankind, and he was reprobated for the sake of his own election and the election of all humankind in him. The election of the man Jesus, which includes and presupposes his reprobation, was to manifest God's righteousness: "[Christ's election] is the highest righteousness of this God—and Jesus himself is surely God's Son—to be the reprobated human in our place and to bear our punishment himself."[65]

In this way double predestination is for Barth not balanced equilibrium but sublation (*Aufhebung*, sometimes translated as "supersession," literally meaning "lifting up": this is the Hegelian notion of the negation of a negation, resulting in the abrogation of the negatives while preserving their rationality and fulfilling their purpose): "But as God's righteousness is determined and executed here, as our reprobation becomes manifest and surely manifest in its justice here, as God's elect [Jesus Christ] accepted it in faith and took it upon himself, our reprobation is sublated [*aufgehoben*]."[66] That is, reprobation is God's eternal negation of humanity's sin that negates God's grace, and this negation of negation in Christ is sublated in the event of election. "Only if we see it [reprobation] as having been sublated do we see it truly. But where we see its having been sublated, we see it truly, and there is no evasion from or revolt against the free and in-its-freedom-justified decision of God."[67] In a word, Christ was reprobated vicariously for the sin of all humankind, so that all humankind, partaking of him, may be elected in and with him.

Part three: Election as Aufhebung: *The complexity of Barth's lapsarianism.* In light of Barth's christological rendition of double predestination as *Aufhebung* of the divine No against sin, we may now proceed to delve

---

[64] Ibid., 21.
[65] Ibid.
[66] Ibid., 22.
[67] Ibid., 23.

deeper into the lapsarianism that underlies his doctrine of God's gracious election. Recall that according to supralapsarianism God issued forth election-reprobation irrespective of human sin. Reprobation, in particular, is simply God's decree to manifest God's glory in justice, but the object of this justice is God's eternal conception of unfallen humanity. In other words, on the supralapsarian view, double predestination does not logically presuppose humanity's sin. By contrast, infralapsarianism holds that the object of double predestination is *homo lapsus* (fallen humanity), not in historical actuality, but strictly as God's eternal conception of humanity before the actual creation of the world. Accordingly, double predestination is God's plan to take care of the problem of sin, the dark element that God freely presupposed in the double decree of election and reprobation.

Now, when Barth formulates double predestination as christological *Aufhebung*, the element of sin is undeniably presupposed in God's gracious election. Barth states that there is no election without reprobation: election is the sublation of reprobation, while reprobation is the negation of sin. For Barth, Golgotha reveals that Christ took on the sin of humanity and was vicariously reprobated for humankind from all eternity, and precisely in this eternal act of willing and doing God's will on the cross is the man Jesus, who is himself God, revealed to be God's elect.

Barth's notion of predestination as *Aufhebung* of God's No against sin is such that Christ took on humanity's reprobation so that humankind may participate in his election. Strictly speaking, however, although Christ is the only reprobate (Barth already hints at this in *Gottes Gnadenwahl*, though he does not spell it out as explicitly or extensively as he does in *CD* II/2), reprobation is in fact God's will against humankind's sin: Christ is "reprobated human *in our place*."[68]

Now the question is: in *Gottes Gnadenwahl*, is the object of divine reprobation and election fallen or unfallen humanity? The following passage makes it clear: "Just as the law of God can kill and must kill human beings who are contemptuous of grace (grace is the mystery of the law), just as God charges, banishes, condemns and, with temporal and eternal death, punishes the sinner, so everything becomes manifest here: God's holy justice in

---

[68] Ibid., 21.

his eternal reprobation of the *massa perditionis*."[69] In other words, God's justice in the act of reprobation is against the sin of *homo lapsus*.

In this light, Christ's vicarious reprobation is for Barth God's eternal negation of humanity's sin, and this negation of negation is presupposed in election as the *Aufhebung* of reprobation, manifested in the actuality of Christ's resurrection. Barth's understanding of double predestination as christological *Aufhebung* is basically infralapsarian: double predestination deals with the element of sin, and the *obiectum praedestinationis* is *homo lapsus*.

Of course, with regard to teleology, Barth's understanding of election-in-Christ in terms of the logic of *Aufhebung* resonates more with supralapsarianism, because supralapsarians tend to ascribe teleological priority to election more than infralapsarians. That is to say, with respect of teleological order, humanity's sin as negation of God's grace serves to occasion the cross that manifests the reprobation that Christ endures in our place, and this reprobation serves the purpose of election. This is the supralapsarian aspect of Barth's understanding of election as a process of *Aufhebung*.

In terms of the *ordo decretorum*, then, there is a clearly supralapsarian aspect in Barth's doctrine of God's gracious election. However, the *Aufhebung* process also involves an infralapsarian *ordo*: election presupposes reprobation, and reprobation presupposes humanity's sin, as sin is humanity's negation of God's grace, and reprobation is God's negation of sin, and this negation of negation leads to election as the sublation of reprobation. Even this infralapsarian aspect of the *ordo*, however, contains within it a supralapsarian element, as the grace that humanity sinfully negates *is* God's electing grace in Jesus Christ (i.e., humanity's sin presupposes God's electing grace). In the current analysis, then, the *ordo decretorum* in *Gottes Gnadenwahl* is a robustly complex and dialectical combination of both supra- and infralapsarian patterns of thinking.

If Barth's christological doctrine of election in *Gottes Gnadenwahl* can be described as "basically infralapsarian," it is because the object of God's electing grace is sinful humanity. Again, by describing Barth as *basically* infralapsarian, my intention is to stress that there are supralapsarian em-

---

[69] Ibid., 22.

phases in his formulation of election-in-Christ. Not only is this so with regard to the *ordo*, but his view of the *obiectum praedestinationis* is not simply infralapsarian either. It must be emphasized that for Barth, Christ in his human nature is properly and directly the object of divine election and reprobation, and fallen sinners are elected *in* and *with* him. For Barth, Christ in his own human nature is certainly without sin, and it is by *imputation* and *participation* that Christ took on the sin of all humankind. Therefore, Christ as the proper *obiectum praedestinationis* is not *simpliciter homo lapsus*, even though the human race reprobated and elected in and with him is unquestionably fallen.

Part four: Election of all in Christ. Having asserted in part three that double predestination is not "balanced equilibrium" but *Aufhebung*, Barth proceeds to part four to claim that the grace of election is for all humankind. He begins by stating: "We are not in the place to make the declaration, who is elected and who is rejected."[70] In fact proponents of the classical Reformed doctrine of election have made the same statement too. Therefore, in order to distinguish his own doctrine from historic Calvinism, Barth contends that "we must go even further: we are not in the place to make the general declaration either, that there are two classes of humans as elects and reprobates."[71]

This is in fact not the first time in his career that Barth takes issues with the classical Reformed understanding of the *decretum absolutum*, the doctrine that humankind is inflexibly divided by an absolute and unsearchable divine decree into two masses as elects and reprobates. Recall from chapter three that in *Romans* II Barth cited Romans 11:32 ("for God hath shut up all unto disobedience, that he might have mercy upon all" [ASV]), contending that this is the passage whereby "the final meaning of 'Double Predestination' seeks to make itself known."[72] Barth argued there that while election appears to be dividing humankind into believers and unbelievers in the here and now, on the eternal-eschatological level reprobation is only a means toward the goal of the election of all humankind

During the Göttingen-Münster period (see chapter four), Barth retained this exegesis of Romans 11:32: "The way leads fundamentally from rejection

---

[70]Ibid., 26.
[71]Ibid.
[72]*Römerbrief* II, 407; ET 421.

to election, not vice versa. God has shut up all in disobedience in order to have mercy upon all."[73] However, in this phase of his development he no longer differentiated between God's eternal will and actualistic work. The distinction was now between the side of God's decree and the side of the elect that might perish against this decree. For this reason, Barth rejected the notion of any absolute assurance of being chosen on the part of the elect. Yet in contending for a relative assurance, the Barth of Göttingen-Münster still held that in the death and resurrection of Christ we see a movement of God's will from reprobation to election.

In *Gottes Gnadenwahl*, Barth again appeals to Romans 11:32 to interpret double predestination as a universal movement—a process of *Aufhebung*—of all humankind from reprobation to election.

> The insight that we gain from the recognition of gracious election is the twofold insight of faith in Jesus Christ. By faith in Jesus Christ, Paul wrote—and by the same faith we are to recognize and confess: "God hath shut up all unto disobedience, that he might have mercy upon all" (Rom 11:32). All: that is to say without doubt from the meaning and the context: all, upon whom God decides and shall have mercy in Jesus Christ. . . . All: precisely because all are ones upon whom God decides and shall have mercy in Jesus Christ, the notion that there might be elects who are not threatened with reprobation or reprobates who are not promised with election is firmly excluded.[74]

That is, in Christ all humans are placed under the threat of reprobation in order to be elected.

> "God hath shut up all unto disobedience": that is the threat from which we have been freed through the promise freely given to us in Jesus Christ. . . . The fact that all of us, the good and the evil, the pious and the ungodly, belong in this prison [of the threat of reprobation] is shown to us by God's wrath from Gethsemane to Golgotha, shown to us by the matter-of-fact [*Tatsache*] that the one elect who has never sinned bears this wrath as righteous wrath.[75]

In a word, "By faith in Jesus Christ we cannot avoid the recognition that our reprobation is determined and deserved and really executed."[76]

---

[73] *Unterricht* 2:193; ET 461.
[74] *Gottes Gnadenwahl*, 27.
[75] Ibid.
[76] Ibid.

Yet that our reprobation has been executed in Christ leads to the very next step of the *Aufhebung* process: "'that he might have mercy upon all': that is the promise."[77] As Barth has just stated, this promise frees humankind from the threat of reprobation. However, "it does not eliminate the threat. The promise presupposes that our reprobation is determined, deserved and really executed. The threat was and is thus not a game."[78] In other words, there is no election without reprobation. Election is "reprobation sublated [*aufgehoben*] in the promise": in election the purpose and rationality of reprobation are fulfilled and preserved.[79]

In this way the vicarious reprobation that Christ suffers in the stead of all sinners constitutes all humankind's election in him who is the one elect of God—this is for Barth the core meaning of the doctrine of God's gracious election: "that God—God in Jesus Christ—is with us on the way through such threat and promise in this double and yet unbalanced [*ungleichen*] foreordination, holding us in his hand: that is the insight that we gain from the recognition of gracious election."[80]

Now it is clear again from the foregoing discussions that the *obiectum praedestinationis*, that is all humankind in Christ, is *homo lapsus* (fallen humanity) for whose disobedience Christ is vicariously reprobated from eternity. Election as a process of *Aufhebung* presupposes reprobation, and the reprobation of all humankind is God's act whereby "God hath shut up all unto disobedience." In other words, for the Barth of *Gottes Gnadenwahl*, reprobation is not a divine fiat whereby God arbitrarily condemns the reprobate, but rather God's substitutionary punishment (we have seen in numerous passages that Barth does use penal-substitution language, however much his view of the atonement might be closer to a *Christus Victor* model) of Jesus Christ on the ground of humankind's disobedience unto which God has shut them all up. This aspect of Barth's complex and dialectical lapsarianism is what makes it basically infralapsarian.

Barth explicitly states, "Outside of the promise, [the threat] exists in force with the full severity of a real and necessary judgment of God: shut up in

---

[77]Ibid., 27-28.
[78]Ibid., 28.
[79]Ibid.
[80]Ibid., 28-29.

disobedience. It is this disobedience of our own being and action; but even so, it is by divine reprobation that God... shuts us up in this prison wherein we are without grace and in conflict with the grace of our own Lord" (recall that Barth had earlier defined sin as being in conflict with grace).[81]

Here Barth's notion of reprobation must be understood as comprising two distinct but inseparable aspects: the reprobation of all humankind in Christ, and the vicarious reprobation that Christ suffers in the place of all humankind. The abiding distinction and inseparable union of these two aspects are predicated on a basically Chalcedonian understanding of humankind's *participatio Christi*: human beings participate in Christ without ever becoming identical to Christ, but they and Christ are really one such that they are indivisibly and inseparably united to Christ, in much the same way as Christ's two natures are joined together in the person of the Son.

Now, because of the abiding distinction between Christ and the rest of humankind that participates in him, the reprobation of all humankind in Christ must be distinguished from the vicarious reprobation that Christ suffered for all humankind. In the former aspect, God shut up all in disobedience by the decree of reprobation; in the latter, God reprobated Jesus Christ on the ground of the guilt of the disobedience of all humankind transferred (via *participatio*) to him who is in himself guiltless.

It is important to note here that of these two aspects of divine reprobation, it is the latter that is constitutive and determinative of the former. That is, for Barth, God's decree in Christ is definitive of the state of humankind as *homo lapsus*. This makes Barth's lapsarian thinking complex and dialectical, at once exhibiting supra- and infralapsarian incentives and patterns of thinking. If Barth can be described as basically infralapsarian, it is because the decree of reprobation, consisting of two distinct but inseparable aspects, is not two but one, and in the constitutive and determinative aspect of this decree the *obiectum praedestinationis*, Christ, is reprobated on the ground of humanity's guilt of disobedience.

In other words, by God's decree of reprobation, humankind is confined to the prison of disobedience, and the vicarious reprobation that Christ endures is for disobedient humans whom God has pronounced guilty (*die*

---

[81]Ibid., 27.

Schuldiggesprochenen).[82] The object of God's electing grace as a process of *Aufhebung* is thus *homo lapsus*.

Implications of *Gottes Gnadenwahl*

Having given an exposition of Barth's Christocentric revision of predestination in *Gottes Gnadenwahl*, some concluding observations are now in order.

Actualism and critical realism. First, with his Christocentric revision of the doctrine of election, Barth has resolved a contradiction between his actualism and critical realism that marked the chief defect of his theology from GD to CD I/1. Recall that in GD Barth rejected the claim of any knowledge of an eternal predestination of God above and behind the eternity-in-actuality intuitable to human beings in space and time. Double predestination must and can only be understood actualistically as manifested in the Holy Spirit's work in the here and now. Christ's death and resurrection mirrors a movement in God's will from reprobation to election, but there is no absolute assurance that all are elected in Christ, or that a believer will always remain an elect, for to claim such assurance would be to speculatively probe into a will of God above and behind God's revelation-in-act, that is, revelation in the divine act of double predestination in the here and now.

This premature version of Barth's actualism would carry two possible implications, both of which would contradict his own axiomatic "critical realism." The first possible implication would be that the electing God is indeed objectively real in eternity above and behind temporal actualities (this is Barth's "realism"), but humans can only come to know the God self-revealed in temporal actualities without also knowing the eternal God in Godself. This could not have been Barth's contention, for it would have amounted to positing the existence of a deity apart from the God self-disclosed in the act of revelation, which Barth would have found uncritically metaphysical. If Barth were to accept this possible implication of his actualistic doctrine of election in GD, his theological realism would have ceased to be critical (i.e., it would violate Kant's critique of human reason).

Moreover, as we saw in chapter four, Barth's intention in GD was precisely to establish that God in Godself is one and the same as the God who has

---

[82]Ibid., 28.

entered into the veil of objectivity without ceasing to be the Subject. To say that believers may know of God's election-in-act without knowing election-in-eternity would be to contradict this very intention.

The second possible implication would be that there is no God apart from the God whose eternity is bound to temporal actualities. If Barth were to accept this implication, he would indeed have avoided uncritical speculations about the existence of a deity above and behind God's revelation-in-act, but then his theological realism would have been compromised, since this possible implication of his actualistic doctrine of election would have erased the distinction between the electing God's objectively real being and God's temporal acts. As George Hunsinger points out, although God's being and act are inseparable in Barth's thought, there is always a distinction between the two.[83] In the language of his mature theology, God is being-in-act rather than being-as-act (note in passing that so-called revisionists often make the mistake of construing Barth's actualism as a notion of divine being-*as*-act): God and God's act are not *simpliciter* identical, but rather God's being, distinct from God's act, is *in* act so that God's being cannot be known apart from God's act. This distinction is crucial to Barth's mature theology, for blurring this distinction would lead to a denial of the objective reality of God's transcendent being that is in act.

Now, if Barth's actualistic doctrine of election in GD is taken to imply that there is no distinction between the electing God-in-eternity and the electing God self-disclosed through the temporal actuality of faith and unfaith, then an eradication of the distinction between God's being and act would be inevitable, which would then amount to denying the objective reality of God's transcendent and eternal being. While some have found this possible implication of a sort of process theology in the earlier Barth appealing,[84] it blatantly contradicts his intentions.

In either case, then, Barth's earlier actualism would have contradicted one or another aspect of his critical realism. This defect in Barth's theology from GD to CD I/1 is resolved by his Christocentric revision of the doctrine of

---

[83]George Hunsinger, "Election and the Trinity: Twenty-Five Theses on the Theology of Karl Barth," *Modern Theology* 24 (2008): 180.
[84]For example, Robert Jenson, *God After God: The God of the Past and the God of the Future as Seen in the Work of Karl Barth* (Minneapolis: Fortress, 2010).

election in *Gottes Gnadenwahl*, where he develops the notion—though not yet the precise terminology and all the implications—of God's being-in-act for the first time in his career.

In *Gottes Gnadenwahl*, predestination no longer consists in merely temporal actualities. Rather, predestination really is God's eternal act of election and reprobation. Incarnation, which is now identified with predestination, is also eternal. This eternity, moreover, is not merely eternity-in-time. It is an objectively real eternity that has entered into temporality without ceasing to be eternal.[85] Predestination is thus God's eternal being *in* God's eternal act, transcendent over time and space, entering into time by the Christ event while remaining transcendent as ever. The being of the eternal God-in-Christ is made known to humans through Christ's birth, death and resurrection in history. These historical works of God in Christ actualistically correspond to God's eternal act of predestination-incarnation: "What took place on Golgotha for us and unto us, which became manifest on Easter—although it took place in time—is our eternal election."[86]

With this new actualism in which God's works and acts perfectly correspond to God's being with abiding distinction, Barth is now able to say that God's objectively real being in eternity is made knowable and indeed known to humans through God's works in fallen creaturely time and space. In other words, Barth's Christocentric revision of the doctrine of election has harmonized his actualism and critical realism, which had previously stood in mutual contradiction as well as contradiction to some of his other methodological axioms. It is with this notion of God as being-in-act that he is able to say that God's gracious election is not *Denknotwendigkeit* or *Erfahrungsgegenstand*, but *Offenbarungswahrheit* (as I have already demonstrated in this chapter).

Christocentric particularism. With his Christocentric notion (though

---

[85]Barth's understanding of eternity is at once traditional and modern. Reappropriating an Augustinian-Boethian understanding, Barth sees eternity as "in some strong sense" timeless and successionless (Hunsinger). Yet with reference to Whitehead and Hegel, Barth also thinks of eternity as involving a kind of temporality and procession. Barth's notion of eternity is grounded on his trinitarian thought, which I shall not discuss here. Suffice it to say that for Barth eternity as God's time is wholly other than creaturely and fallen temporality. See George Hunsinger, "*Mysterium Trinitatis*: Karl Barth's Conception of Eternity," in *Disruptive Grace: Studies in the Theology of Karl Barth* (Grand Rapids: Eerdmans, 2000), 186-209.

[86]*Gottes Gnadenwahl*, 16.

not yet the terminology) of God as being-in-act now in place, Barth's "particularism" also becomes concentrated in the person and work of Christ. Hunsinger explains the meaning of this term: "Particularism means that Barth strove to take his bearings strictly from the particularities of the biblical witness, especially its narrative portions. The particulars from which he wanted to move toward general theological constructions were the events of grace as attested in scripture and centered on Jesus Christ."[87]

Particularism and actualism are closely related in Barth's theology. He refuses to begin with general statements about reality in his theological constructions. The classic instance is his treatment of the biblical predication "God is love." He insists that one should not probe into what God is by examining general truths about love. For Barth, such *analogia entis* would lead to what Ludwig Feuerbach famously calls the "anthropological essence" of religion. Interestingly, Barth finds that Feuerbach is "no mere sceptic and nay-sayer" in his charge of anthropomorphism and idolatry against Christian theology.[88] It has too often been the case that in Christian theology, especially in the various traditions of natural theology, divine attributes are understood in light of human attributes, and as Barth sees it Feuerbach is certainly right in pointing out that "if the divine predicates are attributes of the human nature, the subject of those predicates is also of the human nature."[89] Barth thinks that such *analogia entis*[90] is the seed of the so-called anthropological turn to the subject in theology that culminated in neo-Protestantism. In an attempt to counter Feuerbach's charge of anthropomorphism, Barth challenges Feuerbach's assumption that "what the subject is lies entirely in the attributes of the subject," and insists that in Christian theology it is the divine subject that defines the attributes, not vice versa.[91]

Thus Barth stresses that in the biblical statement "God is love"—Feuerbach

---

[87]George Hunsinger, *How to Read Karl Barth* (Oxford: Oxford University Press, 1991), 33.

[88]Karl Barth, *Die Theologie und die Kirche* (Zollikon-Zurich: Evangelischer Verlag, 1928), 291; ET *Theology and Church*, trans. L. P. Smith (Eugene, OR: Wipf and Stock, 2015), 222.

[89]Ludwig Feuerbach, *The Essence of Christianity*, trans. George Eliot (New York: Prometheus, 1989), 25.

[90]Amy Marga has argued that despite Barth's avowed antagonism toward natural theology, he in fact allows room for some form of an *analogia entis* during his Göttingen-Münster years. Marga suggests at the end of her book that Barth's theology from 1936 onward might leave even more room for the *analogia entis*. See Amy Marga, *Karl Barth's Dialogue with Catholicism in Göttingen and Münster: Its Significance for His Doctrine of God* (Tübingen: Mohr Siebeck, 2010), 172.

[91]See Feuerbach, *Essence of Christianity*, 25.

is fond of saying that Christianity ascribes to the divine object the human attribute of love—it is the subject that defines the predicate, and not vice versa: God is love, but love is not God. To know what love is, then, one must first know the God who is love—this is one important principle of Barth's *analogia fidei* (see chapter five).

Yet because of the epistemological gulf between God and sinful creatures, direct human knowledge of God's being is impossible, thus one may know the God who is love only by knowing God's particular act of love. (In Barth's mature theology, God's act of love would be entirely centered on Jesus Christ.) To know God's act of love is to know the God who is love, for God is being-in-act.

Now, since Barth's actualism from *GD* to *CD* I/1 was not yet the Christocentric notion of God's being-in-act, but a trinitarian understanding of God's revelation-in-act, his particularism was also not yet Christocentric. For the Barth of *GD*, God's act of double predestination is known through subjective human experiences of existential faith-obedience and unbelief-disobedience in the here and now. Although these experiences are described as God's sovereign act in the person of the Holy Spirit, human knowledge of divine predestination still in one sense begins with a general *Erfahrungsgegenstand* (object of experience, alluding to Kant's analytic/synthetic and a priori/posteriori distinctions). This would violate the (neo-)Kantian rejection of the empiricist view of experience.

In *Gottes Gnadenwahl*, however, all human knowledge of God's gracious election is centered on Jesus Christ, and Barth has now made the attempt to strip away every last element of epistemological subjectivism (that is, establishing human knowledge of God on the ground of the subjective consciousness or experience of human individuals): recall from earlier that Barth would now insist that knowledge of God's gracious election is neither *Erfahrungsgegenstand* (object of experience) nor *Denknotwendigkeit* (conceptual necessity), but *Offenbarungswahrheit* (revelational truth), which is *Wahrheit in Christus* (truth in Christ).[92] Logical necessity or general observations of existential faith and unbelief no longer provide any sort of starting point for Barth's theological reflection on divine predestination. The particular person and work of Christ have now become the sole ground for

---

[92]*Gottes Gnadenwahl*, 11.

Barth's theological inquiry. Thus we find in *Gottes Gnadenwahl* a thoroughly Christocentric particularism, which was not yet in place in the previous phase of Barth's development.

Christological-objectivist soteriology. The next point of observation concerns the development of Barth's "christological objectivism," also known as his "objectivist soteriology." As already noted, one crucial difference between *Gottes Gnadenwahl* and his Göttingen-Münster theology is that rather than ascribing double predestination to the subjective sphere of faith and obedience in the here and now, Barth now describes election as a completely objective reality eternally accomplished in Christ.

As Hunsinger points out, Barth's objectivism is both epistemological and soteriological: "Objectivism . . . has two important aspects. The one concerns knowledge of God, the other, salvation in Christ."[93] In chapter five we saw that in *CD* I/1 Barth had already asserted that revelation *is* reconciliation. This soteriological emphasis on the doctrine of the Word of God was a slight improvement on his Göttingen-Münster theology, where, as we saw in chapter four, even its basically Chalcedonian Christology was formulated in a primarily epistemological rather than soteriological setting. This is not to say that soteriology was absent in Barth's Göttingen-Münster theology, since Barth has always considered the concept of revelation as one in which the sin of humanity must be overcome. However, in the Göttingen-Münster period, Barth's primary concern was with the possibility of revelation, and soteriology was in many ways subservient to epistemology. In *CD* I/1, the emphasis had shifted a bit such that soteriology and epistemology began to carry more or less equal weight in the doctrine of the Word of God, the center of which was the person and work of Christ.

In *Gottes Gnadenwahl*, soteriology has become the central focus of Barth's Christology, and some epistemological principles have governed his construction of the doctrine while other epistemological implications will follow from this new Christocentric doctrine of election.[94] Barth's main

---

[93] Hunsinger, *How to Read Karl Barth*, 35.
[94] Some have called this a "christological ontology" and deduced elaborate implications that Barth never stated explicitly. See Bruce McCormack, "Grace and Being: The Role of God's Gracious Election in Karl Barth's Theological Ontology," in *The Cambridge Companion to Karl Barth*, ed. John Webster (Cambridge: Cambridge University Press, 2000). Also see Aaron Smith, "God's Self-Specification: His Being is His Electing," *Scottish Journal of Theology* 62 (2009): 1-25.

concern now is how Christ has defeated sin by the eternal act of double predestination, rather than how humanity may come to know God through Christ. To be sure, the concept of revelation still carries substantial weight in Barth's thought, but it has now made way for a soteriological emphasis in his Christology.

The great import of Barth's soteriology in *Gottes Gnadenwahl* is that humankind's salvation is entirely determined in Christ from all eternity, and no subjective element from the human side may have any effect on an individual's status as elect or reprobate. This differs from the actualistic rendition of predestination in *GD*, where whether a person is elect or reprobate is determined by his existential status of faith or unbelief (though the Barth of *GD* would emphasize that this takes place by the sovereign decision of God through the work of the Holy Spirit).

This thoroughgoing Christocentrism in *Gottes Gnadenwahl* carries far-reaching implications for Barth's theological method: he would now treat every theological topic in light of his new Christocentrism. We shall explore these implications in chapters eight. Suffice it now to say that Barth's Christocentric epistemology developed in *Gottes Gnadenwahl* is aimed at ensuring that "the knowledge of God as confessed by faith is objective in the sense that its basis lies not in human subjectivity but in God."[95]

Conclusion: the Centrality of Lapsarianism

Finally, we return to the topic of Barth's lapsarianism. In this chapter we have seen how Barth's Christology and doctrine of election converge through his treatment of the reprobation and election of all humankind in Christ as a process of *Aufhebung*. I have demonstrated the complex and dialectical nature of Barth's lapsarianism in his christological doctrine of election set forth in *Gottes Gnadenwahl*: it brings together supra- and infralapsarian incentives and patterns of thinking in a robust manner, though it might be described as basically infralapsarian in that the object of God's electing grace is fallen humanity—*homo lapsus*.

This robustly complex lapsarian scheme that Barth develops in *Gottes Gnadenwahl* subtly holds together all the themes I have just treated in the

---

[95]Hunsinger, *How to Read Karl Barth*, 35.

foregoing discussion, as it constitutes the very core of Barth's mature Christocentric doctrine of election.

First of all, Barth's mature notion of God's being-in-act is predicated on his lapsarian thinking. Of course, with regard to Barth's understanding of the Trinity, whether God's being-in-act presupposes election has been a subject of debate for a number of years now. I leave this discussion for chapter eight. Suffice it now to say that when I assert that Barth's notion of God's being-in-act is predicated on his lapsarianism, I am not referring to God's trinitarian acts *ad intra*, but to God's being in the act of election.[96]

According to Barth's mature theology that found its inception in *Gottes Gnadenwahl*, God's act of election is the act of becoming human without ceasing to be God in order to take on and defeat humanity's sin from all eternity by enduring reprobation in the place of all humankind for the sake of the election of all in Christ. This is the act in and by which the objective reality of God's transcendent being is mediated and revealed to sinners.

Now, without the infralapsarian aspect of this notion of God's being-in-act (that is, if God's act of election does not presuppose humanity's sin), Barth's actualism would be void of its central soteriological-epistemological import. The reason is self-evident: Barth's critically realistic theology is not about a paradise where creatures are immediate to God, but finds it setting in a world plagued by the plight of sin and separation from God; thus he cannot claim direct knowledge of God's being *ad intra*. By speaking of God as being-in-act, he begins not with the immanent Trinity, but with the particular person and work of Christ as God's act of election, which mediates and reveals God to sinners, and since this act of election is to take care of the problem of sin, it carries a deeply infralapsarian aspect and is identified as the *Aufhebung* of God's No to sin rather than "balanced equilibrium." It is this infralapsarian aspect of Barth's thinking that gives to his mature actualism its soteriological-epistemological import in the setting of a critically realistic theology.

The same may also be said about Barth's Christocentric particularism. As I just pointed out in the last paragraph, when he discusses God's being-in-act

---

[96]One of the most important works in this area of Barth studies in recent years is Paul Nimmo, *Being in Action: The Theological Shape of Barth's Ethical Vision* (London: T&T Clark, 2007). See especially 4-12, 110-35 and 161-67.

(without yet using this terminology, of course), he begins with the particular person and work of Christ. The reason is simple: he is doing theology in the setting of a critical realism in which humankind is found in the plight of sin and separation from God, and for him, there is nowhere else to begin than the person and work of Christ, since the incarnation—identified with election in Christ—is God's act of overcoming humanity's plight. This again reflects an infralapsarian Christology married with a basically infralapsarian doctrine of election.

Finally, Barth's christological-objectivist soteriology is also predicated on the infralapsarian aspect of his complex and dialectical treatment of the lapsarian problem. The "purification" of his doctrine from the classical Reformed understanding of the *decretum absolutum* implies that human faith and unbelief by no means reflect divine election and reprobation as two sides of a decree standing in balanced equilibrium. For Barth the temporal realities of faith and unbelief cannot alter the objective reality of the eternal election of all in Christ.

Moreover, the soteriological character of Barth's christological objectivism also reflects the infralapsarian aspect of his formulation of God's gracious election. He does not speak of the objective reality accomplished in Christ through election-incarnation as unfallen creatures' union with God. Rather, for Barth, the objective reality eternally accomplished in Christ is the mediation between God and fallen humankind. The incarnation was made necessary by God's decision to negate humanity's sin—it is for our salvation (this is the basic claim of infralapsarian Christology); the object of election is sinful humanity (this is the basic conviction of predestinarian infralapsarianism). It is this infralapsarian aspect in both Barth's Christology and doctrine of election that gives to his mature christological objectivism its central soteriological character. In the next chapter we shall see how he develops his lapsarian thinking into maturity in *CD* II/2.

7

CD II/2 (1939–1942)

Christ as Electing God and Elected Human—Lapsarianism "Purified"

This chapter looks into the lapsarian thinking underlying *CD* II/2 (begun in the winter semester of 1939/1940, and published in 1942), a half-volume in which Barth develops his Christocentrism from *Gottes Gnadenwahl* (1936) into maturity. In the last chapter we saw that the Christology of *Gottes Gnadenwahl* is expressed in basically infralapsarian terms while the doctrine of election is a robust and dialectical combination of supra- and infralapsarianism. When we come to volume two of the *Church Dogmatics*, however, we see that the lapsarian position of Barth's Christology becomes much more complex. In *CD* II/1 (published in 1940), his discussion of God's love and freedom in terms of God's being-in-act employs deeply supralapsarian christological expressions, which are qualified by definitively infralapsarian statements in II/2.

Recall that predestinarian supralapsarianism is the position that the object of election-reprobation is God's eternal conception of unfallen humanity (*homo labilis* or *homo nondum lapsus*), while the infralapsarian thesis is that the object of double predestination is God's eternal conception of fallen humanity (*homo lapsus*). When applied to Christology, supralapsarianism holds that God's will to become incarnate logically precedes God's will to deal with humanity's sin, and infralapsarianism asserts that God's decision to become incarnate proceeds from God's consideration of sin.

In the previous chapter we looked into how Barth's struggles with the lapsarian problem led to some decisively new understandings of election-in-Christ in *Gottes Gnadenwahl*. The task of this chapter is to give an exposition of Barth's full-fledged Christocentric doctrine of election in *CD* II/2 to explore how he developed his new understandings into maturity from 1936 to 1942, also on the basis of his treatment of the lapsarian problem.

CD II/2: Jesus Christ as Electing God and Elected Human

Volume two of the *Church Dogmatics* is titled *The Doctrine of God*, with its second half-volume (*CD* II/2) comprising two chapters, "The Election of God" and "The Command of God." In the introductory summary to §32, "The Problem of a Correct Doctrine of the Election of Grace," found at the very outset of *CD* II/2, Barth states:

> The doctrine of election is the sum of the Gospel because of all words that can be said or heard it is the best: that God elects man; that God is for man too the One who loves in freedom. It is grounded in the knowledge of Jesus Christ because He is both the electing God and elected man in One. It is part of the doctrine of God because originally God's election of man is a predestination not merely of man but of Himself.[1]

It is not an exaggeration on Barth's part to call the doctrine of election "the sum of the Gospel," for all of his subsequent doctrinal writings are predicated on his christological understanding of election (though he offers a highly historical-actualistic revision thereof in *CD* IV/1).

Barth's identification of Jesus Christ as both electing God and elected human is of central importance to *CD* II/2. As we saw in the last chapter, this idea was only latent in the 1936 *Gottes Gnadenwahl*. It is in *CD* II/2 that it is fully developed: Jesus Christ in both his deity and humanity as at once electing God and elected human is the beginning of all God's ways and works. As stated in the quotation above, the ontological identification of the incarnate Christ as electing God and elected human carries epistemological significance: the doctrine of election is "grounded in the knowledge of Jesus Christ because He is both the electing God and elected man in One."

---

[1] *KD* II/2, 1; ET 3.

In *Gottes Gnadenwahl* Barth's focus was on the knowledge of humanity's election in Jesus Christ; in *CD* II/2 the emphasis is on the knowledge not only of election as an act of God but also of Jesus Christ as both God's act and being, that is, as both God's election and the electing God. In other words, since the incarnate one, who is the electing decree of God, is himself the electing God, to know Jesus is to know the God who elects. Thus in *CD* II/2 Barth describes God's being as epistemologically accessible. Of course the idea of God's being-in-act was already developed in *Gottes Gnadenwahl* (as I argued in chapter six), but it is in *CD* II/1 that Barth uses the precise terminology and gives a full exposition of this actualism, as it has often been called, and in II/2 that Barth begins to emphasize that to know Christ is to know God's gracious election and the graciously electing God.

Furthermore, Christ the electing God is knowable to humankind because he is also the elected human. More concretely, as Barth puts it in the quotation above, Christ is "electing God and elected man *in One*." Here Barth is intimating what might be called a "basically Chalcedonian" understanding of humanity's participation in Christ: human beings are united to Christ on the basis of their consubstantiality with Christ.[2] Meanwhile Christ is truly and fully God who became truly and fully human without ceasing to be truly and fully God. Thus to know Christ is to know God, and to participate in Christ is to share in God's election of the human Jesus Christ.

Yet, as we saw in the quotation above, "God's election of man is a predestination not merely of man but of Himself." Expressions like this in Barth's later writings have spurred much debate in recent years, which I shall address in chapter eight. Suffice it now to say that I see in Barth a consistent

---

[2]See George Hunsinger, "Karl Barth's Christology: Its Basically Chalcedonian Character," in *Disruptive Grace: Studies in the Theology of Karl Barth* (Grand Rapids: Eerdmans, 2000). There are debates as to how "Chalcedonian" Barth's Christology is. See Bruce McCormack, "Karl Barth's Historicized Christology: Just How 'Chalcedonian' Is it?," in *Orthodox and Modern: Studies in the Theology of Karl Barth* (Grand Rapids: Baker Academic, 2008). Also see Paul Nimmo, "Karl Barth and the *Concursus Dei*—A Chalcedonianism Too Far?" *International Journal of Systematic Theology* 9 (2007): 58-72. Nimmo cautions on historical, material and methodological grounds that the term "Chalcedonian" as a description of Barth's theology should not be used without discretion. However, Hunsinger points out that "Barth saw the Chalcedonian Definition as a regulative framework, not as a substantive position," and with convincing textual evidence Hunsinger shows that Barth may be rightly described as Chalcedonian. See George Hunsinger, *Evangelical, Catholic, and Reformed: Doctrinal Essays on Barth and Related Themes* (Grand Rapids: Eerdmans, 2015), 160. I shall argue in chap. 8 that Barth in fact retains aspects of classical substantialism in his actualism.

concern to maintain the perfect correspondence between God's act and being. In the act of election God has chosen to *become* human, but what becomes of the life of the triune God in the act of election does not alter what God necessarily and unchangeably *is* in God's eternal trinitarian act *ad intra*. It must be remembered that Barth describes God as being-*in*-act rather than being-*as*-act (see chapters six and eight).

It is with the understanding that God became human without ceasing to be God that Barth writes in the quotation above, "God is for man *too* the One who loves in freedom." God in Godself is the *I am that I am* who *loves* in the perfect freedom of God's trinitarian acts *ad intra*, and God *pro nobis*, the God who elects humankind in Christ, is the very same God who loves in perfect freedom.

Since Barth's treatment of God's love and freedom is important for understanding the complexity of the lapsarianism underlying his formulation of God's being in the act of election, I will offer a discussion of it before proceeding to an exposition of Barth's doctrine of election itself.

From* CD II/1 *to* II/2: *God's love—freedom or caprice? The theme of God's love and freedom in the act of election is found at the very beginning of *CD* II/2, §32. This is an application of Barth's notion of "the being of God as the One who loves in freedom" (*CD* II/1, §28) to the doctrine of election. More precisely, this central notion in Barth's doctrine of God is the preliminary assumption in Barth's treatment of election.

On one hand, God is love: love is intrinsic to God's very being, or, better put, God's being is always in the act of love—we know this from the love of God in Christ. On the other hand, God is free, and God loves in complete freedom—we know this from the divine sovereignty that Christ manifests even in his death. The question, then, is this: How are we to think after (*nach-denken*) the fact that love is intrinsic to God's being while God's love is completely free?

First, negatively speaking, Barth's notion of divine freedom is that of aseity and unconditionedness—though, as we shall see anon, Barth, on the supposition of this view of divine aseity and unconditionedness, qualifies this very notion in a significant way in light of Jesus Christ: "He [God] ordains that He should not be entirely self-sufficient as He might be."[3] Before

---

[3] *KD* II/2, 9; ET 10.

going there, however, we must understand the supposition of divine aseity and unconditionedness. Barth writes in *CD* II/1: "He is the same even in Himself, even before and after and over His works, and without them. They are bound to Him, but He is not bound to them. They are nothing without Him. But He is who He is without them."[4] Timothy Bradshaw explains: "The free God is self-grounded and unconstrained God. This means that God is free in that he is unconditioned, which can be seen as a freedom defined by absence of another conditioning factor."[5] In describing God's love as free in this sense, Barth's implicit presupposition is trinitarian: God's being is eternally in the act of the loving fellowship of the Father, Son and Holy Spirit.

Now, love is an act toward an object. If God subsisted in one hypostasis, then to say that God's being is eternally in the act of love would imply that there is an object of divine love that is not God. This would mean that the predication "God is love" can be true only insofar as this object of divine love exists, be it creation, humankind, the world, a second god or what not: in other words, God would be love not in and of Godself, but only in relation to the object that is not God. If that were so—if God subsisted in only one hypostasis—the aseity of God could not be maintained.

For Barth the freedom of God's love first means the aseity and utter independence of the God whose being is love: God is love regardless of whether the object of divine love exists or not. To think after the truth of the freedom of God's love, then, is to think after the truth of the triune God: God is love in and of Godself as God's being is eternally in the act of loving communion of Father, Son and Holy Spirit. Thus Barth in *CD* II/1:

> We have seen that the freedom of God, as His freedom in Himself, His primary absoluteness, has its truth and reality in the inner Trinitarian life of the Father with the Son by the Holy Spirit. It is here, and especially in the divine mode as the Son who is the "image of the invisible God" (Col. 1:15), in God Himself, that the divine freedom in its aspect of communion with the other, i.e., the secondary absoluteness of God, has its original truth. . . . God Himself becomes Another in the person of His Son. The existence of the world is not

---

[4]*KD* II/1, 291; ET 260.
[5]Timothy Bradshaw, "Karl Barth on the Trinity: A Family Resemblance," *Scottish Journal of Theology* 39 (1986): 146.

needed in order that there should be otherness for Him. Before all worlds, in His Son He has otherness in Himself from eternity to eternity.[6]

Therefore, while Barth affirms "positively" in *CD* II/2 that "in the free decision of His love, God is God in the very fact and in such a way, that He does stand in this relation, in a definite relationship with the other [viz., the object of divine love that is not God]," he sets forth the axiomatic predication: "God is love. But He is also perfect freedom. Even if there were no such relationship [between God and the other], *even if there were no other outside of Him, He would still be love.*"[7]

In other words, for Barth, God's freedom first entails God's aseity and thus utter independence. As Bradshaw puts it, "Barth rejects definitely any suggestion that the world is 'needed in order that there should be otherness for Him' [*CD* II/1, 137]. Rather: 'Before all worlds, in His Son, He has otherness in Himself from eternity to eternity [ibid.]. The inner being or history of God is utter freedom complemented, in supreme harmony, by the 'foil' of the Son's otherness."[8] This is the first sense in which Barth describes God's love as free.[9]

Second, dialectically, in addition to (but not in denial of) Barth's own claim of divine freedom as aseity and unconditionedness, he states that God's love is free in the sense that God's act of entering into loving covenant with the creature is completely sovereign. In fact, in his typically antimetaphysical manner, Barth insists that while it is necessary to posit the aseity and unconditionedness of God in Godself, it would be quite meaningless and speculative, even idolatrous, to talk about what God's freedom might have been like apart from God's covenantal relation with us.

Therefore, after asserting God's freedom as aseity and unconditionedness in *CD* II/1, Barth immediately qualifies: "In the light of what He is in His works it is no longer an open question what He is in Himself. In Himself He

---

[6]*KD* II/1, 357; ET 317.
[7]*KD* II/2, 4; ET 6 (emphasis added).
[8]Bradshaw, "Barth on the Trinity," 148.
[9]On this point I do not entirely agree with Paul Jones, who argues that this understanding of the self-sufficiency of the immanent Trinity applies only to *CD* I, but in *CD* II "a clean distinction between God's immanent existence qua Son and God's economic activity qua Son no longer holds." See Paul Jones, *The Humanity of Christ: Christology in Karl Barth's Church Dogmatics* (London: Continuum, 2008), 64-65.

cannot, perhaps, be someone or something quite other, or perhaps nothing at all. But in His works He is Himself revealed as the One He is."[10]

This carries two implications: first, God's freedom is not even constrained by aseity and independence, but God is free to bind Godself to covenant with the creature without altering God's own necessary properties; second, even in this covenant God remains utterly free. Bradshaw explains:

> Barth's view is that God's freedom is not conditioned even by this freedom from any constraining or correlating factor.... Divine free transcendence is not only sheer unconditionedness..., "but furthermore and supremely in the fact that without sacrificing His distinction and freedom, but in the exercise of them, He enters into and faithfully maintains communion with this reality other than Himself" [CD II/1, 103]. God's love, his overflowing generosity, and God's freedom, a freedom which transcends simply freedom from being conditioned, are the two main *foci* in Barth's vision of God.[11]

Thus Barth in *CD* II/2:

> To be truly Christian, the doctrine of God must... [make] the Subject known as One which in virtue of its innermost being, willing and nature does not stand outside all relationships, but stands in a definite relationship *ad extra* to another. It is not as though the object of this relationship... constitutes a part of the reality of God outside of God.... It is not as though God is forced into this relationship.... It is not as though He is in any way constrained or compelled by this other.[12]

This passage shows that for Barth God's election to enter into loving covenant with humankind in Christ is not an absolutely necessary act (even though it was made necessary by God's free decision) on God's part, nor does Barth think of God's act of election-incarnation as constituting the basis of God's being *ad intra* in such a way that election logically precedes God's triunity. Rather, God's covenantal love perfectly corresponds to the intratrinitarian love between Father, Son and Holy Spirit, and this love draws the creature into union with God in Christ. As Bradshaw puts it, "God the Trinity not only corresponds with himself *ad extra* in the event of

---

[10] KD II/1, 291; ET 260.
[11] Bradshaw, "Barth on the Trinity," 146.
[12] KD II/2, 4; ET 5-6.

revelation and the knowledge of God, but also establishes man in participation with God thereby. For Barth the divine reality and self-knowledge exist as the primary entity and, by virtue of their movement into the creaturely sphere, the covenant union of God with man occurs."[13]

For Barth, God's entry into covenantal union with the creature is irrevocable and determinative of God's being *pro nobis*.

> Jesus Christ is the decision of God in favour of this attitude or relation. He is Himself the relation. It is a relation *ad extra*, undoubtedly; for both the man and the people represented in Him are creatures and not God. But it is a relation which is irrevocable, so that once God has willed to enter into it, and has in fact entered into it, He could not be God without it. It is a relation in which God is self-determined, so that the determination belongs no less to Him than all that He is in and for Himself.[14]

Hunsinger explains that Barth draws a distinction between the *constitution* of God's being and God's self-*determination*: God's eternal trinitarian acts *ad intra* constitute God's triune being, while divine self-determination is an act of God's will that presupposes God's being.[15] God eternally determines to be *pro nobis* in Christ, and this eternal decision "presupposes the creation and fall of the world" (this is the infralapsarian thesis!): it is a completely free act on God's part, though it corresponds perfectly to God's being.[16] For Barth, the act of God's will does not ontologically precede or supersede God's being, but the two are equally basic and imply each other: God is being-in-act.

In a word, divine self-determination logically presupposes God's triune being-in-act. Therefore, when Barth states in the block quote above that God "could not be God without" the covenant relationship, he means that God could not choose to contradict or revoke what God has elected: one of Barth's concerns in *CD* II/2 is to avoid portraying divine predestination as the "caprice of a tyrant."[17]

---

[13]Timothy Bradshaw, "Trinity and Ontology: A Comparative Study of the Theologies of Karl Barth and Wolfhart Pannenberg" (PhD diss., University of Nottingham, 1984), 9.
[14]*KD* II/2, 6; ET 7.
[15]George Hunsinger, "Election and the Trinity: Twenty-Five Theses on the Theology of Karl Barth," *Modern Theology* 24 (2008): 181.
[16]Ibid., 193.
[17]*KD* II/2, 45; ET 43. Kevin Hector rightly recognizes God's act of election as "volitionally neces-

This concern is already explicit in *CD* II/1, where Barth emphasizes that "there is no caprice about the freedom of God."[18] On the basis of his understanding of God as being-in-act, which he sets forth at the very outset of §28, he states that God's fellowship with us perfectly corresponds to the inner fellowship of the triune God.

> As and before God seeks and creates fellowship with us, He wills and completes this fellowship in Himself. In Himself He does not will to exist for Himself, to exist alone. On the contrary, He is Father, Son and Holy Spirit and therefore alive in His unique being with and for and in another. The unbroken unity of His being, knowledge and will is at the same time an act of deliberation, decision and intercourse. He does not exist in solitude but in fellowship. Therefore what He seeks and creates between Himself and us is in fact nothing else but what He wills and completes and therefore is in Himself.[19]

For this reason the God who loves necessarily within God's inner triunity is the very God who loves the world in utter freedom.

> God's loving is necessary, for it is the being, the essence and the nature of God. But for this very reason it is also free from every necessity in respect of its object. God loves us, and loves the world, in accordance with His revelation. But He loves us and the world as He who would still be One who loves without us and without the world; as He, therefore, who needs no other to form the prior ground of His existence as the One who loves and as God. Certainly He is who He is wholly in His revelation, in His loving-kindness, and therefore in His love for us.[20]

In a consistent effort to maintain both the constancy and freedom of God's love, Barth writes in *CD* II/2,

> The fact that God makes this movement, the institution of the covenant, the primal decision "in Jesus Christ," which is the basis and goal of all His works—that is grace. Speaking generally, it is the demonstration, the overflowing of *the*

---

sary." However, in defending McCormack's take on election and Trinity in Barth, Hector wrongly takes Barth's epistemological refusal to regress to a *Logos asarkos* logically prior to election to be an ontological denial of the logical priority of divine triunity. I will address this debate in chap. 8. See Hector, "Immutability, Necessity and Triunity: Towards a Resolution of the Trinity and Election Controversy," *Scottish Journal of Theology* 65 (2012): 64-81.

[18]*KD* II/1, 358; ET 318.
[19]Ibid., 309; ET 275.
[20]Ibid., 315; ET 280.

love which is the being of God, that He who is *entirely self-sufficient*, who even within Himself cannot know isolation, *willed* even in all His divine glory to share His life with another, and to have that other as the witness of His glory.[21]

In this passage, when Barth comments that God "within Himself cannot know isolation," he is implying that God is eternally and immutably triune. God is love in and of Godself: God's love is free in the sense of the utter aseity of the God whose being is the intratrinitarian act of love—"the love which is the being of God." Meanwhile, God "willed . . . to share His life with another": it was God's free decision to enter into loving covenant with humankind.

God's act of entering into this loving relationship with humankind in Christ is completely free on God's part. Yet God's will corresponds perfectly to God's being, which is "entirely self-sufficient" just as it is in the intratrinitarian act of love. Precisely because election corresponds perfectly to God's being-in-act *ad intra*, it is a decision that God does not revoke. For this reason, God "cannot be God without" the loving relationship into which God has decided to enter.[22]

Paul Nimmo offers an incisive exposition—notwithstanding the questionable "actualistic ontology" he deduces from it—of these relations of correspondences and distinctions between God's love *ad intra* and the covenantal relationship that God has elected in Christ.

> For Barth, the covenant relationship effected and revealed in Jesus Christ repeats for God "*ad extra* a relationship proper to Himself in His inner divine essence" [*CD* III/2, 220]. This means that the relationship between God and the true human revealed in Jesus Christ is analogous to the prior intra-Trinitarian relationship of God the Father to God the Son. These two relationships are analogous not in terms of any correspondence of similarity of being, an *analogia entis*, but in terms of what Barth calls "an *analogia relationis*" [ibid.]. Jüngel asserts that this *analogia relationis* is "a correspondence of relationships which are constituted by . . . the 'Yes' of the free love of God, which the Trinitarian God speaks to Godself and which God then also speaks to God's creature, thereby creating its correspondence."[23]

---

[21]*KD* II/2, 9; ET 10 (emphasis added).
[22]Ibid., 5; ET 7.
[23]Paul Nimmo, *Being in Action: The Theological Shape of Barth's Ethical Vision* (London: T&T Clark, 2007), 89. See Eberhard Jüngel, *Barth-Studien* (Gütersloh: Mohn, 1982), 221-22.

This understanding of the *analogia relationis* implies that the triune God freely elected to enter into loving covenant with humankind, and it is by this free decision that God "could not be God without" the covenant, for God's freedom is not the caprice of a tyrant, but the "overflowing" of the constancy of the unchanging "love which is the being of God" (see preceding quotations).

Actualism and lapsarianism. Underlying the foregoing discussions about Barth's notion of the love and freedom of God as being-in-act is a complex and dialectical treatment of the lapsarian problem in both Christology and the doctrine of election. In *CD* II/1, §28, Barth's treatment of the incarnation as the central and defining act of God's love *ad extra* does not involve extensive discussions of divine consideration of sin. It would thus seem that in §28 Barth sets forth a view of the incarnation resonating with supralapsarian Christology.

He first lays down his understanding of God's freedom in relation to creation, and of creation as a natural expression *ad extra* of God's being: "Before all worlds, in His Son He has otherness in Himself from eternity to eternity. But because this is so, the creation and preservation of the world, and relationship and fellowship with it, realised as they are in perfect freedom, without compulsion or necessity, do not signify an alien or contradictory expression of God's being, but a natural, the natural expression of it *ad extra*."[24] On this basis he immediately proceeds to claim,

> The world is, because and as the Son of God is. . . . When we now learn that, over and beyond all this, it is said of the same Son of God: σὰρξ ἐγένετο (Jn. 1¹⁴), that therefore, besides being Creator, He became creature, it is clear that in this singular and supreme relationship and fellowship between God and the world realised in the incarnation we have the quintessence of all possible relationship and fellowship generally and as such, and that in the transcendent freedom of God thus expressed we see the archetype and the norm of all the possible ways in which He expresses His freedom in this relationship and fellowship.[25]

In other words, resonating with supralapsarian Christology, Barth is stating here that God's purpose in becoming incarnate is to enter into fellowship

---

[24] *KD* II/1, 357; ET 317.
[25] Ibid.

with the creature. On the surface this would seem to imply that Barth either jettisoned the basically infralapsarian view of the incarnation from *GD* to *Gottes Gnadenwahl* in favor of a supralapsarian outlook, or that his Christology in the second volume of *CD* is complexified by an incoherent admixture of competing lapsarian positions.

The fact, however, is that Barth gives to this supralapsarian claim an infralapsarian qualification, and the result is a dialectical combination of supra- and infralapsarian patterns of thinking. Barth writes: "Creation itself . . . is already a seeking and creating of fellowship. This seeking and creating is heightened in the work of revelation itself, which is not so much a *continuation* of creation as its *supersession*, and is identical with the reconciliation of sinful man in the incarnation, death and resurrection of the Son of God."[26]

In other words, with supralapsarian overtones Barth has claimed that the incarnation is for the purpose of God's will to seek and create fellowship with the creature, but he gives to this claim an infralapsarian qualification: this seeking and creating of fellowship already began with creation, and the incarnation, which is for the "reconciliation of sinful man," is not a *continuation* but a *supersession* of the work of creation. That is to say, this qualification modifies Barth's supralapsarian claim in such a way that it approaches infralapsarianism: God's purpose in the incarnation is to seek and create fellowship with—mark well—the *sinful* creature.

This dialectical lapsarian scheme would shed light on Barth's explanation of the actualistic relation between God and the fallen creature in §28: "Everything beside and outside Him [the triune God] . . . exists only on the basis of His gracious creation and providence, conditioned by His gracious reconciliation of the sinner, and with a view to His future redemption. And it can be known only by God's Word and revelation."[27]

Christ as election. The foregoing discussions have focused on *CD* §28 and §32, which address prolegomenal issues concerning the doctrine of election,

---

[26]Ibid., 307; ET 274 (emphasis added). This is not a word-by-word translation, but is true to the original text: *Es potenziert sich aber dieses Suchen und Schaffen in dem die Schöpfung nicht sowohl fortsetzenden als überbietenden Werk der Offenbarung selber: identisch mit der Versöhnung des sündigen Menschen in der Fleischwerdung, im Tode und in der Auferstehung des Sohnes Gottes.* The verb *überbieten* means "to surpass," with the connotation of "to eliminate" (as in a competition), and is rendered here brilliantly as "supersession."

[27]Ibid., 305; ET 272.

while §33, titled "The Election of Jesus Christ," sets forth the heart of the doctrine, comprising two sections: "Jesus Christ, Electing and Elected" and "The Eternal Will of God in the Election of Jesus Christ."

Before stating the radical idea of Jesus Christ as electing God and elected human in one, Barth first states the central thesis of §33, that election is *in* Christ. As mentioned earlier, in *CD* II/2 Barth consistently stresses that human beings can know no other God than the God who has entered into loving covenant with humankind. Concretely speaking, Christ *is* this covenant. Otto Weber calls this the "ground-laying thesis" of Barth's doctrine of election, of which Weber offers the following summary: "When we talk about God's election, we are not talking about some dark secret beside, behind or above the revealed God, but rather we gaze exclusively 'upon the name Jesus Christ and the existence and history [*Geschichte*] of the people actualized [*verwirklichte*] in Him, whereof the beginning and end are determined in the mystery of His name."[28] Methodologically, this implies that Barth's theology is antimetaphysical and Christocentric: "We do not talk about an abstract God, but about God in Christ."[29]

Insisting that predestination must be understood christologically, Barth identifies Christ as "Electing and Elected" just as he is very God and very human.[30] At the beginning of §33 Barth expounds on this notion: "Between God and man there stands the person of Jesus Christ, Himself God and Himself man, and so mediating between the two."[31] Yet before explaining that Christ is at once "Electing" and "Elected," Barth first identifies Christ as election—God's absolute decree.

> He [Christ] is the decree of God behind and above which there can be no earlier or higher decree and beside which there can be no other, since all others serve only the fulfilment of this decree. . . . He is the election of God before which and without which and beside which God cannot make any other choices. Before Him and without Him and beside Him God does not, then, elect or will anything.[32]

---

[28]Otto Weber, *Karl Barths Kirchliche Dogmatik: Ein einführender Bericht* (Neukirchen-Vluyn: Neukirchener Verlag, 1975), 69 (translation mine).
[29]Ibid., 70 (translation mine).
[30]*KD* II/2, §33.
[31]Ibid., 101; ET 94.
[32]Ibid.

This brings us back to Barth's notion of the freedom of God's love. As noted earlier, God's free decision to enter into loving covenant with humankind in Christ is not the "caprice of a tyrant." Rather, it is an immutable decree that binds God to the covenant in such a way that "once God has willed to enter into [covenant relationship with humankind], and has in fact entered into it, He could not be God without it."[33]

Now Barth is restating the same thesis in more concretely christological terms: Drawing on Chalcedon, Barth insists that Christ's deity and humanity are united inseparably. Therefore Barth speaks of Christ as God's absolute decree "before which and without which and beside which God cannot make any other choices." In other words, God's eternal decision to become incarnate determine God's being in such a way that God could no longer be without human agency, and that God could no longer make any decision apart from Christ the God-man proleptically present in pretemporal eternity by virtue of divine election to be the beginning of all God's ways and works.

Barth's innovative reappropriation of Chalcedon in identifying Christ as God's immutable decree is a maneuver to engage with the notion of *decretum absolutum* in Reformed orthodoxy. Recall that in Reformed orthodoxy the *decretum absolutum Dei*—"absolute decree of God"—is an immutable decision whereby God inflexibly divides humankind into two masses for election and reprobation from all eternity. Barth agrees with Reformed orthodoxy that God's decree of election is immutable once it has been issued. However, he insists that election must not be understood abstractly apart from Christ. Rather, election is immutable because Christ *is* God's very decree of election.

Furthermore, when Barth states that "Jesus Christ is Himself the divine election of grace," he means to say that God's ways and works *ad extra* in the person of Christ correspond perfectly to God's inward being: "He, Jesus Christ, is the free grace of God, provided that this *not only* remains identical with the inward and eternal being of God, but is active in the ways and works *ad extra* of God."[34]

---

[33]Ibid., 6; ET 7.
[34]Ibid., 102. *Er, Jesus Christus, ist die freie Gnade Gottes, sofern diese* nicht nur *mit Gottes innerem, ewigem Wesen identisch bleibt, sondern in Gottes Wegen und Werken nach außen kräftig ist* (translation mine). Original translation is on ET 95 (emphasis added).

Here Barth clearly affirms that in operating *ad extra* Christ remains identical with the eternal God in Godself, positing God's immanent existence qua Son, "the inward and eternal being of God." In becoming human, Christ does not cease to be God—for Barth this is the central meaning of the statement that "Jesus Christ is Himself the divine election of grace."

Christ as electing God and elected human. Having thus expounded on the meaning of the statement that Jesus Christ is God's decree of election, Barth proceeds to identify Christ as electing God and elected human. First, as God's Son, Christ is the electing God; as Son of Man, Christ is the elected human in whom all humankind is elected. What is groundbreaking in Barth's identification of Jesus Christ as electing God is that the incarnate God-man, and not just the *Logos asarkos*, is the beginning of all God's ways and works from and to all eternity. This radical idea, which *Gottes Gnadenwahl* only anticipates, has led a group of scholars to deduce elaborate ontologies in which election-incarnation constitutes God's triune being. As much as this might construe "a 'thoroughly modern Barth' without the supposed encumbrances of 'classical metaphysics' and 'substance ontology,'" Hunsinger reminds us that "only the [rationalistically] deduced Barth teaches that there is no Trinity prior to election."[35]

Note that in speaking of Christ as "Electing and Elected," a basically Chalcedonian view of Christ's deity and humanity undergirds Barth's doctrine of election: "The name of Jesus Christ has within itself the double reference: the One called by this name is both *very God and very man*. Thus the simplest form of the dogma may be divided at once into the two assertions that Jesus Christ is the electing God, and that He is also elected man."[36]

Hunsinger demonstrates with the idea of *prolepsis* what is radical about the statement that Christ is electing God: "in the mind of God the earthly Jesus is already present as such to the eternal Son and assumed into hypostatic union with him in pretemporal eternity."[37] It is by virtue of God's election, not of the actualization of existence, that Jesus is present at the

---

[35] George Hunsinger, *Reading Barth with Charity: A Hermeneutical Proposal* (Grand Rapids: Baker Academic, 2015), 79.
[36] *KD* II/2, 110; ET 103 (emphasis added).
[37] Hunsinger, *Reading Barth with Charity*, 63.

beginning of all God's ways and works: "In and through the decision of the electing Son, Jesus is present before he exists as 'the man who was in the beginning with God.'"[38]

Barth's basically Chalcedonian rendition of the doctrine of election entails an *abiding distinction* between Christ's two natures and thus the subject and object of election in the person of Christ. Thus Barth comments that Christ constitutes "God's dealings with the reality which is *distinct* from Himself."[39] Properly speaking, Jesus of Nazareth participates in the Son's eternal act of election only by virtue of the hypostatic union and by virtue of his proleptic presence in eternity through this act.

Likewise, Hunsinger observes that in *CD* II/2, "Jesus Christ is also present by virtue of God's eternal will, according to which he is the object of pretemporal election."[40] What is radical about the idea that Christ is elected human is that the Son of God, and not merely the human Jesus, is the object of election.

However, Barth is very careful to state that "as the Son of the Father He has no need of any special election."[41] Here, again, we see that Barth posits the immanent Trinity and the Son *asarkos* as a logical presupposition of election and incarnation: the preincarnate Son in Godself has no need of any special election, and the election of the Son presupposes the *assumptio* of human agency.

Now, since Christ's deity and humanity are inseparably united in one divine person, whatever may be said about the one can also be said about the other in a derivative sense. It is in this derivative sense that the Son is elected by the Father in eternity. Barth states: "Because as the Son of the Father He has no need of any election, we must add at once that He is the Son of God elected *in His oneness with man*."[42]

Note here that Barth's understanding of the election of Christ intimates an infralapsarian understanding of the logical relations between election and creation, even though the fall is not yet mentioned: if election presupposes Christ's union with the creature, then, as Hunsinger puts it, "[election] presupposes the creation . . . of the world"—recall that this is the infra-

---

[38]Ibid.
[39]*KD* II/2, 109; ET 102 (emphasis added).
[40]Hunsinger, *Reading Barth with Charity*, 63.
[41]Ibid., 110; ET 103 (emphasis added).
[42]Ibid.

lapsarian view against the supralapsarian understanding that election does *not* presuppose God's decree of creation.[43]

These logical relations among the Trinity, election and the incarnation bring us back to the theme of God's freedom in the act of election: the eternal election of the Son, unlike God's inner-trinitarian act of the eternal generation of the Son, is God's decision that God could have chosen otherwise, though once God has made this decision, "God could not be God" without it. In other words, for Barth, God's freedom in election is implicit in the abiding distinction between God and the reality that is not God: "It is as God's election that we must understand the Word and decree and beginning of God over against the reality which is *distinct* from Himself. When we say this, we say that in His decision all God's doings [*Tun*], both 'inward' and 'outward,' rest upon His freedom."[44]

As a note of explanation, in the earlier volumes of the *Church Dogmatics*, including II/2, Barth distinguishes between God's work (*Werk*), doing (*Tun*) and act (*Tat*). When he uses the words *Werk* or *Tun*, he never refers to God's trinitarian *opera ad intra*, to which he usually designates the word *Tat*. *Werk* usually refers to God's dealings with the actually existent reality that is not God, such as the works of creation and reconciliation, but excludes the eternal act of election. By contrast, the word *Tat* can refer to the inner-trinitarian acts of God, the eternal act of election or the historical acts of reconciliation, and it is with this word that Barth speaks of God's being-in-act (*Sein in der Tat*). The word *Tun* is often used synonymously with *Tat*, but does not cover the trinitarian *opera ad intra*. Therefore, in the quote above, by "God's doings, both 'inward' and 'outward,'" Barth is referring to the eternal actuality of election and the historical actuality of God's works of reconciliation. He is saying that God's eternal election, just as God's works of reconciliation in the here and now, rests completely on God's free decision, since God's dealings with the reality that is distinct from God are always free on God's part.

Meanwhile, though there is an abiding distinction between God's eternal act of election and the historical actuality of God's works of reconciliation, Barth also stresses the perfect correspondence between them.

---

[43]Hunsinger, "Election and the Trinity," 193.
[44]*KD* II/2, 107; ET 99 (revised).

> For these are two separate things: the Son of God in His oneness with the Son of Man, as foreordained from all eternity; and the universe which was created, and universal history which was *willed for the sake of this oneness*, in their communion with God, as foreordained from all eternity.... On the one hand, there is God's eternal election of grace, and, on the other, God's creation, reconciliation and redemption *grounded in* that election and ordained *with reference to it*.[45]

Note that Barth says here that the historical actuality of God's works are *grounded in* God's eternal election: the actuality of God's dealings with the historical reality that is distinct from God was "willed for the sake of this oneness," that is, for the sake of the incarnation and thereby the communion of all creatures with God. For this reason Christ's being elected as a creature corresponds perfectly to his divine act of election: "Even the fact that He is elected corresponds as closely as possible to His own electing."[46] This is because from all eternity God willed "the closest possible union" with God's covenant partner.[47] It is in the hypostatic union of the electing and the elected that "the inner glory of God overflows."[48]

Wrestling with lapsarianism: Election as Aufhebung. But why was the hypostatic union in the divine act of election necessary for the sake of the communion between God and creatures? The reason is that for Barth, the divide between God and creation is not merely ontological. The election of Christ is to overcome the gulf of sin and death that separates the world from God, which Barth describes as follows: "Face to face with temptation [man] cannot maintain the goodness of his creation in the divine image and foreordination to the divine likeness.... Exposed to the power of the divine negation, he is guilty of death."[49]

Therefore Barth, in line with the infralapsarian (i.e., the object of election is fallen humanity; election presupposes the fall) aspect of his predestinarian scheme in *Gottes Gnadenwahl*, maintains in *CD* II/2 that election-in-Christ includes within itself reprobation and judgment.

---

[45]Ibid., 111; ET 104.
[46]Ibid., 112; ET 105.
[47]Ibid., 130; ET 121.
[48]Ibid.
[49]Ibid., 131; ET 122-23.

"The Word became flesh" (Jn. 1¹⁴). This formulation of the message of Christmas already includes within itself the message of Good Friday. For "all flesh is as grass." The election of the man Jesus means, then, that a wrath is kindled, a sentence pronounced and finally executed, a rejection actualized. ... From all eternity judgment has been foreseen—even in the overflowing of God's inner glory.⁵⁰

As we saw in chapter five, in *CD* I/2 Barth already stated that Christ took on a "flesh of sin."⁵¹ The "sanctification," "obedience" and "sinlessness" of Jesus is such that "he has judged sin in the flesh, whereby he set the Reconciliation in order, that is, whereby he, *in the place* of a sinner, was struck down under divine judgment and alone implored the grace of God."⁵²

In *CD* II/2, §33, Barth retains this infralapsarian-christological understanding of the incarnation (i.e., the view that God's decision to become incarnate logically follows God's permission of the fall) and applies it to the doctrine of election, stating that "the rejection which all men incurred, the wrath of God under which all men lie, the death which all men must die, God in His love for men transfers from all eternity to Him in whom He loves and elects them, and whom He elects as their head and in their place."⁵³ Barth then maintains that Christ became a sinner as humanity's sin—which is not Christ's own—is transferred to him from all eternity, and Christ alone suffered divine judgment in the place of all humankind; thus there is "other than Him no reprobate."⁵⁴

It should be stressed, however, that this statement needs qualification. In one sense Christ is the only reprobate; in another sense all humans are reprobated in and with Christ: since all humans participate in Christ from all eternity, the reprobation that Christ alone suffered also applies to all humankind that is in him. Moreover, strictly speaking not the Son of God but the human Jesus is the reprobate, and he who is sinless is reprobated for the sin of all others.

Note here that it is "from all eternity" that "the elected man Jesus was foreordained to suffer and to die."⁵⁵ Now, as we saw in chapter six, in *Gottes*

---

⁵⁰Ibid., 131; ET 122.
⁵¹Ibid., 171; ET 155.
⁵²Ibid., 172; ET 157 (translation mine).
⁵³Ibid., 132; ET 123.
⁵⁴Ibid., 389; ET 353 (revised).
⁵⁵Ibid., 131; ET 122.

Gnadenwahl Barth had developed a basically infralapsarian understanding of election as the sublation (*Aufhebung*) of reprobation: reprobation is God's act of negating humanity's sin that negates God, and this negation of negation is sublated in election. (Again, the supralapsarian aspect of this *Aufhebung* process must not be overlooked: in terms of teleological order, humanity's sin serves to occasion the cross and the reprobation of Christ, while this vicarious reprobation serves the purpose of election.) On this view, double predestination presupposes sin.

Barth retains the same understanding in *CD* II/2, in which reprobation is described as God's defeat of humanity's sin that negates God and God's grace. Since Christ was reprobated from eternity in order to be elected from and to all eternity, in *CD* III/2 Barth would describe sin as having been defeated "a priori" (*zum Vornherein*). Sin is thus an "ontological impossibility": when humans choose to sin, they are choosing that which they cannot choose.[56]

Although Barth does not develop this language of impossibility, which he draws from his own *Romans* II, until *CD* III (see chapter eight), the idea is already implicit in *CD* II/2 or even *Gottes Gnadenwahl*, where he speaks of sin as having been eternally rejected in Christ. This does not mean that humans cannot or do not sin. What Barth means is that sin is an absurd and unexplainable reality, or, better put, an ontological nonreality that is nevertheless existentially real. As we shall see in the next chapter, sin, which is a form of "nothingness" (*das Nichtige*), exists only by God's nonwilling—recall that in his mature doctrine of election Barth is emphatic that God's will never contradicts God's being, as God's freedom in election is not caprice.

Once again, when the "ontological impossibility" of sin is understood in light of election as *Aufhebung* of God's No against sin, the teleological nature of Barth's rendition of double predestination becomes apparent. While Barth would agree with Reformed orthodoxy that double predestination is God's immutable decree, he would insist against Reformed orthodoxy that Christ is this very decree, and in Christ we see a definite teleological movement from reprobation to election. For Barth, double predestination

---

[56]*KD* III/2, 174; ET 146. ET renders "from the very first."

is not a balanced equilibrium—it is not the kind of *decretum absolutum* of which Reformed orthodoxy speaks. Rather, the purpose of reprobation is election. Daniel Migliore's words succinctly describe the understanding of double predestination as a process of *Aufhebung*: "The grace of God includes judgment, and the judgment of God serves the purpose of grace."[57]

Precisely because in *CD* II/2 Barth insists on understanding election as divine *Aufhebung* of reprobation, he emphasizes, as he already did in *Gottes Gnadenwahl* (see chapter six), that there is no election without reprobation. That is, for Barth, predestination has to be *double* predestination. What is decisive, however, is not reprobation but election, since election is the purpose of reprobation—this, again, is a supralapsarian aspect of Barth's christological doctrine of election. As Hunsinger puts it, "Although God's grace never occurs without judgment, nor God's judgment without grace, *in* Jesus Christ it is always God's grace, Barth believes, that is decisive."[58]

The preposition "in" is key to understanding this sentence. For Barth, to be *in* Christ "does not simply mean *with* Him. . . . Nor does it only mean *through* Him."[59] Humans are elected *with* and *through* Christ on the basis of their being *in* Christ, that is, their objective participation in Christ from all eternity. This *participatio* is an ontological union with Christ's human nature, and through this union all humans participate also in the being of God, since Christ is very electing God as he is very elected human.

Moreover, recall Barth's "actualism": God is being-in-act. Therefore *participatio Christi* also implies participation in God's act of election, that is, in God's eternal covenantal decision *pro nobis* in Christ. Therefore Barth states that to be *in* Christ "means in His person, in His will, in His own divine choice, in the basic decision of God which He fulfils over against every man."[60] Note here that for Barth, participation in Christ means participating in the very "basic decision of God."

Now, since this basic decision of God is a twofold will constituting an *Aufhebung* that moves from reprobation to election, the participation of all humans in Christ means that the sin and evil that assail them are "sublated

---

[57]Daniel Migliore, *Faith Seeking Understanding* (Grand Rapids: Eerdmans, 2004), 187. This quote is not a commentary on Barth's theology, but it serves well as a summary of Barth's position.
[58]George Hunsinger, *Disruptive Grace*, 142.
[59]*KD* II/2, 125; ET 117.
[60]Ibid.

[*aufgehoben*] in the positive will" of God, so that they are all elected in Christ.[61] Thus understood, not only is the communion between God and humankind the purpose of election as *Aufhebung* of the divine No, which we already saw earlier, but it also serves as the basis whereupon God executes, as it were, the act of election.

Election is God's free and gracious Yes to all humankind. Yet, just as Barth had stated in *Gottes Gnadenwahl*, God's Yes—because it is *Aufhebung*—presupposes God's No. By describing double predestination as a process of *Aufhebung*, Barth wants to emphasize that God's No is not the caprice of a tyrant, but rather a rejection that corresponds to God's unchanging love overflowing from God's immutable inner being for the fallen covenant partner in Christ. It is with this basically infralapsarian—dialectically carrying deeply supralapsarian aspects to be sure—understanding of election-in-Christ that Barth renders reprobation a noncapricious No of God.

Lapsarianism "Purified"

As we saw in chapter two, in a lengthy excursus in *CD* II/2, §33, Barth calls his doctrine of election a "purified Supralapsarianism."[62] Having seen some key features of Barth's formulation of the doctrine in *CD* II/2, we are now ready to consider (1) what the adjectival participle "purified" means and how this is important for understanding Barth, and (2) how Barth's robust and complex appropriation of both supra- and infralapsarian patterns of thought in fact places him closer to the latter.

It might be helpful to briefly revisit the definitions of *supralapsarianism* and *infralapsarianism* before proceeding. According to infralapsarianism, the object of double predestination is fallen humanity (*homo lapsus*). Note that *homo lapsus* is God's eternal conception of humanity guilty of sin, but not actually created and fallen human beings. On the infralapsarian view, then, double predestination logically follows God's eternal decision—but not the historical event—of effectually permitting the fall.

By contrast, supralapsarianism is the position that in God's eternal plan the object of double predestination is God's conception of human individuals as unfallen (*homo labilis* or *homo nondum lapsus*). For supralapsarians,

---
[61] Ibid., 189; ET 175 (revised).
[62] Ibid., 153; ET 140.

double predestination does not presuppose the fallenness of the object of predestination. On the contrary, the divine decree to permit humanity's fall logically precedes double predestination.

Before discussing Barth's "purification" of lapsarianism, which is my main intention in this section, we may briefly revisit a question addressed in chapter two, namely, why Barth calls his doctrine a "purified *supralapsarianism*." As Barth sees it, the infralapsarian *ordo decretorum* (order of decrees) is formulated on the basis of the historical economy of salvation. Moreover, the *ordo* begins with the decrees of creation and permission of the fall rather than election-reprobation, and so the purposes of these two decrees are attributed to an arbitrary will of God apart from election. For Barth, this opens up an avenue for natural theology. (Contra Barth, we have seen in chapter one that the infralapsarian *ordo* is in fact not a teleological order. Rather, the claim that election-reprobation presupposes the fall is meant to convey the conviction that the object of election is *homo lapsus*.) By contrast, the supralapsarian ordering of divine decrees, on Barth's understanding, allows him to seek to know all God's ways and works as finding their beginning in the election of Jesus Christ. This of course is Barth's own reading of the two lapsarian positions, but in reality there is no evidence that the supralapsarian *ordo* in the original Lapsarian Controversy was aimed at avoiding metaphysical speculation.

Now, before proceeding to identify Barth's christological doctrine of election as basically in line with the infralapsarian thesis that the object of God's electing grace is sinful humanity, it is necessary to clarify some crucial points on which he differs from traditional supra- and infralapsarians, and how he "purifies" the classical Reformed doctrine of predestination from certain presuppositions that he considers dangerous.

In the lapsarian excursus of §33, Barth claims that his "purification" is of the supralapsarian doctrine, which he considers, unlike infralapsarianism, worthy of salvage.[63] However, as I showed in chapter two, what Barth calls supralapsarianism is ambiguous, and his definition of it might well be applied to infralapsarianism. Therefore, when Barth claims that he is "purifying" the supralapsarian doctrine from its "dangerous" presuppositions, we may understand him as engaging with Reformed orthodoxy in general,

---

[63]Ibid., 155; ET 143.

supra- and infralapsarianism alike. In what follows, then, I shall speak of Barth's "purification" of the theological starting points of Reformed orthodoxy, rather than of supralapsarianism alone.

Barth outlines four common presuppositions of supra- and infralapsarianism that he finds fatal in Reformed-orthodox formulations of the doctrine of predestination. First, according to Barth, in Reformed orthodoxy "the *obiectum praedestinationis* is the individual abstractly understood." If this is so, says Barth, "then it is most dangerous to seek God's primal and basic purpose in election and reprobation."[64] The keyword here is "abstractly": for Barth, to be "abstractly understood" is to be considered detachedly from Jesus Christ. Regardless of whether Barth is entirely accurate in his understanding and criticism of Reformed orthodoxy, his main intention is to revise the Reformed doctrine in strictly christological terms.

The second "common presupposition" in Reformed orthodoxy Barth names is that "predestination consists in the eternal setting up of that fixed system which governs all temporal reality"; the third is that "within that system election and reprobation are evenly balanced."[65] He criticizes these presuppositions: "It is most dangerous so unconditionally to carry through the thought of the divine sovereignty that the fall and evil are understood as means foreseen and foreordained by God to the attainment of the finally good purpose which He has willed."[66] Barth's concern is that Reformed orthodoxy (as he understands it) does not sufficiently describe reprobation, the fall and evil in terms of God's absolute nonwilling, as something absolutely alien to God's will and being. In this way Barth thinks that Reformed orthodoxy, especially supralapsarianism, is prone to render God the author of evil.

Finally, according to Barth, the Reformed-orthodox understanding of the *decretum absolutum* "is the last possible word concerning the basis of divine predestination."[67] His critique of this presupposition is that "it is most dangerous to think of God as the One who sees and plans and achieves His own glory in the foreordaining of a certain number of individuals irresistibly to heaven and of a certain number of individuals no less irresistibly to hell."[68]

---

[64]Ibid., 153; ET 140.
[65]Ibid.
[66]Ibid.
[67]Ibid.
[68]Ibid.

Additionally, "it is most dangerous to believe that for this purpose God created the world, and permitted and to that extent willed the existence of sin and then the devil, and then of course, in line as it were with these prior acts, accomplish the work of redemption."[69] Even more:

> It is most dangerous to believe that, in virtue of His over-all determination, this redemptive work must itself mean both calling and also hardening, that it must be a means of election and also a means of rejection—and both with that unshakeable fixity, both in that indestructible equilibrium, both as the fulfilment of that secret good-pleasure of God which is wholly anonymous and completely close in upon itself.[70]

In a word, Barth's main criticism of Reformed-orthodox formulations of the doctrine of election is that in positing a *decretum absolutum Dei*, along with the decree of the fall, above, behind and thus detachedly from the God self-revealed in Christ as being-in-act, they inevitably render God's eternal will arbitrarily capricious and rigidly tyrannical. That is, Barth thinks Reformed orthodoxy, by engaging in metaphysical speculation about God, fails to understand predestination christologically, thus detaching God's act of predestination from the constancy of God's love-in-freedom. Regardless of how accurate Barth is in his evaluation of Reformed orthodoxy, his intention in "purifying" classical Reformed lapsarianism is, as stated early on in *CD* II/2, to avoid making double predestination the "caprice of a tyrant."[71]

Barth's solution is that instead of considering election and its object *in abstracto* as he thinks Reformed orthodoxy does, he insists on treating them *in concreto*, which for him means *in Christo*.[72]

Barth agrees with Reformed orthodoxy that Scripture indeed teaches both election and reprobation. Yet for him the elect and the reprobate are not to be considered as two classes of individuals. Rather, all are reprobated in and with Christ so that all may be elected in and with him. Thus Barth: "[the elect man] should testify to His Yes and to what He wills, and he should also testify to His No and to what He does not will."[73]

---

[69]Ibid.
[70]Ibid.
[71]Ibid., 45; ET 43.
[72]Ibid., 153; ET 140.
[73]Ibid.; ET 141.

What God does not will is humankind's fall into sin: "It is not God's will that elected man should fall into sin. But it is His will that sin, that which God does not will, should be repudiated and rejected and excluded by him."[74] As we shall see in more detail in chapter eight, for Barth sin as that which God does not will exists only on the basis of God's absolute non-willing and reprobation. Yet in order for the elected human to actually manifest God's Yes as sublation (*Aufhebung*) of God's No to the sin that negates God, the elected human herself must also "repudiate what He repudiates."[75] Paradoxically, then, sin became absurdly actual, though having no part whatsoever in God's will, in order that it be actually repudiated by God's covenant partner.

In this actualistic scheme with which Barth counters what he thinks to be Reformed orthodoxy's description of predestination as rigid (in the sense that it is not understood as the activity of God's being) and capricious (in the sense that it is described detachedly from the constancy of God's being-in-act), he appeals to a basically infralapsarian pattern of thinking, identifying the "elected man" as "sinful man": "God does not will and affirm evil and the fall and an act of sin on the part of this man, but for the sake of the fullness of His glory, for the sake of the completeness of His covenant with man, for the sake of the perfection of His love, He wills and affirms this man as sinful man . . . , as the one foreordained to utter the same No and thus to corroborate the divine Yes."[76]

Note again the actualistic nuance of this basically infralapsarian assertion. I have already talked about Barth's notion of God's being-in-act in his discussion of God's love-in-freedom: God's works in history perfectly correspond to God's eternal being-in-act. Because of this principle of correspondence, humankind's fall into sin could not possibly be an act or work of God, otherwise there would have corresponded to the absurd element of sin a dark, capricious secret in God's being. If the history of humankind is to correspond to the history of the electing God's free love in Christ, the creaturely covenant partner must utter the same noncapricious No to sin and "thus to corroborate the divine Yes" in history.

---

[74]Ibid.
[75]Ibid.
[76]Ibid.

In the case of the elected human, then, "the defeat of this evil power cannot be so self-evident as it was in God's case. In his [the elected human's] case it must take on the character of an *event*. It must become the content of a history: the history of an obstacle and its removing; the history of a death and a resurrection; the history of a judgment and a pardon; the history of a defeat and a victory."[77] This is not the case for God—"in God Himself there is a simple and immediate victory of light over darkness."[78] In the "creaturely sphere," however, God's eternal act of double predestination "must take on historical form, thus becoming an event in time."[79]

By God's act of election, then, God "wills the confrontation of man by the power of evil."[80] That is, in the language of Reformed orthodoxy, God wills *obiectum praedestinationis* as *homo lapsus*. God "does so in order that man should proclaim His glory as the one who is freed by Him from the dominion of sin, the one who is saved by Him from death the consequence of sin, the one for whom He Himself must and will and does act as Pledge and Substitute if he is really to take this path."[81]

In a word, "God wills *homo labilis* [sic: Barth actually refers to *homo lapsus* according to the definition given in the original Lapsarian Controversy], not in order that he may fall, but in order that *when he has fallen* he may testify to the fullness of God's glory."[82] The following summarizes what Barth calls "purified supralapsarianism," which, as I have argued, is in fact closer to infralapsarianism:

> The existence of this man, the predestined bearer and representative of the divine Yes and the divine No, foreordained to victory over sin and death but also to the bearing of the divine penalty, is the divine promise, the divine Word, in which the God who elects from all eternity confronts all humanity and each individual, in which His electing will encounters us and through which He Himself has dealings with us.[83]

---

[77]Ibid.
[78]Ibid.
[79]Ibid.
[80]Ibid.
[81]Ibid.
[82]Ibid., 153; ET 141-42.
[83]Ibid., 154; ET 142.

"Such, then," says Barth, is the lapsarian theory "as detached and purified from the doubtful presuppositions of the older theology."[84] In this "purified" lapsarianism Barth intends to "remove completely . . . the thought of the foreordination of a rigid and balanced system of election and reprobation. Above all, we [have expunged] completely the idolatrous concept of a *decretum absolutum*."[85] In place of these Reformed-orthodox presuppositions, Barth introduces "the knowledge of the elect man Jesus Christ as the true object of the divine predestination," thus developing lapsarianism "in a Christological direction."[86]

Concluding Remarks

In this chapter we have seen how Barth "purifies" his christological doctrine of election from Reformed-orthodox assumptions regarding the *decretum absolutum*, and how this doctrine is a robustly complex and dialectical combination of supra- and infralapsarian patterns of thought. If it may be described as basically infralapsarian, it is because Barth sees the object of election as sinful humanity. Even with regard to the *obiectum*, however, Barth's basic lapsarian thesis does not resonate with infralapsarianism in any simple way: for him the object of election is first and finally Jesus Christ, who is in himself without sin and became sin for us only by imputation and participation. Sinful humanity is the object of election only by participation in Christ.

With regard to Christology, we have seen that in *CD* II/1 and II/2 Barth has developed two related lapsarian theses. In his discussion of the love and freedom of God as being-in-act (§28 and §32) he describes the incarnation as having proceeded from God's decision to enter into fellowship with the creature, a supralapsarian claim that is qualified by the statement that the incarnation, unlike creation, which is also God's seeking and creating fellowship with the creature, is for the salvation of sinners. As a result Barth would see the incarnation as God's seeking and creating fellowship with the *sinful* creature, rather than the neutral creature as in the work of creation. When he applies his notion of the love and freedom of God as being-in-act

---

[84]Ibid.
[85]Ibid.; ET 143.
[86]Ibid.

to the doctrine of election (§33), he makes the assertion that the incarnation was made necessary by God's decision to defeat sin on behalf of God's covenant partner. In this way Barth has developed a basically infralapsarian Christology dialectically incorporating both supra- and infralapsarian patterns of thinking.

While the actualism of *CD* II/1-2 already addresses the correspondence between God's eternal act and the history of God's covenant partner in Christ, Barth has not yet developed a strong notion of the history (*Geschichte*) of God's being-in-act by Christ's assumption of Adamic history. In the next chapter we will see how Barth develops his Christocentrism in a highly historical and actualized direction in *CD* IV/1 on the basis of his complex lapsarianism.

8

CD IV/1 (1951–1953)

ADAMIC HISTORY AND HISTORY OF CHRIST —INFRALAPSARIAN TENDENCIES IN BARTH'S DOCTRINE OF SIN

THIS CHAPTER IS ON CD IV/1, §60, "The Pride and Fall of Man." In the last two chapters we examined Barth's development of his Christocentric doctrine of election in which God is described as being-in-act. In *CD* II/2 Barth points to an actualistic correspondence in Christ between God's election of humankind and humankind's election of God: "The decision of the sovereign God, His election of grace . . . has as its sole content that God elects humanity in order that it be awakened and called, that it might also elect God."[1] Needless to say, in the *Geschichte* of Christ the activity of God always takes precedence, and human action only mirrors divine election. In *CD* II/2 the emphasis on the objectivity of the accomplished reality of God's election of all in Christ seems almost overwhelmingly determinative of the entire course of human history. As if to repudiate the charge of "Christomonism,"[2] Barth offers a nuanced rendition of incarnational Christology in §59, "The Obedience of the Son of God," which some have described as "historicized."[3]

While much secondary literature has been written on the Christology of *CD* §59 in recent years, this chapter focuses instead on §60 in order to gain

---

[1] *KD* II/2, 198; ET 180.
[2] *KD* IV/1, 763; ET 683.
[3] See Bruce McCormack, "Karl Barth's Historicized Christology: Just How 'Chalcedonian' Is It?" in *Orthodox and Modern: Studies in the Theology of Karl Barth* (Grand Rapids: Baker Academic, 2008).

an understanding of the christological doctrine of election underlying Barth's development of the notion of human sin and fallenness. Here he develops his Christocentrism in a highly historicized and actualistic direction in order to stress God's absolute nonwilling of and nonrelation to sin. I will show that in so doing, Barth in his doctrine of sin everywhere presupposes a basically infralapsarian Christology, and that underlying his notion of fallen Adamic history is a doctrine of election that leans heavily toward infralapsarianism, as far as the object of God's electing grace is concerned.

KNOWLEDGE OF SIN IN LIGHT OF CHRIST: BASICALLY INFRALAPSARIAN CHRISTOLOGY

Epistemological considerations. At the outset of an exposition of Barth's doctrine of sin it is important to keep in mind that according to him no true knowledge of sin is possible apart from the believer's knowledge of Christ. As Hans Frei puts it, "For [Barth] . . . , the evil that we believe, do, and feel is unveiled to our self-apprehension not directly, but only as the refracted distortion of Jesus' free, obedient goodness in which God has overcome evil."[4] Therefore, while the material content of his doctrine of sin primarily consists of two parts, "The Pride of Man" and "The Fall of Man," Barth begins with an epistemological-methodological consideration of the doctrine in a section titled "The Man of Sin in the Light of the Obedience of the Son of God."[5]

In this introductory consideration Barth states: "In this section we are apparently going back a step behind the knowledge that we have already won of the salvation which has come to man in the self-sacrifice and death of the Son of God in our flesh and which is revealed in His resurrection."[6] Here we find that for Barth, even though Christ's incarnation, death and resurrection negatively presuppose humanity's sin (hence "going back a step"), when it comes to epistemological considerations knowledge of Christ precedes knowledge of sin.

Barth continues: "We are apparently concerned with the *negative pre-*

---

[4]Hans Frei, *Theology and Narrative*, ed. George Hunsinger and William Placher (Oxford: Oxford University Press, 1993), 174.
[5]*KD* IV/1, 395-458; ET 358-413.
[6]Ibid., 395-96; ET 359.

supposition of this event, the disruption of the relationship between God and man which *made this event necessary* and which was overcome by this event."[7]

This is a clear indication of a basically infralapsarian Christology. Sure enough, the "event" of which Barth speaks here is "the salvation which has come to man in the self-sacrifice and death of the Son of God in our flesh and which is revealed in His resurrection," and so one might argue that this "event" does not refer to the incarnation.[8] However, at the very outset of this selfsame section just on the previous page, Barth states: "We now turn to the question of the perception of the human situation in the light of *the event* in which for our sake the Lord became a servant, the Son was obedient to the Father, the Word became flesh of our flesh, the Judge was Himself judged on the cross of Golgotha."[9] This makes it unquestionable that in this context Barth is speaking of the cross and the incarnation as the same "event" of which sin is the "negative presupposition." R. Scott Rodin thus observes that for Barth, "God did not positively will the Fall . . . , but in His eternal election of Jesus Christ . . . , the Fall is fully assumed as the state of humanity."[10]

This basically infralapsarian treatment of the knowledge of sin is in fact a restatement of Barth's position in *CD* III/3. When he discusses human knowledge of sin, evil and death as "nothingness" (*das Nichtige*) in §50 ("God and Nothingness"), he states: "We know all this [about nothingness] . . . from . . . the knowledge of Jesus Christ. For the revelation of the goodness of God's creation in its twofold form alone, the incarnation of the Word of God *would obviously have been unnecessary*."[11] This is a clear statement of an infralapsarian Christology.

---

[7]Ibid., 395; ET 359 (emphasis added).
[8]Ibid.
[9]Ibid., 394; ET 358 (emphasis added).
[10]R. Scott Rodin, *Evil and Theodicy in the Theology of Karl Barth* (New York: Peter Lang, 1997), 113.
[11]*KD* III/3, 344; ET 303 (translation and emphasis mine). Bromiley wrongly translates the subjunctive (*Konjunktiv* II) into the indicative, thereby misleadingly suggesting a Christology reminiscent of Duns Scotus, who claims to know that God would have become incarnate even if humankind had not fallen into sin: "It must be clearly grasped that the incarnation of the Word of God was obviously not necessary merely to reveal the goodness of God's creation." Original: *Allein zur Offenbarung der Gute der Schöpfung Gottes in ihrer doppelten Gestalt* wäre *die Fleischwerdung des Wortes Gottes offenbar nicht nötig gewesen.*

Sure enough, Barth's ever-present claim that Jesus Christ is the beginning of all God's ways and works carries supralapsarian overtones. However, on Barth's view, the incarnate *Logos* eternally present at that beginning by virtue of God's pretemporal election is revealed by Christ's concrete history to be one who is eternally determined to take on the sin of all humankind, whose incarnation was made necessary by sin.

Barth insists that if sin is not understood christologically, that is, in light of God's rejection of and triumph over sin in Christ, then the "sin" we claim to know is not the true sin of humankind. In *CD* IV/1 he elaborates that humankind's evil "nature and actions," "the imperfection and problematical nature of [human] existence," may be manifestations of sin, but these are "not as such [humankind's] sin."[12] (Here Barth loosely speaks of human nature as "evil," but as we shall see, he stresses that strictly speaking human nature as created by God is and always remains good, and that the sin that extends to every part of the human being is and remains completely alien to human nature.) For Barth, to consider sin independently of Christ as such is to give to sin an ontological status alongside God, thus turning sin into a second god. In order to avoid such idolization of sin, says Barth, one must develop knowledge of sin in light of Christ.

If Christ is the "mirror of sin," as Barth now puts it (in *CD* II/2 he only spoke of Christ as "mirror of election"), the "basic question" would be "to what extent we really have in the obedience of the Son of God and therefore in Jesus Christ the mirror in which we can see the man of sin as such."[13] He makes four rather lengthy points of epistemological consideration. For my purpose of demonstrating the basically infralapsarian character of the christological doctrine of election underlying Barth's discussion of sin, I will skip to the fourth point.

Sin as impossible possibility: Infralapsarian considerations. The point is this: "The knowledge of Jesus Christ is . . . the knowledge of the significance and extent of sin, or in the words of Anselm: *quanti ponderis sit peccatum* [how great the weight of sin is]."[14] Barth's answer to Anselm's question is this: the weight of sin is properly measured "only when it is seen that this

---

[12]Ibid., 397; ET 360.
[13]Ibid., 439; ET 397.
[14]Ibid., 451; ET 407.

was the cost to God—in the person of His Son—of our reconciliation with Him," namely, "that the Judge allowed Himself to be judged and caused the man of sin to be put to death in His own person."[15]

Yet before arriving at this answer, Barth makes a qualification of fundamental importance: "Whatever evil is, God is its Lord."[16] Reiterating his position in *CD* III/3, §50, he comments that "evil is a form of that nothingness which as such is absolutely subject to God."[17] Echoing Luther's notions of God's *opus alienum* and *proprium*, Barth asserts that "in the light of the fact that in Jesus Christ, in His death (the meaning of which is shown in His resurrection to be His victory and the liberation of man), we see evil overcome and indeed shattered and destroyed by the omnipotence of the love and wrath of God."[18] Sin as such "was impressed into the service of God and contrary to its own nature became necessarily an instrument of the divine triumph."[19]

Meanwhile, Barth stresses that sin as an instrument of God is absolutely rejected by God. This is an important emphasis in *CD* III/3. As I have elsewhere argued against meontological interpretations, *das Nichtige*, which Barth defines as "that which is not," is primarily a predestinarian term.[20] Nothingness "is not"—it negates God and creation—because God has negated it. Nothingness exists precisely because of God's absolute rejection, and could not have existed apart from God's "nonwilling." Paradoxically this divine nonwilling becomes the ground whereupon nothingness exists.[21] Only in this sense does Barth speak of divine *permissio* of nothingness.[22] For him God's activity is always a holy activity, and God's being in God's holy activity has absolutely nothing to do with nothingness; God does not even will it for a higher good, since to attribute evil to the act of God's will is to ascribe evil to God's being-in-act. God rejects nothingness absolutely, and

---

[15]Ibid., 457; ET 412.
[16]Ibid., 452; ET 408.
[17]Ibid.
[18]Ibid. Barth describes *das Nichtige* as *opus Dei alienum*. See *KD* III/3, 407-19; ET 353-62. He explains: "Nothingness has no existence and cannot be known except as the object of God's activity as always a holy activity" (*KD* III/3, 411; ET 356).
[19]*KD* IV/1, 452; ET 408.
[20]Shao Kai Tseng, "Karl Barth on Nothingness: A Christological-Predestinarian Defiance of Theodicy," *Sino-Christian Studies* 20 (forthcoming).
[21]*KD* III/3, 407; ET 353.
[22]Ibid., 424-25; ET 367-68.

only in rejecting it does God permit it. For this reason nothingness has no ontological status as "being"—it is neither Creator nor creature. Its existence is absurd and irrational; thus Barth calls it a "paradox"—an "impossible possibility"—that exists absurdly "as inherent contradiction."[23]

This description of nothingness serves as the basis on which Barth sets forth his hamartiology in *CD* IV/1. He writes: "The superiority with which God confronts sin in Jesus Christ is that of His unconditional No to this element and to us as its representatives. It is a No in which there is no hidden Yes, no secret approval."[24] He elaborates:

> Sin has no positive basis in God, no place in His being, no positive part in His life, and therefore no positive part in His will and work. It is not a creature of God. It arises only as the exponent, and in the creaturely world the most characteristic exponent, of what God has not willed and does not will and will not will, of that which absolutely is not, or is only as God does not will it.[25]

On this basis Barth proceeds to discuss the possibility of human sin. Sin as human activity is an a posteriori given. However, "when man sins, he does that which God has forbidden and does not will. The possibility of doing this is not something which he has from God."[26] Against the freewill argument of humanity's fall, Barth contends that the possibility to sin does not pertain to the freedom and rationality of the "creaturely nature of man."[27]

So if the possibility to sin originated from neither God nor the creature, on what basis has it arisen? Barth answers: "It has no basis."[28] The possibility to sin is purely negative in its existence. "It has, therefore, no possibility—we cannot escape this difficult formula—except that of the absolutely impossible."[29]

Here we come back to Barth's notion of sin as "impossible possibility." We have seen from previous chapters that he first developed this formula in *Romans* II to describe faith and human knowledge of God through revelation,

---

[23]Ibid., 405; ET 351. See John McDowell, "Much Ado About Nothing: Karl Barth's Being Unable to Do Nothing About Nothingness," *International Journal of Systematic Theology* 4 (2002): 310-11. Contra Joseph Mangina, *Karl Barth: Theologian of Christian Witness* (Louisville: Westminster John Knox, 2004), 99.
[24]*KD* IV/1, 453; ET 409.
[25]Ibid.
[26]Ibid.
[27]Ibid.
[28]Ibid., 454; ET 410.
[29]Ibid.

and that he rarely used the same dialectic again until *CD* III/3 and IV/1, where the impossible possibility now refers to human sin and unbelief.

This contrast between *Romans* II and *CD* III/3–IV/1 is a significant indicator of Barth's theological development. In *Romans* II the dialectic describes God's acts of overcoming human impossibilities. As long as humankind remains within fallen time, the impossibility that God has made possible remains impossible, hence faith and revelation as impossible possibilities.

In CD III/3–IV/1, by contrast, Barth describes the paradox of sin as the impossible possibility, while election and the economy of divine salvation are no longer impossible possibilities for him. For the Barth of *CD* III/3–IV/1, "paradox" denotes that which is blatantly self-contradictory and irrational. Here he no longer follows Kierkegaard in calling the God-man a "paradox": "It is not paradoxical or absurd that God becomes and is man. It does not contradict the concept of God. It fulfils it."[30] However, "it is certainly paradoxical and absurd that man wants to be as God. It contradicts the concept of man."[31]

When Barth says in *CD* IV/1 that the incarnation "fulfils" the concept of God, he has in mind the divine act of election as discussed in *CD* II/2. Election is God's eternal act of choosing to be God with us through the incarnation. In the act of election God has eternally negated humankind's sin by the incarnation.

This, again, manifests the basically infralapsarian orientation of Barth's christological doctrine of election. In this infralapsarian manner Barth sees the incarnation as fulfilling the very concept of God: Election-in-Christ as manifested in his death and resurrection reveals that in the person of Christ God judges sin in the flesh for the sake of God's love-in-freedom. That is, the incarnation fulfills the concept of God because by the incarnation God rejects that which negates God and God's covenant partner, and remains true to God's absolute perfection. This rejection serves the purpose of the mercy of the God who is immutably love-in-freedom. For Barth, the incarnation is by no means paradoxical or absurd.

Contrarily, it is humankind's sin, the prideful attempt to be as God, that is paradoxical and absurd, for it contradicts the very concept of humanity:

---

[30]*KD* IV/1, 465; ET 419.
[31]Ibid.

to be human is to be God's creature and covenant partner *in Christo*. To be *in Christo* means that sin is impossible: sin is a priori (*zum Vornherein*) negated and defeated in God's eternal double predestination in Christ. (This, again, is basically oriented toward infralapsarianism.) For this reason the human possibility to sin is "absolutely impossible."[32] Thus Barth calls sin an "impossible possibility": "How else can we describe that which is intrinsically absurd, but by a formula which is logically absurd? Sin is that which is absurd, man's absurd choice and decision for that which is not.... Sin exists only in this absurd event."[33] Barth continues: "The possibility [of sin]... can be described only as that which God has denied and rejected and forbidden, as that which is nothing in itself, as that which is as such impossible, which exists only on the left hand of God."[34]

But the question is, "How do we know this?"[35] Barth answers: "We know it, we have to know it, from the fact that sin has been treated in this way by God Himself in Jesus Christ, with an opposition which excludes any compact with it, any explanation or exculpation of the fact that it has taken place, with an uncompromising No."[36] This "No," this "supremely real wrath of God," is "what took place in the death of Jesus Christ at Golgotha."[37]

Yet Golgotha is that event which perfectly corresponds to the gracious reprobation that Christ has sublated from all eternity. Thus we see again that Barth is basically oriented toward infralapsarianism in both his Christology and his doctrine of election: the incarnation is for the purpose of defeating humankind's sin, while election as the *Aufhebung* of reprobation presupposes the sin of all humankind communicated to Christ.

Understanding this basically infralapsarian orientation of Barth's christological doctrine of election would shed light on his insistence that only in Christ is the weight of sin truly revealed.

> The truth is that Anselm's question: *quanti ponderis sit peccatum?* is given an answer either from the cross of Christ or not at all.... The serious and terrible nature of human corruption, the depth of the abyss into which man is about

---

[32] Ibid., 454; ET 410.
[33] Ibid.
[34] Ibid.
[35] Ibid.
[36] Ibid.
[37] Ibid., 455; ET 411.

to fall as the author of it, can be measured by the fact that the love of God could react and reply to this event only by His giving, His giving up, of Jesus Christ Himself to overcome and remove it and in that way to redeem man, fulfilling the judgment upon it in such a way that the Judge allowed Himself to be judged and caused the man of sin to be put to death in His own person.[38]

Sin as Human Pride in Light of an Infralapsarian Christology

Actualism revisited: Human act of sin as paradox. Having established that sin must be understood christologically, Barth proceeds to ask: "But what is sin as seen from this place?"[39] He answers: "The sin of man is the pride of man."[40] To be sure, this is not an exhaustive definition, but neither is it "just a part of the content" of sin.[41] While it is also to be defined in other ways, "sin in its unity and totality is always pride."[42]

Human pride is the concretion of disobedience and unbelief. Here Barth sets forth the thesis that in light of Christ, the general acts of disobedience and unbelief are revealed concretely as humankind's pride. Now what remains to be seen is how Barth substantiates this statement. He begins by asking: "What is it that God does in Jesus Christ?"[43]

What God does in Christ, says Barth, is an obedient act of *humility*: in obedience the Son "gives Himself and humbles Himself to go into the far country, as very God to become ... man, flesh of our flesh, to take to Himself human existence not only in its creaturely limitation but in its sinful contradiction and misery."[44] The act of incarnation is the event of "divine obedience and humility."[45]

Here Barth stresses that this act of obedience and humility by no means takes away God's freedom. In basically Chalcedonian grammar he states that "the Lord becomes a servant but does not cease to be the Lord," stressing that

---

[38]Ibid., 456; ET 412.
[39]Ibid., 457; ET 413.
[40]Ibid.
[41]Ibid.
[42]Ibid.
[43]Ibid., 462; ET 417.
[44]Ibid.
[45]Ibid.

"as a servant He is truly the Lord in His very Godhead."[46] This is basically another way of saying that the incarnation fulfills the concept of God rather than contradicting it. Christ's servanthood is a perfect manifestation of rather than contradiction to divine lordship. In the act of incarnation God "does not give Himself away or give Himself up, but offers Himself in His divine lordship, and as such maintains Himself."[47]

At this juncture Barth revisits an important theme in *CD* II/2, which I addressed in chapter seven, namely, the notion of God's love and freedom. Recall that for Barth true freedom is not caprice. Thus in *CD* IV/1 he again rejects any voluntaristic understanding of divine freedom: God does not elect to become human "in the chance of a caprice or variation of His divine being."[48] On the other hand, to say that the incarnation is a free act of God is to say that it is not "under the compulsion of any inward or outward necessity."[49]

On this point, Bruce McCormack, notwithstanding voluntaristic tendencies in his reading (see footnote 50), issues the helpful caveat that Barth's understanding of "God's freedom cannot be exhaustively described when reference is had only to such negations."[50] Positively stated, McCormack

---

[46]Ibid.
[47]Ibid.
[48]Ibid.
[49]Ibid.
[50]Bruce McCormack, "Election and the Trinity: Theses in Response to George Hunsinger," *Scottish Journal of Theology* 63 (2010): 223. While McCormack's "thesis" on and "explanation" of Barth's understanding of divine freedom are helpful, and granted that for Barth "God is what he is in the eternal decision of election," I am not quite sure how McCormack arrives at the conclusion that with regard to logical relationship, Trinity presupposes election. In fact, McCormack himself concedes that "where the logical relationship of election to trinity is concerned," his "foregoing considerations," including those on divine love and freedom, "would allow us to take either element as a starting point" (223). That is, to say that God is what God is in the eternal decision of election does not necessarily imply that Trinity presupposes election. McCormack seems to have provided little textual evidence to sustain this inference. The closest one he provides, it seems to me, is found earlier in his article (218): "God is not *in abstracto* Father, Son and Holy Ghost, the triune God. He is so with a definite purpose and reference" (*CD* II/2, 79). However, this "definite purpose and reference," which Barth identifies in the selfsame sentence that McCormack does not quote, is "the love and freedom in which *in the bosom of His triune being* He has foreordained himself from and to all eternity" (*CD* II/2, 79). That is, God foreordained Godself from and to all eternity unto this definite purpose and reference of love and freedom *in the bosom of God's triune being*: election presupposes the Trinity. Of course, Barth states in the same excursus that we "cannot speak of the being of God without at once speaking of this *interna actio* of His being, i.e., the election" (*CD* II/2, 79). However, here Barth does not indicate what the logical relation between Trinity and election is. My reading of Barth is such that election logically presupposes the Trinity. I shall provide more textual evidence to sustain this reading later.

comments, "God's freedom is the freedom of the love that God is to set itself in concrete relationship to that which is other than itself."[51] Thus Barth immediately proceeds to state that God elected to become a servant "in the determination of His free love on the basis of His eternal election in fulfillment of the eternal decree of His mercy."[52]

To recapitulate what I have already argued in chapter seven, Barth's notion of the freedom of God's love in the act of election is such that it is neither the voluntaristic "caprice of a tyrant," as Barth puts it, nor the compulsion of any inward or outward necessity on God's part, but *perfect correspondence* between God's being-in-act *ad extra* and *ad intra*. By virtue of this actualism, God's election to assume the form of a servant is to be understood as a perfect manifestation of God's lordship.

Moreover, it must be stressed that the incarnation is God's sovereign election to be *pro nobis*: "It is for our sake (*pro nobis*) that God determined and came to this action which cuts right across all human belief and surmise and thought about God, this action in which His Word becomes flesh."[53]

Now, if God's eternal election is *for us*, and if, in Paul Nimmo's words, "the activity of God and the activity of the creature are ... inseparable and must be understood 'as a single action' [*CD* III/3, 132]," then there should correspond to God's eternal election a human act of faith and obedience *for God*.[54] This is indeed true in the human Jesus, whose acts of humility and obedience perfectly correspond to God's act of election *pro nobis*.

Yet, as God carries through with the act of election, this act does not stop short at the point of Christ's obedience and humility. The whole human race must also act in correspondence to God's act *pro nobis*—in *CD* II/2 Barth already intimates such an actualistic correspondence between divine election of humanity and human election of God.[55]

---

[51] Ibid.
[52] *KD* IV/1, 462; ET 417.
[53] Ibid., 463; ET 418.
[54] Paul Nimmo, "Karl Barth and the *Concursus Dei*—A Chalcedonianism Too Far?" *International Journal of Systematic Theology* 9 (2007): 60. We shall see anon that Nimmo's caveats against "a Chalcedonianism too far," though helpful in some respects, are in fact based on an "actualistic ontology too far" that tries to strip away every last element of classical theistic substantialism from Barth.
[55] *KD* II/2, 198; ET 180.

In *CD* IV/1 Barth reiterates the same notion: "If it is not in vain that He [God] does what He does [namely, electing to be *pro nobis*], then it is right and proper that we should turn from His action to ours, that we should ask concerning the *correspondence* of our actions to His action, concerning our own form as reflected in what God does, and does for us."[56] In Barth's discussion of justification by faith in *CD* IV/1, he shows that human faith and obedience have indeed become actual in the here and now by the Holy Spirit, and points to an eschaton in which the faith-obedience of all humankind becomes fully actual.

But before going there, Barth stresses that in the here and now human sin as pride is still actual, because, as Nimmo puts it, "Jesus Christ corresponds perfectly, in his existence, to that which—in the event of election—he determined and was determined to be in essence. Barth writes of Jesus Christ that 'as a man He exists analogously to the mode of existence of God' [*CD* IV/2, 166]. The creature, however—through sin—does not."[57]

In *CD* IV/1 this is the juncture where the notion of sin comes sharply to the foreground: sin is "the pride of man" as "a terrible *paradox*, that man is the being whose attitude not only does not *correspond* to the attitude of God as revealed and active in Jesus Christ, but contradicts it and actively opposes it, that the two attitudes move in a diametrically opposite direction."[58] The actuality of sin is paradoxical because it does not correspond to God's gracious election. The prideful human "loves and chooses the inner nothingness which can only reveal itself to his shame in the impotence of his action," and "the omnipotent act of [Christ's] humility exposes us as proud men."[59]

Four key points: Basically infralapsarian Christology. On this ground Barth proceeds to delineate four main points to explain how sin is always human pride. First, sin is the human attempt to be as God. Sure it is "paradoxical and absurd that man wants to be as God," and "the only result of his attempts is the revelation of his impotence to do so."[60] Yet "the impotence of the enterprise does not alter the fact that for all its perversion it does take

---

[56]*KD* IV/1, 464; ET 418 (emphasis added).
[57]Nimmo, "*Concursus Dei*," 67.
[58]*KD* IV/1, 464; ET 418 (emphasis added).
[59]Ibid., 465; ET 419.
[60]Ibid.

place."[61] To this extent sin is "something actual."[62] But it is actual only as that which God has already rejected in Christ. It is precisely God's omnipotent act of election-in-Christ that the human act of sin is revealed to be impotent. Likewise, God's attitude of humility in becoming human reveals and overcomes the pride of humankind in trying to become as God: "To that attempt of man to become as God . . . , God has made answer with the gracious and triumphant act that He Himself became as man: 'The Word was made flesh.'"[63]

Second, Christ reveals the prideful character of human sin by taking on the form of a servant. "The Lord became a servant": this is what Barth calls the "main Christological definition," "the humility of the act of God which took place for us in Jesus Christ."[64] This reveals the prideful character of sin, since "the man for whom God is God in this [humble] way in Jesus Christ is the very opposite—the servant who wants to be lord."[65]

Third, Barth revisits the notion of Christ as "the Judge judged in our place" (*CD* IV/1, §59, section 2), foreshadowing a key element in his doctrine of justification, namely, that God does not neglect human sin, but actually judges sin in Christ: "The real Judge not only wills to accuse and sentence and judge, but does so."[66] The Judge judges the sin of all by taking on our very sin and being judged in our place. Properly speaking, God—and Christ is God—is the Judge. Yet at Golgotha, sinners attempted to judge the Judge judged in their place. The Judge humbly justifies the sinner, yet the sinner condemns—with no power or validity—the Judge. This paradox, again, reveals the prideful character of sin.

Fourth, the "free grace" of justification that God has accomplished in Christ reveals that human attempts at "self-help" are not only futile but also sinfully prideful: "The man whose place and kind God made His own in Jesus Christ is, in clear antithesis to the One who in this way humbled Himself for him, the man who has always thought and still thinks that he can help himself and that in this self-help he has a claim to the help of God."[67]

---

[61] Ibid.
[62] Ibid.
[63] Ibid., 470; ET 423.
[64] Ibid., 479; ET 432.
[65] Ibid.
[66] Ibid., 495; ET 446.
[67] Ibid., 509; ET 458.

Here Barth is repudiating every possible form of synergism, the idea that humans can help themselves to merit God's help. In an exegetical excursus on Genesis 3, Barth describes Adam's fall as a "move to self-help in paradise."[68] First, they ate the fruit to help themselves attain unto autonomous knowledge of good and evil. Then, for a second time they committed the prideful sin of self-help when they vainly attempted to cover their shame with fig leafs. Finally, Adam attempted to help himself with the "pitiable excuse" that the woman made him eat the fruit, and Eve in turn tried to help herself with the "pitiable excuse" that the serpent made her eat it.[69] The result is that humankind became "catastrophically helpless."[70] This is precisely the very helplessness that Christ took on himself. On behalf and in the stead of all humans who helplessly try to help themselves, "Jesus cried on the cross, the helpless One taking the place of all those who gaily help themselves: 'My God, my God, why has thou forsaken me?'"[71] It is in Christ's humbly vicarious helplessness, then, that human attempts at self-help are revealed to be futile and sinfully prideful.

Now, if we reflect on these four key points regarding the christological notion of sin as pride, we recognize a basically infralapsarian Christology underlying Barth's doctrine of sin. Recall that he begins his discussion of Christ's revelation of sin as human pride by asking, "What is it that God does in Jesus Christ?"[72] What God does in Jesus Christ is, as we saw in the four key points above, the following: (1) God became human without ceasing to be God; (2) the Lord became a servant without ceasing to be Lord; (3) the Judge became the judged without ceasing to be the Judge; (4) the Helper became helpless without ceasing to be the Helper. As we have seen, all these four aspects of what "God does in Jesus Christ" are predicated on and for the purpose of overcoming humankind's sin.

Recall that according to supralapsarian Christology, God would have become incarnate regardless of humanity's sin. In the current analysis this is clearly not the case for the Christology underlying Barth's understanding of human sin as pride: for Barth, God's determination to become incarnate

---

[68]Ibid., 518; ET 466.
[69]Ibid.
[70]Ibid.
[71]Ibid.
[72]Ibid., 462; ET 417.

is God's decision to defeat sin on behalf of God's covenant partner. In this respect the basic orientation of Barth's Christology is infralapsarian. The supralapsarian overtones in his claim that Jesus Christ is the beginning of all God's ways and works do not alter the fact that for Barth the eternal determination of the *Logos incarnandus* and *incarnatus* has always involved God's decision to overcome sin.

The Sinner as Fallen: Infralapsarian *Homo Lapsus*

Having discussed human sin as pride, Barth proceeds to expound on the statement that "the man of sin is fallen man."[73] To be precise, humankind has fallen into the state of corruption. But, he asks, "what is the *status corruptionis* which is set aside by [Christ's] intervention but cannot be set aside except by His intervention?"[74]

Barth answers immediately: "Our corruption cannot be any different, it cannot be greater and it cannot be less than that on account of which, and to overcome which, He suffered and died for us on the cross."[75] So, then, Barth proceeds to put the question more concretely: "What is this corruption of ours which is shown to us by Him as the Saviour who is as such the living Word of God to us?"[76] That is, how does Jesus Christ reveal to us what our fallenness is?

The weight of sin: God's Son among **homo lapsus**. Barth answers this question with three basically infralapsarian propositions. First, the *status corruptionis* "consists in the fact that man is God's debtor."[77] Here Barth is explicitly engaging with Anselm's satisfaction theory set forth in *Cur Deus Homo*. Barth agrees with Anselm that human sin consists in an infinite debt that the creature owes to the Creator, and that this "disturbance...has to be followed by some action which radically reverses it."[78] The reason, as Anselm puts it, is that "it does not befit God to allow anything inordinate in his kingdom."[79] Thus far Barth is in agreement with Anselm, but he takes

---

[73] Ibid., 531; ET 478.
[74] Ibid., 538; ET 484.
[75] Ibid.
[76] Ibid.
[77] Ibid.
[78] Ibid., 540; ET 486.
[79] Ibid. See Anselm, *Cur Deus Homo* 1.12 (translation mine).

issues with Anselm's conclusion from these statements that "it is not worthy of God to forgive man his sin *sola misericordia* [by mercy alone]."[80]

Anselm's position here is known as the "absolute necessity" view of the atonement, according to which God's forgiveness of humankind's sin is impossible without Christ's work of satisfaction—divine mercy alone is not sufficient to forgive humankind's sin. Note that although Barth opposes this view, he does not subscribe to its opposite either, namely, the "hypothetical necessity" view of the atonement, which states Christ's work of atonement is necessary only on the supposition of God's decision, and that God could have decided to forgive sin without Jesus Christ. For Barth, both these views err in detaching Christ and his works as pretemporally determined in God's act of election from the mercy of God's being, failing to see that Christ is the "full actuality of the grace of God."[81] Recall that for Barth, the incarnation does not contradict the concept of God, but fulfills it. Similarly, the atonement, which for Barth is objectively accomplished in the eternal act of incarnation, is "the action of His perfect righteousness as well as that of His pure mercy, and therefore supremely worthy of God."[82]

Here again, Barth's actualism comes to the foreground: God is being-in-act and as such God's act never contradicts God's being. On this point Barth not only departs from Anselm in the doctrine of the atonement but also carries Anselm's classical theism in an actualistic direction. As George Hunsinger points out, "With Anselm, [Barth] adopted many of the divine predicates associated with classical theism. With Hegel, however, he stressed that God's inner being was dynamic and not static."[83]

The incarnate act and atoning works of the Son "overflowed" from God's triune being *ad intra* "in the form of avenging righteousness . . . , so that in face of this opposition [from fallen creatures as debtors] His forgiveness was His . . . sword of justice. This God, the God who judges this way, is God alone, in His *unchanging being and essence*."[84] Thus Hunsinger (contra "revisionist" views) says, "Here in IV/1 we have Barth saying . . . that God is not filling up

---

[80]Ibid.
[81]Ibid.
[82]Ibid., 542; ET 487.
[83]George Hunsinger, *Reading Barth with Charity: A Hermeneutical Proposal* (Grand Rapids: Baker Academic, 2015), 128.
[84]*KD* IV/1, 542-43; ET 487-88 (emphasis added).

a perfection that needs no filling, but that God allows his antecedent perfection to overflow toward the world in a gracious superfluity."[85]

Now, underlying Barth's actualistic understanding of God's immutability in incarnation and atonement is a basically infralapsarian Christology, namely, the conviction that the Word became flesh to be among fallen creatures and make restitution on behalf of the human debtor: "This God who is *the same in every part of His being* is the God attested in Holy Scripture, and decisively with the witness of His appearance and action in the manifestation and revelation of His own Son *amongst fallen men*."[86] On the basis of this basically infralapsarian Christology Barth concretely sets forth his first proposition in answer to the question of human corruption (the following passage is clearly against "revisionist" readings—see footnote 87).

> It is clear that the God who in sheer mercy encounters the man who has become His debtor, as the God who forgives him his sin, is the God who, without being untrue to Himself but supremely true, is gracious to man, because first He is gracious in Himself, in His own inward being, and that as such He is almighty and holy and righteous, the Creator of heaven and earth, the Lord of His covenant with man.[87]

---

[85] Hunsinger, *Reading Barth with Charity*, 95.
[86] *KD* IV/1, 542; ET 487 (emphasis added).
[87] Ibid. Note here that Barth distinguishes between God's "inward being" and God as "Lord of His covenant with man." The latter presupposes the former: God is "*first* gracious . . . in His own inward being," and then as such God is "the Lord of His covenant with man." By the same token, incarnation logically presupposes the *Logos asarkos*; election presupposes the immanent Trinity. Of course, in this very part-volume (IV/1), Barth states that "we must not refer to the second 'person' of the Trinity as such, to the eternal Son or the eternal Word of God *in abstracto*, and therefore to the so-called λόγος ἄσαρκος" (55; ET 52). He emphasizes that the Son of God *is* Jesus of Nazareth. Yet Barth is here making an *epistemological* rather than *ontological* statement. As Hunsinger puts it, Barth's rejection of the *Logos asarkos* "pertained more to the knowledge of God than to the doctrine of God." See Hunsinger, *Reading Barth with Charity*, 157. For Barth there is no point in regressing to the concept of a *Logos asarkos* above and behind the *Logos ensarkos* when all that we may know of the Son is the one self-revealed in history as Jesus of Nazareth—such regression "would be tantamount to natural theology" (ibid.). This does not mean that Barth treats the *Logos asarkos* as *simpliciter* identical with the *Logos* eternally *incarnandus*. In fact, Barth acknowledges the *Logos asarkos* as "the content of a necessary and important concept in trinitarian doctrine when we have to understand the revelation and dealings of God in the light of their free basis in the inner being and essence of God" (*KD* IV/1, 55; ET 52). McCormack recognizes this too (see Bruce McCormack, "Grace and Being: The Role of God's Gracious Election in Karl Barth's Theological Ontology," in *The Cambridge Companion to Karl Barth*, ed. John Webster [Cambridge: Cambridge University Press, 2000], 193), but he thinks that this is an inconsistency on Barth's part. On my reading, the "Son of God in Himself" is a concept that Barth presupposes, even though he refuses to probe into it because in *CD* IV/1 he

Fallen humanity: Unaltered good nature and total corruption of being.
Barth's second proposition is this: "The fact that Jesus Christ died totally for the reconciliation of every man as such, for the man who exists in this way, means decisively that this corruption is both radical and total."[88] Here Barth expressly indicates that he is using Kantian language.[89] While he appeals to Kantian notions in explaining the radicalness and totality of human corruption, his deeply Christocentric understanding of salvation stands in sharp contrast to Kant's idea of a universal moral vocation to restore the good predispositions within all humans.[90]

For Barth, Kant's moral religion would be in agreement with "the Roman-Catholic-Neo-Protestant side" of the debate on human nature.[91] Barth insists against this view that there is no "relic or core of goodness which persists in man in spite of his sin.... The only relic that we can speak of is that of God's good and gracious will operative to man and over him—the being of man before God, as the object of His grace even in the form of judgment."[92] Barth agrees with Kant that fallen humanity "lives by an 'evil principle,' with

---

is "concerned with the revelation and dealings of God, and particularly with the atonement, with the person and work of the Mediator," and "it is pointless, as it is impermissible, to return to the inner being and essence of God and especially to the second person of the Trinity as such, in such a way that we ascribe to this person another form than that which God Himself has given in willing to reveal Himself and to act outwards" (*KD* IV/1, 55; ET 52). In other words, in a way akin to Kant's transcendental method of positing God's existence without claiming any theoretical knowledge thereof, Barth posits the concept of the *Logos asarkos* as a necessary presupposition of God's election to become incarnate, but refuses to claim knowledge of the preincarnate Son above and behind the incarnate *Logos* "proleptically" present in eternity by virtue of divine election as revealed in Christ (see Hunsinger, *Reading Barth with Charity*, 62-71): "The second 'person' of the Godhead in Himself and as such is not God the Reconciler. In Himself and as such He is not revealed to us. In Himself and as such He is not *Deus pro nobis*, either ontologically or epistemologically" (*KD* IV/1, 55; ET 52). That is, the God made known to humankind is the *Deus revelatus*, *Deus pro nobis*, while the *Deus absconditus*, *Logos asarkos*, God in Godself, is transcendentally posited as a necessary presupposition of the incarnation, but one cannot claim theoretical knowledge thereof. For Kant's transcendental argument for God's existence, see Kant, "The Only Possible Argument in Support of a Demonstration of the Existence of God," in *Theoretical Philosophy, 1755-1770*, ed. and trans. David Walford (Cambridge: Cambridge University Press), 107-202. Also see Clifford Anderson, "A Theology of Experience? Karl Barth and the Transcendental Argument," in *Karl Barth and American Evangelicalism*, ed. Bruce McCormack and Clifford Anderson (Grand Rapids: Eerdmans, 2010), 91-110.

[88] *KD* IV/1, 548; ET 492.
[89] Ibid., 551; ET 495.
[90] Immanuel Kant, *Religion Within the Bounds of Bare Reason*, trans. Werner Pluhar (Indianapolis: Hackett, 2009), 31-43.
[91] *KD* IV/1, 548; ET 492.
[92] Ibid., 549; ET 493.

a 'bias towards evil,' in the power of a 'radical evil' which shows itself virulent and active in his life . . . , with which he is not identical, but to which he commits himself and is committed."[93] Yet the fact that Jesus died totally for every human being means for Barth that "there is . . . no 'nature-reserve'" that fallen humans can restore by the kind of synergism for which Kant, as with Roman Catholicism and neo-Protestantism, hopes.[94]

On the other hand, Barth also takes issues with the "Augustinian-Reformed" side of the controversy over human nature.[95] He insists that humankind "has not lost—even in part—the good nature which was created by God, to acquire instead another and evil nature."[96] He is worried that such a view of human fallenness will lead to a kind of dualism whereby sin is given some sort of an ontological status as human *nature*. (Here Barth, without subscribing to any ontology, retains a substantialist notion of nature.)

To be sure, sinful corruption lies at the "very core of his [humanity's] being—the heart, as the Bible puts it."[97] Yet this radical and total corruption of the human being is not as such any part of human *nature*. While the Barth of 1936 still considered humankind "by nature sinful,"[98] he now contends that "man himself in his nature and determination and attitude and capacity as they are still good is not a quantum which is confronted by his sinfulness as a greater or lesser quantum . . . , failing to [counterbalance it] according to the pessimistic view of Augustine and the older Protestantism."[99]

For Barth, this Augustinian-Reformed understanding of fallen human nature is "quite untenable," as "the Bible accuses man as a sinner from head to foot, but it does not dispute to man his *full and unchanged humanity*, his *nature as God created it good*."[100] For Barth, sin as nothingness is completely foreign to the human nature that God created good.

Of course, Barth recognizes that Ephesians 2:3 speaks of the fallen human being as "'by nature' a 'child of wrath,'" and that the Heidelberg Catechism,

---

[93] Ibid., 551; ET 495.
[94] Ibid., 552; ET 496.
[95] Ibid., 548; ET 492.
[96] Ibid.
[97] Ibid., 550; ET 494.
[98] Karl Barth, *Gottes Gnadenwahl* (Munich: Kaiser, 1936), 6.
[99] *KD* IV/1, 549; ET 493.
[100] Ibid., 548; ET 492.

which he regards highly, also describes the inclination of human nature as sinful.[101] Thus he concedes that "it is perhaps permissible to speak of the 'poisoned' nature of fallen man" in a certain sense. However, he stresses: "But in order to put the matter exactly, avoiding that idea of the fatefulness of man's being in sin—to which even the term 'poisoned nature' might give rise—I would prefer, if we are going to use the word 'poison,' to describe man as one who poisons himself in his pride."[102] In a word, Barth rejects the notion that humankind is by *nature* sinful, fallen or poisoned.

This does not mean that Barth fails to treat human fallenness seriously. In fact, "the seriousness of [humanity's] situation is much greater than can be expressed by the idea of a setting aside or damaging of his nature which is good."[103] The seriousness of the radical and total corruption of fallen humankind, with its "consequent sinful perversion that extends to the whole of his being without exception,"[104] consists in the fact that "the one whole man whom God created good ..., whom He does not cease in the very least to recognise and honour and claim as His covenant-partner, that this man elected and willed and ordained and equipped for the service of God has turned away from Him and is now ... corrupt and guilty."[105]

Without ever ceasing to be God's good creature and covenant partner elected in Christ, the sinner actually gives in and falls prey to that inner nothingness that is not and has never been and will never be a part of human nature. Thereby sin corrupts the human being to the very core.

Sin not only consists in the *acts* of humankind; it extends to every part of the human *being*-in-act: "He sins, but more than that, he is a sinner."[106] It is in this sense that Barth describes humanity's fall with the term "original sin."[107] On his view, however, the *peccatum originale* should not be taken as the hereditary sin of which the early church speaks. "'Hereditary sin' has a hopelessly naturalistic, deterministic and even fatalistic ring."[108] What the term "original sin" should convey is rather "the original and radical and

---

[101] Ibid., 550; ET 494.
[102] Ibid.
[103] Ibid., 549; ET 493.
[104] Ibid., 548; ET 492.
[105] Ibid., 549-50; ET 493-94.
[106] Ibid., 551; ET 495.
[107] Ibid., 557; ET 500.
[108] Ibid., 558; ET 501.

therefore the comprehensive and total *act* of man, with the imprisonment of his existence in that circle of evil being and evil activity."[109] In other words, by "original sin" Barth means that fallen humans are corrupt not only in their sinful acts but also in their very being—extensively and radically so. (As we shall see, this has profound implications for Barth's understanding of the sinlessness of Christ's *act* as well as Christ's human *nature*.)

This is the point where Barth's basically infralapsarian Christology comes into play: Christ reveals human corruption to be original and radical, since the incarnation is God's act to eradicate this sinful origin in order to bestow on humankind the true origin to which God has elected all humans from eternity. Barth comments that Christ took the place of a human being "to set aside this false beginning and origin in order that he may be born again from above by the Spirit, in order that by that new beginning and origin he may be a new man."[110] That is, the Son of God became incarnate *in order to* take care of the problem of sin. It will become even clearer anon that for Barth the incarnation *is* Christ's assumption of fallen Adamic history; thus it would be quite meaningless and speculative in Barth's view to speak of the possibility of an incarnation regardless of sin.

Alive but dead: A basically infralapsarian exegesis of Romans 11:32. Barth's third proposition in answer to the question of human corruption is especially dense and complex. Here he cites Romans 11:32 to offer an actualistic account of a basically infralapsarian formulation of double predestination on the basis of his basically infralapsarian Christology. The proposition is this: "The fact that God willed to have mercy and did have mercy on all men in the sacrifice of Jesus Christ, means that 'He hath concluded them all in disobedience.'"[111]

Recall that in *Romans* II and the *Göttingen Dogmatics*, Barth appealed to Romans 11:32 to describe reprobation as the divine conclusion of all in disobedience (see chapters three and four). This is no longer the case in *CD* IV/1, where reprobation is the No of God vicariously suffered by Christ for the eternal sublation of sin with the election and justification of all, while the divine conclusion of all in disobedience is a description of humankind's

---
[109]Ibid., 557; ET 500.
[110]Ibid., 552; ET 496.
[111]Ibid., 558; ET 501.

fall into the *status corruptionis*. To be sure, this divine "concluding" does imply that God placed sinners under the verdict of divine reprobation, but these two concepts are not identical. Barth explains: "'Concluded' means that He has placed them under an authoritative verdict and sentence which cannot be questioned or disputed, let alone resisted, with all the consequences which that involves."[112]

According to Romans 11:32 this divine "concluding" serves the purpose of God's mercy. Barth interprets the teleological language of this biblical verse in a nuanced, actualistic way: "This presupposition [of divine concluding] *corresponds* to the mercy of God."[113] With this actualistic interpretation, Barth's aim is to avoid attributing sin to God's being-in-act. On one hand, he insists, as he did in *CD* III/3, that humanity's fall into sin is completely under God's sovereign ruling. On the other hand, he refuses to describe God as having caused humankind's sin in any sort of way. Humanity's fall is indeed *opus Dei* in a certain sense, but it is absolutely *alienum* to God. As *opus Dei* it somehow corresponds to God's inward being, but by no means does this imply that there is a dark, evil or capricious side of God to which humanity's fall corresponds. Rather, as a negative "presupposition" of election-in-Christ as the *Aufhebung* of reprobation, humanity's fall corresponds to God's act of mercy in Christ, and only by corresponding to this act does the divine concluding also, *secundum quid*, correspond to the mercy of God's immutable and never-capricious being.

Additionally, as Hunsinger points out, Barth assigns to the word "all" in Romans 11:32 an exegetical importance that sets him quite apart from the entire Western (Latin) theological tradition.[114] Barth comments, with reference to Romans 9:15: "Those on whom He willed to have mercy and did have mercy are the very ones that He had concluded or placed under this verdict. In both cases the reference is to all men."[115] These are the two "unities" wherein "all men stand according to the order and will of God."[116]

---

[112]Ibid.
[113]Ibid.
[114]See George Hunsinger, "A Tale of Two Simultaneities," in *Conversing with Barth*, ed. John McDowell and Mike Higton (Aldershot: Ashgate, 2004), 77.
[115]*KD* IV/1, 558; ET 501.
[116]Ibid.

The definitive unity is the actual union of all humans with Christ. In one sense, this union has been objectively accomplished from all eternity. In another sense, human actions in the here and now as characterized by pride and disobedience still do not correspond perfectly to Christ's eternal act of humility and obedience in the incarnation.

There is thus an eschatological aspect to Barth's actualistic understanding of the unity of all humans *in Christo*. Therefore, he comments that "the unity of the divine mercy" is one that "embraces them [all humans] *prospectively, in their future being.*"[117] This unity of the divine mercy, though futuristic in the here and now, "is shown to them as the Son of God *has come* to them in the far country."[118] That is, the eschatological aspect of divine mercy has its objective basis in what Christ has eternally and actually accomplished: the future tense corresponds perfectly to the perfect tense.

By contrast, the divine "concluding" as "the unity into which God has fused them [all humans] and as which He sees and addresses and treats them" is one that "embraces them retrospectively, in their past being."[119] As real as the disobedience of all humans may appear in the here and now, it has no ontological status. It belongs to "man's past, with the being which lies behind him."[120]

That is, the state of disobedience into which God concluded all humans has been eternally sublated in and by Jesus Christ. Therefore, even the perfect tense in German (logically equivalent to the past tense) is insufficient to describe this past unity. It can only be described properly in the "pluperfect tense": "The kingdom of darkness is the conclusion in disobedience, the unity into which the divine verdict *had* previously fused all men."[121] With reference to the definitive unity of God's will for all humans *in Christo*, the kingdom of darkness pertains to an eternal past already negated and was never real in any ontological sense.

Now, underlying this entire actualistic interpretation of divine mercy and concluding in Romans 11:32 is a basically infralapsarian understanding of both predestination and incarnation, which for Barth are inseparable

---

[117] Ibid. (emphasis added).
[118] Ibid. (emphasis added).
[119] Ibid.
[120] Ibid., 559; ET 502.
[121] Ibid.

because predestination is *in Christo*. Barth sees God's electing grace in Christ, "*the* mercy of God," as presupposing the divine concluding of all in the state of disobedience: "Those on whom He willed to have mercy and did have mercy are the very ones that He had concluded or placed under this verdict."[122] That is, the object of God's gracious election is *homo lapsus*.

Furthermore, the incarnation is for the salvation of all from the "state and being of disobedience," which "is the unity of their being in the far country in which God has sought them in His Son to call and bring them home."[123] Combining this basically infralapsarian Christology and doctrine of predestination, Barth contends that "the one who was set aside in Jesus Christ [i.e., elected in Christ] and who is defined and claimed and described as such in the divine verdict *is the man of sin*."[124]

History of Christ and Fallen World-History

Moving on, Barth concludes his exegesis of Romans 11:32 by turning to a discussion of Adam and the history of fallenness, or the fallenness of Adamic history. Noteworthy here is the fact that Barth does not use the word *Historie* to denote the "godless" (illusorily so—the history of God's covenant partner cannot possibly be Godless!) history of the world. Readers of Barth recall that in *CD* I/1 Barth distinguishes between *Geschichte* and *Historie*: the former denotes revelational history as God's act, while the latter is plain history as understood by historians with their naturalistic assumptions— *bloss historisch*. In *CD* IV/1 he no longer uses the binary concept of *Geschichte*-versus-*Historie*, but he still uses the word *Geschichte* with more or less the same meaning, even though his understanding of God's being-in-act has undergone significant maturation. It is thus surprising that instead of referring to the apparently and illusorily godless history of the world and the naturalistic literary genre associated therewith as *Historie*, Barth chooses the word *Geschichte*.

In *CD* IV/1 Barth distinguishes between two kinds of *Geschichte* that are inseparable, albeit with abiding distinction. The first is Adamic history—humanity's history of fallenness—which he always identifies clearly either by

---
[122] Ibid., 558; ET 501.
[123] Ibid.
[124] Ibid., 559; ET 502.

the context or by the term "world-history" (*Weltgeschichte*). This *Weltgeschichte* is distinct yet inseparable from the *Geschichte* of Christ, which Barth defines as the history of obedience of the Son of God.

For the Barth of *CD* IV/1, there is no history that falls outside of God's *Geschichte* in Christ; thus Adamic history has no independent status. The *Weltgeschichte* of Adam's fall took place because God has rejected it absolutely in Christ's *Geschichte*, and in rejecting Adamic history Christ took it on himself in order to sublate it. There could have been no *Weltgeschichte* without the Christ-*Geschichte*: *Weltgeschichte* is, so to say, the negative presupposition of the Christ-*Geschichte*. (Here again we have a reference to Barth's basically infralapsarian Christology, with a doctrine of election dialectically combining supra- and infralapsarian elements.)

Barth begins his discussion of humanity's fallenness as *Weltgeschichte* by commenting that in Romans 11:32, "when the word 'all' is used . . . it is very much to the point to think of what we mean by the word 'history.'"[125] That is to say, "world-history is concluded in disobedience."[126] World-history as such is "apart from the will and Word and work of God."[127] To be sure, "this does not mean that it is outside the divine control, that it is abandoned to chance, or fate . . . , or indeed that it stands under the dominion of the devil. . . . The history of the world which God made in Jesus Christ, and with a view to Him, cannot cease to have its centre and goal in Him."[128] Yet this "goal" is God's Yes as the *Aufhebung* of God's No to "the history which is grounded and determined and characterized by . . . corruption."[129] World-history as such, then, is "grounded on the ignoring and rejection of the will and Word and work of God and determined [that is, constituted] in this way, by this ignoring and rejection."[130]

Already here the basically infralapsarian orientation of Barth's christological understanding of double predestination is clear: God's Yes in Christ to world-history is not just a Yes, but a Yes presupposing a No, and this No

---

[125] Ibid., 563; ET 505.
[126] Ibid., 564; ET 506 (translation mine). In many instances, Bromiley's English translation renders *Weltgeschichte* as either "history of the world" or simply "history" without the predicate, which tends to blur the distinction between Adamic history and the history of Christ.
[127] Ibid., 563; ET 505.
[128] Ibid., 564; ET 506.
[129] Ibid.
[130] Ibid., 563; ET 505.

is to the fallenness and corruption of Adamic history. That is, election presupposes the fall (though, of course, the fall would not have been possible without election—one must not neglect the dialectical nature of Barth's theology); the object of election is *homo lapsus*. (Again one must remember that for Barth, Christ as elected human is without sin, and this *homo lapsus* refers to humankind elected in and with Christ.) As Barth now sees it—a view of history that was still quite implicit in *CD* II/2—by the act of election-in-Christ God participates in humankind's history of fallenness so that world-history may in turn participate in God through Christ.

In a move somewhat reminiscent of Kant, Barth identifies world-history and all humans therein, "concluded in disobedience," as Adam: "The Bible gives to this history and to all men in this sense the general title of Adam."[131] Barth clarifies that "the meaning of Adam is simply man, and as the bearer of this name which denotes the being and essence of all other men, Adam appears in the Genesis story as the man who owes his existence directly to the creative will and Word and act of God without any human intervention, the man who is to that extent the first man."[132]

Here we see that Barth does not deny the real existence of Adam as the first human directly created by God. Yet Barth does not use the term "historical Adam" to denote this first human, because the genre of historiography deals with natural events, but the creation of Adam was supernatural. Thus Barth resorts to the category of saga, a genre that, in his view, may be used to properly narrate God's participation in the creaturely realm.

It must be noted that by using the term "saga" Barth is not claiming that the creation story is a figment of the imagination or that what is narrated in Genesis 1-2 did not really happen. Barth is aware that "saga" is generally understood as the literary "form which, using intuition and imagination, has to take up historical narration at the point where events are no longer susceptible as such to historical proof."[133] As Barth sees it, this general description applies to the biblical saga as well, but he emphasizes that "within this *genre* biblical saga is a special instance which cannot be compared with others but

---

[131] Ibid., 565; ET 507.
[132] Ibid., 566; ET 507-8.
[133] Ibid., 567; ET 508.

has to be seen and understood in and for itself."[134] Biblical saga is special because therein "intuition and imagination are used but in order to give prophetic witness to *what has taken place* by virtue of the Word of God in the (historical or pre-historical) sphere where there can be no historical proof."[135]

The creation of Adam, then, pertains to the prehistorical "sphere of biblical saga."[136] It was in this sphere, too, that "there took place the fall, the fall of the first man."[137] According to Barth, "the biblical saga tells us that world-history began with the pride and fall of man."[138] Recall that world-history, as he defines it, is the sphere and genre that ignores and rejects the will and Word and work of God. For Barth, "it is the name of Adam the transgressor which God gives to world-history as a whole."[139]

If world-history is Adamic history as such—as fallen history and the history of fallenness—then in world-history "there never was a golden age. ... The first man was immediately the first sinner."[140] Here Barth identifies Adam, the first human, as *primus inter pares* (first among equals). However, this does not imply for Barth a doctrine of inherited sin.[141] Adam "has not poisoned us or passed on a disease. What we do after him is not done according to an example which irresistibly overthrows us, or in an imitation of his act which is ordained for all his successors. No one has to be Adam. We are so freely and on our own responsibility."[142]

Now, if the relationship between Adam and all other humans is not "one which is pragmatically grounded and demonstrable, nor is it one which can be explained in terms of a transmission between him and us," then how is this relationship to be understood?[143] Again Barth's answer, as always, is that this relationship must and can only be understood in light of Christ, the Word of God. "It is the Word of God which gives this name and title [Adam] to mankind and the history of man," since "it is God's Word which fuses all men into unity

---

[134] Ibid.
[135] Ibid. (emphasis added).
[136] Ibid.
[137] Ibid.
[138] Ibid.
[139] Ibid.
[140] Ibid., 568; ET 509.
[141] For a succinct discussion of this topic, see John Webster, *Barth's Moral Theology: Human Action in Barth's Thought* (London: T&T Clark, 1998), 73.
[142] *KD* IV/1, 568; ET 509.
[143] Ibid., 569; ET 510.

with this man as *primus inter pares*."¹⁴⁴ The Word of God forbids us to "dream of any golden age in the past or any real progress within Adamic mankind and history or any future state of historical perfection," because the only hope of humankind is in "the atonement which has taken place in Jesus Christ."¹⁴⁵

More concretely, Barth proposes to turn to Romans 5:12-21 in order to understand why and to what extent all humankind has been concluded in the disobedience of Adamic history.¹⁴⁶ This is the biblical passage setting forth the famous Pauline dialectic of Christ and Adam. As Barth understands this passage, "Jesus Christ takes the first place as the original, and Adam the second place as 'the figure of him that was to come.'"¹⁴⁷ For this reason, Barth contends that Paul "knew Jesus Christ first and then Adam."¹⁴⁸

The Christ-Adam dialectic in *CD* IV/1 is again to be understood in terms of the Hegelian logic of *Aufhebung*. The one end of the dialectic "does not balance" the other.¹⁴⁹ Adam "has no independent existence," but exists only as, "as it were, the negative side of Jesus Christ."¹⁵⁰ Adamic history as a history of rejecting God has no autonomous status; it owes its existence to the No of God that has rejected it. Christ is the Yes of God as the (divine) rejection of (human) rejection, and it is in the history of Christ as such that Adamic world-history has been allowed to exist in order to be sublated.

Here we may note again that Barth's interpretation of the Christ-Adam relation is basically infralapsarian in both the christological and predestinarian senses: election-in-Christ presupposes Adamic fallenness just as the incarnation is Christ's participation in fallen world-history drawing Adam's fallen race into *participatio Christi*.

The Christ-Adam Dialectic: Election and the Trinity in Recent Debates

Bruce McCormack: Barth's "historicized Christology." At this juncture we might note that there are various interpretations of Barth when it comes

---

¹⁴⁴Ibid.
¹⁴⁵Ibid.
¹⁴⁶Ibid., 571; ET 512.
¹⁴⁷Ibid., 571-72; ET 512-13.
¹⁴⁸Ibid.
¹⁴⁹Ibid., 572; ET 513.
¹⁵⁰Ibid.

to his Christology in *CD* IV/1. Bruce McCormack contends that in *CD* IV/1 Barth formulates a "historicized Christology" in which he replaces the Chalcedonian "category of 'nature with the category of 'history' and then integrating 'history' into his concept of 'person.'"[151] McCormack rightly observes that the Christology of *CD* IV/1 is developed in a much more actualistic and historical direction than I/2 (the first part-volume wherein Barth sets forth his Christology in the *CD*). As early as 1993 McCormack noted that "Barth did not understand human nature in substantialist terms. He understood 'nature' to be a function of decision and act."[152] Though in 1993 he applied this description to both *CD* I/2 and IV/1 and did not recognize the significant development in the latter's "historicized Christology," this is certainly not a wrong interpretation of the later Barth. The more complicated question, however, is how much and which aspects, if any, of traditional substantialist ontology Barth retains in his historicized Christology.

Like Nimmo, who requires that "we ... choose between an 'actualist' and a 'substantialistic' ontology," McCormack sets up a questionable dichotomy between "Chalcedonian" (on his view substantialist) and "historicized" (antimetaphysical) Christology, leaving no choices in between.[153] To begin with, McCormack's (and Nimmo's) understanding of Chalcedon starts on slippery footing, not acknowledging that "Barth saw the Chalcedonian Definition as a regulative framework, not as a substantive position. ... The terms *hypostasis* ('person') and *physis* ('nature') had no fixed meaning in the fifth century."[154]

Further, given that Chalcedon does rely heavily on classical substantialism (hence the *homoousion*), there is no reason to suppose that the modern antimetaphysical impulse in Barth must lead to a complete rejection of every last element of substantialism—for that matter there is no reason to suppose that Chalcedon itself uncritically adopted a substantialist ontology rather than simply relied on substantialist concepts without accepting

---

[151]McCormack, "Karl Barth's Historicized Christology," 222. Also see Nimmo, *"Concursus Dei."*
[152]Bruce McCormack, *For Us and Our Salvation: Incarnation and Atonement in the Reformed Tradition* (Princeton: Princeton Theological Seminary, 1993), 21.
[153]Hunsinger, *Reading Barth with Charity*, 76.
[154]George Hunsinger, *Evangelical, Catholic, and Reformed: Doctrinal Essays on Barth and Related Themes* (Grand Rapids: Eerdmans, 2015), 160.

any system of metaphysical ontology as a whole. As Hunsinger points out, and as my exposition of *CD* IV/1 will demonstrate anon, "Barth was not replacing one ontology with another. . . . He was simply using Chalcedon to regulate his thinking as he strove to work out the theological and Christological implications of the biblical narratives."[155]

The crucial question here is: given Barth's ever-critical attitude toward classical ontology, what aspects of substantialist understandings of the category of "nature" does Barth retain? Without examining the intricacies underlying this question and the distinction between "nature" and "history" in Barth's usage, which I have already discussed, McCormack mistakenly asserts that Barth describes Christ as having assumed "fallen human nature"—this mistake is not even remedied by qualifying "fallen human nature" as "reconciled."[156] Note that the term "fallen human nature" never appears even in the passage that McCormack quotes from *CD* I/2 in support of his fallenness view. As we shall see in the next section, the Barth of *CD* IV/1 is all the more emphatic that Christ assumed *sinless* human nature even as he took on himself humankind's history of sin.

For one thing, McCormack's assertion that Barth has "replaced" the Chalcedonian category of "nature" with the category of "history" is in need of more intricate qualifications to address the way Barth uses the term "nature" with reference to an enhypostatic-anhypostatic Christology on numerous occasions in *CD* §57–59. On this note, Paul Jones's contention that Barth "effectively discards the language of 'nature' in his mature Christology" also seems exaggerated, notwithstanding his otherwise sophisticated arguments.[157] I will devote the next section to discussing Jones's important work on Christ's humanity in Barth's Christology.

For now, suffice it to say that Barth *does* use the language of "nature" in *CD* IV/1, and as we have seen, he defines human nature in a meaningful way that retains certain aspects of substantialist ontology: God created human nature to be good and it remains good even in the *status corruptionis*, as sin is an alien element that never becomes a part of what God has created. In

---

[155]Ibid., 162.
[156]McCormack, *For Us and Our Salvation*, 21.
[157]Paul Jones, *The Humanity of Christ: Christology in Karl Barth's Church Dogmatics* (London: T&T Clark, 2008), 28.

this usage of the term "nature" Barth retains the Creator-creature distinction as an aspect of the substantialist ontology of classical theism, even though he does not accept metaphysical substantialism as a whole. According to the substance ontology (or ontologies) of classical theism(s), "nature" pertains to the idea of "being." There are only two kinds of beings: eternally self-existent being and creatures that derive their being from the Creator. Divine nature is uncreated and human nature is created, and there is not a third kind of "nature," hence sin, evil and death—neither creatures nor second creators—as *das Nichtige* ('that which is not').

For Barth, the Chalcedonian notion of "nature" as set within a metaphysical framework of classical substantialism "gave the impression of being static and immobile (IV/1, 127). Like any grammar, it did not stand on its own but needed to be fleshed out. Barth did that in an 'actualistic' way."[158] In "actualizing" and perhaps in a way "historicizing" the Chalcedonian Definition, Barth formulates the doctrine of the incarnation as the description of one single event in process rather than a static system of metaphysical truths, just as he would describe God as being-in-act in contradistinction to classical substantialism's static notion of God as being.

However, Barth does not simply supplant substantialist ontology with a Christocentric or actualistic one. Hunsinger puts it best: "Barth does not abandon his 'perfect being' theology for the sake of his 'actualism.' On the contrary, he incorporates his actualism into his perfect-being theology. Actualism is developed as an inner aspect of God's perfect being."[159]

Barth retains in his actualism the Creator-creature distinction in classical-substantialist theistic ontology and makes a stronger case for it than even Calvin and other strict adherents to the Chalcedonian tradition: Barth insists that human *nature* as *created by God* must remain ever sinless and unfallen.

There is for the Barth of *CD* IV/1 a strict distinction between *nature* and *history*. He does not, as McCormack would have it, "historicize" the category of nature in such a way that it is completely absorbed into the category of history and process. Retaining the Creator-creature distinction of classical substantialism in defining human nature, Barth states that Christ as very

---

[158] Hunsinger, *Evangelical, Catholic, and Reformed*, 162.
[159] Hunsinger, *Reading Barth with Charity*, 133.

God assumes human nature in order to be the *sinless* bearer of our "flesh" (this point will become clearer in the next section). He writes:

> Who the one true God is, and what He is, i.e., what is His being as God, and therefore His deity, His 'divine nature,' which is also the *divine nature of Jesus Christ* if He is very God—all this we have to discover from the fact that as such He is very man and a *partaker of human nature*, from His becoming man, from His incarnation and from what He has done and suffered in the flesh. For—to put it more pointedly, the mirror in which it can be known (and is known) that He is God, and of the divine nature, is His becoming flesh and His existence in the flesh.[160]

Again: "[The assumption of *forma servi*] corresponds to and is grounded in His *divine nature*."[161] In a brief exegesis of John 1:14 ("the Word became flesh . . ."), Barth comments that "'flesh' is the concrete *form* of *human nature* and the being of man in his world under the sign of the fall of Adam—the being of man as corrupted and therefore destroyed, as unreconciled with God and therefore lost."[162] That is to say, "flesh" denotes human nature, which is in and of itself God's good creation, under the sign of Adam's fall that is alien to this nature. Recall that for Barth the human *being* is in the *condition* of corruption, but human *nature* as created by God in Christ remains good.

In any case, the foregoing discussion issues the caveat that when we talk about Barth's "historicized Christology"—if we are to use the term at all—we must not lose sight of the Creator-creature distinction as an aspect of substantialist ontology that he retains. It would be erroneous to think that Barth would simply reject or redefine everything in substantialist ontology and classical theism in constructing some modern sort of "ontology."

McCormack on election and Trinity: Basically infralapsarian interpretation. Furthermore, McCormack's proposal of a historicized Christology in *CD* IV/1 as one possible way of reading the Christ-Adam dialectic is related to his understanding of the logical relation between incarnation and

---

[160]*KD* IV/1, 193; ET 177 (emphasis added).
[161]Ibid., 198; ET 182 (emphasis added).
[162]Ibid., 180; ET 165 (emphasis added).

the Trinity.¹⁶³ According to McCormack, if Barth were always consistent with the "Christocentric ontology"¹⁶⁴ developed in *CD* II/2, then he would not have, as he did at times, posited a *Logos asarkos* as the necessary presupposition of (i.e., logically preceding) God's election to become incarnate. McCormack is worried that regressing to the notion of a *Logos asarkos* above and behind the *Logos incarnandus* self-revealed in Jesus Christ would constitute natural-theological speculation. On McCormack's interpretation of Barth's mature theological "ontology," the *Logos* is eternally and necessarily *incarnandus*, as there is no God in Godself logically prior to the God *incarnandus* and *incarnatus* as self-revealed in Jesus Christ. On this view, election-incarnation constitutes God's triune being; the Trinity is a function of and logically follows God's decision to be incarnate.

When this scheme is applied to *CD* IV/1, McCormack would say that human history in Christ participates in God's very being as what God eternally is. Hunsinger comments on the "revisionists" who follow McCormack: "They think that [the history of God's works and acts *ad extra*] is at least as fundamental to the constitution of God's being as [the history of God's triune life *ad intra*] (if not more so)."¹⁶⁵ McCormack's position raises some difficult questions when we take into account what Barth has said about history: as we have just seen, Adamic history, which participates in the history of Christ, is the sinful history of humanity's rejection of God. Some of McCormack's critics might be worried that this would give to Adamic history, with all its corruption and prideful fallenness, an ontological status with its locus in the very being of God.

Though I do not agree with McCormack's interpretation, I prefer to read him with charity. True enough, oftentimes the "revisionist Barth" is too reminiscent of Hegel, but we should at least credit McCormack for explicitly

---

¹⁶³More recently McCormack defended this interpretation in "Election and the Trinity." In an earlier work he directed his arguments against van Driel: "Seek God Where He May Be Found: A Response to Edwin Chr. van Driel," *Scottish Journal of Theology* 60 (2007): 62-79.

¹⁶⁴George Hunsinger cautions that "ontology" in the stricter sense of the word as a branch of metaphysics must be distinguished from its extended meaning that refers loosely to any "general area of action, inquiry, or interest" that addresses ontological topics. He points out that McCormack and so-called revisionists "do not take sufficient pains to distinguish" between the two, and "too often ... seem to trade on the ambiguity, appearing to speak of [the latter] while slipping into [the former]." See Hunsinger, *Reading Barth with Charity*, 2.

¹⁶⁵Ibid., 127.

rejecting the "most popular route at present" to "follow Hegel in making a direct identification of the second person of the Trinity with the human Jesus."[166]

Commenting on "the kind of Christology worked out by Barth," McCormack observes that "*kenosis* is by addition and not by subtraction."[167] This implies that fallen human history assumed by Christ is not proper of the second person of the triune God. To be sure, "for the Barth of *CD* IV/1 . . . , the 'humiliation of the Son' in time has its root in the humility of the Son in eternity—which means that it has its root in the eternal relation of the Son to the Father."[168] Christ's humility in eternity is defined by the eternal relation of command and obedience between the Father and the Son. It is by the "eternal relation in which the Father 'commands' and the Son 'obeys'" that "God freely constitutes his own being in eternity"—this is how election constitutes the Trinity on McCormack's reading of Barth.[169] According to this interpretation, "the 'humiliation' of the Son in time" and "the 'humility' of the Son in eternity" are not *simpliciter* identical: "What happens in time . . . *corresponds* to what happens in eternity."[170] In eternity the human history of fallenness has already been rejected, and as much as Christ's participation in the *status corruptionis* corresponds to this rejection, in God's eternal being-in-act there is no room for any sinful activity.

Note here that McCormack's interpretation of the Christology of *CD* IV/1 as "historicized"—problematic as it may be (I will discuss this issue later)— leans heavily toward infralapsarianism. According to this "historicized Christology," the incarnation is necessarily bound up with fallen history, thus a supralapsarian Christology claiming that God would have become incarnate regardless of humanity's fallenness is ruled out.

This means that a simply supralapsarian understanding of the object of election is also excluded in McCormack's interpretation of Barth. Barth describes election in terms of God's faithfulness to God's covenant partner in Christ, who as electing God is himself also God's very covenant partner elected from all eternity. According to McCormack's understanding of Barth,

---

[166]See Bruce McCormack, "Karl Barth's Christology as a Resource for a Reformed Version of Kenoticism," *International Journal of Systematic Theology* 8 (2006): 247.
[167]Ibid., 247-48.
[168]Ibid., 248-49.
[169]Ibid., 249.
[170]Ibid.

God's electing grace could not have been apart from or without regard to the fallen Adamic history that has been taken up into Christ and in which Christ participates. Thus, despite his questionable "historicized Christology," McCormack rightly identifies "the object of God's electing grace" as "the sinful human," as we saw in chapter two.[171]

Speaking of Christ as the object of election in Barth's "Christocentric ontology," McCormack stresses that "God's eternal will is for fellowship with fallen, sinful human beings."[172] This is the basic contention of infralapsarianism.

George Hunsinger and the "traditionalists." As much as the "revisionist Barth" might appear thoroughly modernized, the real Barth in fact posits a preincarnate Trinity and thus a *Logos asarkos* as the necessary presupposition of (i.e., logically preceding) election and incarnation. On the view of those who take Barth at his word, God is in and of Godself triune and by a free decision became the electing God *incarnandus* without ceasing to be the same *Logos asarkos*. God in Godself, in God's "inward being" (a term that Barth himself uses, as we saw earlier), does not participate in history, nor history in God in Godself.[173] Humanity, which for the Barth of *CD* IV/1 is in one sense synonymous with world-history, is what God has assumed by the pretemporal act of election, and this act presupposes the triunity of God's inward being.

Arguments for this view have been advanced by the so-called traditionalists, including George Hunsinger, Paul Molnar and Edwin van Driel, among others.[174] I have defended this interpretation in two earlier footnotes in this chapter, and my intention now is to engage this reading of Barth with my understanding of his christological doctrine of election—especially the nuanced version set forth in *CD* IV/1—as basically infralapsarian.

"Traditionalist" interpretation: A supralapsarian solution? In adopting this interpretation of Barth on election and Trinity, one would be tempted

---

[171] Bruce McCormack, "*Justitia aliena*: Karl Barth in Conversation with the Evangelical Doctrine of Imputed Righteousness," in *Justification in Perspective: Historical Development and Contemporary Challenges*, ed. Bruce McCormack (Grand Rapids: Baker Academic, 2006), 191.

[172] McCormack, "Grace and Being," 198.

[173] "The second 'person' of the Godhead in Himself and as such is not God the Reconciler. In Himself and as such He is not revealed to us. In Himself and as such He is not *Deus pro nobis*, either ontologically or epistemologically." See *KD* IV/1, 54; ET 52.

[174] See, for example, Paul Molnar, "The Trinity, Election and God's Ontological Freedom: A Response to Kevin Hector," *International Journal of Systematic Theology* 6 (2006): 294-306; Edwin van Driel, "Karl Barth on the Eternal Existence of Jesus Christ," *Scottish Journal of Systematic Theology* 60 (2007): 45-61; Hunsinger, "Election and the Trinity."

to resort to a supralapsarian view of his christological doctrine of election in order to steer away from some theological difficulties. According to Barth, election is God's eternal covenantal act to be *for* and *with* God's covenant partner by the act of incarnation. In this act God becomes what the covenant partner is, namely, human, without ceasing to be God. By this act, then, God actually takes humanity into what becomes of the life of the triune God. Now, if the covenant partner to whom God has pledged faithfulness, the *obiectum praedestinationis*, is sinful humankind—*homo lapsus*—would this not imply that by the incarnation God actually took sin into God's very own being-in-act? Does the incarnation not make the Son of God a sinner and a reprobate?[175]

I wonder whether van Driel's proposal of a supralapsarian reading of Barth is partly driven by the concern to avoid ascribing sin to the Son of God and thus to what becomes of the life of the triune God. (I have explained van Driel's supralapsarian interpretation of Barth in chapter two.) Van Driel contends that "we have on Barth's side ... the decree of election, which is not part of God's nature, but dependent on the divine will, and contingent, since God could have been God without being the God of election."[176] So far so good—by this maneuver van Driel (as well as Molnar and Hunsinger for that matter) avoid attributing sin to God's nature in a way that some think McCormack's reading of Barth might. Yet as if worried that election might be described as an act of taking sin into God's nature, van Driel asserts that in Barth's theology "the ontological and epistemic principles that govern divine revelation are not a result of sin, but given with the nature of Creator and creation. Incarnation, as the necessary means of divine self-disclosure, is therefore a supralapsarian event."[177] That is, the incarnation was God's act of revealing Godself to humankind regardless of sin, and thus the humanity that God has taken unto Godself is unfallen. In this way van Driel's supralapsarian interpretation of Barth can avoid attributing sin to God's being in any way.

However, as I have argued, Barth clearly indicates that God's covenant partner is *sinful humanity*, and that the incarnation—as depicted in *CD*

---

[175] I am indebted to Professor Paul Fiddes for putting this question to me and encouraging me to think it through.
[176] Van Driel, "Eternal Existence," 53.
[177] Edwin van Driel, *Incarnation Anyway: Arguments for Supralapsarian Christology* (Oxford: Oxford University Press, 2008), 77.

IV/1—is God's act of assuming humanity *in Adam*. The Adamic history that the Son of God has assumed by the incarnation began with the fall, and in it there is no "golden age" whatsoever. As I argued in chapter two, the mainstream understanding of Barth is such that both election and incarnation presuppose the fallenness of humanity. Of course the converse is also true, namely, that humanity's fall presupposes election and God's decision to become incarnate: one must not neglect the dialectical nature of Barth's theology. However, as we have seen, the supralapsarian contention, in light of which van Driel interprets Barth, is that election and incarnation *do not* presuppose the fall. This obviously contradicts Barth's lapsarian thinking. In other words, as much as van Driel may succeed in rescuing Barth, as it were, from ascribing sin to God's being, his interpretation contradicts what Barth expressly states and how the majority of mainstream scholars understand Barth's view of election, incarnation and the fall.

George Hunsinger's rejoinder. It is none other than Hunsinger who, as if in dialogue with van Driel, states that in Barth's theology, election (and thus the incarnation) "presupposes the creation and fall of the world."[178] So how might Hunsinger avoid describing Barth's view of the incarnation as an act whereby God took sin into the triune being?

The key here is to recognize the *abiding distinction* between the deity and humanity of Christ, and thus between the Son of God in Godself and the human Jesus. Hunsinger writes: "When Barth states that Jesus Christ is 'the subject of election' he is not speaking without qualification (*simpliciter*) but only in a certain respect (*secundum quid*)."[179]

What Hunsinger means to say might be summarized by a statement that Barth himself makes in *CD* II/2: "As the Son of the Father He [Jesus Christ] has no need of any special election."[180] Christ is elected human first in his humanity and derivatively as the Son of God. By the same token Christ is electing God first as Son of God and derivatively as Son of Man, who was present in the Son's pretemporal act of election not by virtue of actual existence but "proleptically" (Hunsinger) by virtue of God's decision. These two are not *simpliciter* identical. They are one and inseparable for sure, but there

---

[178] Hunsinger, "Election and the Trinity," 182.
[179] Ibid., 182.
[180] *KD* II/2, 110; ET 103 (emphasis added).

is an abiding distinction between Christ's deity and humanity such that strictly speaking the one elected is not the Son of God but Jesus the human being in whom all humans participate.

Hunsinger explains this notion of abiding distinction as follows:

> The *logos asarkos* is not eliminated upon becoming *ensarkos*. On the contrary, as intimated by the doctrine of the extra Calvinisticum, the Logos subsists in two modes (*asarkos* in eternity/*ensarkos* in history) simultaneously (through a pattern of unity-in-distinction). It is one and the same unabridged Logos in two simultaneous modes of existence—*totus/totus*, primary and secondary objectivity. The *logos asarkos* becomes the *logos ensarkos* without ceasing to be the eternal *logos asarkos* in God's relationship in and for himself to all eternity.[181]

In this way, when Christ assumed human nature and took up Adamic history into his own person, the Son qua Son and therewith the inner being of the triune God remained unchanged and untainted by fallen world-history.

This is not to say that the contingent properties God has chosen in electing to be incarnate makes no difference in God's being-in-act. Hunsinger agrees with Paul Dafydd Jones, whose nuanced interpretation of Barth's Christology we will discuss anon, that "once chosen, God's contingent properties do indeed define his identity in a way that makes a difference for him. God will never be another than the One incarnate in Jesus Christ, who took suffering, sin, and death into his divine being in order to destroy them."[182] However, "the difference they make is by addition and self-qualification, not by essential transformation. God's contingent properties represent the way in which he actualizes himself *ad extra* without losing or essentially altering himself."[183] In other words, by taking up sin in Jesus Christ God does not become a sinner, just as God does not cease to be impassible by taking up suffering and death.

At this juncture I might add that for Barth the human nature Christ has assumed is not in and of itself fallen. Contra the contention that Barth holds to a "fallenness view" of Christ's humanity,[184] he insists that Christ's hu-

---

[181] Hunsinger, "Election and the Trinity," 194.
[182] Hunsinger, *Reading Barth with Charity*, 141.
[183] Ibid.
[184] For example, Oliver Crisp, *Divinity and Humanity* (Cambridge: Cambridge University Press, 2007), 90-93, 98.

manity is in and of itself sinless. The incarnation is such that Christ assumed sinless human *nature* and participates in Adamic *history*, the sinful *condition* of all other human beings, uniting them to his own humanity, thereby taking on the sin of all. Barth makes this point crystal clear in his discussion of the Christ-Adam relation in *CD* IV/1: "This other, too, came directly from God, not as a creature only, but as the Son of God and Himself God by nature. He, too, was a sinner and debtor, but as the sinless and guiltless bearer of the sins of others, the sins of all other men."[185] In other words, human fallenness was transferred to Christ's humanity by means of the union between him and the rest of the human race.

In view of the sinlessness of Christ's own human nature, then, we can see that Hunsinger's understanding of the logical relationship between election and the Trinity in Barth's theology, with infralapsarian impulses underlying it, is safeguarded from describing the humanity of Christ as in itself fallen, much less ascribing sin to the being of the triune God.

"An inconsistency in Barth's thought"? While I follow Hunsinger's interpretation, Paul Fiddes's critical analysis from the 1980s serves as a reminder that the Trinity-election debate in recent Barth scholarship reflects at least a certain tension in Barth's own theology.[186] Fiddes seems to be more in line with Hunsinger when stating that for Barth, "God in himself is holy mystery, but we can be confident that the being of God corresponds to his self-revelation" (it would be more precise to reverse the order and say that God's self-revelation corresponds to God's being), as "there is an 'analogy of relations' between the Triune God in essence and the Triune God as revealed."[187] On this reading of Barth, however, Fiddes comments that "there is . . . bound to be a gap between the immanent and the economic Trinity since this leaves room for God's freedom to reveal himself as a work of sheer grace."[188]

At this juncture, Fiddes's criticism appears to be similar to McCormack's concern that when Barth posits the *Logos asarkos* as a logical presupposition of election-incarnation, Barth is contradicting his own "Christocentric ontology" by engaging in metaphysical speculation about a God-in-Godself

---

[185] *KD* IV/1, 571; ET 512.
[186] Paul Fiddes, *The Creative Suffering of God* (Oxford: Oxford University Press, 1988), 112-22.
[187] Ibid., 116.
[188] Ibid.

back behind the God self-revealed in Christ. Fiddes comments that Barth's treatment of the immanent and economic Trinity "drives too great a wedge between the being of God in himself and his acts in the world."[189]

Similarly, in Barth's own day, Emil Brunner had commented that Barth's Christocentric doctrine of election would lead to the "extraordinary" conclusion that election constitutes the Trinity, though, fortunately in Brunner's view, "Barth does not attempt to deduce [such conclusions]."[190] This seems to be precisely what McCormack calls "an inconsistency in Barth's thought," against which he tries to "register a critical correction."[191]

Whether this is an inconsistency that needs to be corrected or a theological tension that Barth intentionally leaves unresolved is a question that defies any simple answer, though it seems to me that Barth would be willing to pay the price of inconsistency in order to maintain certain theological convictions that he deems fundamental.

What seems lacking in the above-mentioned critics of Barth and the "revisionists" who try to rescue him, as it were, from the alleged inconsistency is "the principle of charity," which entails, inter alia, that "one assumes for the moment that the ideas under consideration, regardless of how difficult they may seem, are both truth and internally coherent."[192] Moreover, "if apparent contradictions are found, an active attempt is made to resolve them."[193] Hunsinger is fair in suggesting that among most of the revisionists, little "active attempt [has] been made to resolve [the alleged contradictions] in Barth's favor."[194]

In any case, what appears to be the consensus now is that Barth does posit the *Logos asarkos* as the logical presupposition of election-incarnation—the debate is as to whether this is an inconsistency on Barth's part that leaves us only with a choice between classical theism/substantialist ontology and a revisionist "Christocentric/actualistic ontology." The next section will touch on this discussion.

---

[189]Ibid., 122.
[190]Emil Brunner, *Dogmatics*, vol. 1, *The Christian Doctrine of God*, trans. Olive Wyon (Philadelphia: Westminster, 1950), 315.
[191]McCormack, "Grace and Being," 193.
[192]Hunsinger, *Reading Barth with Charity*, xii.
[193]Ibid.
[194]Ibid., xiii.

Christ's Sinlessness and Human Nature:
In Dialogue with Paul Dafydd Jones

We now return to the topic of Christ's sinlessness. My understanding of Barth's notion of the sinlessness of Christ's humanity, as delineated in the foregoing discussions, is of course not the only possible interpretation. Paul Jones's treatment of this topic in his brilliant contribution, *The Humanity of Christ: Christology in Karl Barth's Church Dogmatics*, offers a different perspective. The book itself is among the most sophisticated studies of the development of Christology in the *Church Dogmatics* to date. In what follows I shall show that although I read Barth differently from Jones when it comes to the question of how Barth treats the Chalcedonian category of "nature" (*physis*), he and I share the same understanding that in Barth's mature theology Christ's person cannot be discussed without soteriological reference (i.e., Barth's Christology is basically infralapsarian in that Jesus Christ, who is the beginning of all God's ways and works, is concretely determined to be the Reconciler between God and sinners), and that election goes hand in hand with God's rejection of sin (i.e., Barth's doctrine of election is basically infralapsarian in that the humankind elected in and with Christ is *homo lapsus*, even though Christ as elected human is in himself without sin).

While Jones's reading of Barth's notion of Christ's sinlessness is for the most part thorough and convincing, one of his assertions seems somewhat overstated, namely, that Barth "effectively discards the language of 'nature' in his mature Christology."[195] Here Jones is in agreement with McCormack's assessment of Hunsinger's description of Barth's mature Christology as "basically Chalcedonian": they are of the opinion that the term "Chalcedonian" might not be entirely helpful in describing Barth's mature Christology because he has discarded Chalcedon's substantialist category of "nature."

I have already shown earlier that McCormack has yet to recognize the intricate distinctions in Barth's usage of the terms "nature" and "history" in *CD* IV/1. While McCormack's proposal of understanding Barth's mature Christology as "historicized" is concerned with *CD* IV/1, Jones, recognizing Barth's habitual use of the word "nature" in this part-volume, goes even further than McCormack, claiming that "*Natur* and *Wesen* take up no

---

[195] Jones, *Humanity of Christ*, 28.

meaningful role in *Church Dogmatics* I/2 and thereafter."[196] Jones's strategy is to conflate "nature" and "history" in Barth's usage, claiming that Barth has completely redefined the notion of "nature" by historicizing it. This enables Jones to uphold his thesis regarding Barth's disposal of the Chalcedonian category of nature while liberally quoting passages in which Barth explicitly uses the term *Natur* or *Wesen*.[197]

Hunsinger's recent contribution challenges Jones's application of this reading strategy to Christ's divine nature and thereby God's eternal properties: Jones "sometimes writes as if God's contingent properties serve to 'transform' his noncontingent properties (like eternality, simplicity, impassibility, and immutability) into something essentially other than they were before."[198] Hunsinger is worried that in Jones's historicized Christology, "God somehow historicizes his eternal being."[199] Approving of Jones's emphasis "that God's decision to become incarnate in pretemporal election affects God's concrete identity materially and radically, especially because it leads God himself to suffer and die for us in Christ on the cross,"[200] Hunsinger warns that Jones "is oblivious to Barth's clear use of Chalcedon to establish the grammar by which these two 'histories' (eternal and temporal) are inseparably related while also remaining abidingly distinct. He stresses their oneness but obscures their distinction."[201]

What I offer in the following discussions is on a related theme: Jones not only tends to blur the distinctions between God's noncontingent and contingent properties by conflating the Son's eternal and temporal histories (as Hunsinger points out), but also historicizes Christ's human nature in much the same way as to render the notion of *nature* completely meaningless on its own apart from the notions of *history* and *act*. In other words, just as Jones, like McCormack and Nimmo, tends to slip into interpreting Barth's notion of God as being-*as*-act rather than being-*in*-act, he is also inclined to obscure the distinction between Christ's human *nature* and *history*, *act* or *condition*.

---

[196]Ibid., 33.
[197]Ibid., 43.
[198]Hunsinger, *Reading Barth with Charity*, 140.
[199]Ibid., 143.
[200]Ibid., 156.
[201]Ibid., 143.

Jones needs to defend his approach to Christ's human agency with more efforts, as he has yet to successfully account for Barth's meaningful discourse on human nature in CD IV/1, which I have discussed at length in this chapter. Jones's chapter on *CD* IV/1, like McCormack's essay on Barth's "historicized Christology," focuses on §59. Of course, this is completely warranted, since §59 is *the* paragraph in which Barth sets forth his actualistic-historical rendition of the incarnation under the rubric "The Obedience of the Son of God." However, as Jones astutely observes, "no single paragraph, chapter or part volume conveys the essence of Barth's Christology. Conversely, *every* paragraph chapter and part volume of *Dogmatics* conveys some part of Barth's Christology."[202] In light of this insight, Jones might have considered modifying his thesis regarding Barth's use of the term "nature," had he paid closer attention to the Christology that underlies §60, "The Pride and Fall of Man."

As I have shown, in §60 "human nature" is a meaningful and significant ontological concept in Barth's usage. Here Barth retains the Creator-creature distinction as an aspect of the substantialist ontology on which Chalcedon relies: a thing is by nature either eternal and self-existent, as in the case of God as being (according to classical theistic ontology) or being-in-act (according to Barth's actualism), or creaturely and derivative from the Creator as in the case of human beings.

For this reason Barth calls sin that which is not: *das Nichtige*. It is not created and it is not a second god. He finds it idolatrous to speak of sinful human *nature*. God created human nature to be good, and it remains good despite humankind's fall into corruption. Whatever is corrupt and sinful about the human being does not pertain and is absolutely alien to its *nature*, since sin as a form of nothingness can never be a part of the good human nature that God created.

When Barth says that Christ took on human nature, then, it could not have been sinful nature. As I pointed out earlier, according to Barth, Christ assumed human nature that is in and of itself sinless, but in the very meantime, by taking on human nature he participates in the corrupted condition of Adamic history. The sin of all humankind is, to use Barth's own language adopted in *CD* II/2, *transferred* to Christ by means of *participatio*.

---

[202]Jones, *Humanity of Christ*, 16.

Of course, I am not contending that Barth's use of the term *nature* is statically substantialist, but it would be erroneous to conclude that he has completely discarded every last vestige of substantialist ontology. It seems that Jones's study on Christ's humanity in Barth's Christology could have paid more attention to this discourse in *CD* §60.

Without appreciating Barth's use of the category of nature as a means of drawing a distinction between humanity as *created* and as *fallen*, one result is that Jones interprets Barth's formulation of Christ's sinlessness as consisting in *act* alone and not in essence or nature—Jones thinks that Barth has effectively discarded the category of nature. Thus Jones sees the following passage as Barth's own definitive word on Christ's sinlessness: "Jesus' 'sinlessness was therefore not his condition, but rather the act of his being in which he fought off temptation in his condition, which is ours, in the flesh' (IV/1, pp. 258-9 rev.)."[203]

On Jones's reading, Barth replaces the category of nature with the historical category of "condition," and Christ's sinlessness does not consist in his condition but the act of his being. True enough, Christ did not enter a sinless human condition, and his sinlessness primarily consists in the act of his being. However, Barth never completely dispensed with the Chalcedonian category of nature, and it is safe to say that he would also affirm the sinlessness of Christ's human nature, even though Jones is certainly right in pointing out that Barth's emphasis is on Christ's concretely active and actual sinlessness.

In light of Barth's treatment of the category of human nature in *CD* IV/1, Jones's thesis that Barth has completely discarded the category of nature is difficult to sustain. In fact, in the same passage from which Jones retrieves the quotation above, Barth states that Christ "was a man as we are. His condition was no different from ours. He took our flesh, the nature of man as he comes from the fall."[204] Note, again, that Barth does not speak of human nature itself as fallen, but the nature (which, as we have seen, was created good and always remains good) of humankind in the condition and under the sway of fallenness—"the nature of man *as he comes from the fall*." Because the human being whose nature remains good is in the historical

---
[203]Ibid., 176.
[204]*KD* IV/1, 285; ET 258.

condition of corruption, Barth states that Christ's "sinlessness was not therefore His condition."

As we have seen, in *CD* IV/1 Barth distinguishes between "condition" and "nature." Humankind is in the condition of corruption—that is what "flesh" denotes for Barth—but human nature has remained good even in the condition of fallenness. This condition, moreover, must not be thought of as original sin *inherited* from Adam: as we have seen, Barth rejects the traditional notion of hereditary sin. For this reason, Christ's entry into the condition of human "flesh" does not entail that he inherited original sin from Adam. Rather, Christ has taken on the condition of corruption in the sense of "placing Himself in the series of men who rebelled against God," the "series" of which Adam is *primus inter pares*, the "series" in which each member becomes and *is* Adam "freely and on our own responsibility."[205] That is, to be in the Adamic condition of corruption does not necessarily entail being sinful in act or nature.

In this light, what Barth is really saying in the passage quoted by Jones, then, is that the human condition in which Christ participates is the condition of fallenness, while Barth's emphasis is that by Christ's human act of obedience that perfectly corresponds to the inner-trinitarian relation of the Son's obedience to the Father, Christ overcomes sin in the flesh. It is not merely a passive sinlessness—Barth would indeed affirm that Christ is without original sin in his human agency since for Barth original sin describes something that each human person actively chooses—but an active and actual obedience. That is, Christ is indeed sinless in his human nature, but what is of central soteriological import is his act of perfect obedience as the Son of God and as Jesus of Nazareth.

Jones's basically infralapsarian reading. Despite what might be a slight shortcoming in Jones's treatment of Barth's usage of the term nature, his interpretation of Barth's notion of Christ's sinlessness lends support to my contention for a basically infralapsarian reading of Barth: the incarnation is Christ's act of taking on the sin of all humanity one way or another; humanity's sin is presupposed in the divine decision to become incarnate. Thus Jones comments on the Christology of *CD* I/2: "It follows that Christ's person

---

[205]Ibid., 568; ET 509-10.

must not be described without reference to his action and its salvific consequences."[206] When Barth revised his doctrine of election in light of this infralapsarian Christology in 1936–1942, the result was a basically infralapsarian doctrine of election. Thus Jones: "The description of Christ as 'electing God' adverts Barth's remarkable understanding of the atonement. . . . God's elective action, in Christ, goes hand in hand with God's rejection of humanity's sinful waywardness."[207]

In *CD* IV/1, where Barth's Christocentric doctrine of election takes on deeply historical-actualistic nuances, the *Geschichte* of Christ becomes even more deeply entangled with the sinful *Weltgeschichte* of Adam. On this point, Jones's summary serves as a nice conclusion to my exposition of the basically infralapsarian orientation of the Christ-*Geschichte* in *CD* IV/1:

> IV/1 provides an extensive articulation of [Christ's reconciling life-unto-death as the way of covenant fulfillment]. Christ's "history must be a history of suffering (*Leidensgeschichte*)" (IV/1, p. 175) in which he accepts and enacts the transition from election to rejection. In order that humanity's complicity with sin and death be permanently undercut, rendered part and parcel of a superseded and "old" humanity, God wills that Jesus Christ's reiteration of God's No against sin and death merge into his *bearing* God's No, suffering the punishment of sinful humankind. Christ therefore constitutes himself as the object of this punishment; his death completes a history in which he absorbs both the waywardness of humankind and its rejection. Only in this way is the human made new.[208]

Conclusion

In previous chapters I have repeatedly argued that from the development of a Christocentric doctrine of election in 1936–1942 on, Barth held to a basically infralapsarian view that the incarnation presupposes humanity's sin and the object of election is sinful humanity. However, we had not yet come to see how Barth defines "sin" and "fallen humanity" concretely until this chapter.

Here I use the word *concrete* in a technical sense: for Barth, to know something concretely is to understand it christologically. Christological

---

[206]Jones, *Humanity of Christ*, 43.
[207]Ibid., 86.
[208]Ibid., 199.

understanding consists in knowledge *of* and *in light of* the *history* of Jesus Christ. This emphasis on history, though already present in *Gottes Gnadenwahl* and *CD* II/2, is given especial prominence in *CD* IV/1.

As I have argued in this chapter, Barth's notion of the history of Christ involves the element of human sin in a profound way. Christ's history is the history of the way of the Son of God into the far country; it is the history of the Word's becoming flesh; it is the history of the Son's participation in world-history. As we have seen, world-history began with Adam's fall; without the fall there would have been no *Weltgeschichte*. World-history *is* the history of human fallenness and the fallen history of humanity, and by God's eternal decision in Jesus Christ it could not have been otherwise.

So could there have been a different *Geschichte* of Christ, a different history of the incarnation, in which Christ participates in an Adamic history that is unfallen? That is, had humankind not fallen into the *status corruptionis*, would the Word still have become human, without at once becoming "flesh" also? For the Barth of *CD* II/2, this is a question that is, in the words of George Hunsinger, "speculative and unanswerable."[209] This would remain so for *CD* IV/1. This is not to say that God *could not have* decided to become incarnate even if humanity had not fallen into sin—God certainly has the freedom to do so. This is only to say that God has elected only one *Geschichte* of Christ, and by God's decision an incarnation regardless of sin has been excluded, because God has decided that Christ's history should be one to which fallen *Weltgeschichte* is united. (Recall that both supra- and infralapsarian Christology are concerned with the logical order between God's decisions to become incarnate and to overcome sin.)

Thanks to recent studies on the category of history in *CD* IV/1 to which Bruce McCormack, Paul Jones and others have called attention, in this chapter we have come to recognize further developments in Barth's lapsarian thinking in the early 1950s: by his emphasis on history Barth has become more infralapsarian in his Christological doctrine of election than he had been in 1936–1942. While the Barth of, say, *CD* II/2 would have left room for the possibility of a prelapsarian incarnation, in *CD* IV/1 Christ's history is so covenantally bound to the history of sinful humanity that the proposition

---

[209] George Hunsinger, *Disruptive Grace: Studies in the Theology of Karl Barth* (Grand Rapids: Eerdmans, 2000), 204.

"God became human" is inseparable from the statement "the Word became flesh." The incarnation *is* the history of the electing God's entrance into the history of God's fallen covenant partner, in order to sublate the latter's history of fallenness *for the sake of* and *in* the election of all in Christ.

On this note we come to a fitting end to this book. Of course, a discussion of sin and divine reprobation could never have been the last word in Barth's theological discourse, and to end my book on Barth with a chapter on sin seems to do him injustice. But bear in mind that part of his theological agenda was to expose what he thought to be nineteenth-century neo-Protestantism's optimism of human nature and to treat sin seriously. To investigate the development of his lapsarian thinking is precisely to look into how he understands the notion of sin (in light of God's sovereign grace in Jesus Christ!) in various phases of his theology. It is thus appropriate to end this book with a chapter on Barth's doctrine of sin set forth in a part-volume in which his theology has arguably developed into full maturity.

My conclusion for this chapter is quite simple: in this (arguably) final phase of Barth's theological development, his understanding of the *Geschichte* of election-in-Christ leans more heavily toward infralapsarianism than ever before, as this *Geschichte* cannot be otherwise than Christ's participation in the *Weltgeschichte* of God's covenant partner, who is radically and totally fallen in historical actuality. Christ the electing God has said No to Adam's sin, but as Barth sees it this No as revealed in the concrete history of Christ's death and resurrection is not the final word out of the caprice of a tyrant, but the never-capricious No of the electing God that serves the purpose of and is sublated in the Yes pronounced in God's unchanging love-in-freedom.

Conclusion

RECAPITULATING THE ARGUMENTS

A conclusion is now in order, and I begin by briefly reprising the main arguments of this book. First, I have argued that despite his avowed sympathy for the supralapsarian ordering of divine decrees, Barth's Christocentric doctrine of election developed in 1936–1942 has in fact been a robustly complex scheme in which supra- and infralapsarian theological incentives and patterns of thinking, in both the predestinarian and christological senses, have been dialectically interwoven. This has been demonstrated throughout the book with the following considerations:

1. From 1936 onward, Barth described election-in-Christ as an absolute, never-capricious *Aufhebung* (the Hegelian understanding of dialectical progress or *Bildung* in which the new annuls the old in form, but in a sense preserves the rationality of the old) of reprobation: reprobation as manifested in Christ's death and resurrection is God's gracious negation of humankind's sin that negates God, and this negation of negation is for the purpose of the election of fallen humankind, to which God has pledged covenant-faithfulness in Christ. This grammar of *Aufhebung* carries a supra- as well as an infralapsarian aspect. In terms of teleological order, sin serves to occasion the cross, which corresponds to Christ's triumph over nothingness, and the cross that corresponds to divine reprobation serves God's highest purpose of election as manifested in Christ's resurrection. This teleological ordering is unquestionably on the supralapsarian side. However, the logic of *Aufhebung* also involves an infralapsarian *ordo* in that reprobation as God's re-

jection of nothingness presupposes the dark element that assails the creature, and election as the sublation of reprobation also presupposes God's decision to confront nothingness.

2. Related to the first point above is Barth's insistence that humanity's sin was eternally rejected by God, and could not have come into existence without God's *permissio, quodam-modo*, thereof in the form of absolute rejection, which is the No that cannot be detachedly considered from and serves the purpose of God's Yes in Jesus Christ. On this view, God's permission of sin, as it were, presupposes election, without which sin could not have been permitted to come into existence. This is another supralapsarian aspect of Barth's treatment of the lapsarian problem.

3. Dialectically, the second point above also leads to the appreciation of an infralapsarian aspect in Barth's doctrine of election: for Barth, God's Yes as revealed in the concrete history of Jesus Christ sublates and thus presupposes the No to sin, just as Christ's resurrection presupposes death on the cross for the triumph over sin. This infralapsarian *ordo* is another way of describing the *Aufhebung* process as discussed in the first point above.

4. In his formulation of "creation as the external basis of the covenant" and "covenant as the internal basis of creation," the dialectical nature of Barth's lapsarian thinking comes to the foreground once more. In terms of teleological order, he is on the supralapsarian side: God created the world for the sake of bringing about the covenant, which is God's election in the form of pledging fidelity to Jesus Christ as the head of the human race. While the covenantal grace of election is the purpose fulfilled in creation (i.e., covenant as the internal basis of creation), however, the covenantal purpose is conversely fulfilled on the very basis of creation. Although the fall is not explicitly mentioned here, Barth's application of the covenant theology developed in *CD* III/1 to his discussion of nothingness in *CD* III/3 and IV/1 shows that God's covenantal purpose is fulfilled on the basis of a creation already threatened by the alien element. To be sure, God was under no external or internal compulsion to permit nothingness to accompany creation. Yet God so decided that the Yes should be accompanied with a No, and so in God's primal decision God's covenant is with the fallen creature. With regard

to the object of election, then, Barth's covenant theology is on the infralapsarian side.

5. Barth's own treatment of the Lapsarian Controversy in *CD* II/2 also deserves consideration. He rejects the infralapsarian ordering of divine decrees, because he sees it as opening up an avenue for natural theology. Whether his opinion on infralapsarianism is correct is to be decided in the field of Puritan and Reformation studies. What is noteworthy for those interested in Barth is his reason for favoring the supralapsarian *ordo*: as he sees it, this *ordo* ascribes teleological priority to the decrees of election and reprobation, and when these two decrees are reinterpreted christologically as a process of *Aufhebung*, the last vestiges of natural-theological speculation can be eliminated. It is for this reason that in the various descriptions of Barth's complex lapsarian scheme outlined in the foregoing points, he always sides with supralapsarianism when it comes to teleological ordering. However, concerning the more decisive question of the *obiectum praedestinationis*, which mainstream scholars in the field of Puritan and Reformation studies generally understand to be the definitive watershed between supra- and infralapsarianism, Barth would be basically on the infralapsarian side. In the lapsarian excursus of *CD* II/2, he explicitly describes the object of election as humanity "sinful and lost."

6. With regard to the *obiectum praedestinationis*, although Barth is basically on the infralapsarian side, his formulation is much more complex than a straightforwardly infralapsarian thesis because of the christological emphasis in his doctrine of election. Barth identifies Christ, who is without sin in himself and took on the sin of all humanity by *participatio*, as the primary object of election. Election is first and finally of Jesus Christ, and sinful humanity is elected not directly, but *in* and *with* Christ. That is, the *obiectum praedestinationis* in Barth's theology is *homo lapsus*, but not *simpliciter* so.

7. The point above leads to considerations of lapsarianism in Barth's Christology. Once again, his position is a dialectical admixture of supra- and infralapsarian patterns of thinking, even though it can be described as basically infralapsarian, as I have contended in this book.

The supralapsarian aspect of Barth's Christology lies primarily in his axiomatic claim that Jesus Christ is the beginning of all God's ways and works. Creation and God's rejection of nothingness, as well as everything God wills and does, all proceed from God's primal decision to become incarnate. Yet, even in this identification of Jesus Christ as *en archē*, there is a more decisive infralapsarian aspect. For Barth, the *Logos* eternally *incarnandus*, the incarnate God-man "proleptically" (Hunsinger) present in the beginning by virtue of divine election, is revealed in the concrete history of the incarnation as determined from the very beginning to be Reconciler between God and fallen sinners. There has never been and will never be a moment in the entire history of Jesus Christ, who is the very beginning of all God's ways and works, in which he is not determined to be the bearer of and victor over humankind's sin—this point is made especially clear in *CD* IV/1.

8. In one particular instance, Barth makes a christological assertion that approaches the supralapsarianism of Duns Scotus. In *CD* II/1 Barth discusses the love and freedom of God as being-in-act, an important theme and axiom that undergirds Barth's doctrine of election in II/2. There he asserts that God's purpose in becoming incarnate is to seek and create fellowship with the creature. However, he qualifies this almost supralapsarian assertion by distinguishing between creation and incarnation. Creation is already God's seeking and creating fellowship with the creature regardless of sin. The incarnation, however, is the event of revelation that is *identical* to divine reconciliation with the sinner. With this qualification, the claim that the incarnation proceeded from God's will to enter into fellowship with the creature, despite its supralapsarian overtones, is given a basically infralapsarian underpinning: unlike creation, the incarnation is God's will to establish fellowship with the *fallen* creature. In this instance, Barth's Christology, though dialectically incorporating both supra- and infralapsarian patterns of thinking, is closer to infralapsarianism.

9. On a related note, George Hunsinger has observed that for Barth "the incarnation resolves a plight [of creation] logically independent of sin,

namely, the plight of transitoriness and dissolution into nonbeing."[1] While Barth's view of the incarnation approximates Duns Scotus's supralapsarianism in this particular regard, he never ventures far enough to make the quintessential supralapsarian claim that God *would have* become incarnate regardless of sin. Rather, in Hunsinger's words, "whether God would have become incarnate even if the world had not fallen into sin was . . . a question that" Barth regarded "as speculative and unanswerable."[2]

10. Barth's Christology can be described as basically infralapsarian in that the incarnation presupposes God's decision to deal with the nothingness that assails God's covenant partner in Jesus Christ. It is not straightforwardly infralapsarian, however, as the logical relation between God's primal decision to become incarnate and God's decision to reject sin is not unilateral. For Barth, the two divine decisions cannot be separated, as they dialectically presuppose one another. God's decision to confront sin in Jesus Christ clearly presupposes God's decision to become incarnate, but Barth also states that the latter was made necessary by the former. While this makes Barth's Christology somewhat of an admixture of supra- and infralapsarian claims, it would still be basically infralapsarian because the dialectical relation between incarnation and sin in his thinking rules out the supralapsarian claim of certainty that God *would have* become incarnate even if humanity had not been allowed to fall into sin. Of course, the defining infralapsarian aspect of Barth's theology does not go to the extent of agreeing with Aquinas that God *would not have* become incarnate had humanity not fallen into sin. Sure, Barth would not deny that God *could have* become incarnate regardless of sin, but the order of God's decisions as revealed in the concrete history of Christ, determined by God's *potentia ordinata*, is that the incarnation does presuppose the fall. The following quotation, from R. Scott Rodin, which we saw in chapter two, serves to make this point clear: "To hold to such a distinction between incarnation and atonement, between the assuming of human essence and the assuming of sinful humanity, is to

---

[1]George Hunsinger, *Disruptive Grace: Studies in the Theology of Karl Barth* (Grand Rapids: Eerdmans, 2000), 204.
[2]Ibid.

misread Barth's intentions. Barth never sees God as envisaging a creation which would be fulfilled by incarnation alone."[3]

The foregoing observations of the complexity of Barth's predestinarian and christological lapsarianism are the result of examining the development of his lapsarian thinking through the successive phases of his career. In his early theology, Christology and predestination began as two separate doctrines, but as predestination, which was inconsistently supralapsarian in the first phase of the development, gradually came to merge with Christology, which carried infralapsarian tendencies in *Romans* II and became basically infralapsarian in the Göttingen-Münster period, his doctrine of predestination began to carry more characteristically infralapsarian patterns of thinking, and then after the Christocentric revision of the doctrine of election in 1936–1942 he developed a robustly complex lapsarian scheme adopting the basic infralapsarian thesis in both Christology and predestination.

This study has shown that Barth's struggle with the lapsarian problem is one chief factor driving his theological development through the successive stages of his career. For Barth scholars interested in his theological development, this would seem enough to demonstrate the significance of lapsarianism to the theological enterprise.

Topics for Further Exploration

However, it is still worthwhile to consider again a question to which I alluded more than a few times in this book: Who (except perhaps some Barth scholars) cares if Barth is supra- or infralapsarian in his Christology and doctrine of election? I have continually suggested that the lapsarian problem is by no means a vainly scholastic inquiry detached from the life of the church. As Barth himself sees it, the lapsarian problem is most crucial because it struggles with the perplexing reality of humankind's fallenness in light of God's universal sovereignty and immutable holiness—he expressly states that this is the primary theological problem that *Gottes Gnadenwahl* tackles—even though he takes issue with the ways the answers have been formulated and the problem has sometimes been framed in classical Reformed theology, as he understands (and sometimes misunderstands) it.

---

[3]R. Scott Rodin, *Evil and Theodicy in the Theology of Karl Barth* (New York: Peter Lang, 1997), 87.

Beyond theodicy. In this book I have pointed out some doctrinal implications of Barth's lapsarian thinking, such as his attitude of defiance toward the theodicy problem, at which chapter eight hints.[4] In fact, the implications of Barth's lapsarian treatment of the problem of nothingness go beyond doctrinal theology. For instance, Barth's defiance of the theodicy problem in *CD* III/3 has been famously dubbed "Mozartean" as it echoes the joyousness of Mozart's music so characteristic of a triumphal Christian attitude against nothingness. As Barth himself puts it, "In face of the problem of theodicy, Mozart had the peace of God which far transcends all the critical or speculative reason that praises and reproves. . . . In the music of Mozart . . . we have clear and convincing proof that it is a slander on creation to charge it with a share in chaos because it includes a Yes and a No."[5] As we saw in chapter eight, Barth's formulation of sin, evil and death as *das Nichtige* carries deeply infralapsarian incentives. So how might Barth's lapsarian thinking shed light on his love for Mozart? This is one question that might be of interest to those who would like to look into Barth's musical temperament in relation to his theology, as well as his appreciation for culture and the arts in general. For that matter, Paul Brazier has argued that Barth's affection for Dostoevsky during the 1910s has much to do with the theme of sin and grace, and one might wonder if this would hint to struggles with the lapsarian problem in the early Barth.[6]

Public theology. Additionally, Barth's lapsarian thinking in his public theology has also been documented in the secondary literature. In a book on the topic of culture and common grace, Richard Mouw observes that Barth developed his lapsarian position in such a way that "created humanness . . . [cannot] be understood apart from redemption."[7]

While Mouw does not take note of the complexity of Barth's lapsarian thinking, we might consider how Barth's political theology differs from supralapsarian thinkers such as, say, the neo-Calvinist Abraham Kuyper.

---

[4] More thorough discussion of Barth's treatment of the theodicy problem can be found in my article, "Karl Barth on Nothingness: A Christological-Predestinarian Defiance of Theodicy," *Sino-Christian Studies* 20 (forthcoming).

[5] *KD* III/3, 338; ET 298-99.

[6] Paul Brazier, *Barth and Dostoyevsky: A Study of the Russian Writer Fyodor Mikhailovich Dostoyevsky on the Development of the Swiss Theologian Karl Barth* (Colorado Springs: Paternoster, 2007).

[7] Richard Mouw, *He Shines In All That's Fair: Culture and Common Grace* (Grand Rapids: Eerdmans, 2001), 69.

According to Kuyper there is a will of God for creation logically independent of God's redemptive will in Christ. For Kuyper, Christ's redemptive work is in line with and serves the purpose of God's prelapsarian mandate for creation, issued apart from Christ. The correlation of this understanding to Kuyper's supralapsarianism has been well documented.[8] It is not hard to see that on the supralapsarian view, God's ultimate purpose for creation in the decree of double predestination is logically independent of humankind's fall, while the infralapsarian view insists that double predestination, also understood as God's highest purpose, presupposes human fallenness. The supralapsarian view would imply that there is a will of God for creation that is apart from and logically prior to God's will in the redemptive work of Christ. Supralapsarians like Kuyper believe that God's will revealed in the work of creation, which for them is knowable to all humankind by means of common grace and general revelation, is logically independent of the matter-of-fact that the world is fallen.

Barth's public theology is strikingly different from this supralapsarian outlook on one crucial point: he rejects any logical separation between creation and redemption, and wipes out the distinction between common and special grace.

It has been observed that Barth's political theology is part and parcel of his rejection of natural theology.[9] Supralapsarians of neo-Calvinist convictions, including Kuyper, also reject natural theology, but for them there was a prelapsarian stage in the history of humankind in which natural theology was still viable. For Barth, natural theology is untenable because there is no will of God for this world and the entirety of its history apart from Christ, who was determined from the beginning to be Reconciler between God and sinners. Furthermore, not only does Barth reject Roman Catholic versions of natural theology, but also in his famous *Nein!* to Emil Brunner he denies traditional Calvinist distinctions between common and special grace, or general and special revelation.

To be sure, when Barth debated Brunner and drafted the Barmen Decla-

---

[8]See, for instance, John Bolt, *A Free Church, A Holy Nation: Abraham Kuyper's American Public Theology* (Grand Rapids: Eerdmans, 2001), 459.
[9]For example, George Hunsinger, "Barth, Barmen, and the Confessing Church Today," in *Disruptive Grace*, 80.

ration in the first half of the 1930s, he still posited a prelapsarian state in which humankind existed in immediacy to God, but this *Ursprung* is pretemporal and prehistorical. While Barth posited the *Ursprung*, he denied the possibility of any knowledge thereof—we saw this in chapter five. Barth writes in his polemical response to Brunner: "Man is of himself unable to find access to the revelation of God. Just because Christ is born, we have to regard the world as lost in the sight of God."[10]

Here the infralapsarian aspect of Barth's Christology is obvious: the event of the incarnation reveals the world to be fallen. This is in line with the Anselm book and *CD* I/1, in which the Word of God is addressed to fallen, rather than paradisiacal, humanity. There is no prelapsarian revelation apart from the Word of God in Jesus Christ in the veil of secularity.

What might Barth's basically infralapsarian Christology from his Bonn years imply for his political theology during the rise of the Third Reich? For one thing, note that the Barmen Declaration is thoroughly *theological*. Unlike neo-Calvinist supralapsarians, Barth does not think of politics as a science belonging to a sphere separate from that to which theology pertains. To be sure, for Barth there is an abiding distinction between theology and politics, but Barth is of the conviction that the church's political stance and actions must remain faithful to and be guided by the Word of God; thus ecclesial participation in politics must be a *theological* science. So how is Barth's conviction to be understood in light of his lapsarian thinking? Here I leave this question for further consideration on the reader's part—I am just trying to give an example to show that Barth's lapsarian thinking has far-reaching implications for his thought, life and actions in each stage of his theological development.

Barth on the analogia entis. Another related question that has piqued some scholarly interest in recent years is the development of Barth's stance on the possibility of natural theology. Understanding the development of Barth's lapsarian thinking would in fact shed much light on this topic. For example, Amy Marga's 2010 book on the role and place of the *analogia entis* in Barth's theology during the Göttingen-Münster period repeatedly alludes

---

[10]Karl Barth, "No! Answer to Emil Brunner," in Karl Barth and Emil Brunner, *Natural Theology, Comprising "Nature and Grace" by Professor Dr. Emil Brunner and the Reply "No!" by Dr. Karl Barth*, trans. Peter Fraenkel (Eugene, OR: Wipf and Stock, 2002), 116.

to the lapsarian problem, though she does not treat it explicitly. In a chapter titled "The Incarnation and Its Presuppositions," for instance, she discusses Barth's dictum that "revelation means reconciliation."[11] This is a theme that we treated in chapter five.

Marga describes Barth's understanding of the incarnation as presupposing creation and reconciliation, but despite this infralapsarian aspect of his Christology, the Barth of Göttingen and Münster, according to Marga, still allows room for a certain kind of *analogia entis*. In light of the development of Barth's lapsarian thinking, we can see that this has to do with how Barth's doctrine of election during this period was still inconsistent in its lapsarian aspect, as Barth still spoke of "a God apart from God's revelation in Christ."[12]

One question that Marga leaves open is what Barth's view on the *analogia entis* would be like after the christological reorientation of the doctrine of election in 1936, though she suggests that this Christocentrism would leave more room for natural theology.[13] Whether or not this is so is a question that I, too, leave open. However, my discussion of Barth's notion of God as being-in-act, part and parcel of the Christocentric doctrine of election developed in 1936, would suggest that the *analogia entis* would be quite untenable in Barth's mature theology. As we have seen, although on one occasion in *CD* II/1 Barth still speaks of the purpose of the incarnation apart from the actual account of the history of Jesus Christ, from *CD* II/2 onward Barth begins to make every effort to avoid any speculation about God apart from the concrete *Geschichte* of Christ's a priori (*zum Vornherein*) triumph over nothingness. The correlation of this deeply lapsarian Christocentric doctrine of election to Barth's stance against natural theology would be a key to answering the question whether, in what sense and to what extent the later Barth might allow for any sort of *analogia entis*.

God's Gracious Reprobation

The brief examples above show that the lapsarian problem plays an important role in Barth's thought, life and actions in his career as a theologian.

---

[11] Amy Marga, *Karl Barth's Dialogue With Catholicism in Göttingen and Münster: Its Significant for His Doctrine of God* (Tübingen: Mohr Siebeck, 2020), 93.
[12] Ibid., 170-71.
[13] Ibid., 172.

While nineteenth-century dogmatics has generally deemed the Lapsarian Controversy to be speculatively metaphysical, Barth is convinced that "we are not in any position to dismiss the seventeenth-century problem as superfluous, or to abandon the problem to merely capricious solution."[14] Rather, he believes that seventeenth-century lapsarianism can "shed light upon the path which we have to tread."[15]

As Barth sees it, confronting the lapsarian problem is worthwhile and necessary, but the solutions formulated by seventeenth-century Reformed orthodoxy inevitably posit a God above and behind the God self-revealed in Jesus Christ. Whether he is right on Reformed orthodoxy is for experts in Puritan and Reformation studies to decide—I have shown that he does not demonstrate thorough familiarity with Reformed orthodoxy.

Whatever the case, Barth's own theological intention in developing a "purified" version of the lapsarian doctrine is clear: he wants to make sure that the electing God of whom his theology speaks is none other than Jesus Christ, the Word of God revealed, and that God's act of double predestination, including reprobation, is not out of the "caprice of a tyrant," but perfectly corresponds to the being of the God who is always in the free act of love. In Jesus Christ God is immutably God, and Christ is the unchangeable *decretum absolutum Dei* in whom God's gracious No against sin eternally negates the nothingness that threatens God's covenant partner, so that God's Yes to all in Christ is the final and definitive Word whereby all of history is determined in and by the history of Christ.

---

[14]*KD* II/2, 136; ET 127.
[15]Ibid.

Bibliography

Primary Sources by Karl Barth (German)
Anselm: Fides quaerens intellectum. Zurich: TVZ, 1931.
Die christliche Dogmatik im Entwurf, 1. Band: Die Lehre vom Worte Gottes, Prolegomena zur christlichen Dogmatik, 1927. In Gesamtausgabe 2.14. Zurich: TVZ, 1982.
Gottes Gnadenwahl. Munich: Kaiser, 1936.
Die Kirchliche Dogmatik. 4 vols. in 12 parts (I/1–IV/4). Zollikon-Zurich: Evangelischer Verlag, 1932–1970.
Die Protestantische Theologie im 19. Jahrhundert: Ihre Geschichte und ihre Vorgeschichte. Zurich: TVZ, 1994.
Der Römerbrief 1919. In Gesamtausgabe 2.16. Zurich: TVZ, 1985.
Der Römerbrief 1922. 16th ed. Zurich: TVZ, 1999.
Die Theologie Calvins 1922. In Gesamtausgabe 2.23. Zurich: TVZ, 1993.
Die Theologie der reformierten Bekenntnisschriften 1923. In Gesamtausgabe 2.32. Zurich: TVZ, 1998.
Die Theologie und die Kirche. Zollikon-Zurich: Evangelischer Verlag, 1928.
Unterricht in der christlichen Religion. 3 vols. In Gesamtausgabe 2.17, 20, and 38. Zurich: TVZ, 1985–2003.

Primary Sources by Karl Barth (English and English Translation)
Anselm: Fides Quaerens Intellectum. Translated by Ian Robertson. London: SCM, 1960.
Church Dogmatics, all volumes. Edited by Geoffrey W. Bromiley and T. F. Torrance. Translated by Geoffrey W. Bromiley. Edinburgh: T&T Clark, 1936–1975.
The Church and the Churches: A Message from Prof. Barth to the "World Con-

ference on Faith and Order" which is to meet in Edinburgh, Scotland, in the year 1937. Grand Rapids: Eerdmans, 1936.

The Epistle to the Romans. Translated by Edwyn Hoskyns. Oxford: Oxford University Press, 1933.

The Göttingen Dogmatics. Vol. 1, *Instruction in the Christian Religion*. Edited by Hannelotte Reiffen. Translated by Geoffrey W. Bromiley. Grand Rapids: Eerdmans, 1991.

"No! Answer to Emil Brunner." In Karl Barth and Emil Brunner, *Natural Theology, Comprising "Nature and Grace" by Professor Dr. Emil Brunner and the Reply "No!" by Dr. Karl Barth*. Translated by Peter Fraenkel. Eugene, OR: Wipf and Stock, 2002.

Protestant Theology in the Nineteenth Century. Translated by Brian Cozens and John Bowden. London: SCM, 2001.

Primary Sources by Other Authors

Anselm of Canterbury. *Cur Deus Homo*. Translated by Sidney Deane. Chicago: Open Court, 1903.

Baynes, Paul. *A Commentary upon the First Chapter of the Epistle to the Ephesians*. London, 1618.

Beza, Theodore. *Tractationum theologicarum*. Vol. 3. Geneva, 1582.

Buber, Martin. *I and Thou*. Translated by Walter Kaufmann. New York: Scribner's Sons, 1970.

Calvin, John. *Concerning the Eternal Predestination of God*. Translated by J. K. S. Reid. Philadelphia: Westminster, 1961.

———. *Institutes of the Christian Religion*. Edited by John T. McNeil. Translated by Ford Lewis Battles. Philadelphia: Westminster, 1960.

Charnock, Stephen. *The Existence and Attributes of God*. Vol. 1. Grand Rapids: Baker, 1996.

Cyril of Alexandria. *On the Unity of Christ*. Translated by John A. McGuckin. Crestwood, NY: St. Vladimir's Seminary Press, 1997.

Edwards, John. *Veritas Redux*. Andover, UK: Gale, 2010.

Feuerbach, Ludwig. *The Essence of Christianity*. Translated by George Eliot. New York: Prometheus, 1989.

Gillespie, Patrick. *The Ark of the Covenant Opened*. London: Parkhurst, 1677.

Goodwin, Thomas. *The Works of Thomas Goodwin*. 12 Vols. Grand Rapids: Reformation Heritage Books, 2006.

Heppe, Heinrich. *Die Dogmatik der Evangelisch-Reformierten Kirche*. Whitefish, MT: Kessinger, 2010.

———. *Reformed Dogmatics*. Edited by Ernst Bizer. Translated by G. Thomson. London: Wakeman, 2010.

Kant, Immanuel. *Kritik der reinen Vernunft*. Wiesbaden: Fourier, 2003.

———. "The Only Possible Argument in Support of a Demonstration of the Existence of God." In *Theoretical Philosophy, 1755–1770*, 107-202. Edited and translated by David Walford. Cambridge Edition of the Works of Immanuel Kant. Cambridge: Cambridge University Press, 1992.

———. *Religion Within the Bounds of Bare Reason*. Translated by Werner Pluhar. Indianapolis: Hackett, 2009.

Kierkegaard, Søren. *Concluding Unscientific Postscript to the Philosophical Crumbs*. Edited and translated by Alastair Hannay. Cambridge: Cambridge University Press, 2009.

———. *Sickness unto Death*. Translated by Alastair Hannay. Radford: Wilder, 2008.

Kuyper, Abraham. *Lectures on Calvinism*. Grand Rapids: Eerdmans, 1931.

Luther, Martin. *Against Latomus*. In *Luther's Works* 32. Edited by George Forell and Helmut Lehmann. Translated by George Lindbeck. Philadelphia: Muhlenberg, 1958.

———. *The Bondage of the Will: A New Translation of De Servo Arbitrio (1525), Martin Luther's Reply to Erasmus of Rotterdam*. Translated by J. I. Packer and O. R. Johnston. Old Tappan, NJ: Revell, 1957.

Maccovius, Johannes. *De aeterna Dei electione*. Franeker, 1618.

Maury, Pierre. "Erwählung und Glaube." In *Theologische Studien* 8. Zurich: Evangelischer Verlag, 1940.

Moltmann, Jürgen. *The Experiment Hope*. Edited and translated by M. Douglas Meeks. Philadelphia: Fortress Press, 1975.

———. *Hope and Planning*. Translated by Margaret Clarkson. London: SCM, 1971.

———. *Religion, Revolution, and the Future*. Translated by M. Douglas Meeks. New York: Charles Scribner, 1969.

———. "Toward a Political Hermeneutics of the Gospel." In *Union Seminary Quarterly Review* 23 (1968).

———. *The Way of Jesus Christ*. Minneapolis: Fortress, 1993.

Owen, John. *The Works of John Owen*. Vol. 1, *The Glory of Christ*. Philadelphia: Banner of Truth, 1991.

———. *The Works of John Owen*. Vol. 10, *The Death of Christ*. Philadelphia: Banner of Truth, 1991.

———. *The Works of John Owen*. Vol. 12, *The Gospel Defended*. Philadelphia: Banner of Truth, 1991.

Perkins, William. *A Treatise of the Manner and Order of Predestination, and of the Largeness of Gods Grace* in *Works*. London, 1606.

Schaff, Philip, ed. "The Canons and Decrees of the Council of Trent." In *The Creeds of Christendom*. Vol. 2. Grand Rapids: Baker, 1983.

Schleiermacher, Friedrich. *On Religion: Speeches to its Cultured Despisers*. Edited and translated by Richard Crouter. Cambridge: Cambridge University Press, 1988.

Schweizer, Alexander. *Die Glaubenslehre der evangelisch-reformierten Kirche, dargestellt und aus den Quellen belegt*. 2 vols. Zurich: Orell, Füssli, 1844-1847.

Tillich, Paul. *Systematic Theology*. Vol. 2. Chicago: Chicago University Press, 1957.

Torrance, T. F. *Space, Time and Resurrection*. Edinburgh: T&T Clark, 1976.

———. *Theology in Reconciliation*. Eugene, OR: Wipf and Stock, 1996.

Turretin, Francis. *Institutes of Elenctic Theology*. Vol. 1. Edited by James Dennison Jr. Translated by George Giger. Phillipsburg, NJ: P&R, 1992.

———. *Institutio Theologicae Elencticae*. Volume 1. Geneva, 1679.

Secondary Literature

Allen, Michael. "Jonathan Edwards and the Lapsarian Debate." *Scottish Journal of Theology* 62 (2009): 299-315.

Anderson, Clifford. "A Theology of Experience? Karl Barth and the Transcendental Argument." In *Karl Barth and American Evangelicalism*, edited by Bruce McCormack and Clifford Anderson, 91-110. Grand Rapids: Eerdmans, 2010.

Armstrong, Brian. *Calvinism and the Amyraut Heresy: Protestant Scholasticism and Humanism in Seventeenth-Century France*. Madison: University of Wisconsin Press, 1969.

Asselt, Willem van. "On the Maccovius Affair." In *Revisiting the Synod of Dordt*, edited by Aza Goudriaan and Fred van Lieburg, 217-41. Leiden: Brill, 2006.

Balthasar, Hans Urs von. *The Theology of Karl Barth: Exposition and Interpretation*. Translated by Edward T. Oakes. San Francisco: Ignatius, 1992.

Bavinck, Herman. *The Doctrine of God*. Translated and edited by William Hendriksen. Grand Rapids: Eerdmans, 1951.

———. *Reformed Dogmatics*. Vol. 2, *God and Creation*. Edited by John Bolt. Translated by John Vriend. Grand Rapids: Baker Academic, 2004.

Becker, Dieter. *Karl Barth und Martin Buber, Denker in dialogischer Nachbarschaft? Zur Bedeutung Martin Bubers für die Anthropologie Karl Barths*.

Göttingen: Vandenhoeck & Ruprecht, 1986.

Beeke, Joel, and Mark Jones. *A Puritan Theology: Doctrine for Life*. Grand Rapids: Reformation Heritage Books, 2012.

Beintker, Michael. *Die Dialektik in der "dialektischen Theologie" Karl Barths*. Munich: Kaiser, 1987.

———. "Unterricht in der christlichen Religion." *Verkündigung und Forschung* 30, no. 2 (1985): 45-49.

Berger, Peter. *The Sacred Canopy: Elements of a Sociological Theory of Religion*. New York: Anchor, 1969.

Berkhof, Louis. *Systematic Theology*. Edinburgh: Banner of Truth, 1958.

Berkouwer, Gerrit. *The Triumph of Grace in the Theology of Karl Barth*. London: Paternoster, 1956.

Bertram, Robert. "'Faith Alone Justifies': Luther on *Iustia Fidei*." In *Justification by Faith: Lutherans and Catholics in Dialogue*. Vol. 7. Edited by H. George Anderson, T. Austin Murphy and Joseph A. Burgess. Minneapolis: Augsburg, 1985.

Beza, Theodore. *The Christian Faith*. Translated by James Clark. Lewes: Focus Christian Ministries, 1992.

Boersma, Hans. *Nouvelle Théologie and Sacramental Ontology: A Return to Mystery*. Oxford: Oxford University Press, 2009.

———. *Violence, Hospitality, and the Cross: Reappropriating the Atonement Tradition*. Grand Rapids: Baker Academic, 2004.

Boettner, Loraine. *The Reformed Doctrine of Predestination*. Philadelphia: P&R, 1932.

Bolt, John. *A Free Church, A Holy Nation: Abraham Kuyper's American Public Theology*. Grand Rapids: Eerdmans, 2001.

Boughton, Lynne C. "Supralapsarianism and the Role of Metaphysics in Sixteenth-Century Reformed Theology." In *Westminster Theological Journal* 48 (1986).

Braaten, Charles, and Robert Jenson, eds. *Union with Christ: The New Finnish Interpretation of Luther*. Grand Rapids: Eerdmans, 1998.

Bradshaw, Timothy. "Karl Barth on the Trinity: A Family Resemblance." *Scottish Journal of Theology* 39 (1986): 145-64.

Busch, Eberhard. *Die Anfänge des Theologen Karl Barth in seinen Göttingen Jahren*. Göttingen: Vandenhoeck & Ruprecht, 1987.

———. *Barth*. Nashville: Abingdon, 2008.

———. *Karl Barth: His Life from Letters and Autobiographical Texts*. Translated by John Bowden. Munich: Kaiser, 1975.

Chung, Sung Wook, Ed. *Karl Barth and Evangelical Theology*. Grand Rapids: Baker Academic, 2006.

Cortez, Marc. "What Does It Mean to Call Karl Barth a 'Christocentric' theologian?" *Scottish Journal of Theology* 60 (2007): 127-43.

Crisp, Oliver. *Divinity and Humanity*. Cambridge: Cambridge University Press, 2007.

———. "Karl Barth on Creation." In *Karl Barth and Evangelical Theology*. Edited by Sung Wook Chung. Grand Rapids: Baker Academic, 2006.

Dever, Mark. "Moderation and Deprivation: A Reappraisal of Richard Sibbes." *Journal of Ecclesiastical History* 43 (1992): 396-413.

DeVries, Dawn. "Does Faith Save? Calvin, Schleiermacher and Barth on the Nature of Faith." In *The Reality of Faith in Theology: Studies on Karl Barth—Princeton-Kampen Consultation 2005*. Edited by Bruce McCormack and Gerrit Neven. Bern: Peter Lang, 2007.

Driel, Edwin van. *Incarnation Anyway: Arguments for Supralapsarian Christology*. Oxford: Oxford University Press, 2008.

———."Karl Barth on the Eternal Existence of Jesus Christ." In *Scottish Journal of Theology* 60 (2007): 45-61.

Dulles, Avery. "Two Languages of Salvation: The Lutheran-Catholic Joint Declaration." *First Things* 98 (1999): 25-30.

Ebeling, Gerhard. "Glaube und Liebe." In *Martin Luther: 450 Jahre Reformation*, edited by Helmut Gollwitzer, 69-80. Köln: Dumont, 1967.

Fesko, John. *Diversity Within the Reformed Traditions: Supra- and Infralapsarianism in Calvin, Dort, and Westminster*. Greenville, SC: Reformed Academic Press, 2001.

———. "Lapsarian Diversity at the Synod of Dort." In *Drawn into Controversie: Reformed Theological Diversity and Debates Within Seventeenth-Century British Puritanism*, edited by Michael A. G. Haykin and Mark Jones, 99-123. Göttingen: Vandenhoeck & Ruprecht, 2011.

———. *The Theology of the Westminster Standards: Historical Context and Theological Insights*. Wheaton, IL: Crossway, 2014.

———. "The Westminster Confession and Lapsarianism: Calvin and the Divines." In *The Westminster Confession into the Twenty-First Century*, edited by Ligon Duncan, 2:477-525. Fearn, Scotland: Mentor, 2004.

Fiddes, Paul. *The Creative Suffering of God*. Oxford: Clarendon, 1988.

Ford, David. *Barth and God's Story*. Eugene, OR: Wipf and Stock, 1985.

Franks, Robert. *A History of the Doctrine of the Work of Christ*. 2 vols. London: Hodder and Stoughton, n.d.

Frei, Hans. *The Doctrine of Revelation in the Thought of Karl Barth, 1909 to 1922.* PhD diss., Yale University, 1956.

———. *Theology and Narrative.* Edited by George Hunsinger and William Placher. Oxford: Oxford University Press, 1993.

Furry, Timothy. "Analogous Analogies? Thomas Aquinas and Karl Barth." *Scottish Journal of Theology* 63 (2010): 318-30.

Garcia, Mark. *Life in Christ: Union with Christ and Twofold Grace in Calvin's Theology.* Milton Keynes, UK: Paternoster, 2008.

Gavrilyuk, Paul. *The Suffering of the Impassible God: The Dialectics of Patristic Thought.* Oxford: Oxford University Press, 2004.

Gerstner, John. *The Rational Biblical Theology of Jonathan Edwards.* Vol. 2. Sanford, FL: Ligonier, 1992.

Gibson, David, and Daniel Strange, eds. *Engaging with Barth: Contemporary Evangelical Critiques.* Nottingham: Apollos, 2008.

Glomsrud, Ryan. "Karl Barth as Historical Theologian" in *Engaging with Barth: Contemporary Evangelical Critiques.* Eds. D. Gibson and D. Strange. Nottingham: Apollos, 2008.

———. *Karl Barth Between Pietism and Orthodoxy: A Post-Enlightenment Ressourcement of Classical Protestantism.* DPhil thesis, University of Oxford, 2009.

Gockel, Matthias. *Barth and Schleiermacher on the Doctrine of Election: A Systematic-Theological Comparison.* Oxford: Oxford University Press, 2006.

Gollwitzer, Helmut, ed. *Martin Luther: 450 Jahre Reformation.* Köln: Dumont, 1967.

Greggs, Tom. "'Jesus Is Victor': Passing the Impasse of Barth on Universalism." *Scottish Journal of Theology* 60 (2007): 196-212.

Gunton, Colin. *The Barth Lectures.* New York: T&T Clark, 2007.

Hart, Trevor. "Barth and Küng on Justification: 'Imaginary Differences'?" *Irish Theological Quarterly* 59 (1993): 94-113.

Hastings, Ross. "Discerning the Spirit: Ambivalent Assurance in the Soteriology of Jonathan Edwards and Barthian Correctives." *Scottish Journal of Theology* 63 (2010): 437-55.

Hector, Kevin. "Immutability, Necessity and Triunity: Towards a Resolution of the Trinity and Election Controversy." *Scottish Journal of Theology* 65 (2012): 64-81.

Hendry, George. "The Transcendental Method in the Theology of Karl Barth." *Scottish Journal of Theology* 37 (1984): 213-27.

Hick, John. *Evil and the God of Love*. New York: Macmillan, 1977.

Horton, Michael. *Thomas Goodwin and the Puritan Doctrine of Assurance: Continuity and Discontinuity in the Reformed Tradition, 1600–1680*. PhD diss., Wycliffe Hall, Oxford and Coventry University, 1995.

Hunsinger, George. *Disruptive Grace: Studies in the Theology of Karl Barth*. Grand Rapids: Eerdmans, 2000.

———. "Election and the Trinity: Twenty-Five Theses on the Theology of Karl Barth." *Modern Theology* 24 (2008): 179-98.

———. "*Fides Christo Formata*: Luther, Barth and the Joint Declaration." In *The Gospel of Justification in Christ: Where Does the Church Stand Today?* edited by Wayne Stumme, 69-84. Grand Rapids: Eerdmans, 2006.

———. *How to Read Karl Barth: The Shape of his Theology*. Oxford: Oxford University Press, 1991.

———. "Karl Barth's *The Göttingen Dogmatics*." *Scottish Journal of Theology* 46 (1993): 371-82.

———. "A Tale of Two Simultaneities: Justification and Sanctification in Calvin and Barth." In *Conversing with Barth*, edited by John C. McDowell and Mike Higton, 68-89. Aldershot: Ashgate, 2004.

Jenson, Robert. *God After God: The God of the Past and the God of the Future as Seen in the Works of Karl Barth*. Minneapolis: Fortress, 2010.

John Paul II, Pope. *Savifici Doloris: The Salvific Value of Suffering: Apostolic Letter on Suffering*. London: Catholic Truth Society, 1984.

Johnson, William Stacy. *The Mystery of God: Karl Barth and the Postmodern Foundations of Theology*. Louisville: Westminster John Knox, 1997.

Jones, Mark. *Why Heaven Kissed Earth: The Christology of the Puritan Reformed Orthodox Theologian, Thomas Goodwin (1600–1680)*. Göttingen: Vandenhoeck & Ruprecht, 2010.

Jones, Paul. *The Humanity of Christ: Christology in Karl Barth's Church Dogmatics*. London: T&T Clark, 2008.

Jüngel, Eberhard. *Gottes Sein ist im Werden*. Tübingen: Mohr, 1965.

———. *Justification: The Heart of the Christian Faith*. Edinburgh: T&T Clark, 2001.

———. "Von der Dialektik zur Analogie: Die Schule Kierkegaards und der Einspruch Petersons." In *Barth-Studien*, 127-79. Gütersloh: Mohn.

Krötke, Wolf. *Sin and Nothingness in the Theology of Karl Barth*. Edited and translated by Philip Ziegler and Christina-Maria Bammel. Princeton: Princeton Theological Seminary, 2005.

Küng, Hans. *Justification: The Doctrine of Karl Barth and a Catholic Reflection.* Philadelphia: Westminster, 1981.

La Montagne, D. Paul. *Barth and Rationality: Critical Realism in Theology.* Eugene, OR: Wipf and Stock, 2012.

Letham, Robert. "Theodore Beza: A Reassessment." *Scottish Journal of Theology* 40 (1987): 25-40.

Lohmann, Johann. *Karl Barth und der Neukantianismus.* Berlin: de Gruyter, 1995.

Malloy, Christopher. *Engrafted into Christ: A Critique of the Joint Declaration.* New York: Peter Lang, 2005.

Mangina, Joseph. *Karl Barth: Theologian of Christian Witness.* London: Westminster John Knox, 2004.

Marga, Amy. "Jesus Christ and the Modern Sinner: Karl Barth's Retrieval of Luther's Substantive Christology." *Currents in Theology and Mission* 34 (2007): 260-70.

———. *Karl Barth's Dialogue With Catholicism in Göttingen and Münster: Its Significance for His Doctrine of God.* Tübingen: Mohr Siebeck, 2010.

McCormack, Bruce. "Election and the Trinity, Theses in Response to George Hunsinger." *Scottish Journal of Theology* 63 (2010): 203-24.

———, ed. *Engaging the Doctrine of God: Contemporary Protestant Perspectives.* Grand Rapids: Baker Academic, 2008.

———. "Grace and Being: The Role of God's Gracious Election in Karl Barth's Theological Ontology." In *The Cambridge Companion to Karl Barth*, edited by John Webster, 92-110. Cambridge: Cambridge University Press, 2000.

———, ed. *Justification in Perspective: Historical Developments and Contemporary Challenges.* Grand Rapids: Baker Academic, 2006.

———. "Karl Barth's Christology as Resource for a Reformed Version of Kenoticism." *International Journal of Systematic Theology* 8, no. 3 (2006): 243-51.

———. *Karl Barth's Critically Realistic Dialectical Theology.* Oxford: Clarendon, 1995.

———. "The Ontological Presuppositions of Barth's Doctrine of the Atonement." In *The Glory of the Atonement: Biblical, Theological and Practical Perspectives*, edited by Charles E. Hill and Frank A. James III, 346-66. Downers Grove, IL: InterVarsity Press, 2004.

———. *Orthodox and Modern: Studies in the Theology of Karl Barth.* Grand Rapids: Baker Academic, 2008.

———, ed. *The Reality of Faith in Theology: Studies on Karl Barth.* Bern: Peter Lang, 2005.

———. "Seek God Where He May Be Found: A Response to Edwin Chr. Van Driel." *Scottish Journal of Theology* 60 (2007): 62-79.
———. "So That He May Be Merciful to All: Karl Barth and the Problem of Universalism." In *Karl Barth and American Evangelicalism*, edited by Bruce McCormack and Clifford Anderson, 227-49. Grand Rapids: Eerdmans, 2011.
———. "The Sum of the Gospel: The Doctrine of Election in the Theologies of Alexander Schweizer and Karl Barth." In *Toward the Future of Reformed Theology: Tasks, Topics, Traditions*, edited by David Willis and Michael Welker, 470-93. Grand Rapids: Eerdmans, 1999.
McDonald, Nathan. "The *Imago Dei* and Election: Reading Genesis 1:26-28 and Old Testament Scholarship with Karl Barth." *International Journal of Systematic Theology* 10 (2008): 303-27.
McDonald, Suzanne. "Barth's 'Other' Doctrine of Election in the *Church Dogmatics*." *International Journal of Systematic Theology* 9 (2007): 134-47.
———. "Evangelical Questioning of Election in Barth: A Pneumatological Perspective from the Reformed Heritage." In *Karl Barth and American Evangelicalism*, edited by Bruce McCormack and Clifford Anderson, 250-69. Grand Rapids: Eerdmans, 2010.
———. *Re-Imaging Election: Divine Election as Representing God to Others and Others to God*. Grand Rapids: Eerdmans, 2010.
McDowell, John. "Learning Where to Place One's Hope: The Eschatological Significance of Election in Barth." *Scottish Journal of Theology* 53 (2000): 316-38.
———. "'Mend Your Speech a Little': Reading Karl Barth's *das Nichtige* through Donald MacKinnon's Tragic Vision." In *Conversing with Barth*, edited by John McDowell and Mike Higton, 142-72. Aldershot: Ashgate, 2004.
———. "Much Ado About Nothing: Karl Barth's Being Unable to Do Nothing about Nothingness." *International Journal of Systematic Theology* 4 (2002): 319-35.
McGrath, Alister. "Justification: Barth, Trent and Küng." *Scottish Journal of Theology* 34 (1981): 517-29.
———. "Karl Barth's Doctrine of Justification from an Evangelical Perspective." In *Karl Barth and Evangelical Theology*, edited by Sung Woo Chung, 172-90. Grand Rapids: Baker Academic, 2006.
———. *Luther's Theology of the Cross: Martin Luther's Theological Breakthrough*. Oxford: Blackwell, 1990.
McMaken, W. Travis. "Election and the Pattern of Exchange in Karl Barth's Doctrine of the Atonement." *Journal of Reformed Theology* 3 (2009): 202-18.

Migliore, Daniel. *Faith Seeking Understanding: An Introduction to Christian Theology*. Grand Rapids: Eerdmans, 2004.

Molnar, Paul. "The Trinity and the Freedom of God." *Journal for Christian Theological Research* 8 (2003): 59-66.

———. "The Trinity, Election and God's Ontological Freedom: A Response to Kevin Hector." *International Journal of Systematic Theology* 6 (2006): 294-306.

———. "'Thy Word Is Truth': The Role of Faith in Reading Scripture Theologically with Karl Barth." *Scottish Journal of Theology* 63 (2010): 70-92.

Mouw, Richard. *He Shines in All That's Fair: Culture and Common Grace*. Grand Rapids: Eerdmans, 2001.

———. "Some Reflections on Sphere Sovereignty." In *Religion, Pluralism, and Public Life: Abraham Kuyper's Legacy for the Twenty-First Century*, edited by Luis Lugo, 87-109. Grand Rapids: Eerdmans, 2000.

Muller, Richard. *Christ and the Decree: Christology and Predestination in Reformed Theology from Calvin to Perkins*. Grand Rapids: Baker, 1986.

———. *Dictionary of Latin and Greek Theological Terms Drawn Principally from Protestant Scholastic Theology*. Grand Rapids: Baker Academic, 1985.

———. *Post-Reformation Reformed Dogmatics*. Vol. 1, *Prolegomena to Theology*. Grand Rapids: Baker Academic, 2003.

———. "Revising the Predestination Paradigm: An Alternative to Supralapsarianism, Infralapsarianism, and Hypothetical Universalism." Lecture for the Mid-America Fall Lecture Series. Mid-America Reformed Seminary, Dyer, Indiana, 2008.

Murphy, Francesca Aran. *God Is Not a Story: Realism Revisited*. Oxford: Oxford University Press, 2007.

Myers, Benjamin. "Predestination and Freedom in Milton's *Paradise Lost*." *Scottish Journal of Theology* 59 (2006): 64-80.

Neder, Adam. *Participation in Christ: An Entry into Karl Barth's Church Dogmatics*. Louisville: Westminster John Knox, 2009.

Nimmo, Paul. *Being in Action: The Theological Shape of Barth's Ethical Vision*. London: T&T Clark, 2007.

———. "Karl Barth and the *Concursus Dei*—A Chalcedonianism Too Far?" *International Journal of Systematic Theology* 9 (2007): 58-72.

Pattison, George. *God and Being: An Enquiry*. Oxford: Oxford University Press, 2011.

Penner, Myron. "Calvin, Barth, and the Subject of Atonement." In *Calvin, Barth and Reformed Theology*, edited by Neil McDonald and Carl Trueman, 118-46. Eugene, OR: Wipf and Stock, 2008.

Price, Daniel. *Karl Barth's Anthropology in Light of Modern Thought*. Grand Rapids: Eerdmans, 2002.
Rasmussen, Joel. *Between Irony and Witness: Kierkegaard's Poetics of Faith, Hope and Love*. London: T&T Clark, 2005.
Reymond, Robert. *A New Systematic Theology of the Christian Faith*. Nashville: Thomas Nelson, 1998.
Richards, Guy M. "Samuel Rutherford's Supralapsarianism revealed: A Key to the Lapsarian Position of the Westminster Confession of Faith?" *Scottish Journal of Theology* 59, no. 1 (2006): 27-44.
Rodin, R. Scott. *Evil and Theodicy in the Theology of Karl Barth*. New York: Peter Lang, 1997.
Ruschke, Werner. *Entstehung und Ausführung der Diastasentheologie in Karl Barths zweitem* Römerbrief. Neukirchen: Neukirchener Verlag, 1987.
Scaer, David. "The Concept of *Anfechtung* in Luther's Thought." *Concordia Theological Quarterly* 47 (1983): 15-30.
Sibbes, Richard. "To the Reader." In Paul Baynes, *A Commentary Upon the First Chapter of the Epistle to the Ephesians*. London, 1618.
Smith, Aaron. "God's Self-Specification: His Being Is His Electing." *Scottish Journal of Theology* 62 (2009): 1-25.
Spiekermann, Ingrid. *Gotteserkenntnis: Ein Beitrag zur Grundfrage der neuen Theologie Karl Barths*. Munich: Kaiser, 1985.
Stumme, Wayne, ed. *The Gospel of Justification in Christ: Where Does the Church Stand Today?* Grand Rapids: Eerdmans, 2006.
Swinburne, Richard. *Providence and the Problem of Evil*. Oxford: Clarendon, 1998.
Tanner, Kathryn. "Creation and Providence." In *The Cambridge Companion to Karl Barth*, edited by John Webster, 111-26. Cambridge: Cambridge University Press, 2000.
Torrance, Thomas F. *Karl Barth: An Introduction to His Early Theology 1910-1931*. Edinburgh: T&T Clark, 1962.
———. *Space, Time and Resurrection*. Edinburgh: T&T Clark, 1976.
Trueman, Carl R. "Calvin, Barth, and Reformed Theology: Historical Prolegomena." In *Calvin, Barth and Reformed Theology*, edited by Neil MacDonald and Carl Trueman, 3-26. Eugene, OR: Wipf and Stock, 2008.
———. *The Claims of Truth: John Owen's Trinitarian Theology*. Carlisle: Paternoster, 1998.
———. *John Owen: Reformed Catholic, Renaissance Man*. Aldershot: Ashgate, 2007.
———. "John Owen's *Dissertation on Divine Justice*: An Exercise in Christo-

centric Scholasticism." *Calvin Theological Journal* 33 (1998): 87-103.
Turchin, Sean. "Examining the Primary Influence on Karl Barth's *Epistle to the Romans*." MARS thesis, Liberty University, 2008.
Walker, Ralph. "Kant and Transcendental Arguments." In *The Cambridge Companion to Kant and Modern Philosophy*, edited by Paul Guyer, 238-68. Cambridge: Cambridge University Press, 2006.
Ward, Graham. "Barth, Modernity, and Postmodernity." In *The Cambridge Companion to Karl Barth*, edited by John Webster, 274-95. Cambridge: Cambridge University Press, 2000.
―――. "Barth, Hegel and the Possibility for Christian Apologetics." In *Conversing with Barth*, edited by John McDowell and Mike Higton, 53-67. Aldershot: Ashgate, 2004.
Watson, Gordon. "Karl Barth and St. Anselm's Theological Programme." *Scottish Journal of Theology* 30 (1977): 31-45.
Weber, Otto. *Karl Barths Kirchliche Dogmatik: Ein einführender Bericht*. Neukirchen-Vluyn: Neukirchener Verlag, 1975.
Webster, John. *Barth's Earlier Theology*. London: T&T Clark, 2005.
―――. *Barth's Moral Theology: Human Action in Barth's Thought*. London: T&T Clark, 1998.
―――, ed. *The Cambridge Companion to Karl Barth*. Cambridge: Cambridge University Press, 2000.
―――. *Karl Barth*. 2nd ed. New York: Continuum, 2004.
―――. "'There Is No Past in the Church, so There Is No Past in Theology': Barth on the History of Modern Protestant Theology." In *Conversing with Barth*, edited by John McDowell and Mike Higton, 14-39. Aldershot: Ashgate, 2004. Also in John Webster, *Barth's Earlier Theology*, 91-118. London: T&T Clark, 2005.
Wigley, Stephen. "The von Balthasar Thesis: A Re-Examination of von Balthasar's Study of Barth in the Light of Bruce McCormack." *Scottish Journal of Theology* 56 (2003): 345-59.
Wolterstorff, Nicholas. "Barth on Evil." *Faith and Philosophy* 13 (1996): 584-608.
Wübbenhorst, Karla. "Calvin's Doctrine of Justification: Variations on a Lutheran Theme." In *Justification in Perspective: Historical Perspectives and Contemporary Challenges*, edited by Bruce McCormack, 99-118. Grand Rapids: Baker Academic, 2006.

Author Index

Anselm of Canterbury, 23, 31, 35, 43, 127, 148-62, 165, 168, 171, 183, 189, 245, 249, 256-57
Asselt, Willem Van, 51, 59
Athanasius of Alexandria, 181
Augustine of Hippo, 45-46, 48, 53, 181, 206, 260
Balthasar, Hans Urs von, 27, 35, 148, 150-51, 157-59
Bavinck, Herman, 25, 51, 56, 72
Beintker, Michael, 113, 150
Berger, Peter, 26-27
Berkhof, Louis, 48-49
Beza, Theodore, 46, 55-56, 59-60, 67, 69, 196
Boethius, 48, 206
Boettner, Loraine, 24, 53, 56
Bradshaw, Timothy, 217-20
Bromiley, Geoffrey W., 244, 266
Brunner, Emil, 27, 29, 151, 281, 297-98
Buber, Martin, 118
Bucanus, Guliemus, 50, 69
Busch, Eberhard, 118-19
Calvin, John, 45-47, 67, 83, 91, 112-14, 129-32, 135, 138, 177, 180-81, 191, 196, 200, 272
Charnock, Stephen, 54
Cocceius, Johannes, 51-52, 181
Cyril of Alexandria, 115
Dostoyevsky, Fyodor, 296
Driel, Edwin van, 31, 74-78, 276-78
Edwards, John, 55
Edwards, Jonathan, 67, 69
Fesko, John, 47-48, 50, 56, 61, 141
Feuerbach, Ludwig, 66, 207
Fiddes, Paul, 277, 280-81
Ford, David, 77
Frei, Hans, 150, 243

Gillespie, Patrick, 50-51
Glomsrud, Ryan, 42
Gockel, Matthias, 103, 107, 178-82
Gogarten, Friedrich, 118, 176
Goodwin, Thomas, 44, 51, 57-59, 227
Hegel, G. W. F., 36, 197, 206, 257, 269, 274-75, 290
Heppe, Heinrich, 36, 42-45, 49-50, 56, 69, 71-73, 108, 110-11, 114, 130
Hume, David, 190
Hunsinger, George, 24, 75, 78, 114-17, 167, 205-7, 209, 215, 220, 227-29, 251, 257-59, 271-72, 274, 276-83, 288, 293-94
Jenson, Robert, 88, 102, 205
Jones, Mark, 24, 58
Jones, Paul Dafydd, 171, 218, 271, 279, 282-87
Jüngel, Eberhard, 150, 163, 222
Kant, Immanuel, 83-84, 89, 98-100, 115-16, 119, 155, 189-90, 204, 208, 259-60, 267
Kierkegaard, Søren, 84-85, 100, 104, 115, 121, 248
Knox, John, 181-82
Kuyper, Abraham, 29, 296-97
Letham, Robert, 67
Locke, John, 190
Luther, Martin, 93, 96, 100, 246
Maccovius, Johannes, 59, 140-41
Marga, Amy, 119, 207, 298-99
Maury, Pierre, 177-82, 184, 192
McCormack, Bruce, 32, 35, 77-78, 84, 98, 102-3, 115, 123, 126-27, 148-56, 177-82, 209, 215, 221, 251, 258-59, 269-77, 280-84, 288

McNeill, John T., 67
Meister Eckhart, 33
Migliore, Daniel, 233
Mouw, Richard, 296
Mozart, Wolfgang Amadeus, 296
Muller, Richard, 43
Nimmo, Paul, 123, 215, 222, 252-53, 270, 283
Origen, 33
Owen, John, 44, 51, 56-59, 66, 73-74, 79
Packer, J. I., 23
Pattison, George, 22
Perkins, William, 46-47, 69
Polanus, Amandus, 42, 50, 72
Rasmussen, Joel, 85
Rijssen, Leonard van, 71
Rodin, R. Scott, 77, 244
Rutherford, Samuel, 44, 55-56, 59
Schweizer, Alexander, 42-43
Scotus, John Duns 31, 33, 244, 293-94
Sibbes, Richard, 44, 49
Simons, Menno, 33
Tanner, Kathryn, 25, 68, 71, 74
Thomas Aquinas, 31, 118, 153, 294
Thurneysen, Eduard, 118, 176
Tillich, Paul, 99
Torrance, T. F., 84, 115, 150
Trueman, Carl, 43, 57-58
Turretin, Francis, 42, 44, 46-47, 53-54, 60-61, 69, 71
Twisse, William, 69
Ward, Graham, 155
Weber, Otto, 225
Webster, John, 26, 86, 161, 175, 168
Whitehead, Alfred North, 206

Subject Index

actualism, 105, 114, 118-19, 123, 130-42, 153-56, 161-64, 183-84, 204-9, 211, 215-16, 222-24, 233-41, 250-52, 272, 284
    and Thomist metaphysics, 118, 153-55
    See also *actus purus*; *analogia fidei*; being-in-act; revelation-in-act
actus purus, 118, 153. *See also* actualism
analogia fidei, 150-57, 160-62, 168-70, 184, 207. *See also* actualism
anthropology as essence of theology (Feuerbach), 22, 135, 207
apocatastasis, 138-39
aseity, 118, 153, 216-18
atonement, 75, 95, 202, 257-59, 69, 287, 294
    Christus victor model of the, 202
    and incarnation, 75, 157-59, 244, 294
    necessity (absolute/hypothetical) of the, 257
    penal-substitutionary model of the, 197-98, 202, 239, 287
Aufhebung, 36, 64-65, 85, 87, 92-93, 195-200, 201-4, 210-11, 230-34, 238, 249, 263-69, 290-92
    election/double predestination as, 195-200, 230-34
    Hegelian grammar/logic of, 36, 197, 269, 290
being-in-act, 66, 105, 114, 142, 155, 162, 192-93, 206-16, 220-23, 233, 237-41, 252, 261-65, 272, 275-79, 283-84, 293. *See also* actualism

Chalcedon, symbol of, 115, 117, 123-27, 203, 209, 215, 226-28, 250-51, 270-72, 282-85
    category of nature in the, 259-62, 270-73, 277-80, 282-86
    grammar/patterns of the, 123-27, 250, 272, 283
    substantialist ontology of the, 215, 227, 252, 260, 270-73, 281-82, 284-85
    See also Christology, Barth's basically Chalcedonian
Christocentrism
    of Barth, 36, 62-63, 114-15, 174-76, 177-84, 195-96, 204-11, 214, 225, 242, 259, 287, 290, 295, 299
    in Reformed orthodoxy, 57-59, 73-74, 182, 227
    See also ontology, Christocentric
Christology
    Barth's basically Chalcedonian, 123-27, 203, 209, 215, 227-28, 250-51, 254, 282-85.
    Barth's basically infralapsarian, 35, 108-110, 127-29, 146-49, 158, 166-71, 212, 241-62, 265-66, 287-88, 298
    historicized, 34-35, 123, 215, 242-43, 269-70, 273, 275-76, 282-83
    infralapsarian, 23, 31-33, 74
    supralapsarian, 23, 31-33, 74, 108, 128, 146, 173, 223, 255, 275
    See also Chalcedon, symbol of; incarnation
common grace, 29, 296-97
consciousness theology, 90, 116, 155

covenant, 28, 37, 64, 76-78, 178, 218-23, 225-26, 230, 233-34, 238, 241, 248-49, 256, 258, 261, 265, 275, 277, 287, 287-94, 300
    and creation, 291
    of redemption (intratrinitarian covenant, *pactum salutis*), 50-58
creation
    decree of, as logical presupposition of election in Barth's theology, 33, 62, 71, 75-78, 143, 146, 166-67, 190, 220, 228-30, 244, 278, 293, 295
    as external basis of the covenant. *See* covenant, and creation
    original, 85, 89-90, 107, 109, 118-19, 128, 167-69, 190
crisis, 88, 92-95, 98, 103
critical realism, 89, 110, 120, 131, 155-56, 204-6, 211-12
decretum absolutum, 64-65, 72, 103, 135-36, 138, 141, 185, 196, 200, 212, 226, 233, 236-37, 240. *See also* predestination, double
dialectic(s)
    Hegelian. *See Aufhebung*, Hegelian grammar/logic of
    Kierkegaardian, 84-85, 115, 121, 150, 248
    possibility-impossibility. *See* impossible possibility
    subject-object, 118-22, 130
    See also infralapsarianism, and supralapsarianism, Barth's dialectical combination of

Dort, Canons/Synod of, 46-47, 53, 59, 140-42, 144, 146
election
   Barth's Christocentric revision of, 34-35, 149, 162, 175-76, 179-84, 197, 204-12, 295
   Barth's early actualistic rendition of, 114, 130-39, 164-69, 172-76, 180-84
   Christ as object of, 24-25, 36, 62-64, 79, 106, 214-16, 227-30, 233, 238-39, 267, 278, 282
   Christ as subject of, 36, 64, 70, 106, 174, 178, 204-5, 213-5, 225-30, 23, 238, 275-78, 287-89, 300
   of *homo lapsus* (in Barth's theology), 30, 37, 62-63, 70, 77, 106, 140, 195, 198-200, 202-4, 210, 213, 230, 234, 259
   as sublation of reprobation. See *Aufhebung*
   and Trinity, debate on. See Trinity, and election, debate on
epistemology, 66, 84, 99, 115-16, 120, 123, 126-27, 208-11, 124-15, 221, 243-45, 258-59, 276
eschatology, 95-97, 101-3, 105-7, 110, 122, 127-29, 138-39, 200, 253, 264
eternality of divine decrees (in Reformed orthodoxy), 48-52, 69
eternity
   Augustinian definition of, 45-46, 48, 206
   Boethian definition of, 48-49, 206
   Hegelian view of. See Hegelianism, eternity, time and succession
evil, problem of. See theodicy
fall of humankind, 89-90, 256-62, 265-69
   divine permission of the, 28, 45-47, 54, 63, 72-73, 137, 141, 144-45, 237, 246-47

as logical presupposition of election, 32, 77-78, 106-10, 230-38, 267
as logical presupposition of incarnation, 77, 127-28, 231, 243-44, 246, 291
as pretemporal, nonhistorical event, 90-95, 106, 119
as saga. See saga
fallenness view of Christ's human nature/agency, 31, 271, 279-80
Geschichte, 35, 225, 241-42, 265-66, 287-89
   and *historie*, 265
Hegelianism, 36, 197, 206, 257, 269, 274-75, 290
   and classical theism, 257
   eternity, time and succession according to, 206
   trinitarian doctrine in, 206
   See also *Aufhebung*
Heidelberg Catechism, 114, 127, 196, 260
historicism, 90, 116
human nature, 245, 259-62, 270-73, 279-80, 284-86
   of Christ. See Chalcedon, symbol of: category of nature in the Christ's sinless, 231, 262, 280, 282-86
I-thou philosophy, 118
impossible possibility, 86-88, 91, 95-99, 101-5, 107, 109-11, 116-18, 122, 159, 164, 245-50
   Kierkegaardian dialectic of the, 84-86
   of sin, evil and death, 245-50
   See also sin, as ontological impossibility
incarnation, 31-33, 74-78, 108-110, 122-29, 133-34, 146-47, 156-57, 169-74, 182-83, 192-95, 212, 223-24, 227-31, 240-45, 248-52, 257-59, 272-78, 280-81, 284, 286-89, 293-95

infralapsarianism
   assumptions shared between supralapsarianism and, 45-52, 54
   Barth's misnomer of, 30, 42-45, 67-74, 107-8, 139-46, 188-89
   in Barth's theology, 36, 108-10, 127-28, 139-42, 163-71, 194-95, 197-200, 202, 212, 224, 239-40, 243-45, 248-49, 256-65, 269, 273-76, 278, 282, 286-87, 290-95
   Christological. See Christology, infralapsarian
   definition of, 21, 27-31, 53-55, 56, 60-61, 67-74, 213, 234
   and supralapsarianism, Barth's dialectical combination of, 23-24, 29-32, 41, 63, 79, 197-200, 202-3, 218, 223-24, 234, 241, 266, 290-95
Kantianism. See Kant, Immanuel (Author Index)
   See also synthetic *a priori* judgments
Krisis. See crisis
Lapsarian Controversy
   Barth's excursus on the, 42-43, 62-74, 79, 108, 234-39, 292
   See also supralapsarianism; infralapsarianism
metaphysics, 21-22, 65-66, 118, 152, 191, 227, 235, 270-72
   Aristotelian and Classical, 118, 153, 227, 270-72, 281, 284
   Kantian critique of, 84, 98, 120, 153, 175, 190-91, 196, 225, 227, 237, 270-72
Thomist. See Thomism
natural theology, 22, 65-66, 118, 151-53, 207, 235, 258, 274, 292, 297-99
   analogia entis, 119, 151-53,

Subject Index

158, 207, 222, 298-99
  See also metaphysics
neo-Calvinism, 296-98
neo-Kantianism (Marburg),
  27, 84, 89, 98, 100, 155, 208.
  See also transcendental
  argument
neo-Protestantism, 27, 83,
  90-91, 116, 207, 259-60, 289
nothingness (*das Nichtige*), 22,
  29, 35, 64, 87, 159, 232, 244,
  246-47, 253, 260-61, 272, 284,
  290-91, 293-94, 296, 299-300
  sin, evil and death as, 64,
    244, 272, 296
  and the theodicy problem.
    See theodicy
obiecum praedestinationis. See
  supralapsarianism;
  infralapsarianism,
  definitions of
objectivism, soteriological
  and Christological, 114,
  174-75, 209-10, 212
ontology, 21, 152, 181, 220-21,
  227, 232, 233, 245-47, 260,
  270-74, 281, 284-85
  actualistic, 222, 227, 252,
    272
  Barth's rejection of the
    method of, 270-71
  Christocentric, 181, 209,
    214, 227, 270-74, 276, 280
  substantialist. See
    Chalcedon, symbol of:
    substantialist ontology
    of the
ordo rerum decretorum. See
  supralapsarianism;
  infralapsarianism,
  definitions of
particularism, Christocentric,
  175, 206-209
pneumatology, 114, 116-17, 121,
  129-35, 139, 142, 147, 165-67,
  172-75, 183, 190-92, 204, 208,
  253
*potentia absoluta/ordinata
  Dei*, 32, 172-73, 294. See also
  predestination, double
predestination, double, 21, 49,
  60-61, 64-65, 87, 91, 93, 97,

102-7, 134-39, 185, 188,
  191-201, 232-35, 239, 262-66,
  300
  in Romans 11:32
    (according to Barth's
    exegesis), 97, 104-5,
    137-39, 200-204, 262
  See also *decretum
    absolutum Dei; potentia
    absoluta/ordinata Dei*
process theology, 205
psychologism, 90, 110
reprobation
  of Jesus Christ, 36-37, 64,
    185, 196-98, 202-3,
    231-32, 237, 277
  as negative
    presupposition of
    election in Barth's
    theology. See *Aufhebung*
  See also double
    predestination
revelation-in-act, 114, 142,
  153-58, 162, 166, 204-8. See
  also actualism
romanticism, 128
saga, 267-68
Scots Confession, 181-82
sin
  Augustinian-Reformed
    view of, 130-31, 260-61
  Catholic and neo-
    Protestant view of,
    259-60
  as fallenness, 256-65
  hereditary, 261, 286
  history of, 265-69
  Kantian view of, 259-60,
    267
  as nothingness. See
    nothingness
  as ontological
    impossibility, 232. See
    also impossible
    possibility, sin as
  original, 71, 261-62, 286
  as paradox, 250-53
  as pride, 253-56
  weight of, 256-59
supralapsarianism
  Barth's misnomer of. See
    infralapsarianism,

Barth's misnomer of
  definition of, 21, 24, 28, 41,
    47, 52-61, 213, 234-35
  and infralapsarianism,
    Barth's dialectical
    combination of. See
    infralapsarianism
  pure (in Reformed
    orthodoxy), 58-59
  purified, 29, 34, 63-66, 73,
    212, 234-40, 300
synthetic *a priori* judgments,
  189-90, 195, 208. See also
  Kantianism
theodicy, 26-28, 246, 296
  lapsarianism as, 27-28, 47
Thomism. See Thomas
  Aquinas (index of names).
  metaphysics in, 118, 152-53
  See also *actus purus*;
  analogia entis
transcendental argument, 84,
  92, 98, 259. See also
  neo-Kantianism (Marburg)
Trinity
  Barth's doctrine of the,
    114-15, 121, 155, 206, 208,
    211, 216-22
  and election, debate on,
    78, 211, 216-22, 227-29,
    251, 258-59, 269-82
  as ground of divine love
    and freedom, 216-22
  See also covenant of
    redemption (*pactum
    salutis*, intratrinitarian
    covenant)
Ursprung. See creation,
  original
Word of God, 147, 149, 154,
  160, 163, 166-73, 179, 184
  infralapsarian
    formulation of the,
    166-71
  proclaimed, 161, 163, 167-70
  revealed, Christ as, 166-75,
    184, 189-91, 195-96
  Scripture as, 167-70
  threefold form of the,
    167-71, 190
  written, 167-70

New Explorations in Theology

Theology is flourishing in dynamic and unexpected ways in the twenty-first century. Scholars are increasingly recognizing the global character of the church, freely crossing old academic boundaries and challenging previously entrenched interpretations. Despite living in a culture of uncertainty, both young and senior scholars today are engaged in hopeful and creative work in the areas of systematic, historical, practical and philosophical theology. New Explorations in Theology provides a platform for cutting-edge research in these fields.

In an age of media proliferation and academic oversaturation, there is a need to single out the best new monographs. IVP Academic is committed to publishing constructive works that advance key theological conversations. We look for projects that investigate new areas of research, stimulate fruitful dialogue, and attend to the diverse array of contexts and audiences in our increasingly pluralistic world. IVP Academic is excited to make this work available to scholars, students and general readers who are seeking fresh new insights for the future of Christian theology.

DISTINCTIVES OF NEW EXPLORATIONS IN THEOLOGY:

- Best new monographs from young and senior scholars
- Volumes explore systematic, historical, practical and philosophical theology

VOLUMES INCLUDE:

- *Karl Barth's Infralapsarian Theology: Origins and Development, 1920–1953*, Shao Kai Tseng
- *The Reality of God and Historical Method*, Samuel V. Adams

    Forthcoming

- *A Shared Mercy: Karl Barth on Forgiveness and the Church*, Jon Coutts

Finding the Textbook You Need

The IVP Academic Textbook Selector
is an online tool for instantly finding the IVP books
suitable for over 250 courses across 24 disciplines.

www.ivpress.com/academic/

www.ingramcontent.com/pod-product-compliance
Lightning Source LLC
Chambersburg PA
CBHW020110010526
44115CB00008B/769